Teacg Emple

Teaching Empire

Native Americans, Filipinos, and US Imperial
Education, 1879–1918

ELISABETH M. EITTREIM

UNIVERSITY PRESS OF KANSAS

Published by the University Press of Kansas (Lawrence, Kansas 66045), which was organized by the Kansas Board of Regents and is operated and funded by Emporia State University, Fort Hays State University, Kansas State University, Pittsburg State University, the University of Kansas, and Wichita State University

© 2019 by the University Press of Kansas
All rights reserved

Library of Congress Cataloging-in-Publication Data

Names: Eittreim, Elisabeth M., author.
Title: Teaching empire : native Americans, Filipinos, and US imperial education, 1879–1918 / Elisabeth Eittreim.
Description: Lawrence, Kansas : University Press of Kansas, [2019] | Includes bibliographical references and index. | Identifiers: LCCN 2019019300
    ISBN 9780700628575 (cloth)
    ISBN 9780700628582 (paperback)
    ISBN 9780700628599 (ebook)
Subjects: LCSH: Indigenous peoples—Education—United States—History. | Indigenous peoples—Education—Philippines—History. | Indigenous peoples—Cultural assimilation—United States. | United States Indian School (Carlisle, Pa.)—History. | Indians of North America—Education—History. | Indians of North America—Cultural assimilation. | Teachers—United States—Attitudes.
Classification: LCC LC3731 .E58 2019
DDC 371.829—dc23
LC record available at https://lccn.loc.gov/2019019300.

British Library Cataloguing-in-Publication Data is available.

Printed in the United States of America

10 9 8 7 6 5 4 3 2 1

The paper used in this publication is recycled and contains 30 percent postconsumer waste. It is acid free and meets the minimum requirements of the American National Standard for Permanence of Paper for Printed Library Materials Z39.48–1992.

For Alice, Benjamin, and Cole

CONTENTS

ACKNOWLEDGMENTS

I would first like to extend my sincere admiration to the diverse indigenous Native American and Filipino peoples of both the past and present for their boldness, resilience, and resolve in the face of American empire. I am humbled by your stories and strength, and following your lead, I am committed to striving for a more equitable, hopeful, and humane future.

I would like to thank Kim Hogeland of the University Press of Kansas for believing in this manuscript and providing consistent guidance and support. Countless thanks also to the press's editorial and production teams for their patience, insights, and suggestions each step along the way, especially that of Larisa Martin. Sincere thanks to the faculty of the Rutgers University History Department for their inspiration and encouragement in devising and developing this project during my doctoral studies. Without the support of the Warren Susman Dissertation Completion Fellowship, Andrew W. Mellon Foundation summer grants, and History Department Fellowship funding, the initial research and writing would not have been possible.

Ten years in the making, this book is a testament to the dedication and commitment of my doctoral advisor, Nancy Hewitt. I am forever grateful that she agreed to take me on as one of her last doctoral students. Her guidance, constructive criticism, and brilliance supported and propelled every stage of the dissertation and continued to inspire the manuscript. Her thorough and timely critiques enabled me to write, revise, and rewrite several drafts of each dissertation chapter, and knowing that I could count on her insights and optimism inspired me to continue moving forward. As doctoral co-advisor, Benjamin Justice's enthusiasm and knowledge similarly motivated me to pursue this work. His suggestions of primary and secondary sources and brainstorming on theoretical frameworks enriched and guided my scholarly journey, and his steadfast support throughout the many years of researching and writing helped to sustain my commitment to the project. I would also like to thank Judy Gerson and Cami Townsend for their expertise and service on the dissertation committee. From the dissertation proposal to the final draft, they pushed me to consider new ways of understanding this project, both inside and outside of the discipline of history. Many thanks also to Suzanne Lebsock, who provided me with critical feedback in the planning stages of this project.

Teaching Empire took me to archives near and far. Thank you to all of the archivists, librarians, and researchers who gave me access to the thousands of primary documents that form the basis of this work. In particular, I would like to thank the archivists with whom I worked at the Cumberland County Historical Society in Carlisle, Pennsylvania; the National Personnel Research Center in St. Louis, Missouri; and the Bentley Historical Library in Ann Arbor, Michigan. My gratitude also extends to the many archivists who guided me through the significant holdings at the National Archives in Washington, DC; the National Archives in College Park, Maryland; the Library of Congress; and Yale University's Beinecke Rare Book and Manuscript Library. In addition, I thank all of the individuals who assisted in my research at universities I was unable to visit but who made photocopies and digital images in my stead. Thank you all for your commitment to preserving, organizing, and making available the sources that make the writing of history possible.

I would also like to extend my sincere thanks to the dozens of scholars who have inspired and challenged me, shaping how I have understood the Carlisle and Philippines experiments. In particular, I would like to thank historian David Adams for taking my scholarship seriously from the very beginning and encouraging me to consider archival and publishing possibilities; Solsiree del Moral for her insightful critique of excerpts from chapter 4 that I presented at the November 2016 History of Education Society Conference; the anonymous peer reviewer who pressed me to refine my argument; and the scholars at the New-York Historical Society's Center for Women's History for their feedback and encouragement during the 2017–2018 Early Career Workshop. Special thanks also to my students, from middle schoolers to undergraduates, who have taught me so much.

On a personal note, I would like to thank and acknowledge my family—both immediate and extended—and the many caretakers who helped me to balance my home and work life. Many thanks to my parents, Peggy and Rich Eittreim, for believing in me from day one and for their ongoing encouragement, as well as countless days of watching their grandchildren as I delved into research and writing over the past decade. Thanks also to my in-laws, Sue and Jim Harbison, who also helped care for the children as I studied and researched, providing consistent support and inspiration. In addition to helping out with the kids, many thanks to my sister, Sam Eittreim, who also kept me grounded with her witty sense of humor. And, thanks, too, to my brother, Ted Eittreim, who although not geographically close, regularly reminds me of the importance of family. Sincere thanks also to Geta Mardari, Beth Kashuba, Ann Forbes, Dawn Greenleaf, and Kerry Kevill, who have cared for the kids and managed the household while I researched and wrote; it really does take a village.

A special thank you to my husband, Tommy Harbison, who has encouraged me throughout, providing his editorial and scholarly expertise and, more importantly, for helping to raise our children, even turning the many research trips into family vacations. Finally, thank you to Cole, Benjamin, and Alice for your patience, love, hugs, and giggles. This project is for you.

INTRODUCTION

AN INTIMATE AND FRAGILE EMPIRE

In the front row of Uncle Sam's imperial classroom—imagined by artist Louis Dalrymple and published as the centerfold illustration in the January 25, 1899, issue of the satirical magazine *Puck*—sit the newest group of students purportedly requiring an education in "Civilization": Philippines, Hawaii, Porto Rico, and Cuba. These four dark-skinned students stare up, frowning at their old white teacher, having only recently been transferred from the Spanish to the American imperial classroom and not (yet) complacent members of the growing US empire. Uncle Sam's whiteness and the white students seated in the second tier of desks contrast with the brown- and black-skinned students, both in posture and dress. The Philippines figure in the front row appears frightened yet also shocked and angry, with his hands in a defensive posture, flanked by other new students who embody similarly noncompliant or frightened positions: with arms crossed, hands in pockets, or leaning back.[1] Uncle Sam's pointer directs the viewer's attention to an otherwise ignored student seated in the back of the classroom; a Native American figure, slouched over an upside-down alphabet book, seemingly engrossed in his reading. Several other students in the classroom represent a multitude of peoples and places that encountered or were taught about the apparent superiority of US customs and values, some more learned (and welcomed) than others.[2]

Here Dalrymple criticized American imperialism for its (and Uncle Sam's) short-sightedness, laying bare the supposed hierarchy of race central to its mission. By setting the scene in an American classroom, he elevated education—and teaching empire—to center stage, reflecting the reality that schooling played in assimilating peoples often resistant to US authority. Fundamentally, the political cartoonist questioned the presumed benevolence of the emerging US superpower as the new century approached and challenged his audience to do the same.

As the image suggests, at the turn of the twentieth century the US government celebrated a particular brand of civilization—one that held mainstream Anglo-American culture in the highest esteem, purportedly to benefit "others" who adopted that culture's norms and ideals, including

"Uncle Sam (to his new class in Civilization): Now, children, you've got to learn these lessons whether you want to or not! But just take a look at the class ahead of you, and remember that, in a little while, you will feel as glad to be here as they are!" (*Puck*, January 25, 1899, centerfold; Louis Dalrymple, artist.)

American Indians and Filipinos. In the late nineteenth century, the debate among white Americans over whether Indians could be "civilized" was considered part of a broader "Indian problem"—how to deal with a people who insisted on maintaining their autonomy in spite of US domination of their homelands.[3] For many reformers, education offered one crucial answer, and in 1879 the Carlisle Indian Industrial School opened its doors in hopes that reeducating Indian youth would "save" the race via cultural transformation. The first of its kind, Carlisle was a government-sponsored off-reservation boarding school, established a few years before the more far-reaching Indian School Service.

Almost twenty years later, as the United States extended its boundaries across the Pacific and gained control of the Philippine Islands in 1898, reformers again touted education as the best means to assimilate, or at least pacify, the American empire's newest colonial subjects. Beginning in 1901 the US government sent hundreds of teachers across the Pacific to set up a modern school system amid a continuing rebellion launched by Filipinos.[4] To much different scales, both experiments—the Indian boarding school in Carlisle, Pennsylvania, and the educational initiative in the Philippines—represent the US government's initial attempts at imperial education to appease, and from its perspective, "civilize" a "backward" and largely reluctant people. In the case of Carlisle, policymakers hoped to scale up the school's successes and create enough boarding schools to educate all indigenous children, with the ultimate objective to "uplift" all American Indians within one generation.[5] Although this proved impossible, efforts in the Philippines started just as grand: with the aim of sending enough teachers to the islands to build a US-styled school system from the bottom up, throughout the 7,000-plus-island archipelago. In both cases US ambition outpaced reality, and the imperial dilemma over how to assimilate a people who did not want to or seem to "fit in" fell to teachers.

This study draws from the records of fifty-five Carlisle teachers and thirty-three American teachers sent to the Philippines, including five who worked in both locations. Their stories reveal the challenges of translating imperial policy into practice, even for those most dedicated to the mission. The schools they helped to establish struggled to attract and retain students, perhaps not surprising since their goal was to effectively displace native customs with white "American" cultural norms.[6] These educators, who worked on behalf of the US government, sought to meet expectations of policy bureaucrats and supervisors while contending with leadership crises on the ground. To different degrees, these teachers encountered disease and death, risking their lives and those of their students, particularly in the Philippines due to the ongoing military conflict. Ultimately, in both projects, teachers faced problems common to all classrooms—how to manage students and convey knowledge—but in the imperial classroom, the stakes seemed higher.[7] Thus, in these and other ways, the teachers' work was complicated by unique circumstances but remained constant at its core as educators, on behalf of the US government, sought to "pour in" knowledge, purposefully dismissing and undermining the values, desires, and protests of the receiving communities.[8]

How might some of the teachers who worked on behalf of American empire at Carlisle and in the Philippines have reacted to Dalrymple's depiction or other criticisms of their work? Although perspectives would have varied, two teachers—Emma Lovewell of Carlisle and Frederick Behner of the Philippines—illustrate what working on behalf of US imperial education looked like on the ground and allow us to speculate on their reactions to this satirical portrait. Their stories reveal both the complexity and fragility of implementing US imperial education policy and signal the importance of understanding teachers' perspectives. While government authorities and education leaders imagined the classroom as an intimate space—one where teachers could effect profound cultural change through their personal interactions and relationships with students—building an empire from the bottom up proved tenuous as teachers contended with infrastructural deficiencies, personnel disputes, and environmental hazards, as well as political and sexual scandal in the all-consuming work environments of Indian boarding and Filipino schools. Of course, teachers brought their own visions, hopes, dreams, and biases with them, largely reflecting turn-of-the-twentieth-century Protestant, white, middle-class values, with some exceptions.[9] Ultimately, while it is true that teachers developed a unique understanding of their students by virtue of living and working among them, translating education policy into practice remained a complicated and often fraught endeavor, even for the most loyal agents of empire.

In 1869, a decade before Carlisle opened its doors, fifteen-year-old Emma Lovewell began teaching.[10] At twenty-one, she married and left the classroom, committing the next fifteen years to motherhood and domesticity. When Lovewell's husband died in 1890, she returned to teaching to support herself and her only son.[11] She taught in public schools until she joined the Indian Service in 1904, initially working as a matron and seamstress at the school in Flathead, Montana. Like many Indian Service employees, she moved frequently. Over the next two years, she transferred to Indian schools in Oklahoma and then North Carolina, working as an assistant matron. In 1907 Lovewell passed the Indian Service teacher examination and was sent to work at the Indian school in Fort Shaw, Montana, for two years before transferring to Carlisle in 1909.[12] Lovewell was happy to leave the bitter cold behind and settle closer to her son, who was then living in Washington, DC.[13] By the time she joined the teaching force at Carlisle, she was fifty-five, older than most teachers in the broader Indian Service, but not unusual for those at the Pennsylvania boarding school.[14]

At Carlisle, Lovewell first taught fourth grade and took up the "voluntary work" expected of all teachers at the school, including "decorating on special occasions, taking part in Sunday School work, drilling for entertainments and the like."[15] In her first couple of years, she was liked by her colleagues and recognized for her strong work ethic, earning a promotion to teach the more challenging seventh-grade class, which led her to request a raise.[16] However, evidence shows that by 1912 Lovewell faced challenges from colleagues regarding her professionalism, and she fought back. That fall, Carlisle's music director made a formal complaint that questioned the merit of a student performance under Lovewell's charge. She defended herself and her students by noting that the audience had demanded an encore and colleagues commended her for organizing the concert. Moreover, she argued, the song they presented aligned with temperance values prioritized by the Indian Office. Lovewell then wrote to her supervisor, "I have never presented a number but that would help raise the moral standard of the school, for I have the Indian at heart."[17] In this case, Lovewell presented herself as firmly committed to her students, the school, and the broader Indian Service, believing in its mission of education and assimilation above all else, despite her colleague's criticism.

In 1914 Lovewell joined others in publicly condemning Carlisle's leadership and direction, though she continued to proclaim her commitment to Indian "uplift." When she had first arrived at Carlisle in 1909, superintendent Moses Friedman was in his second year at the school and working to distance himself from the prior administration's financial mismanagement and a covered-up sex scandal. However, within a couple of years Friedman found himself at odds with some senior teachers and staff members, and from there tensions and rumors escalated. Following a federal investigation, the US Congressional Joint Commission to Investigate Indian Affairs conducted hearings on Indian schools, including Carlisle. In February and March 1914, Lovewell was one of several teachers who testified on the national stage against Superintendent Friedman for his role in purportedly leading the school into moral and professional decline.[18] Although these hearings will be discussed in length in Chapters 3 and 5, in brief, Lovewell characterized Carlisle's disciplinary methods under Friedman as ineffective and suggested that this led to an increase in students' "immoral" behavior; in other words, sex that resulted in pregnancy. She blamed the superintendent for his inability to gain respect and control of students for their own apparent lack of respectability. Although Lovewell may have seen Dalrymple's stone-faced Uncle Sam as too harsh, or perhaps as lacking empathy, she, like many other civil service educators, believed that Indian children's hearts, minds, and bodies needed to be "rescued" from the "backward" influences of their native culture and the barbaric impulses attributed to their perceived lack of civilization.[19]

Whether it was students' illicit sexual relationships or habitual unruliness in the classroom, Lovewell saw herself as having her students' best interests at heart and thought it necessary to impart firm discipline in severe cases of misconduct. In an April 1914 letter to her supervisor, Lovewell explained that she addressed the occasional disorderly students by giving them "gentle reprimands and good motherly talks," and when this was not enough, she isolated an "insolent" student from the rest of the class, sometimes making the student scrub floors. Still, Lovewell expressed concern for even the most misbehaved child and held out hope that such students could reform their behavior.[20] Rather than giving up on a child—as the *Puck* cartoon suggests by the isolated Indian at the edge of the classroom reading a book upside-down—Lovewell proclaimed her commitment to the most difficult of students, even as the record suggests her own feelings of racial and cultural superiority. Moreover, she would certainly have defended the broader Indian education system against critics who accused it of ignoring Indians' humanity, despite its entanglement in federal scandal. Although she testified against the administration's and school's failings, she emphasized the constant care that she and other teachers exhibited toward students, even the most rebellious. Ultimately, she saw herself, Carlisle, and the Indian Service as a force of good—trying to save Indians from themselves—even if it was flawed.[21]

By the end of December 1914, Lovewell had had enough. She resigned on December 31 at the age of sixty, after having been hospitalized for about a month. At the time, her attending physician advised her not to return to the "arduous duties required of an employee in the Indian School Service."[22] Not only was the work considered physically challenging, but the round-the-clock work cycles were also deemed emotionally draining. Nevertheless, Lovewell sought reinstatement, but a year later recanted. On December 10, 1915, Lovewell wrote to Commissioner of Indian Affairs Cato Sells:

> Kindly cancel my request for reinstatement.
> The Indian Service will never be a success while young frivolous incompetent persons of *influence* are appointed, (I say this advisedly) and promoted over those of sterling worth and experience . . . and I trust that you, Honorable Commissioner, in your wise judgment will bring about different conditions in the near future.[23]

Here, Lovewell ardently faulted the Indian Service for improper hiring practices, casting blame well beyond the failings of Superintendent Friedman, whom she had helped get suspended back in February 1914. She revealed what she believed were critical qualities for an Indian Service employee to possess—"worth and experience"—and identified cronyism as the reason for *her* decision not to return to the service. Having not yet secured reappointment herself, in this letter to Commissioner Sells she reclaimed power and asserted authority while exhibiting deference for those she deemed to be honorable service members as well as the larger mission of assimilation.

Overall, Lovewell was proud of her work at Carlisle. She once wrote, "I believe my influence has been a power for good. I feel an interest—personal interest in the Indian and I have always worked for his uplift."[24] Although she ultimately chose not to return to the classroom, her record demonstrates that she believed in the work of "uplift" as a benevolent means of helping native peoples, even if this involved severe, even harsh treatment of Indian children. Like the hundreds of other Indian Service teachers, Lovewell prided herself for working on behalf of a government that strove to assimilate its Native American "wards" into white, middle-class, Protestant culture through schooling, believing that only such work could save Indians from themselves.[25] Still, she was neither just a cog in the machine nor simply a female version of Dalrymple's overbearing tyrant; instead, her strong will and genuine interest in Indians guided Lovewell even as her assumptions about how best to achieve their advancement were constrained by cultural and racial biases.

Like Lovewell, Frederick Behner faced many challenges working on behalf of US empire, although his experiences demonstrate how teaching in the Philippines oftentimes posed severe, even life-threatening risks. Born in 1874 in northwestern Ohio, Behner had no formal schooling until he attended North Central College in Illinois, where he graduated as valedictorian of his class. Like many other teachers sent to the Philippines, his high academic achievements earned him a place aboard the USS *Thomas* in July 1901.[26] He was one of several hundred individuals nominated by colleges and universities across the country to venture across the Pacific to establish US-style schools, all of whom came to be collectively known as Thomasites, whether or not they had traveled to the Philippines aboard the USS *Thomas* in 1901.[27] Soon after arriving in the Philippines, Behner and another teacher, B. N. Blakeslee, were assigned to teach in Banton, several days' journey from Manila.[28] There, they reported being the only white men on the island, after US soldiers left to subdue outbreaks of violence elsewhere.[29] Given weapons for self-protection, they remained almost constant companions over the next year. They faced typhoons and earthquakes, took care of one another during illness, and helped local Filipinos who were sick or injured, all while teaching day and night schools that often challenged village norms.[30] A year later, as Behner recorded dozens of people dying of cholera each day, he admitted that he sometimes found his responsibilities overwhelming.[31] Soon after, Blakeslee was sent home due to illness and Behner was transferred to Boac on the island of Magpag.[32]

Over the next three years, Behner continued to face daunting challenges as he battled disease in a region ravaged by military violence, and until 1904— when he was reassigned to work among a group of Americans—he often did so without the company of any countrymen. Considering the trying and often unpredictable factors that influenced Behner's efforts to educate Filipinos, he likely would have disagreed with Dalrymple's depiction of Uncle Sam as a domineering, seemingly unchallenged presence in the classroom of "Civilization." Although Behner, like Uncle Sam, was often the *only* symbol of US power in a given community—granting him a certain level of authority—he was also at times paralyzed by his isolation and unable to effect significant change. Moreover, insurrection, disease, and environmental crises all made his—and "Uncle Sam's"—job much harder. Still, Behner remained in the Philippines beyond his three-year contract after many of his colleagues had left. Despite his personal suffering—evident through diaries in which he logged his headaches, fevers, delirium, and other illnesses as well as the violence of war and crippling isolation—he remained resolute, continuing to establish schools and teach Filipinos in an often-hostile environment.[33]

During Behner's almost four-year tenure in the Philippines, he transferred job assignments four times, not unusual for teachers in the islands. At each new post he compared his new students with his old, noting their relative intelligence and academic experience. In the Boac elementary schools, he found the children to be "brighter" than those at Banton.[34] The following year he moved up to the high school in Boac, and at year's end he regretted having to leave, although he admitted that the students "could not be improved upon in P.I."[35] Soon after moving to his final post in Lucena, Behner wrote, "These people know much more Geography than those at Boac but, aside from that I think the old Boac people surpass them and in speaking Eng."[36] Yet, by year's end Behner reported that all of the Lucena high school students passed their exams, "the only school where I have heard of no failures."[37] In this and other ways, Behner noted differences among the communities and peoples with whom he worked in the archipelago, and at times he revealed a certain amount of pride regarding the more accomplished students. For him, moving among schools and grade levels alerted him to Filipinos' varied intellectual abilities and influenced his beliefs regarding students' potential, which he more often described as quite limited. Education officials held similar beliefs, particularly that certain groups of Filipinos were more adept at learning and more capable of sufficient self-government than others. While Behner noted differences of academic performance, some early education officials in the islands classified Filipinos based on class, racial, and religious backgrounds, predicting potential for success according to such characteristics.[38]

Yet despite his varied experiences and his recognition of the conditions that constrained Filipino schooling, Behner persisted over nearly four years in implementing US imperial education efforts in the islands. Although other teachers facing disease, death, and military violence revealed doubts about their mission, Behner repeatedly noted in his diaries his continued faith in the larger US mission. He also voiced his pride in being a champion of morality on the islands, not surprising considering his ultimate vocation as a minister. Early on, he wrote of Filipinos' propensity to "lie, gamble, and cheat all possible ways" and noted in his diary that he "hope[d] that my record will be for righting such serious drawbacks to civilization."[39] By the end of four school years, Behner concluded:

> A year of teaching gone. Its fiestas came and went with their usual music, lunching and dancing which is the Philippines passime [sic]. This and their church are their only diversions except cockfighting. The last is prohibited, the second is corrupt that it may be for the best that they have dancing until something can be substituted. Nearly four years have taught me that the Philippines is unmoral rather than immoral but decidedly immoral from one standpoint.[40]

For Behner, Filipinos appeared amoral. Their culture was not necessarily depraved but offered them few "moral" or "right" options. Ultimately, he felt conflicted about the people among whom he had worked for so long but still largely supported US intervention in the archipelago—militarily, educationally, and morally.

From Behner's perspective, Dalrymple did not capture the differences among Filipinos (and perhaps among colonized groups generally) or recognize the many constraints on Uncle Sam's ability to implement his civilizing vision. Still, he seems to have embraced the kind of imperialist views that Dalrymple captures and thus continued to believe that US educational intervention was among the tools necessary for Filipinos and others to be assimilated into Anglo-American "civilization."

As illustrated by the cases of Emma Lovewell and Frederick Behner, this study engages teachers' perspectives, revealing the messiness, complexity, and intimacy of building empire from the ground up and exposing both the strengths and vulnerabilities of a seemingly omnipresent imperial power and the programs it designed. These and other stories reveal the many layers of the teachers' dilemma as they sought to impart "civilized" lessons in what might be described as somewhat "uncivilized" environments, hampered by insufficient leadership and general instability. Like the hundreds of other teachers who worked for the Indian and Filipino School Services around the turn of the twentieth century, Lovewell and Behner were driven by diverse motivations, demonstrated commitment to their work, were frustrated by the conditions they faced or the authorities who controlled their destiny, and confronted both common and *uncommon* challenges. Like all teachers, they experienced varied levels of "success" in educating and "civilizing" their subjects, reflecting the tenuous and subjective nature of such work. And, like other teachers at Carlisle and in the Philippines, their work was both propelled and impeded by personal and structural racism. At the same time, Lovewell and Behner represent the gendered character of US imperial education, with government leaders recruiting women to teach in the Indian Service and men for the Philippine Service, believing each particularly suited for such work. Overall, although entangled in US imperial ambitions, racist norms, and gendered assumptions, teachers exhibited significant agency, wielding their authority with students and the institutions they worked for and negotiating their roles as powerful purveyors of cultural knowledge, often reinforcing but rarely challenging dominant understandings of "civilization."

This study uses the years of Carlisle's operation—from 1879 to 1918—as the chronological framework for understanding both the Indian and Philippine projects. Overlapping in time and purpose, these missions both aimed to "civilize" distinct populations via education around the turn of the twentieth century. Although efforts to educate North America's native peoples had begun as early as European settlement, Carlisle's opening in 1879 signaled the increasing role of the US government in Indian education as well as its growing confidence in schooling to effect rapid cultural transformation and assimilation.[41] The first federally funded off-reservation boarding school, Carlisle soon came to be a part of the larger Indian School Service, a national program formally established in 1882 that focused on educating Indian children in the ways of the dominant, largely middle-class white culture, both on and off the reservation.[42] Twenty years after Carlisle opened, Spain ceded the Philippine Islands to the United States as part of the treaty that ended the War of 1898, and government officials endeavored to implement a program on the islands similar to that which had been used among American

Indians.[43] This Philippine Civil Service employed hundreds and eventually thousands of Americans who endeavored to teach Filipinos more "civilized" ways of being, with the end goal of ostensibly preparing these colonial subjects for democratic self-government.[44] In establishing the Indian School and Philippine Civil Services, reformers imagined these institutions as temporary, necessary only until the targeted populations became assimilated to white culture. For Indians the measuring stick was their adherence to US law and customs; for Filipinos, their capacity for self-rule. In fact, both services persisted for several decades, beyond the one generation initially thought necessary for assimilation and self-sufficiency. Although the US government continued to guide Indian and Filipino education after 1918, its entrance into World War I shifted American priorities. In that year, Carlisle closed its doors to students and opened them to wounded US troops, while the Philippines, an American colony, was drawn into (what was idealistically dubbed) the "war to end all wars." Thus, it was between 1879 and 1918 that US government efforts to assimilate American Indians and Filipinos rested predominately, in both word and deed, on teachers.

The US government launched the Carlisle and Philippine experiments during a period of heightened US imperialism, or what scholars refer to as the Age of Empire.[45] In terms of formal empire building, the United States significantly increased its territorial holdings abroad in 1898, annexing Hawaii and occupying Cuba, Puerto Rico, and the Philippines. However, the United States had demonstrated its imperial appetite well before 1898. In fact, as several scholars have shown, imperial desires helped to found the United States and continued to inspire cross-continental and transpacific expansion into the twentieth century. By the time Carlisle opened its doors in 1879, the United States was well versed in what historian Walter Nugent characterized as the "habits of empire."[46] Scholarship on US empire-building flourished in the 1960s, with historians like William Appleman Williams asserting that the United States consistently used its authority to control less-powerful peoples to its own advantage. Williams and others recognized that US imperialism was distinctive in its "informal" character, defined broadly as government control over other peoples or states via political, social, cultural, and, most often, economic structures.[47] Viewed in this way, US education efforts among Indians and Filipinos were an extension of a much longer history of American empire.

More recently, scholars have directly compared US involvement with American Indians to Filipinos, noting both similarities and differences. Some research points to parallels between these two projects, arguing that

US government and military officials looked to Indian policy as precedent to justify and organize occupation of the Philippines, including its use of schooling as a means of forced assimilation.[48] Despite such noted similarities in policy and practice, scholars also point to the profound discontinuities that existed between the American Indian and Philippine imperial projects as well as particularly localized forces, which forced US administrators to adapt to the unique circumstances of each situation. Sociologist Julian Go critiques scholarship that denies the existence of American empire as well as revisionist histories that simply condemn the archipelago as an object of US imperial greed. He and other scholars rightly emphasize the role of colonized peoples in shaping imperial efforts and reframe the making of empire and power as somewhat negotiable, or at least, consistently contested.[49] *Teaching Empire* builds on the rich scholarship that delves into American empire more broadly, as well as US imperial policies among American Indians and Filipinos more specifically, framing the US experiments at Carlisle and the Philippines as part of a long history of American expansion, noting continuities while, at the same time, examining their distinctive goals, unique characteristics, and local struggles for power.

Regarding the topic of "imperial education," some foundational literature emphasizes the role of the state in establishing educational structures within newly acquired overseas territories and gives less attention to similar efforts closer to the center of power. Wherever states intervened, such schooling systems tended to mimic the uneven power relations between the colonizer and the colonized, ultimately reinforcing colonial rule.[50] Of course, as discussed above and at the heart of this book, the US government's interventions with North America's indigenous population as well as with Filipinos sought to effectively create "outsiders" within and beyond the physical borders of the nation. The US takeover of American Indian and Filipino education developed within traditional spheres of empire—based, in part, on the heightened military and political power of the metropole but also as part of an intensifying cultural imperialism.[51] In each case the goal was to displace a people's way of life with one deemed superior. These and other projects fundamentally sought to expand US power at the expense of others' sovereignty, attempting to reinforce the state's control over marginalized peoples via education.[52]

Of course, postcolonial scholars have aptly challenged the terms "colonizer" and "colonized," demonstrating the fluidity of such categories, and have similarly debunked the seemingly impervious divide between "insiders" and "outsiders," East and West. In this way, the ubiquitous power of empire has been undermined, challenged, and proven fallible as "colonized peoples" found ways to demonstrate agency and shape the "empire."[53] Still, uneven power relations continued to exist between the metropole and periphery. Despite significant resistance among those subject to such efforts, US educational regimes ultimately shaped Indian and Filipino life, and lives, in crucial ways. Nevertheless, further study comparing teachers and their colonial subjects' struggle over power and the significance of imperial education would be a critical addition to the field. This book mostly emphasizes teachers' perspectives and experiences.

In addition to the imperial implications of US intervention in American Indian and Filipino education around the turn of the twentieth century, these projects were shaped by reform efforts typical of the Progressive Era. In the decades from roughly 1890 to 1920, the problems wrought by rapid industrialization, urbanization, and immigration inspired social activists to offer education, alternative home environments, and workplace improvements to people suffering from poverty and other social ills. Like many who worked on behalf of American Indians and Filipinos, those who embraced progressive reforms believed that the nation could be improved by "uplifting" those who had not yet gained entrée to the American way of life. This perspective, however, materialized in a variety of ways, fostering social as well as political change—prompting, for instance, grassroots activists to establish settlement homes and government officials to impose increased regulations. At the same time, many progressives lauded efforts that promoted efficiency, ridding society of the burdens of waste and corruption. As the Age of Empire overlapped with an "age of reform," many political leaders and reformers embraced education as an answer to both domestic and imperial challenges. Streamlining American Indian education and establishing a public school system in the Philippines emerged in this context, and teachers, influenced by the political and social norms of the time period, were central to these efforts.[54]

To devastating consequence, misguided but common turn-of-the-century beliefs about race, propelled by so-called scientific claims, intersected with and too often propelled such progressive reform. Building upon centuries of colonial policies and practices that came to privilege those who were deemed "white" and condemn people of color, by the 1830s phrenologists pointed to brain size and development as apparent evidence of white superiority, erroneously rationalizing the continued mistreatment of enslaved African Americans and displaced American Indians, among others. By the late nineteenth century, the eugenics movement took hold, wrongly proclaiming that genetics predisposed certain peoples to a higher or lower status in society. Such erroneous "science" held great sway within the popular imagination and the progressive movement, greatly influencing new modes of educational reform—including schooling efforts aimed at Native Americans and Filipinos.[55]

Of course, the Carlisle and Philippine educational ventures did not emerge full-blown in the late nineteenth century but rather followed a half-century of school-based reform. Beginning in the 1830s and 1840s, the common school movement sought to establish elementary schools across the nation, aiming to provide children with academic and moral training to prepare them to be capable, conscientious, and productive citizens. Reformers imagined that such a system would equip (mainly white, native-born) children with the skills they needed to thrive individually and to help build a prosperous nation. Moreover, such an educational structure would enhance a developing sense of nationhood, reduce societal ills, and promote a distinctive American culture among the diverse groups that inhabited the United States. However, not all children or cultures were welcomed into the schoolhouse. Catholics formed parochial schools to counter the Protestant values endorsed by the common schools; racial segregation kept most nonwhite children out, with enslaved peoples forcefully denied any formal education; and many white working-class families could not send their children to school since they relied on their labor or income. Furthermore, nineteenth-century curricula was gendered, with boys being groomed to be active in what was imagined to be the public sphere through business, politics, and trades and girls to take charge in the complementary private sphere or household, albeit with ultimate deference to a husband. Although such white, middle-class gendered norms were reinforced in school and largely revered across the social strata, many people were barred from adopting such ideals in their own lives due to economic, racial, and other structural constraints.[56]

By 1880 an educational structure had been established that largely maintained existing class, racial, and gendered boundaries and thus reflected a seemingly "natural" hierarchy of power within the nation. Carlisle, which opened at this critical moment in US educational history, merged a schooling structure that too often entrenched inequality with the effort to assimilate people not considered properly "American" into the body politic. The educational bureaucracy that blossomed in the 1870s and 1880s to address the needs of newly emancipated African Americans, immigrants, and Native Americans was further expanded two decades later to forge proper "Americans" out of populations brought into the US orbit by wars of empire—including Filipinos.[57]

The US government described the Carlisle and Philippines projects as benevolent, intended to *help* "backward" peoples. US economic, political, and cultural exploitation was thus reframed as a gesture of goodwill and a means of conveying modernity to a people otherwise condemned to a life of barbarism. In this way, imperialists viewed the nation and its assimilationist efforts as exceptional, unlike its European cousins who ostensibly grabbed territory out of greed.[58] Of course, US benevolence was a matter of perspective, despite policymakers' efforts to justify and soften their interventions. Carlisle opened as the last phase of US conquest of the Indian, yet whites touted the school as a means of rescuing a "dying race." The US government's efforts to educate Native Americans was rationalized as a matter of education or extinction, with white reformers believing that schools could help to assimilate Indians into the dominant culture and thereby save the race from disappearing altogether.[59] However, as David Adams argues in his foundational study, *Education for Extinction*, Indian boarding schools often served "as a method of saving Indians by destroying them"—severing children from their homes, families, and cultures.[60] Similarly, in the case of the Philippines, Benjamin Justice characterizes US schooling on the islands as "education at the end of a gun," pointing to the profound disconnect between American policy on the ground and the celebratory rhetoric of US salvation.[61] Although government officials sought to frame their intervention as altruistic, the US occupation of the Philippines brought violence, both military and cultural. In both contexts, some teachers recognized the profound dissonance between the positivist rhetoric and the more complex, often cruel, reality on the ground, although they reacted to such discord in a variety of ways.[62]

As mentioned earlier, some scholarship on imperial education and reform points to significant parallels between the American Indian and Philippine experiments, although few are in-depth. One exception is Anne Paulet's work, including her dissertation, whose subtitle succinctly sums up her central argument: "The Use of United States Indian Policy as a Guide for the Conquest and Occupation of the Philippines, 1898–1905." Embedded in her larger argument, Paulet points to education as a particularly "powerful method of destroying Native American culture" and goes on to detail schooling efforts at Carlisle and Indian education more broadly. She concludes her discussion of such schooling by arguing, "If, at the end, the children were not all little 'white' Americans, they were also not 'blanket'

Indians any longer. The disjuncture education created in Native American society was, in essence, what whites were after. Thus the entire educational process was successful enough to become a cornerstone of American overseas policy."[63] Arguably, as Paulet suggests, policymakers may have deemed cultural "disjuncture" among generations of Native Americans a partial success and thus scaled-up educational efforts on the archipelago. Unlike the Indian Service—which built on missionaries' decades-long (even centuries-long) efforts and which utilized a multi-tiered method of both off-reservation boarding schools like Carlisle and on-reservation day schools—policymakers created a virtual army of American teachers for the Philippines who were to quickly take over what US troops had recently begun. In fact, beyond traditional military deployment, some American soldiers were ordered to set up classrooms in remote outposts scattered across the archipelago.[64] Thus, some American teachers in the Philippines literally picked up where US soldiers left off. Seeing the potential of such soft imperial methods, government officials charged US teachers with dismantling Spain's system of Catholic education to replace it with a secular, American-style public school system on the islands, ostensibly easing the transfer from one imperial power to another and with the stated purpose of creating a citizenry who would eventually be deemed "capable" of self-rule. In this way, teachers arrived in the Philippines with great fanfare and quickly dispersed throughout the archipelago, although their preparation—like that of their counterparts among Native Americans back in the states—varied greatly.

Other scholars note comparisons between the Philippines and American Indian projects, though to lesser degrees. In *Federal Fathers and Mothers*, Cathleen Cahill acknowledges the similarities between the civil service programs that the US government designed for American Indians and Filipinos, although her primary focus is on the multifaceted Indian Service, of which schooling was one part. In presenting a social history of the Indian Service, she uses Ann Laura Stoler's theoretical framework of "intimate colonialism" to better understand how government employees "translated policy into practice on the Indian reservations and in the schools" and the significance that gender played in shaping their work.[65] However, Cahill's analysis does not explore teachers' classroom work or their interactions with students much beyond a theoretical level. Ultimately, Cahill argues that the Indian Service strengthened US empire as it gained increasing control over its Indian wards but does not attempt a close reading of teachers' everyday work or interrogate the extent to which they truly served as agents of empire.

Teaching Empire repurposes Stoler's study of "the intimate" in another way: to interrogate teachers' daily lives—their interactions inside and outside of the classroom—and argues that the US government's efforts depended upon a workforce who embodied the imperial mission. While some teachers willingly and whole-heartedly immersed themselves in and furthered such efforts despite facing severe challenges, others burned out, lasted a short while, or otherwise suffered from the stresses of the job and lifestyle. Still other participants moved on, seeking opportunities elsewhere to better fit their personal needs. Ultimately, this dependence on teaching personnel proved both a strength—a means of creating intimate, sincere relationships between imperial agents and wards—and a weakness, as teachers were only human, some able to withstand only so much, some incapable of forming bonds with students or one another, and all working at the behest of what became large bureaucracies, systems that often transferred workers before such deep, close bonds proved possible. Thus, even when teachers employed the imperial mission with their wholes selves, the fragility of US empire became apparent, as it depended upon people and a system that could not always be depended upon.

Still other studies have looked at either the US approach to American Indian or Filipino reeducation using alternative comparative frameworks. Margaret Jacobs's *White Mother to a Dark Race* compares US child removal policies that separated Native American families vis-à-vis white-run boarding schools for indigenous children (of which Carlisle was the first) with those in Australia that took aboriginal children from their homes and placed them in state institutions and white homes. Although Jacobs notes differences between the cases, she argues that in both the United States and Australia, white women played a primary role in advocating for and enacting these policies. At the turn of the twentieth century, many American and Australian white women believed in their racial superiority to the point where separating Indian and aboriginal children from their mothers offered, in their minds, the best opportunity for all children, families, and, by extension, nations. In this way, white women helped to displace indigenous peoples from their families, culture, and land, enabling colonial efforts to claim resources by disrupting the most intimate relationships.[66] Setting up yet another global framework in his book *Innocents Abroad*, Jonathan Zimmerman examines American teachers who ventured overseas to various countries over the course of the twentieth century and argues how their rationale for engaging in such work changed over time, particularly before and after World War II. Looking closely at teachers' personal records as well as state policies, Zimmerman begins with the largest project ever to send American teachers overseas—those sent to the Philippines—and suggests that they and those who followed their lead in the early decades of the twentieth century believed in their mission as a positive good. In contrast, teachers who ventured abroad in the postwar period, according to Zimmerman, were often more humbled in their endeavors, expressing concerns regarding US hegemony but still eager to engage with cultures outside their own.[67] Like Jacobs, who weaves her own personal narrative—as a beneficiary of colonialism and a mother—into the heart-wrenching stories of indigenous children separated from their families, Zimmerman is driven in part by his own experiences, having joined the Peace Corps in Nepal in the 1980s. Thus, these authors have unique perspectives and objectives—for Jacobs, to expose the American and Australian histories and legacy of child removal, and for, Zimmerman, to account for teachers' work overseas as the United States rose to become a world superpower. Both historians tell compelling stories as they recount colonial teachers' personal reflections—and in Jacobs's account, relay indigenous perspectives—alongside analyses of state policies, thereby accounting for the most intimate experiences as well as the most bureaucratic.[68]

Inspired by the deep and comparative research of such scholarship, this book examines two examples of US imperial education as a means of better understanding race, empire, and education around the turn of the twentieth century. Like both Zimmerman and Jacobs, *Teaching Empire* hopes to connect the personal with the collective in an engaging, provocative way; unfortunately, it does not interrogate the records of American Indian or Filipino peoples to a significant degree. However, such work is welcome and would greatly enhance the story told here.[69]

Beyond such comparative studies, far more scholarly attention has been given to the individual projects regarding US involvement in American Indian or Filipino schooling. Several scholars have explored white encroachment in Native American education, with most recognizing Carlisle's profound influence on the development of the entire Indian school system. As previously mentioned, David Adams's foundational study, *Education for Extinction*, examines how the US government used schools for Indian children to indoctrinate them with "'American ways of thinking and living.'"[70] He discusses the founding of Carlisle and its role in promoting ideas and practices of "civilization," rationalized by reformers committed to "saving" the Indian peoples from permanent destruction and their own ignorance.[71] More recently, Jacqueline Fear-Segal's *White Man's Club* and her edited collection with Susan Rose, *Carlisle Indian Industrial School*, offer an intricate perspective on US Indian schools as sites of negotiation, where whites worked to indoctrinate Indian children with ideas that privileged the dominant culture and Indians alternately rejected and adapted to this effort. Both texts highlight Carlisle, with the former examining the ways that the school functioned to maintain control over its students and the latter including American Indian voices on the trauma and resilience of communities directly impacted by the boarding school experience.[72] In addition, *Boarding School Blues*, written by Clifford. E. Trafzer, Jean A. Keller, and Lorene Sisquoc, traces the history of Carlisle and other Indian boarding schools, paying particular tribute to the students who survived them while also acknowledging the complexity of the system, including the varied experiences that students had—both positive and negative—as well as the mixed intentions of teachers and other employees.[73] Still other scholars explore Indian education more broadly, demonstrating the reform movement's significance both for American Indians and for the nation, while monographs focus on individual Indian schools, useful for understanding the particulars of each and for comparing the similarities and differences across the system.[74]

Shifting to scholarship focusing on American education in the Philippines, much of this work is embedded in broader studies on US empire or the nation's rise to global power. Like those of Zimmerman and Justice, discussed above, A. J. Angulo places US ventures in the Philippines within this broader context, arguing how humanitarian and commercial interests vied for control in the region around the turn of the twentieth century. Regarding US schooling efforts on the islands, Angulo focuses on the general shifts among its educational leadership, concluding that efficiency-minded progressives largely prevailed.[75] Texts that focus more specifically on the Philippines often dwell on US military interventions and violence, with less attention to educational endeavors. Still, some of these works relay stories of teachers and how schooling efforts enabled, for example, English to become the common language, uniting the vast archipelago while simultaneously deepening class and other divisions. Stanley Karnow's *In Our Image: America's Empire in the Philippines* notes the successes and shortcomings of American educational policy in the archipelago and gives voice to several US teachers on the islands, although the scope of the book ranges from imperial Spanish control up to the Reagan administration's foreign policy in the region. Other scholarship describes the role that US teachers played in infusing American culture into Filipino lives.[76]

Glenn Anthony May's texts, particularly *Social Engineering in the Philip-*

pines, serve as foundations in the field of US educational intervention in the archipelago. Here, May argues that US policies, including schooling, largely failed to institute fundamental changes on the islands due in part to the difficult circumstances on the ground as well as the conflicting tactics promoted by various US leaders. Tracing the programming developed over the course of three different education administrations between 1901 and 1913, May declares US efforts at "social engineering" a failure.[77] His more recent work continues to frame US educational policies in the archipelago as overly ambitious and only marginally effective. Agreeing with scholars like Paulet, May argues that experimental education projects, namely industrial education, were first attempted in the metropole before being launched abroad.[78] Still, some scholars find fault with such comparisons, fearful that such work might oversimplify, flatten, or ignore the dialectical creation of power between the metropole and periphery.[79]

As suggested from the outset of this book, attention to race—a loaded yet dynamic term and category of analysis—is critical for understanding US teachers' work among Native Americans and Filipinos around the turn of the twentieth century. Teachers in this study did more than simply apply their own racially informed beliefs to their work. Although many clung to or became more firmly committed to ideas of white superiority, even in these cases, teachers' biases were challenged. Many regularly redefined and rooted their own sense of power and place by understanding themselves in relation to "others," as did their students, and these ideas shifted in different contexts. In these and other ways, race mattered, jumpstarting and continually redefining the larger project of American empire and how it manifested on the ground.[80]

Although much of the literature related to these imperial education experiments discusses the significance of race, two scholars particularly influenced my analysis. Paul Kramer points to the dynamic nature of race manifest in the US occupation of the Philippines shaped by transnational forces as well as local realities. He argues that "these two histories—of the racial remaking of empire and the imperial remaking of race—are not separable. It was not simply that difference made empire possible: empire remade difference in the process."[81] Rather than framing US empire as the exportation or reformulation of prior imperial ventures to suit the archipelago, Kramer argues that race and American empire in the Philippines were active, transnational, dialectic forces, shaping one another and influencing power dynamics within the colonial site as well as the metropole. Although Kramer fears that some scholarship works too hard to show parallels between imperial projects and ultimately discusses race in "a static, ahistorical, and decontextualized manner," such problems are not inevitable.[82] *Teaching Empire* recognizes the importance of historical context in shaping systemic and personal ideas regarding race and that such beliefs can change over time and space. Although most US teachers involved in these imperial education ventures subscribed to dominant notions promoted by the white Protestant middle class, their individual ideas of race and "others" were dynamic, somewhat responsive to the gaze and needs of students, and helped to shape larger ideas about race and place in society.

Fear-Segal's *White Man's Club* also debunks race as a static category and focuses on students' participation in making meaning of both Indianness and whiteness, including how their resistance to white authorities undermined the hierarchy of power. She also notes how Indian education reformers changed tactics over time, both influenced by and influencing notions of race. Carlisle's founders, she argues, believed that Indians could assimilate to the dominant culture quickly—within a generation—while later reformers believed that assimilation could only happen over centuries.[83] Thus, Fear-Segal highlights how ideas regarding race can be made or unmade from above as well as below. Ultimately, teachers did not simply carry manufactured racial stereotypes or hierarchies with them, but recreated meanings of race and power in their everyday lives, reshaping their personal biases and notions of self as they strengthened and challenged systemic inequalities, as their students and supervisors did the same.

In addition to race, teachers' work of cultural translation was profoundly shaped by personal, political, and, in some cases, transnational remakings of gender. Cahill's work on the Indian School Service extends the historical beginnings of the "maternalist welfare state"—framed by Linda Gordon and Theda Skocpol as beginning in the 1910s—by arguing that decades earlier the US government recruited women for the Indian Service, believing they were more nurturing and better suited to work with American Indians. According to Cahill, these "federal mothers" of the Indian Service worked to "restructur[e] Native households according to white middle-class gender norms," bolstering US westward expansion via settler colonialism.[84] Scholarship on the Philippine Service does not focus on gender to such an extent, although issues particular to men's and women's experiences are considered. For example, Zimmerman argues that US efforts to recruit men to teach in the Philippines and promote them at higher rates than women reflected American biases "regarding gender and power" rather than, as sometimes claimed by US officials, Filipinos' beliefs. Moreover, Zimmerman points to American norms regarding sex that resulted in the dismissal of several women teachers in the mission's first two years, although no men were sent home for similar transgressions.[85] Vicente Rafael explores the writings of white American women, especially teachers, who ventured to the Philippines at the turn of the century, noting how gender and race influenced ideals of domesticity and power.[86] Although not examining education or intimacy, Kristin Hoganson expands the impact that gender had in shaping US imperial reach into the Philippines, arguing that calls for or against war were framed in terms of the need to protect American manhood.[87] This demonstrates how gender shaped both the design and implementation of these imperial projects, although sometimes teachers wielded agency in ways that defied gendered expectations.

The case studies of Carlisle and the Philippines are largely based on unique sources and types of archival evidence. There are similarities, however, in a few areas. To understand the lives and work of Carlisle teachers, many kinds of primary sources were pieced together, revealing significant evidence on fifty-five teachers. The personal papers of the school's founding superintendent, Richard Henry Pratt, comprise one of the richest Carlisle sources as it includes outgoing correspondence as well as letters from some of the school's founding teachers. After Pratt's twenty years in charge, scandals plagued two of the school's next superintendents. Teachers' perspectives on these scandals were gleaned from congressional hearings as well as the papers of the Executive Committee of Friends on Indian Affairs, housed at Haverford College. Other Carlisle teachers' voices are captured in personnel files housed primarily at the St. Louis Archive and National Archives in Washington, DC, although these archives mainly contain files on those who worked at the school over its last two decades. Further information about Carlisle teachers is gleaned from Pratt's memoir, *Battlefield and Classroom*, as well as a few student memoirs, notably those by Luther Standing Bear, Jason Betzinez, and Asa Daklugie. A source unique to Carlisle is a treasure trove of school newspapers that were published throughout the school's forty years and written for school students, staff, and the broader public. Although they largely served as propaganda, these newspapers served other functions as well and oftentimes reflected the views and experiences of the school's teachers. Other important Carlisle sources are the annual reports of the commissioner of Indian affairs and additional documents that reflect views of the Bureau of Indian Affairs. Overall, the story of Carlisle teachers draws from a wide array of sources and perspectives.

Documentation of Philippine teachers' experiences is primarily derived from their own writing and thus reveals their voices and opinions more clearly than that of the Carlisle teachers. Of the thirty-three Thomasites featured here, several have personal papers housed at universities or national archives. These varied collections include teachers' correspondence, unpublished memoirs, diaries, speeches, and newspaper clippings. The St. Louis Personnel Record Center holds files on several teachers who worked for the Philippine Civil Service, as does the National Archives II in College Park, Maryland, which also houses more general information published by and about the Philippine Civil Service. A couple of published memoirs recount teachers' experiences, as do dissertations written about (and one by) the Thomasites. In addition, a publication titled *The Log of the "Thomas,"* written by recruits as they traveled overseas, details their initial voyage and includes other information about some of the teachers. Together, these sources reveal a rich, personal account of teachers working abroad on behalf of the growing US empire.

Organized into five body chapters plus a conclusion, this book frames "teaching empire" using a comparative lens that leaves room for critical analyses of each case study. Chapter 1 examines the journey to teach and provides a historical background for each mission as well as a context for understanding them as part of turn-of-the-century US imperial ambitions. While Carlisle teachers were part of a small, intimate experiment—only later consumed by the larger work of the Indian Education Service—teachers headed west to the Philippines were part of a grand effort justified by imperial claims from the start. Chapter 2 chronicles life at Carlisle and demonstrates the significance of assimilation efforts as well as everyday life at the Indian boarding school. It details the historical context regarding Indian education more broadly before discussing the school's curricular and extracurricular programming as well as its use of social, familial, and surveillance methods, and the teachers' role throughout. Chapter 3 examines discipline at Carlisle, including methods of punishment, the threat of disease, and political scandal and incompetent leadership at the institution, as well as the fun and friendship teachers and students experienced despite such challenges. Chapter 4 discusses life and death in the Philippines, with teachers adapting to new norms to different degrees and in widely varying circumstances, from managing classrooms to facing more severe challenges like disease, warfare, and famine. Chapter 5 addresses teachers' professional lives after their service at Carlisle and in the Philippines, noting patterns and differences among them, contrasting those who committed their life's work to education with those who left the field for other opportunities, and charting the course of teachers' commitment to imperial education. The conclusion analyzes the legacy of imperial education, noting teachers' contributions and commitment to the larger mission as well as the long-term impacts of such policies, frameworks, and relationships.

Together these chapters examine teachers collectively and as individuals, analyzing the extent to which personal, political, and imperial interests affected them and their work at Carlisle and in the Philippines. This complicates the historical understandings of US expansion and demonstrates how teachers' agency shaped the structure of schooling, and ultimately, the American empire. Although most teachers in the Philippines and at Carlisle viewed their efforts as largely benevolent, their personal diaries and letters reveal how their perceptions of this work changed over time and space. Some teachers became more familiar with their students, more confident in their own teaching, and more committed to Indian or Filipino "uplift." Others became increasingly disillusioned as the hardships they faced on the ground created impenetrable roadblocks for effective schooling. Still, teachers' promotion of the dominant culture within and beyond their classrooms furthered US imperial ambitions, disseminating ideas regarding the righteousness of white middle-class ideals, even as some students and communities rejected such teachings. As mediators, teachers profoundly shaped the experiences of their students as they translated government policies on the ground and helped to build an empire, however fragile, sometimes transforming themselves in the process.

CHAPTER ONE

THE JOURNEY TO TEACH

On June 21, 1901, recent University of Michigan graduate student Ralph Wendell Taylor wrote to his mother, "A rather startling proposition was made [to] me today, in fact about minutes ago. The Secretary of the Appointment Committee asked me if I would care to teach in the Philippines. . . . I could not give him an answer and will not need to for a few days,—that is till I hear from you."[1] Eager to have his mother's blessing before venturing overseas, Taylor, and hundreds of other American teachers like him, had to make a quick and potentially life-changing decision: whether to leave loved ones behind to set up schools in a distant land—one that the United States had recently acquired from Spain following the War of 1898. Explaining the opportunity to his mother, Taylor admitted, "I find myself recalling some indistinct dreams I have had in recent months of going to some place like the Philippine Islands to teach or to take advantage of some of the opportunities there might be in other lives. . . . I have no definite prospect for a school here."[2] Lacking other job offers and following his "indistinct dreams," in less than a month Taylor and hundreds of other men and women from around the country journeyed to San Francisco, where they boarded the USS *Thomas* on July 23, 1901. Bound for Manila, the decommissioned naval carrier transported over five hundred teachers—the largest group sent to set up schools in the Philippines. Although additional teachers traveled via other ships, they all came to be known as "Thomasites."[3]

While the US government sought to set up schools for an entire nation in the Philippines—employing hundreds of teachers like Taylor—it had tried similar experiments before. As discussed in the introduction, in the late nineteenth century US officials built on decades of US-Indian policy and missionary educational endeavors to create a comprehensive, highly stratified Indian School Service.[4] Promising to "uplift" American Indians through education—thereby "civilizing" the colonized peoples living *within* its borders—many practices and policies adopted by the Indian Service were first attempted in 1879 at an abandoned army barracks turned Indian boarding school established in Carlisle, Pennsylvania. This Carlisle Indian Industrial School, the first Indian boarding school established outside of tribal lands, endeavored to assimilate indigenous children into US culture and society more effectively and efficiently than on-reservation day or boarding schools. Like Taylor—who hurriedly chose to go to the Philippines—Carlisle's founding teachers had to quickly decide whether to join the US imperial education mission in Pennsylvania, the first of its kind.

Although the Carlisle and Philippines experiments relied upon teachers to meet a similar goal—to assimilate "other" peoples into the dominant white culture—the US government approached the Indian and Filipino "problems" in distinctly different ways. In the case of Carlisle, students were brought east to the teachers. Thomasites, in comparison, were sent west to their students in the Philippines. In both cases, location mattered. Carlisle was purposefully established far removed from the "backward" influence of reservations and traditional Indian customs, with the hope that a group of mostly white women teachers, committed to the cause of Indian education, could uplift and "save" the race. The Philippines was gained as a bounty of war, and soon after shipping soldiers overseas the United States sent hundreds of American men and women to the archipelago, hoping that they would use their educational expertise and example to civilize those deemed "uncivilized." Overall, although the projects began somewhat hastily—with little time to carefully plan out logistics—they each had lasting impacts upon the individuals involved, the US imperial mission, and the broader Native American and Filipino societies, for better and worse.

Education reformers, who advocated for Indian and later Filipino advancement, rushed to "rescue" these and other colonized peoples in the late nineteenth and early twentieth centuries. In 1883 an elite group of such activists organized the first Mohonk Conference for "Friends of the Indians."[5] Here, they raised their preeminent concerns regarding the best way to "save" the American Indian, which over time came to include what reformer Elaine Goodale Eastman described as engaging "the problems of other 'dependent peoples' belonging to our colonial empire." Elaborating further, Eastman posited that Mohonk conferences "brought together nearly all of the leading workers, and not a few advanced Indians and Filipinos spoke for themselves."[6] Thus, from Eastman and other reformers' perspective, American Indians and Filipinos shared the burdens and problems faced by many "dependent peoples," a fact apparently recognized by some Indian and Filipino leaders as well.[7] Still, little to no attention was paid to Native American or Filipino perspectives and desires, unless they aligned with the "reformers'" goals.

Providing some historical background on US "civilizing" educational efforts among Native Americans and Filipinos and tracing the journeys to these experiments reveals that teachers were largely invested in these imperial education efforts from the start. Rationalizing the need for these projects came relatively easily to reformers, and educators largely followed suit. Significantly, indigenous Americans and Filipinos faced profound challenges and threats as these projects were crafted, and it was not until teachers sought to implement empire in the schoolroom—which will be discussed in later chapters—that their dilemma over how to translate imperial policy into practice arose.

In discussing US involvement in these experiments of "civilization," it is crucial to begin by highlighting their differences as well as similarities in order to demonstrate ways US imperial aims guided educational reform and how this changed over time in each case. As indicated earlier, central to both of these stories is the speed with which reformers and the federal government implemented each mission as they rushed to resolve the Indian and Filipino "problems" before it was deemed too late. Equally important to explore, as this chapter will show, are teachers' motivations and the hiring practices involved in the two cases. Teachers willing to venture to the Philippines often had different reasons for their decisions than those who initially staffed Carlisle, where the school's leaders depended on a preexisting social network to recruit faculty. But eventually the Carlisle School, like the Philippines from the beginning, depended on a growing federal bureaucracy. Whereas some early Carlisle teachers and staff knew each other before arriving at the school, Philippine teachers experienced a kind of rite of passage as they journeyed to the islands, which helped them develop personal relationships and form a collective identity. Finally, examining the experiences of crossover teachers—those who worked both in the Philippines and Carlisle—shows that at least these teachers (and likely others) considered the missions comparable and experienced varying degrees of success in the two locations. For them, as for all the teachers involved, issues of gender, race, class, and bureaucracy shaped their efforts, as did the long history of education as a "civilizing" tool.

Indian education emerged long before Carlisle opened its doors in 1879. Beginning in the colonial era, missionaries and reformers alike strove to "civilize" American Indians by establishing schools across the continent, and by 1868 the federal government "promised a schoolhouse and a teacher for every thirty [Indian] children," although funding for the program did not increase dramatically for another decade. Classified as a "new era in federal Indian education," 1879 marked the beginning of a dramatic increase in government spending on this issue, with monies rising from $75,000 to over $2 million over the next fifteen years. During that period, the US government established twenty off-reservation boarding schools, of which Carlisle was the first, and a federally operated school was opened on every Indian reservation in the country by 1890. In regard to Carlisle in particular, its opening marked a shift from an older, evangelical style of Indian education to a supposedly more progressive approach devoted to the advancement and assimilation of the entire race.[8]

By the late nineteenth century, reformers and advocates of Indian education believed that if Native Americans did not assimilate to the dominant culture, they would die. Carlisle's founder, Richard Henry Pratt, had come to this realization after his experiences in the army. In 1867, a couple of years after his service in the Civil War, Pratt returned to the army and served as a second lieutenant of an all-black regiment, the Tenth United States Cavalry, "sent west to keep the peace and to fight Indians." During the eight years Pratt led his regiment in the West, the lieutenant "came to believe that Indians needed to assimilate to survive."[9] In the spring of 1875 Pratt was ordered to transport and then oversee a group of seventy-two Indian prisoners of war from Fort Sill, Indian Territory, to Fort Marion in St. Augustine, Florida. During the few years that Pratt oversaw the Florida prison, he replaced the inmates' traditional clothing with military uniforms and cut their hair, arranged for them to work in the town, and developed an ad-hoc school for the captives, relying on local sympathizers to teach English.[10] This marked the beginning of Pratt's direct involvement with Indian education. He marveled at the prisoners' quick adoption of white cultural norms and the potential power of education to further assimilate the Indian into white society, all along ignoring how forcing such measures upon the prisoners undermined efforts to "save" the Indian. A few years later, he looked to some of the most active volunteers at Fort Marion to help him recruit and teach the first class at the Carlisle Indian Industrial School.

Pratt was committed to Indian education as a means of accelerating the uplift of the race and sought to convince the federal government of its effectiveness. In 1878, three years into his tenure at Fort Marion, Pratt received federal permission to release the prisoners. Eager to continue his education work, Pratt took twenty-two former prisoners with him to the Hampton Institute in Virginia for further schooling. The Hampton Institute had been established a decade earlier as an industrial training school to uplift African Americans through cultural, moral, and manual training, or what its founder Samuel Armstrong characterized as work of "the head, the heart, and the hand."[11] Pratt spent a little over a year at Hampton and oversaw the former Indian prisoners' education. During that time, US officials asked Pratt to "secure" fifty Indian children from the Nez Perce tribe and the Missouri River agencies by receiving parental permission and bringing them back to the Virginia industrial school.[12] In doing so, the US government showed both its confidence in Pratt and the potential of education to, perhaps quickly, remedy the Indian "problem." These recruitment trips proved foundational for Pratt as he soon ventured west to Indian territory to fill Carlisle's classrooms.[13]

Within a year of arriving at Hampton, Pratt had developed a new vision: to initiate a school strictly dedicated to the Indian. By early 1879 Pratt felt eager to leave the Hampton Institute, believing his duties were "no longer necessary."[14] In addition, he wanted to distance his Indian charges from the racial discrimination borne by blacks at Hampton and hoped to better integrate the Indians into a white community.[15] When Pratt learned that his position at Hampton might become permanent, he rushed to Washington, DC, in the summer of 1879 to discuss alternative appointments. After several meetings with government leaders, and upon his own suggestion, he received orders to transform the abandoned army barracks in Carlisle, Pennsylvania, into a school for Indians. Pratt wrote to his wife, Laura, on August 21, 1879: "Carlisle 'is ours and fairly now.' General Sherman [of the Army] approves. . . . Now the work begins."[16] The next day Pratt again wrote to his wife, this time reassuring her of their next assignment: "Your letter of yesterday told me you were feeling quite badly. I hope dear, little wife that the news I sent you will be good medicine. If we can quietly settle down at Carlisle for a few years, I hope we both may gather up more vigor, and that we may otherwise better our condition."[17] Not knowing the particulars of Laura or Pratt's "condition," it seems likely that after many years of army life, moving had taken a toll on her and the couple. Laura—and, to a certain extent, Pratt—understandably felt anxious to "settle down" somewhere that seemed a bit more permanent. Carlisle became "home" for the Pratts for the next twenty-five years.

Less than two months after having received consent from Sherman, Pratt converted Carlisle's dilapidated army quarters into a school. With approval from the War Department, the barracks at Carlisle were officially turned over to the Department of the Interior on September 6, 1879, with the intention of beginning an Indian boarding school.[18] The school opened its doors just one month later, on October 6, 1879. Moving with amazing speed, between late August and early October, Pratt recruited Indian students and hired staff members while his wife moved their family to Pennsylvania and helped to prepare the run-down buildings for the arrival of Carlisle's first pupils. Pratt's expeditious work in opening the school doors was rooted in his experiences in the West and in Florida. He firmly believed that Indians needed to assimilate quickly into mainstream society to avoid the race's demise.[19] Although much of his work "keeping the peace" in the West involved fighting Indians, his experiences in Florida proved that Indians could adapt to white cultural norms. The improvised schooling Pratt helped to initiate at Fort Marion had "worked"; his Indian prisoners learned English and adopted other white customs. Thus, Pratt concluded that extensive planning was not needed for effective teaching and learning to take place. Rather, he believed that the imminent danger of race extinction necessitated the immediate availability of a school in which Indian youth would be removed from both the "corrupting" influences of reservation life and the racial prejudice borne by African Americans. At a moment when Pratt felt pressure to redirect his military career, Carlisle offered a critical opportunity, both personally and professionally.

In addition to Pratt's individual ambitions in establishing Carlisle, by 1879 the federal government was becoming increasingly desperate to resolve "the Indian problem." Fighting over land and resources had plagued Indian-white relations ever since European settlement, compounding the already devastating rates of disease, which along with conquest and the forced removal from lands resulted in more than an 85 percent loss of the North American indigenous population between 1492 and 1900.[20] By the late 1820s, US government policies forced Indians from their native lands and relocated them west of the Mississippi River. Beginning in the 1850s and increasing steadily by the 1870s, new policies confined Indians to tracts of land or reservations, further limiting their access to food and continuing to destroy indigenous ways of life.[21] As more and more whites moved west, fighting over land and resources continued, resulting in decades of bloody warfare and a devastating assault on indigenous culture and norms.

Attacks on native means of subsistence and indigenous bodies—through warfare, rape, lynching, and other means of terror—ravaged Native American communities. One such assault was brazenly carried out by the federal government and has been deemed the largest mass execution in American history: when President Abraham Lincoln ordered the hanging of thirty-eight Dakota men on December 26, 1862, who were accused of attacking white settlers in the larger theater of the US-Dakota War. The reign of terror brought by white settlers and consistently legitimated or directly ordered by the federal government over the course of the nineteenth century *cannot* be overstated. As a consequence of virtually constant assaults on native peoples, the population of American Indians fell from 600,000 in 1800 to a low point of 237,000 by the 1890s.[22] By the end of the nineteenth century, the rates of American Indian mortality were almost two-thirds higher than that of whites.[23] Despite such devastation, indigenous peoples were resolved to survive. They adapted to white cultural norms and racial hierarchies to differing degrees while, at the same time, continuing to resist, maintaining their dignity, humanity, and pride.[24]

By 1871—having gained increasing control over Western lands and American Indian peoples' lives and livelihoods—the US government officially declared the Indians "wards of the government, a colonized people."[25] At the same time, Congress approved the Indian Appropriations Act, which prevented American Indians from making further treaties with the US government. This legislation took away native peoples' national sovereignty and ultimately created a fully colonized population within the continent's borders. Although Indian rights advocates had long been critical of brutal government policies that decimated Indian tribes and diminished their autonomy, by 1880 they generally agreed with the public consensus that Indians needed to be saved from such ruthless policies as well as from themselves.[26] The reality of high mortality rates among American Indians—due to disease, warfare, and starvation—motivated reformers to try to "save" the "dying race." Thus, by the time Carlisle was proposed as a means of assimilating Indians into white society, government officials and reformers both eagerly supported Pratt's endeavor.

Within two decades, Filipinos joined American Indians as the next group treated as "wards of the government." Beginning in 1899, political leaders sought to assimilate Filipinos via a similar educational program used with American Indians, again ostensibly for their own benefit and that of the greater empire. In fact, soon after the United States acquired the Philippine Islands in December 1898, American officials and reformers pointed to parallels between the nation's newest and oldest colonial subjects, Filipinos and American Indians respectively. According to this logic and ignoring the tremendous diversity within each population, both groups were colonized peoples without full rights of citizenship and both lacked "civilization."[27] Of course, many differences existed between these two peoples, including their particular relationship to the American empire. As argued by sociologist Julian Go, forcible removal of American Indians from their land (and subsequent efforts to assimilate them into mainstream culture) can be understood as an example of "settler colonialism," while the Philippines project falls under the category of "administrative colonialism," whereby the United States sought to exploit the islands' resources and strategic location *without* displacing the Filipino people.[28] Like Go, Ann Paulet notes these and other differences between the two projects but argues that the US government ultimately used its experiences with Native Americans as a model for its policy choices in the Philippine context, deliberately repeating what worked in the American West and avoiding what did not.[29] Significantly, both scholars emphasize that the Carlisle and Philippines projects were examples of purposeful US imperial design. And, in both cases, the US government used education to pacify and transform colonized peoples, claiming purely benevolent intentions while working to strengthen the American empire.

Unlike the long history of American involvement with Indian schools, US interests in Philippine education emerged in earnest only after it occupied the islands following the War of 1898. Moreover, the education mission to the Philippines marked the first time that the US government sent teachers overseas. This particular initiative grew out of a policy dubbed "benevolent assimilation"—a term coined by President William McKinley in a December 1898 speech in which he proclaimed the nation's moral authority following its victory in the war. According to McKinley the US mission was to assure the Filipino people that its occupation of their country would be "substituting the mild sway of justice and right for [the] arbitrary rule" they had known under Spanish dominion.[30] Although the acquisition of the Philippines began as part of a war of conquest, American imperialists framed the war and its aftermath as a progressive movement aimed at helping the Filipino people and thereby distinguishing their efforts from those of European imperialists.[31]

As at Carlisle, the US government moved swiftly to initiate education efforts in the Philippines. Official plans emerged shortly after the Treaty of Paris was signed on December 10, 1898. Just over a month later, on January 20, 1899, President McKinley created the First Philippine Commission, charged with assessing the conditions on the ground, including the status of schools. Tasked with assuming civilian authority over the islands and setting up an American-style government and society, the Philippine Commission was responsible for convincing Filipinos of its government's "benevolent" intentions. Establishing an educational system modeled on the United States became an integral component of these efforts to appease, and from its perspective, civilize, a war-ravaged people.[32] In April 1900 McKinley established the Second Philippine Commission with the primary purpose of focusing on education. On January 21, 1901, that commission passed Act No. 74, which sanctioned the hiring of 1,000 American school-teachers to be sent to the Philippines for the purposes of establishing a public school system akin to that in the United States. Less than six months later, hundreds of American teachers ventured across the Pacific.[33] Thus, within two and a half years of having overthrown the Spanish empire in the Philippines, the United States had surveyed its newest territory, developed policies for its governance, and approved the hiring of one thousand American teachers to establish a US-style school system.

Yet, before recruiting and transporting these American teachers, the United States called upon soldiers to both quell Filipino unrest and demonstrate US goodwill. Filipino rebels' resistance to the American occupation began shortly after the islands were handed over from one imperial power to another. This resistance became increasingly hostile, ultimately sparking the Philippine-American War in February 1899. Soon after this next round of military combat ensued, the US Army commissioned soldiers to set up schools as part of its efforts to prove American benevolence toward Filipino civilians. Thus, as the United States waged war against Filipino rebels, it simultaneously worked to win the hearts and minds of the islands' people through education and other altruistic gestures.[34] In this way, the first phase of the American occupation *overtly* relied upon guns *and* books to ensure Filipino compliance. In fact, the United States rushed to send American teachers overseas in 1901, more than a year before it declared the Philippine-American War officially over in July 1902.[35] Thus, US involvement in Filipino education was mired in military conflict from the beginning, forcing this new colonial power to act quickly to pacify Filipinos and secure American authority on the islands.

Despite complications created by the ongoing war, efforts to recruit American teachers persisted, and perhaps even accelerated. In 1901 the superintendent of instruction in the Philippines, Fred W. Atkinson, largely deferred his power of appointment to educational and political leaders around the country. There were many aspects of the project to oversee, and having local leaders select instructors made the grand task more manageable. As many as 926 teachers served at a time, and sorting through the recorded eight thousand applications for employment within a short amount of time required a large staff.[36] As teachers' personal records suggest, most were likely approached by university and normal school administrators to consider working in the Philippines and, in this way, they were virtually appointed, speeding up the hiring process by effectively minimizing the pool of applicants.[37] Nevertheless, the large number of applications and the more than nine hundred teachers hired within a matter of months suggests that there were effective employment practices in place as well as teachers eager to participate.

Although leaders in the "benevolent" empire sought teachers for the Philippines in order to protect US security and further economic and humanitarian interests, teachers had their own reasons for going.[38] Many were proud to serve and represent the United States government, but they did not dwell upon this in their personal letters or diaries. Most teachers described personal or pragmatic reasons for venturing overseas, and others—including Ralph Taylor, quoted at the opening of this chapter—described dreamlike or opportunistic reasons. Thus, Thomasites were not simply instruments of empire but individuals who exhibited agency, choosing to do what was best for their careers or what might prove most interesting or practical for them as individuals while also expressing an eagerness to teach as part of a new US mission overseas. By the turn of the twentieth century, teachers were working within a new world order, one where the United States strove to prove itself on the global stage. A small but elite anti-imperialist movement vehemently opposed such US expansion overseas, though Thomasites—many elite in their own right—largely did *not* fall in this obstructionist camp.[39] Moreover, as mentioned earlier, teachers usually had little time to think about their decisions before venturing abroad, and officials sought to fill the teaching positions and begin the education experiment as quickly as possible. All in all, and despite the rush on multiple fronts, many teachers were deemed well-qualified, at least on paper, and selected to venture to the archipelago.

Overall, American teachers sent to the Philippines were a highly educated group, most with significant teaching experience and many eager to apply their skills and knowledge to a new environment (see Table 1.1). John Muerman, who received three degrees after teaching in the Philippines, wrote his dissertation in 1925 on the educational experiment there and noted the exceptional qualifications of the Thomasites. Before boarding the USS *Thomas* in July 1901, Muerman had taught for eleven years and served as the superintendent of schools in Moscow, Idaho.[40] Reflecting on the Philippines experiment, he argued in his dissertation, "So far as education and experience goes, it was perhaps the finest trained body of instructors that any nation has ever attempted to send from its shores."[41] In fact, 478 of the 509 teachers onboard the USS *Thomas* in summer 1901 held a higher education degree, including almost fifty teachers earning masters or

Table 1.1: Thomasites' Level of Education

Level of Education	Number of Teachers Aboard USS *Thomas*
No degree or certificate beyond high school diploma	31
Normal school degree	104
Undergraduate degree	309*
Received both normal and undergraduate degree	15
Masters degree	42
Doctoral degree	6
Unknown	2
Total	509

*Eight received two undergraduate degrees
Source: Adapted from Lardizabal, "Pioneer American Teachers and Philippine Education," 22.

doctoral degrees and more than twenty others completing multiple undergraduate or teaching training programs. Although one-fifth of the teachers aboard the *Thomas* did not have teaching experience, many of them graduated from prestigious universities, including Harvard, Yale, Princeton, and Cornell.[42] With such strong professional and education backgrounds, most teachers felt confident in their abilities and eager to prove themselves or try something new.

In his 1924 study, Muerman summed up what he saw as his fellow Thomasites' aims in joining the first large-scale government-sponsored educational mission overseas. He wrote:

> Few Americans went to the Philippines with the intention of making that country their permanent home. In fact the number is so small that it is not worth considering. It is true some went for the pure adventure and to see the world, but the great majority entered the service honestly to give their best to the Filipino children; to educate these children in terms of Filipino life and yet to give them as good an education as the conditions permitted.[43]

Muerman must have considered himself among the "great majority" whom he claimed were "honestly" committed to aiding Filipino children, as his enthusiasm for US educational endeavors in the Philippines ultimately steered his dissertation.[44] Whether it truly was the "great majority" or not, the historical record suggests that many teachers headed to the Philippines eager to participate in the US mission abroad believed that they had something to offer Filipinos. Even so, reflecting upon his own and others' experiences, Muerman qualified teachers' achievements, noting that certain "conditions" hindered what was possible. Thus, even the most-qualified and best-intended teachers could only accomplish so much. Of course, not all teachers were so competent or beneficent, as even Muerman acknowledges. "Some American teachers," he wrote, "did not have a real human sympathy either for the [Filipino] people or for their work," and Muerman expressed relief that such teachers had retired early.[45] Still, as Muerman's account suggests, most teachers—like the mission itself—claimed altruistic motivations; whether they were truly benevolent or not is another question and will be explored in Chapters 4 and 5.

Like Muerman, Philippine native and scholar Amparo Santamaria Lardizabal wrote a romanticized yet similarly significant account of Thomasites' experiences in her 1956 dissertation, "Pioneer American Teachers and Philippine Education." Among other things, she asked these former teachers, "'How did you happen to go there?'"[46] Fourteen respondents indicated that they went primarily to educate Filipinos, eight sought to reunite with a significant other, seven wanted to travel, six needed a job, and four indicated that it was happenstance. A few described wanting adventure or feeling a missionary or pioneering spirit, two hoped to establish their careers, and a handful of others went for miscellaneous reasons, including following in an older brother's footsteps.[47] Overall, like Muerman's dissertation, Lardizabal's study essentially lauds the Thomasites and the schooling system they helped to establish, casting them as pioneers who surmounted obstacles, both treacherous and mundane, and from whom lessons can be learned about teaching in different cultures. She argues that Thomasites' "zeal and earnestness, together with Filipino eagerness for education, made their work a success."[48] Despite such glowing conclusions and the fact that the teachers who responded to her survey were a self-selected group—and as such, had relatively positive experiences—her research captures valuable first-person reflections.

Like Thomasites who published memoirs (including Mary Fee, featured below), Lardizabal's respondents reveal voices and perspectives that would otherwise be lost and give insight into how they remembered and reflected upon their experiences, however biased. In contrast, the majority of the letters, diaries, personal reflections, and personnel files combed for this book were largely intended for a private audience and thus reveal intimate details and perspectives in real time, as the work of building an educational system in the archipelago was ongoing and as yet, uncertain. Overall, most of

Walter Marquardt with local Filipina child, circa 1905. Eager to
venture abroad, Marquardt committed himself to teaching in the
Philippines and worked there for almost four decades. (Walter
W. Marquardt Papers, Bentley Historical Library, University of
Michigan.)

the educators' thoughts captured here paint a less rosy and perhaps more
nuanced, intimate, and diverse portrait of the Thomasites' experiences,
though in all cases, audience and purpose must be taken into account. The
majority of the thirty-three teachers featured here do not outright reveal
their motivations, but some described what prompted them to join the US
mission in the archipelago in the first place.

Aligning with Muerman and Lardizabal's findings, at least two of the thirty-three teachers researched for this book referenced their commitment to teaching abroad—one more enthusiastically than the other. Walter Marquardt, who ultimately remained in the islands for about forty years, remembered that he had hoped for "a chance to see foreign countries and to do work in which I was interested at the same time."[49] A more sentimental yet revealing account is captured in Mary Fee's 1912 memoir. She wrote, "I was going to see the world, and I was one of an army of enthusiasts enlisted to instruct our little brown brother, and to pass the torch of Occidental knowledge several degrees east of the international date-line."[50] In addition to expressing her personal interest in travel, Fee's use of the language "little brown brother"—coined by the 1901 American governor-general of the Philippines, William Howard Taft—drew attention to the racialized framework of the US intervention in the Philippines, which lauded white teachers for bringing Western knowledge to their darker-skinned "brothers" across the Pacific. Such language was not intended as derogatory but was rather an example of "paternalist racism," suggesting that Fee believed that US involvement in the islands was both entirely benevolent and necessary to properly care for an otherwise "backward" people.[51] Other teachers likely shared her ideals.

Still, some teachers claimed more pragmatic reasons for choosing to go to the Philippines, including two teachers who wanted to leave behind difficulties they faced in the United States. John Early remembered feeling "glad of a chance to see the other side of the world" while also detailing some of his troubles in his unpublished memoir titled "Reminiscences." Having worked in the Idaho territory for several years as a newspaper editor, Early wrote that homesteaders were forced to use all of their money on "living expenses" including water instead of cultivating the land since the government was three years behind in providing the people with water. Eager to leave the harsh, impoverished landscape, he welcomed the opportunity to go abroad.[52] Similarly, George Carrothers recalled wanting to escape his dire situation, recounting in his memoir and an interview the desire to leave his Indiana farm so as not to burden his mother with yet another dying son; the family doctor had predicted his early demise. Moreover, having grown up in poverty, Carrothers yearned to see the world despite (or perhaps because of) his grim medical diagnosis.[53] In spite of such troubled backgrounds, both Early and Carrothers went on to have great success teaching in the islands. Their personal memoirs expose multiple reasons for heading overseas, none demonstrably aligned with US imperialist policy, though their ultimate commitment to the work would prove otherwise.

However, as suggested earlier, the majority of Thomasites studied here failed to directly explain their reasons for accepting an appointment in the Philippines, even in their personal diaries and letters to loved ones. While Ralph Taylor suggested that he had dreamed of such an adventure and noted he did not have a "definite prospect" for a job in the States, and others, including Harrie Cole, wrote of needing to earn money, most accounts left no such evidence.[54] Still, it seems clear that several women went to the islands for practical reasons, like being with loved ones, as reflected in Lardizabal's 1956 survey. For example, prior to finishing her undergraduate degree at the University of Michigan, Mary Cole decided to accompany her husband, Harrie, who had already been selected to teach in the Philippines. She then successfully sought a teaching job for herself there. Similarly, Maude Bordner ventured across the Pacific with her husband, Harvey, who had been appointed an administrator, and she then also received a teaching assignment. Other spouses also received positions, such as Willa Rhodes, who married John Early five years into his teaching venture and accompanied him back to the islands after his visit home. By 1915, single women were prohibited from taking the civil service exam to work in the Philippines, as only married women accompanying husbands were allowed entry as teachers. Some teachers, including the Coles and others who married in the islands, like Walter Marquardt and Alice Hollister, depended on two incomes to build up their savings while supporting themselves.[55] Thus, particularly for some women, love and practicality influenced them to teach in the archipelago.

Other Thomasites left even fewer indications of their motivation for heading to the islands. Blaine Moore did not explain why he chose to go but did make a point of saying that he would not tell his family until his appointment was finalized, "for I dreaded the somber emotion and apprehension of impending danger that a trip of ___ miles would engender."[56] A bit of an adventurer, Moore recorded such thoughts in his private diary but was clearly loathe to tell even close family members of his plans. Although John Evans's motivation for boarding the USS *Thomas* in July 1901 is not evident, most likely his younger brother, Glen, headed to the Philippines three years later to follow in his brother's footsteps. A newspaper clipping described the brothers as "restless young men who had to see what lay beyond the confining horizons of an Episcopalian upbringing in Midwest America," and John's letters home may have inspired Glen to head west as well, but their experiences greatly diverged once in the islands.[57] Whereas John remained in the Philippines for sixteen years—during which time he rose to be the governor of the mountain provinces, proving his profound commitment to the US mission abroad—Glen lasted less than a year and was eager to return stateside.

The career paths of others—including Frank Cheney—suggest that some teachers simply wanted to see the world, again aligning with Muerman and Lardizabal's findings. Cheney taught at schools across the United States and around the world over the course of his fifty-six-year career, including a twelve-year stint in the Philippines. Perhaps the diversity of teaching opportunities in the archipelago encouraged him to remain for so many years since he managed to teach at several locations throughout the islands and traveled extensively while stationed there.[58] In Cheney's case, it is unclear how committed he was to promoting American education and culture abroad compared to his persistent wanderlust. For Cheney and other teachers, their actions offer the best insight regarding why they chose to teach in the Philippines.

American leaders in charge of the Philippine schools, in contrast, openly revealed their preferences regarding teaching personnel, particularly in regard to sex. While most schoolteachers in the United States by the turn of the twentieth century were women, government officials initially recruited both men *and* women for the education experiment in the Philippines, believing each sex to be best suited for a particular kind of work. In fact, the majority of Thomasites were men, reflecting, in part, their preferential treatment in hiring practices.[59] In brief, women were deemed better suited to teach in more established schools and towns while men were thought more capable of maintaining the rustic lifestyle necessary to oversee schools in rural areas. A few years into the grand experiment, a December 15, 1904, publication by the Philippine Bureau of Education explained:

> Women teachers, almost without exception, are assigned to duty in the provincial high schools or intermediate schools, where they can have the advantages of American society and an American home. . . . The work of school district supervision, however, is pursued under very different conditions. The teacher usually lives alone in a town separated by some miles from other communities, and very frequently he is the only American resident in a large area . . . traveling sometimes on foot or by horse and vehicle, and sometimes by banca or canoe. . . . This is work which can obviously only be done by a man. For this reason, the greater majority of the teaching force are men. In many cases, however, a man and wife are assigned together to a town, the man carrying the work of

supervision and the woman the instruction of the advanced classes in the central municipal school.[60]

Education officials deemed men's and women's capabilities as fundamentally different, and only in cases of marriage and the support of a husband was it thought that a woman might be able to withstand the pressures of life outside of conventional social comforts. Of course, this line of thinking largely ignored the historical reality of female pioneers who had ventured into the American West, sometimes alone or soon widowed, who created homes, schools, and towns well beyond the reach of established society.[61]

While gendered assumptions about the nature of work largely guided teachers' assignments in the Philippines, "exceptions" did exist. In fact, Thomasite John Muerman reported years later in his dissertation that "over 90% [of teachers] that left Manila [to work in remote villages] stuck to their posts a year, accepted conditions and made the best of them. It was not always the bravest talking pedagogue who proved the best. Often it was a timid young maiden who withstood the hardships with the most fortitude."[62] Thus, in spite of the Bureau's best guess, sometimes single women proved to be the most effective teachers in the challenging circumstances that defined teaching in the Philippines. Defying stereotypes concerning women's dependence on men or on societal comforts, some women remained steadfast in their educational endeavors despite "rustic" island conditions. Indeed, as in Western American towns, some women thrived beyond traditional societal confines.[63]

Twenty years earlier, at Carlisle's founding in 1879, the sex of teachers was never overtly considered. Instead, hiring at the Indian boarding school reflected the national trend whereby single white women comprised the vast majority of teachers. At Carlisle, this pattern continued throughout its forty-year history (see Table 1.2). In fact, the school's first teachers were all women, and this remained true into the 1890s.[64] In the early years, Superintendent Richard Henry Pratt had complete control over hiring at Carlisle, and he likely turned to women automatically because they had, by 1879, become commonly accepted as particularly suited for the teaching profession and for the care of the "needy." Over the course of the nineteenth century, economic demands on the developing public school systems coupled with beliefs concerning women's innate nurturing qualities helped to reshape teaching from a male to a female profession. At the same time, men rose to leadership or "principal" positions to oversee pupils as well as schools' largely female employees.[65] Thus, by 1879 it had become

Table 1.2: Carlisle Teachers' Gender and Marital Status (While Teaching at Carlisle)

Gender	Single	Likely Single	Married	Widow	N/A	Total
Female	25	13	4*	4	2	48
Male	2	—	4*	0	1	7
Total	27	13	8	4	3	55

*One couple met at Carlisle and married.

increasingly common for a male school superintendent, like Pratt, to direct a female teaching faculty.

To staff the new school and alleviate his own uncertainties, Pratt largely looked to women whom he trusted, and they, in turn, looked to one another for inspiration and encouragement. In fact, Carlisle's hiring in its first two decades differed dramatically from the Indian school bureaucracy that developed by the turn of the twentieth century, the latter of which was mirrored in the Philippines. At Carlisle a more intimate social network forged the school's foundation. As Pratt explained, "Finding suitable teachers and employees was a part of the anxieties" in establishing the school.[66] The first person he approached was Sarah Mather, who had taught the Indian prisoners under his care at Fort Marion. Pratt asked Mather to help him recruit students from Western reservations to fill the seats at Carlisle. In reply, Mather suggested that he ask C. M. Semple, whom she believed "would be equally ready" to assist with the work.[67] Pratt had become well acquainted with Miss Semple, superintendent of schools in St. Augustine, Florida, during his years at Fort Marion and trusted her enough to hire her "to take charge of the schoolroom work" during Carlisle's initial stages.[68] Pratt remembered her as "a most efficient New England woman." Another St. Augustine friend of the Indian, J. W. Gibbs, was hired to teach at Carlisle and was delighted to hear that she would be joining Miss Semple there. Acknowledging her own professional shortcomings, Gibbs wrote, "I am so glad to know that Miss Semple is . . . at the head of the school, as I know she will be sweet and gentle [with] one as inexperienced in teaching as myself."[69] Rather than emphasizing Gibbs's inexperience, Pratt remembered her as "most faithful and enthusiastic," qualities he found critical to his pioneering endeavor.[70]

These early hires at Carlisle show how heavily Pratt relied upon people whom he knew and had worked with before and, at the same time, suggests

A portrait photograph of Sarah Mather, who helped to recruit students for Carlisle and was the first teacher hired at the boarding school, circa 1880. Having relied on Mather to educate Indian prisoners held at Fort Marion, Florida, Richard Pratt trusted Mather's educational expertise and commitment to Indian assimilation. (Photo by John N. Choate, courtesy of Richard Henry Pratt Papers, Beinecke Rare Book and Manuscript Library, Yale University.)

how such personal relationships influenced teachers to join the Indian school faculty. Heading a true start-up enterprise, the founder wanted to ensure that he could trust his employees to make the school successful from the beginning.[71] At the same time, teachers were more likely to venture to Carlisle if they felt that they could trust the school's leader. Mather and Semple had worked with Pratt and were excited by the possibilities that Carlisle offered, trusting that their superintendent would provide solid leadership. In addition, Mather's quick acceptance of the job likely influenced Semple to follow her friend and take a chance on the Carlisle venture. This same sentiment influenced Miss Gibbs to accept a post despite her inexperience. Given the short amount of time available to staff the school, Pratt looked to people whom he knew; they, in turn, looked to one another, ultimately building a united workforce from the beginning.[72] The informal social network on which Carlisle was built likely strengthened the teaching force in Carlisle's earliest years, as is evident by the profound commitment that several founding teachers exhibited.

Two such dedicated founding teachers came as a team: Marianna Burgess and Ann Ely were deeply committed to Indian education and helped to guide Carlisle from its earliest days into the twentieth century. At the age of twenty-six, Marianna Burgess sought a position at the school, revealing her forthright disposition in a letter to Lieutenant Pratt, dated October 21, 1879:

> I have seen [in] . . . several prominent papers of the country extended notices of your enterprise of starting an Indian school at Carlisle, Pa. Thousands of people are looking with anxious expectancy to see whether it proves a success or a failure, and a great many more dogmatical unsympathizing individuals are eager for the whole thing to prove an utter failure in order to substantiate the popular theory that the Indian cannot be civilized. I have been a teacher among the Pawnee Indians for more than five years, and very well know the many insurmountable obstacles to meet in attempting to educate Indian children, shrouded as they are by so many counteracting home influences, and can readily see the great advantage of having them removed from the tribe. . . . The object of this letter is to inquire whether I can be of any service to you as teacher.[73]

Having taught indigenous children for several years in Nebraska's Indian Territory, Burgess believed in the promise of Carlisle and endeavored to gain a position there.[74] She was especially supportive of an institution that took children away from the "many counteracting home influences" that she thought hampered the progress of her Pawnee students. Despite the difficulties such separation imposed, Burgess—like Pratt—firmly believed that boarding schools distant from Indian reservations offered the best hope of civilizing, and thus "saving," Indian youth. Though Indian day schools as well as on-reservation boarding schools exposed children to Western education, an off-reservation boarding school like Carlisle promised speedier transformations. Revealing her strong convictions, Burgess wanted to prove wrong those who doubted the benefits that education could have on Indian "uplift."[75]

Burgess's experience teaching Indians and her forthrightness gained her a position at the school as well as her friend, Ann Ely. Significantly older than Burgess, Ely was forty-six when hired at Carlisle and was an experienced educator.[76] Her most recent post had been teaching the Pawnee alongside Burgess. Pratt hired the two women because of their prior work with Indians, professed commitment to Indian education, and glowing recommendation letters from leading Friends.[77] Both Quakers, Burgess and Ely worked for Pratt at Carlisle for more than twenty-five years, during which time their friendship strengthened.[78] And, like Mather, Semple, and Gibbs, their association with one another helped them secure positions at the school.

Unlike Ely's years of experience, which arguably better prepared her for the purported rigor of Indian education, perhaps Burgess tried to minimize her young age and bolster her fitness for such work by appealing to Pratt's anxieties. In her application, she wrote of Carlisle's empty classrooms and emphasized how her experience among the Pawnee could help to recruit Indian children for the school. She claimed, "I have many friends in the Pawnee tribe who entrusted their children to my care, and who earnestly begged for me to remain longer with them." To further strengthen her letter to Pratt, Burgess suggested, "I could obtain a number of Pawnee Children, whose parents would be glad to have them accompany me, should you conclude to need my services."[79] Here, Burgess predicted one of the greatest challenges that Carlisle would face—that of convincing Indian parents to send their children far away from home for several years of schooling among strangers; strangers who resembled, in appearance and behavior, the white men and women who historically and presently broke promises, ultimately stripping indigenous peoples of their land, culture, and livelihood. Burgess sold herself as a valuable asset: an experienced, eager, committed teacher also capable of attracting students to the school, and Pratt felt he needed her expertise.[80]

Yet not everyone was in favor of recruiting Burgess for Carlisle. In spite of Pratt's optimism, he recalled that the commissioner of Indian affairs expressed great dismay when he learned of her appointment. The commissioner referred to Burgess as that "little red-headed thing" and regarded her as "not a suitable teacher," having discharged her from the Indian Service during her time among the Pawnee.[81] Nevertheless, the commissioner agreed to give her a trial period to assess her fitness for the position since Pratt insisted that her "experience" with Indians was invaluable to his work. As Pratt later explained, "Among the many qualities I need here is experience, and persons who know Indians and understand what they will have to do are the ones who can advise and help me best."[82] Ultimately, Burgess proved herself invaluable to Pratt and the school, remaining at Carlisle for over twenty-five years. Indeed, years later Pratt characterized her as "among its ablest and most devoted helpers."[83] Surely, Burgess may just have been the most committed teacher to Carlisle, Pratt, and the broader US imperial mission.

Of the fifty-five Carlisle teachers studied here, a few of the pioneer teachers expressed their enthusiasm and dedication to Indian education and to Carlisle's founder in both words and deeds. Sarah Mather's correspondence with Pratt indicates her profound interest in helping to establish a boarding school dedicated to teaching Indians, as she had helped to do at Fort Marion. Similarly, Marianna Burgess's letter of application clearly reveals her interest in Indian education and in Carlisle as a model for such endeavors. Her twenty-five-year career at the school, followed by over a decade of activism around Indian education, make clear her dedication to this work. Like Burgess, the lengthy Carlisle careers of Ann Ely and Emma Cutter reveal their commitment to Indian education. Ely, a Carlisle faculty member for twenty-eight years, served in many roles, including teacher and manager of the Outing Program, a position that amplified the school's imperial mission of assimilation by sending Carlisle students to live with white families, work the land, attend public school, and learn white customs.[84] Cutter also taught at Carlisle for twenty-eight years and in 1933, fifteen years after the school's closing, expressed her continued admiration for Pratt and the institution's work, explaining, "There was and still is among pupils and employees a spirit of friendliness and loyalty called the 'Carlisle spirit' by those in the Indian Office and others in close contact with work among the Indians, that was due to Gen. Pratt's influence."[85] Although Pratt is often credited with having inspired such sentiment, teachers were equally crucial to fostering this "spirit" at the school and beyond. Indeed, that spirit was likely an outgrowth of the shared experience and general rapport that developed among teachers who believed in the school's civilizing mission.

A few other teachers who nurtured this "spirit" seem to have made more spontaneous decisions to join the Carlisle experiment in the fall and winter of 1879–1880. These included Miss Haskins and Mary Hyde of Massachusetts, as well as Laura Spencer of Carlisle, all single women who joined the faculty without any particular experience teaching Indians. Spencer may have been the woman Pratt found living on the grounds of Carlisle in a vacant building with her mother, a widow of an army officer.[86] Pratt either empathized with this young woman's plight, found her sympathetic to Indian education, or perhaps felt desperate enough to hire any woman that seemed "capable," as hundreds of Indian students made their way east to Carlisle. Whatever his rationale, he hired all three women despite their lack of connection to the networks that provided his first recruits. Regardless of how teachers found their way to Carlisle, they all shared in the unique experience that characterized the school at its foundational stage, and many of them enjoyed the camaraderie that developed over the next several years.

Over time, however, hiring practices at Carlisle changed drastically, often undercutting the personal relationships that had helped to establish the school. Over the first two decades, Pratt hired teachers without much interference. He relied upon his firsthand knowledge of applicants as well as recommendations from friends and colleagues, and he read teachers' letters of application personally. Thus, he decided who best could nurture Indian youth into accepting and adopting white cultural norms.[87] By the late nineteenth century, Pratt's authority began to weaken as the federal Indian Service standardized the employee application process. These policies threatened the personal relationships that had helped to create the school's spirit and the teachers' loyalty. By the late 1880s, Carlisle's hiring process—like that of other Indian boarding schools—became increasingly bureaucratized. Applicants for the Indian Service received a standardized letter detailing the Department of Indian Affairs' high expectations of its employees. This letter explained, "The exigencies of Indian schools are such as to require a higher order of talent to secure success than is required in ordinary teaching. Emphasis is laid upon the fact that those who are engaged in the Indian school service should be persons of maturity, of vigorous health, with some experience in teaching, and with special fitness for the work."[88] Over Carlisle's first decades, Pratt had looked for similar qualities in his employees, knowing the importance of teaching experience, good health, and affinity for the particular work of Indian education.

While Pratt trusted his own instincts, by 1889 the Indian Service asked candidates' references to comment specifically upon an applicant's moral character and qualities and explained that "Special stress is laid upon the moral fitness of the candidates, and, though no religious test is applied, those are preferred who are able to exert a positive religious influence over their pupils."[89] Just as Pratt expected his teachers to conduct moral and religious training with students, both by example and practice, the Bureau of Indian Affairs sought candidates guided by strong moral and religious beliefs.[90] Ultimately, in spite of their differences in hiring practices, both Pratt and the federal Indian bureaucracy maintained similar standards. Nevertheless, Pratt did not trust Washington bureaucrats, whose influence began to jeopardize the relationships that he had created and developed at Carlisle.

The Bureau of Indian Affairs in Washington, DC, made repeated efforts to streamline its expanding Indian School Service to the great dismay of the founding Carlisle superintendent. By the 1890s the Indian Office instituted a civil service exam and appointed teachers to Carlisle based, in part, on their test scores.[91] Pratt became increasingly agitated by the federal government's interference in the school's affairs, and the intimacy of the social networks that had fostered the school's development was further threatened. In particular, Pratt found some of the teachers sent by the Indian Service unfit for work at Carlisle and considered the entire hiring process too slow. In an April 1897 letter to US Senator Knute Nelson, Pratt expressed his outrage:

> That a superintendent of a great school like this [Carlisle] or any of the larger schools in the Indian Service shall be treated with such absolute contempt as to not be allowed to know one iota about a single employe [sic] until that employe [sic] is ordered to report to him, or does report to him, and that the selections for over 200 schools can all be so nicely adjusted and attended to by one person in Washington assisted by his clerk, and in his absence attended to entirely by his clerk, is a proposition so nonsensical and preposterous as to not need any practical demonstration of its harmfulness. . . . The employes [sic] selected and sent to me by the superintendent [of Indian Schools in Washington] have without exception, been incapable of performing their duties.[92]

Clearly, Pratt detested the centralization of hiring in Washington, believing it to be inefficient and ineffective in finding the most qualified candidates for his institution. In addition, this process disrupted the fundamental trust among the staff members who had helped build Carlisle. In fact, Pratt thought the then superintendent of Indian schools, Dr. Hailman, had worked to undermine the success of Carlisle ever since Hailman's daughter had resigned from her position at Carlisle three years prior.[93] In this way, Pratt took the government's intervention as a personal affront and the bureaucratic hiring practices as an attack on the school.

Moreover, Pratt argued that centralized hiring had detrimental effects on the school's ability to function. In September 1898 Pratt included the following in the school's Nineteenth Annual Report:

> The work in the schoolrooms began September 1, 1897, and lasted to the end of June, 1898. Several of the grades were without teachers at the opening of the year, and temporary supplies had to be used. The lack of promptness with which appointments are made by the civil service to fill teachers' vacancies becomes a source of great loss to the pupils and demoralization to the educational work, while the changes

necessary because of the unfitness of many of the appointees is most disheartening.[94]

As Pratt continued to lose control over hiring, he explained how the inefficiencies and impersonal nature of the Indian Office bureaucracy negatively affected the school, forcing it to begin the year without a complete teaching staff. Published within a Department of Interior document that reported on the status of Indian schools more broadly, Pratt made others in the department aware of his discontent and effectively challenged the federal bureau's oversight of hiring for all Indian schools.

In spite of these difficulties, Pratt and the DC bureaucrats whom he undercut agreed on many things regarding employment in the Indian Service. Beyond the physical and moral fitness standards discussed above, the commissioner of Indian affairs explained in a 1901 annual report that he sought teachers for the Indian School Service that were "fitted by natural aptitude and training to carry on the arduous work of Indian civilization."[95] Pratt also believed that educating Indians was particularly demanding work and that teachers needed both innate and learned skills to be successful. Yet, in his experience, the government's hiring practices had time and again failed to appoint teachers fully prepared for work at Carlisle perhaps, in part, because of their impersonal nature. Ultimately, Pratt's refusal to quietly accept federal involvement led to publicized clashes between the Carlisle superintendent and the national leadership, resulting in his forced dismissal in 1904.[96]

For many teachers who worked for the Indian Service in the 1900s and 1910s, Carlisle was only one of several Indian schools in which they taught over the course of their careers, a trend echoed in the Philippines. Unfortunately, it is difficult to compare the hiring practices before and after Pratt's tenure, as the records are inconsistent and many are missing for the early years. Yet, it is known that in the 1890s the Indian Office considered teacher turnover a great problem and noted poor attrition and high transfer rates. Historian David Adams notes, "In 1897 the Indian Office released figures showing that by 1896, over two-thirds of the teachers and three-quarters of the superintendents employed in 1892 had left the service." Although acknowledging that "high turnover" among teachers was similarly problematic in public schools in the late nineteenth century, Indian Service employees were frequently transferred "from school to school" at their own request or that of their supervisors.[97] Similarly, historian Cathleen Cahill points out that "As late as 1911, the commissioner of Indian affairs was still complaining about the 'large numbers of transfers, resignations, and declinations of appointment,'" resulting in teacher shortages.[98] This proved true for several Carlisle teachers, some of whom transferred several times.

Because teachers' employment in the school's first two decades is not as well documented as in later years, Table 1.3 presents the data available regarding thirty-six of the teachers who worked at Carlisle in its last two decades, illustrating the high turnover rates. Of these teachers, only seven (less than 20 percent) did not work at other Indian schools during their careers. As can be seen, Jessie Cook worked at the largest number of Indian schools in her thirty-year teaching career in the Indian Service: ten schools.[99] Of the twenty-seven teachers who worked at multiple schools, they worked at an average of three locations. In addition, ten teachers also worked at public schools over the course of their teaching careers. Thus, movement and change characterized the life of Carlisle teachers in the twentieth century, as they became fully integrated into the larger Indian Service, with fewer developing such loyalty to Carlisle itself.

For teachers working at Carlisle over its last two decades, the question of choice was nearly irrelevant; they taught where the federal government appointed them. However, some teachers revealed their reasons for wanting to work in Indian education, or at Carlisle in particular. As I noted in the introduction, widowed Emma Lovewell joined the Indian Service to support her young son, eventually transferring to Carlisle to live closer to him, as years later he had moved to the District of Columbia for work; she also happily moved out of Montana because of "climatic conditions."[100] Gwen Williams wrote in her "Request for Transfer" application that Carlisle's "locality is more convenient for me."[101] Margaret Sweeney had, on more than one occasion, been called home to Susquehanna County, Pennsylvania, to help care for ailing relatives, and found it easier to work closer to home, as did Emma Hetrick and Clara Donaldson, who missed being near family and felt the need to visit and assist their elderly parents.[102] Jessie Cook had experience volunteering through the Episcopal Church to work with Shoshone Indians before being widowed, suggesting that her experience and religious sentiments initially led her to a career in Indian education.[103] Verna Dunagan took the civil service exam on a bet with her sister, passed, and a week later left her native Indiana, where she was teaching music, and took the train to Carlisle.[104] Clearly, the Bureau of Indian Affairs did sometimes cater to teachers' preferences or, in the case of Dunagan, chance, showing that even as it grew, teachers demonstrated agency.

Of course, Carlisle teachers' individual desires, as well as their practical training and relative privilege, enabled such agency. Unlike their more formally educated and ostensibly higher-achieving counterparts who ventured to the Philippines, most Carlisle faculty's preparation for the Indian classroom came from prior teaching experience.[105] Significantly, almost all Carlisle teachers—and Thomasites—benefited from other advantages, too: namely, white privilege. A checkmark for "white" on Indian and Philippine service personnel records indicated more than one's racial category: it purportedly carried the mark of "civilization." And, the fact that such records were kept reflects the obsession that policy makers had with racial difference, a norm established during the Progressive Era as reformers sought to systematize, calculate, and make the world more efficient. Though otherwise unstated, Carlisle teachers and Thomasites held authority that derived from the ruling class's—and in many cases their own—racist beliefs, backed by false-headed eugenic "science" that privileged white over black, brown, and red. As noted earlier, the work of "civilizing" the natives—whether Native Americans or native Filipinos—was largely motivated by systemic and individual assumptions of "superior" and "inferior" races, cultures, and ways of being. Such assumptions provided the foundation for imperial education within and beyond the continental United States, in Carlisle and the Philippines. Like today, "exceptions" to such norms of "privilege" existed over a century ago, too.

While most of Carlisle's teachers were white, Nellie Robertson Denny (listed in Table 1.3) was one of the few teachers at the school who was of Native American descent. Prior to teaching, Nellie Robertson was a student at Carlisle, having arrived in 1880 and graduated in 1890. A Sioux Indian, she became a teacher at Carlisle in July 1896, switched to clerical work by 1900, and married another former Carlisle student, Wallace Denny, who graduated in 1906. By 1908 she served as the outing manager, remaining with the school until its doors closed in 1918.[106] Pratt held Nellie in high regard, as did successive supervisors. In 1916 interim supervisor O. H. Lipps wrote, "I regard her as the most reliable, competent and dependable educated Indian I have ever known. As manager of the Outing Department she displays a quality of good sense and judgment that would do credit to a captain of industry. I regard her as one of the most valuable employees at this school."[107] Perhaps more than any other teacher, Nellie Robertson Denny embodied Carlisle and its "spirit." She represented what Pratt and Lipps might consider the ideal Carlisle student: one who demonstrated profound commitment to the school's mission, as she dedicated her life to its service. Arriving at Carlisle at the age of ten, Nellie grew up in the institution, became a teacher, married another Carlisle graduate, and remained to

Table 1.3: Indian Service Employment Records of Teachers Who Worked at Carlisle between 1900 and 1918

Teacher	Years Taught in Indian Service Prior to Carlisle	Years at Carlisle	Years Taught in Indian Service After Carlisle	Total Years in Indian Service
Elizabeth Bender	5	1915–1916	N/A	6
Lucy Case	3	1913–1915	3	8
Jessie Cook	4	1898–1904	20	30
Mabel Curtis	4	1911	3	8
Angel DeCora	0	1906–1915	0	9
Elizabeth DeHuff	0	1914	0	<1
John DeHuff	0	1914–1916	9	11
Nellie R. Denny	0	1896–1918*	0	22
Clara Donaldson	0	1914–1918	2	6
Verna Dunagan	0	1915–1918	0	3
Clara May Ellis	0	1908	0	1
Hazel Emery	N/A	1911–1914	N/A	3
Emma Foster	4	1902–1918	0	20
Lottie Georgenson	1	1910–1914 (as teacher); 1918 (as clerk)	4 (as clerk)	13
Emma Hetrick	2	1905** 1908**–1910	0	3
Lida Johnston	1	1907–1912	N/A	6
Elizabeth Jones	6	1913–1914	N/A	1
Mattie Lane	N/A	1911–1912	N/A	1
Dora LeCrone	0	1904–1911	1	8
Emma Lovewell	3	1909–1914	0	8
Royal Mann	0	1913–1915	1	3
Hattie McDowell	1	1904–1918	2	7
Amelia McMichael	2	1906–1909	0	5
Marianna Moore	0	1911–1914	0	3
Adelaide Reichel	N/A	1907–1918	N/A	11
Margaret Roberts	1	1900–1904; 1914–1916	3	10
Frances Scales	3	1902–1908	1	10
Gertrude Simmons (Zitkala-Sa)	0	1898–1900	0	2
Clara Snoddy	2	1914–1918	1	7
Margaret Sweeney	1	1909–1918	N/A	10
Katherine Bingley Tranbarger	2	1908–1911	N/A	5
Fernando Tranbarger	0	1909–1911	~16	18

John Whitwell	3	1907–1914	2	12
Gwen Williams	I	1914–1918	0	5
Idilla Wilson	0	1912–1918	0	6
Mariette Wood	3	1889–1891	N/A	14
		1897–1906** or		
		1909**		

*Nellie R. Denny's time at Carlisle as teacher, then clerk. She arrived at the school in 1880 as a student.
**Conflicting records.
Source: Based on teachers' individual files held at the National Personnel Record Center. Information also drawn from Clara R. Donaldson Folder, Record Group 350, Entry 21, Box 365, NAMD; Mrs. Edward L. Whistler (Verna Dunagan), interview by Dewitt C. Smith, September 1976, transcript, 29–30, Carlisle Indian School Papers, Box 1, Folder 13, WDC; Personal Record of Nellie R. Denny, Record Group 75, Entry 1344A Records Relating to Carlisle School—Personnel, Nellie Robertson Denny Folder, NADC; Shope, "American Indian Artist Angel DeCora"; Claesgens, "Zitkala-Sa (Gertrude Simmons Bonnin) Biography."

work and raise her family there until it closed. Although the details regarding her initial journey to Carlisle as a child are unknown, she was among the first groups of students removed from their homes and brought to the school, likely a shocking and in many ways traumatic experience. While Nellie did not fully elect to go to Carlisle in 1880, she later "chose" to teach in the Indian Service and remained at the school. Thus, her cross-country move, from reservation to boarding school, changed her life. Ultimately, she lived and worked at the school for thirty-five years, longer than any other teacher, and was there almost from its very beginning until its ending days. Moreover, Nellie was deemed an especially essential player to Carlisle and the broader mission of assimilation, as her life and apparent cultural transformation "proved" that an Indian could not only be "saved" but could work to rescue others, too.

Other potentially "saved" teachers of American Indian descent taught at Carlisle, although none for as long or as revered by white authorities as Nellie Robertson Denny. As mentioned above, Nellie's husband, Wallace Denny (Oneida), graduated from Carlisle and remained at the school as a disciplinarian. Former Carlisle student Dennison Wheelock (Oneida) returned to teach music; William Dietz (Dakota), along with his wife, Angel DeCora (Winnebago), taught Native arts in the early 1900s. Elizabeth Bender (Chippewa), educated at the Hampton Institute, worked elsewhere in the Indian Service before teaching at Carlisle for just over a year.[108]

One of the most well-known Native American teachers at the boarding school was Gertrude Simmons, who adopted the pen name Zitkala-Sa (a Lakota word that translates to Red Bird) and became a noted writer and Indian activist. Much of her early work is autobiographical and reflects on her childhood, coming of age, and the struggles she faced as she mediated between Sioux and white cultures. Born on a Sioux reservation in South Dakota, she left home and attended an off-reservation Indian boarding school before enrolling at Earlham College in Indiana. There she excelled at music and earned a place at the Boston Conservatory before moving to Carlisle to teach.[109]

While working at the Pennsylvania boarding school, Zitkala-Sa published her first series of short stories in the *Atlantic Monthly*, revealing her personal journey toward questioning and then rejecting her assimilation into white culture.[110] In the last of these autobiographical vignettes, Zitkala-Sa reflected on her work as a teacher at Carlisle. She described how, soon after arriving at the school, Superintendent Pratt sent her west to secure more students from reservations.[111] During this expedition, she visited with her mother, who warned her repeatedly to "beware of the paleface," who had brought the Sioux both personal and community suffering.[112] When Zitkala-Sa returned to Carlisle, she started to doubt the intentions of many of her white colleagues. She recounted:

> As months passed over me, I slowly comprehended that the large army of white teachers in Indian schools had a larger missionary creed than I had suspected.
>
> It was one which included self-preservation quite as much as Indian education. When I saw an opium-eater holding a position as teacher of Indians, I did not understand what good was expected until a Christian in power replied that this pumpkin-colored creature had a feeble mother to support . . .
>
> I find it hard to count that white man a teacher who tortured an ambitious Indian youth by frequently reminding the brave changeling that he was nothing but a "government pauper."
>
> Though I burned with indignation upon discovering on every side instances no less shameful than those I have mentioned, there was no present help. Even the few rare ones who have worked nobly for my race were powerless to choose workmen like themselves.[113]

The publication of Zitkala-Sa's stories and their condemnations of Carlisle faculty was devastating for the school and the larger assimilation movement, and it encapsulated one of the key criticisms of off-reservation boarding schools that percolated over the first two decades of the twentieth century: that the "eradication of children's native identities" was misguided and cruel.[114] Although she acknowledged the good character of a few somewhat powerless white colleagues, Zitkala-Sa unabashedly denounced the majority, whose intentions and practices she fundamentally questioned. Moreover, she underscored the profound harm of education at Carlisle by showcasing a drug-addicted teacher who was ultimately privileged above the students. Whether she left the Indian boarding school of her own accord or was fired, Zitkala-Sa committed the rest of her life to fighting on behalf of Indians. Indeed, she used her Western education and powerful writing and oratory skills to push for Indian rights and condemn the corruption that plagued federal Indian policy.[115]

Over the school's almost forty-year existence, Carlisle's teachers—whether Native American or white—held varying degrees of allegiance, differing personal or professional motivations for joining the school, and had fundamentally distinct experiences physically moving to the Pennsylvania town. Still, some patterns emerge. First, the significance of teachers' journey to Carlisle is meaningful in terms of race and structures of power. Among Indian teachers, their reasons for joining the faculty were diverse, as was the degree of "choice" they had in the matter. As noted earlier, some Native American teachers grew up at the school and remained, others returned, and still others joined the staff from elsewhere. However they arrived, the journey of Indian teachers to Carlisle was likely quite significant in their lives and that of their communities—likely terrifying, as is suspected in the case of Nellie Robertson Denny, or otherwise life-changing, as for Zitkala-Sa.[117] Historical evidence suggests that for many white teachers (the vast majority of the staff), their journey to Carlisle, Pennsylvania, constituted a much different kind of "choice." It may have drawn them away from the idealized version of a white woman's place in society, as wife and mother, but afforded them an opportunity to be financially independent, largely less confined by gendered societal expectations though still capable of being considered morally upright.

Second, the shift from Carlisle's reliance on social networks to the centrality of a federal bureaucracy—from personal to impersonal hiring practices—also impacted teachers' journeys. Many of the school's white founding teachers respected Superintendent Pratt and valued their colleagues, persuading close friends to join the school's endeavors. In contrast, those appointed during the school's last twenty years were more likely to be placed at Carlisle by administrators much less familiar with the intimate workings of the school.[116] As suggested, the US government's call for teachers to join Pratt at Carlisle in 1879 produced a small cohort of teachers, and even those who had personal ties to Pratt made their journeys alone to the school, only becoming part of a collective endeavor once they reached their new post. Years later, for those who taught in the broader Indian Service for their career, moving from one station to another seems to have become rather mundane. And for those who sought a posting at Carlisle to be nearer family, the journey home did not stand out in their lives. Whether joining Pratt or later superintendents in the small Pennsylvania town, white and Native American teachers exhibited some agency even before arriving at the school's doorstep, or, in Nellie and Wallace Denny's case, in choosing to remain.

As in the case of Carlisle's American Indian teachers, most white teachers left few or no clues behind about their efforts to reach the old army barracks in the small Pennsylvania town. Still, the experiences of a few are worth noting. Among the more dramatic accounts, a flood wrecked Annie Hamilton's train ride in 1889, though she managed to arrive safely at school.[118] Decades later, profound uncertainty preceded Clara Donaldson's appointment in 1914, as her Indian Service assignment was debated during her month-long journey from the Philippines, and she was forced to take a detour to Minnesota before she reached Carlisle.[119] Demonstrative of the haste in which she had to move and in which the Indian Service sometimes made its decisions, she had little time to reacclimate herself to living in the United States before beginning work at the Pennsylvania boarding school. Similarly, Verna Dunagan's story attests to the quickness of her move, as she was expected at Carlisle within one week of passing her exam in 1915. Moreover, Dunagan admitted that until arriving at the Pennsylvania train station she had never interacted with people of different racial backgrounds, having grown up in a segregated Indiana town. She remembered being confused upon her arrival as she did not think that the young man who picked her up appeared Indian, thinking at the time, "Am I coming to an *Indian* School or is this a colored school?" She further explained, "We had no colored people at all in our town . . . in the town I was born in nor in the County Seat where we did business. . . . I just wondered what kind of a school I was coming to."[120] Thus, for Dunagan, her move from a homogenous community to a school that served a nonwhite population proved somewhat shocking, as she did not quite know what to expect. Considering that the vast majority of Carlisle faculty were white women from other small towns and unaccustomed to being around people of different races, many of them likely had similar reactions when they reached the school. Together, these few stories illuminate the swiftness in which the Indian boarding school was staffed and its effects on individuals while also highlighting the significance of race in this imperial project. Other teachers may well have had noteworthy trips to the first federally funded Indian boarding school, but no further accounts have yet been uncovered.

In contrast, teachers' physical journey to the Philippines proved memorable and meaningful. The call for teachers to go to the Philippines in 1901 generated a mass migration of American men and women to the West Coast and then across the Pacific. Many of these teachers left evidence of their journeys via diaries and letters home, and several saw themselves as part of something larger even before their journeys began. Responding to a call for duty at a time of war, teachers often traveled to the islands by the hundreds, taking trains and buses to decommissioned naval vessels at West Coast ports. They met one another along this journey and increasingly felt the gravity of their mission as they made their way to the islands, likely convincing some to keep a record of their experiences. Thus, for teachers headed to the Philippines, their journey to the islands had both personal and symbolic meaning.

Of the thirty-three Thomasites examined here, a few kept detailed accounts as they headed west and across the Pacific, and still others made noteworthy comments about the journey. Norman Cameron left a thorough account of his tenure in the Philippines through a series of five diaries, dating from 1901 to 1904, that reveal both the mundane and bizarre, including ample commentary as he ventured to the islands.[121] Harrie Cole and his wife, Mary, both of the University of Michigan, were initially attracted by the high salaries as well as the allure of travel and enjoyed their westward journey in the summer of 1901. Along the way, they regularly described their experiences in letters to their families.[122] Jules Frelin and Blaine Moore also wrote about their travels to the islands in 1901, as did teachers like H. O. Whiting and Herman Hespelt years later.[123] These and other accounts illustrate the significance of the journey for the teachers and, for many of them, their sense of mission as they witnessed and experienced new things, formed a collective identity, and established new relationships with soon-to-be colleagues.

For most teachers, the trip to the Philippines—beginning with the journey to the West Coast—offered new sights and experiences, some more welcome than others. Norman Cameron, traveling away from home for the first time, commented at length on the landscape, particularly the wide plains, snow-capped mountains, and vegetation along the way.[124] The landscape made a similar impression on H. O. Whiting several years later, as he, too, wrote of agriculture, tunnels, and mountains that blended in with the clouds.[125] It was also Harrie and Mary Cole's first trip across the vast deserts of the Southwest. Harrie wrote to his mother about the almost suffocating heat as they traveled through the seemingly never-ending desert of sagebrush and sand. And though he did not envy those living in the sparse landscape, Harrie marveled at the "cow-boys herding horses . . . and Indian wigwams."[126]

For several teachers, leaving home challenged their norms and values before they even left the country's shores. As Blaine Moore made his way across the vast western deserts, he wrote, "My opinion regarding this country—If I owned New Mexico, Arizona and h-ll I would rent the two former and live in the latter." Beyond finding the landscape uninhabitable, Moore was suspicious of the people he saw out west. He wrote about people whom he described as "Indians" although "not all full blooded by any means. They're a mixture of Indian, Spanish, with some white and negro blood thrown in and & some of them are villainous looking specimens."[127] Clearly Moore was unaccustomed to people who looked different from himself, and he did not trust anyone with such a mixed heritage, particularly those who were not predominantly white. Cameron was similarly wary of some of the people he encountered along the way. After having witnessed two women arrested for drunkenness in San Francisco as well as legalized gambling, he came to the conclusion, "As we go westward the civilization becomes lower and lower."[128] Although alcohol and gambling were often condemned at the turn of the twentieth century for being sinful and corrupting, such activities were more socially acceptable among men. Women, in contrast, were deemed unsexed by such behavior, as codes of proper femininity forbade such unbecoming conduct. For some teachers heading to the Philippines, the line of thinking that equated the western United States and beyond with notions of backwardness and barbarity became increasingly apparent as they made their way to the Philippine Islands.

Still, many teachers forged close bonds with each other as they confronted different peoples and landscapes, and some cemented serious relationships. Cameron wrote, "On my way west, I fell in with several other men also wending their way to Manila."[129] They made acquaintances and friends aboard trains, forming opinions of their future colleagues. Harrie Cole claimed that a group identity began to form as they bumped into one another along the way: "Our trip so far has been quite pleasant as our car is made up of 'Philippinos' as we call ourselves."[130] A decade later, Philippine-bound teachers developed similar camaraderie. In May 1911, Herman Hespelt wrote to his family of meeting "three fellows," then six, and then eighteen all headed to the Philippines aboard the westbound train; his group of "Philippinites, as we chose to call ourselves," grew as they traveled westward and formed "a pretty jolly crowd."[131]

For many, the importance of personal relationships intensified as they prepared to leave familiar surroundings. A couple aboard the train with the Coles confessed that they "hurried up things," marrying sooner than originally planned in order to take advantage of the offer to teach in the Philippines. Other couples married just prior to boarding the USS *Thomas* to ensure that they would be appointed to the same stations once in the islands.[132] Middle-class customs regarding courtship and family weddings were thus cut short as the opportunity of work in the Philippines forced men and women to marry sooner and often far from home. As the teachers learned, they would have to make other swift decisions once their work in the Philippines began.

But, for some teachers, the journey itself proved to be a leisurely affair. This was particularly true for teachers who found others with shared backgrounds. In a July 24, 1901, letter to her family from aboard the USS *Thomas*, Mary Cole wrote, "O, but this is a lazy life. One doesn't have a spark of ambition; We get up for breakfast and then after that, wait for dinner and after dinner, wait for supper and thus the days go by."[133] Similarly, her husband, Harrie, wrote to his mother, "It is so enjoyable to watch the water and visit with others on board that it seems almost impossible to write, read, or do anything but lie around."[134] Although the teachers largely enjoyed the relaxing nature of ship life, they engaged in a variety of activities during the month-long journey. They formed entertainment committees and put on shows, published a newspaper, went to dances, sang college and American songs, and formed clubs. Mary served on one such entertainment committee along with thirteen other men and women. In a letter to her family, she noted, "In the evening, crowds get together and sing college songs, give their yells etc. and have a gay time."[135] Thus, as the teachers ventured westward, they recounted the nostalgia of their college days, making new connections with one another based on such familiarity.

However, some teachers, including Blaine Moore, felt increasingly lonely along the journey. According to Moore, Kansas was not as well represented as some of the other states and colleges aboard, including the Coles's native Michigan. And, while some people enjoyed the freer life aboard, others were offended by card games and gambling, or felt further isolated as they watched others go dancing.[136] Nevertheless, many of the teachers reveled in the camaraderie aboard the ship, in spite of challenges created by loneliness, debilitating bouts of seasickness, or other circumstances.[137] Moreover, their activities and performances enacted and reinforced whiteness while preparing them for their impending work, that of conveying the benefits of the dominant US culture to "others."

In addition to establishing friendships, some teachers apparently engaged in more than friendly alliances while aboard the *Thomas*, with some writing and performing songs that reflected sexual tensions as they crossed the Pacific. On August 21, 1901, Cameron recited the lyrics of "two songs frequently sung by the 'boys.'" The first of these two songs, "Just Because She Made Them Goo-Goo Eyes," was performed on August 7, 1901, by a Mr. Sullivan and was described as "his parody on 'Goo-Goo Eyes.'" The original song "Just Because She Made Dem Goo-Goo Eyes" (1900) was a popular minstrel song by John Queen and Hughie Cannon about a black man in a minstrel show who, attracted to a wealthy black woman in the audience, forgot his lines and ultimately lost both his job and the girl.[138] Sullivan's parody on this song, as recorded in a book compiled by teachers aboard the USS *Thomas*, similarly depicts a deceptive woman who takes advantage of an innocent man:

> In a hammock on the upper deck a couple like to swing
> They ne'er had known of love before—to them 'twas a novel thing;
> 'Twas very sad—
> They had it bad!
> They sat and goo-gooed all the day, at night they goo-gooed more;
> His arm was in a place where many an arm had been before;
> But he knew it not,
> This easy lad!
>
> . . .
>
> Just because she made those goo-goo eyes—
> And all the while he thought he had a prize!
> But she'd played the game before—
> When he finds out he'll be sore,
> He's not the first to see those goo-goo eyes.[139]

Whether or not this song reflected actual behavior aboard ship, it entertained the teachers and was regularly sung by Cameron and "the boys." It suggests that intimacy among the Philippine-bound teachers was at least imagined, if not actualized. And, like the original minstrel song, its portrayal of a sexually experienced girl who takes advantage of a boy in love warned both men and women to beware of behavior unbefitting their sex. Men had to protect their masculinity and avoid being blinded by desire as they sought a sexually pure woman as well as avoid becoming "sore" or infected with a sexually transmitted disease through casual sex. Women were expected to remain chaste until marriage in order to ensure proper femininity. Of course, the racial implications of the original song's lyrics—the stupidity, greed, and barbarity of a black man unable to restrain his sexual desire and hold a job—and its parodied performance by white males may reflect the feeling some felt while onboard the *Thomas*. Far away from the civilized mainland—with its strictures on sex and burdens of work responsibilities—perhaps these performers felt at greater risk of succumbing to such "uncivilized" behavior, deemed in the minstrel song as racially inferior.

For some teachers aboard the *Thomas*, it seems that love, or at least intimacy, did bloom. Considering the predominant demographic of the passengers—many of whom were white, single, young, recent college graduates—romantic relationships were likely to emerge. The second song recorded by Cameron in his diary depicts such romance aboard the *Thomas*. Titled "Home, Boys, Home," the last stanza goes:

> Two, there were, a man and a maid, who'd been lonely all these years,
> Waiting for a kiss to soothe, a hand to dry their tears,
> They met upon the "Thomas," they are happy now for life,
> For the maid has found a husband, the man has found a wife.[140]

Similarly, an article in *The Log of Thomas*, "The Voyage of the 'Thomas'" by C. H. Maxson, uses playful language and euphemism to describe the relationships formed between men and women on their way to the Philippines. Maxson claimed:

> We are a happy family on board the *Thomas* and not without evidences
> of natural affection. Honeymoons by the dozen glow with a soft efful-
> gence fore and aft, while romance spoons in sheltered places, and
> Cupid whispers his secrets under the lee of the life boat. Goo-goo eyes
> look unutterable things to eyes that look again, and love, beautiful to
> behold, flourishes upon the teacher transport like the royal palms in the
> queen's gardens.[141]

Although difficult to ascertain the extent to which romance actually developed among *Thomas*'s passengers during the month-long journey across the Pacific, it is clear that, at least in the realm of imagination, love—or perhaps sex—seemed ubiquitous.

Jules Frelin, who served in the Philippines during the War of 1898, returned to the archipelago to teach in 1901 and recounted both romantic and unromantic ideas during his voyage aboard the *Thomas*. In an August 14, 1901 diary entry, Frelin reported that the YMCA called a meeting to warn the men that syphilis might be contracted aboard the ship, indicating that its members harbored concerns about sexual relationships. Frelin doubted such warnings, ending this long, meandering entry with more romantic thoughts: "That a man's arms about a woman's waist is very pleasant for the arm—That of woman's arms round a man's neck . . . even if gloved, just resting on the back of his neck is very satisfying."[142] Whether Frelin experienced such cuddling onboard or dreamed of it, the sexual tensions intensified during the long voyage across the Pacific, particularly as men and women—including married couples—were housed in separate parts of the ship.[143] Overall, the teachers had a unique experience as they journeyed westward, and many fostered new relationships, both real and imagined, along the way.

For some Thomasites, their trip to the islands was one of two momentous voyages. After working for several years on the islands, at least five Thomasites transferred from the Philippine Service to the Indian Service, ending up at Carlisle. Other Thomasites also joined the Indian Service.[144] In fact, such crossover between stateside and island teaching occurred in both directions, as some Thomasites wrote about colleagues of theirs who ventured to the Philippines after having taught at Indian schools.[145] Some teachers viewed work with Filipinos as preparation for teaching American Indians, and vice versa. For example, Blaine Moore wrote that while aboard the *Thomas*, "A couple of teachers from the Black Feet Indian School of Montana talked this morning telling of their experience with the Indians—many of whom could not speak English."[146] Having worked with non-English-speaking Native Americans, these teachers spoke with some authority on teaching "others," and in this sense helped to prime their fellow Thomasites for what they imagined it might be like working with Filipinos.[147]

The crossover teachers in this study—including Clara Donaldson, John DeHuff, Elizabeth Willis DeHuff, Fernando Tranbarger, and Moses Friedman—similarly envisioned the Philippines and Carlisle as comparable projects, believing that their experience in the Philippines prepared them for working at an Indian school. For some, this proved to be true, including those who formed relationships with one another while in the Philippines. Others met challenges at Carlisle that they could not overcome. And in all cases, teachers moved from one assignment to the next rather hurriedly and without much respite in-between. By virtue of their involvement in both experiments and considering the challenging circumstances of each project (discussed in detail in the next three chapters), these crossover teachers demonstrated profound commitment to US imperial education initiatives as they sought to "uplift" Filipino then American Indian peoples.

Crossover teacher Clara Donaldson gained valuable teaching experience in the Philippines and proved her drive and independence, defying the Philippine Bureau of Education's expectations of a single woman sent to the islands' interior. Recall that by 1904 the bureau declared that differences between men and women's capabilities meant that men were better prepared to work without the comforts of "American society." Donaldson crossed the Pacific with the original Thomasites in July 1901 and taught on the islands through 1914, with only a few leaves of absence spent on the mainland United States.[148] She first worked in a remote village on the island of Luzon—reportedly the only white woman on the island for the first several months—and spent the last few years teaching high school in Manila.[149] Like the stalwart "maiden" Muerman described in his dissertation, Donaldson proved to be a strong woman "who withstood the hardships [in the Philippines] with the most fortitude."[150] In fact, Donaldson proved to be a very successful teacher who thrived in some of the most challenging and isolating circumstances before earning a promotion to teach older students in the nation's capital.

In spite of bureaucratic obstacles, Donaldson's teaching experience and the professional connections she made in the Philippines ultimately helped her receive an appointment at Carlisle. As mentioned earlier, when Donaldson sought transfer to the Indian Service, she, like many of her soon-to-be-colleagues, requested Carlisle specifically due to its location closer to her family, particularly her aging father.[151] Commissioner of Indian Affairs Cato Sells originally rejected Donaldson's appointment on account of her advanced age—fifty-two years—and explained, "My objection to the transfer of Miss Donaldson was her age, as I believe that it is a proper policy to maintain the age limit for entrance to the Indian Service at fifty years."[152] Whereas Pratt had hired teachers of such advanced ages when Carlisle first opened, privileging teaching experience over youth, Indian Service bureaucrats instituted maximum age policies around the turn of the century.[153]

Thus, even with well over a decade of successful teaching in the Philippines, Donaldson was officially ineligible to teach in the Indian Service. However, she was already on her way to the United States in June 1914, having earlier received affirmation from the commissioner's office that she would receive an appointment to teach in the Indian Service.[154] This in addition to two recommendation letters—one written by Carlisle principal teacher (and former Thomasite) John DeHuff and the other a prominent politician— swayed Commissioner Sells to reverse his decision.[155] While US Representative Frank Willis wrote at the urging of Donaldson's sister, DeHuff made a personal plea for Clara's appointment at Carlisle because he knew her to be an accomplished and capable teacher, having worked with her in the Philippines. And, as principal teacher at Carlisle, DeHuff knew what qualities would make a teacher successful at the Pennsylvania Indian school. While Donaldson ultimately found a placement at Carlisle in September 1914, she did not fully know that she would be working there until she reached the States.[156] Having proven herself one of the most highly rated teachers in the Philippines, she became invaluable at Carlisle as well, staying for the final four years of the school's existence.[157] Still, despite her years of experience, Donaldson likely would not have a received a position at Carlisle without having met DeHuff in the Philippines.

Serving as the principal teacher at Carlisle by 1914, John DeHuff had already proven himself an effective educator, rising through the ranks during his twelve years in the Philippines, where he also made lifelong personal connections. Like Donaldson, DeHuff was an original Thomasite, having arrived in the islands in August 1901. He first worked as a classroom teacher in "one of the far inland towns," and by 1904 was promoted to be "Head Teacher" of a province where he proved to be a dedicated supervisor and administrator. He worked as a division superintendent of schools in Bohol and Iloilo from 1906 to 1911 and as superintendent of the Manila City schools from 1911 to 1913. Purportedly embodying "superior intellectual equipment and energy," his last position in the islands was as second in command of the Bureau of Education.[158] In addition to his professional duties, DeHuff acted as head of "Apoyao," a society of Philippine leaders, and was described by one of the organization's members as "scholarly . . . honest, reliable, and true in every way."[159] In applying for a position in the Indian Service, DeHuff wrote that while he found his twelve years working in the Philippines "most gratifying . . . I believe it to be my duty to myself and to those for whom I may become responsible that I establish myself now in my native country and climate."[160] Here, DeHuff was likely referencing his fiancée, Elizabeth Willis, whom he met in the archipelago, and the family they hoped to have together. Although the principal teacher position put him in a leadership role at Carlisle, he sacrificed the prestige he had achieved in the Philippines in addition to accepting a severe salary cut, in part because he believed it better to start a family stateside.

For some teachers, including John DeHuff and Elizabeth Willis, the relationship they formed in the Philippines shaped both their professional and personal lives. Willis's tenure on the islands was much shorter than that of her future husband's, lasting from October 1910 to March 1913, after which she was granted a leave of absence until June 1914.[161] Prior to their marriage that spring, John helped to secure Elizabeth a teaching position at Carlisle, which she filled from late spring through July 1914, at which time she resigned. Although her work at Carlisle only amounted to a few months, and the reason for her resignation is not evident, Acting Supervisor O. H. Lipps considered her to be "a very desirable and competent employee in every way."[162] Considering her recent marriage to John and the fact that they soon had three children, Elizabeth likely resigned in order to care for their growing family.

John served as principal teacher at Carlisle for two years before the family relocated to Santa Fe, New Mexico, in 1916, due in part to his health. Diagnosed with tuberculosis, he received a promotion and became superintendent of the Santa Fe Indian School, where Elizabeth likely served as a substitute teacher and later worked outside of the school system.[163] Although evidence shows that John brought his wife to Carlisle and later to Santa Fe, Elizabeth effectively persuaded her husband to move back to the States, where they established a life and family together. In this way, the intimate relationship that began in the Philippines brought them back to their home country, where they dedicated their lives to working with its indigenous populations.

Of course, relationships between teachers were not always symbiotic, as Fernando Tranbarger and Moses Friedman experienced after transferring from the Philippines to the Indian Service. Both Tranbarger and Friedman received positive evaluations regarding their work in the Philippines. Tranbarger first served in the Philippines as a volunteer in Company "I" during the War of 1898, and after passing the Philippine teacher examination taught on the islands from June 1906 to November 1909.[164] He was one of several military personnel who gladly sought reinstatement in the Philippines following the war, though under a different guise, suggesting that he felt drawn to the islands. Immediately following his service there, Tranbarger taught at Carlisle from November 1909 through August 1911, when he resigned.[165]

Moses Friedman stands out among the crossover teachers for two reasons. First, as discussed in the introduction (and as will be discussed in greater detail in chapters 3 and 5), Friedman was forced to resign from Carlisle's superintendency in 1914 during US congressional hearings investigating the school's mismanagement.[166] Second, unlike the other crossover teachers, Friedman taught in the Indian Service both before and after his stint in the Philippines. He initially taught manual training at the Phoenix Indian School from 1901 to 1903, where his supervisor evaluated his work as exhibiting "eminent satisfaction" and described Friedman "as a young man of excellent character, enthusiastic, inspiring." [167] Transferring to the Philippine Service in January 1904, Friedman spent the next several years teaching manual training at the secondary and then high school on the island of Cebu. According to the principal of the Cebu Secondary School, Friedman quickly gained his students' interest and the community's support, even though he had to "overcome many difficulties," the nature of which are not clear.[168] The division superintendent of Cebu commended Friedman for helping to organize the manual training department at the Provincial High School and for his "willingness to do any outside work that came up, e.g., the making of plans for the barrio school houses and the preparing of an exhaustive report on industrial education in the Philippines."[169] When Friedman finished his contract with the Philippine Service in April 1906, he returned to the States, becoming the assistant superintendent at the Haskell Institute in Kansas, an Indian boarding school.[170] In March 1908 Friedman transferred to Carlisle and became the school's superintendent.[171]

During Friedman's six years as Carlisle's superintendent, he was both commended and criticized by teachers, the Carlisle community, and the Bureau of Indian Education. In fact, Fernando Tranbarger and his wife, Katherine Bingley, whom he met at Carlisle, became some of Friedman's severest critics.[172] Tranbarger worked in the Philippine Service from 1906 to 1909, beginning his work on the islands only days after Friedman had left the archipelago.[173] After teaching in the Philippines for three years, Tranbarger transferred to Carlisle, where he worked under Superintendent Friedman and met his future wife. In August 1911, after almost two years at Carlisle, Fernando and Katherine Bingley Tranbarger resigned, detailing their complaints against the superintendent and his policies in a series of letters to the commissioner of Indian affairs, including unfair treatment regarding payment, unsanitary classrooms, and general mistreatment (see chapter 3 for more).[174] Although Tranbarger and Friedman's work in the Philippines may have better prepared them for working in Indian schools, this common background was not enough to prevent personal conflicts from developing between them at Carlisle. Of course, Carlisle suffered from other interpersonal rivalries among teachers who served solely in the Indian Service, as the next chapter will show. This was the opposite of what had strengthened the school in its earliest days: its intimate social network.

Ultimately, although some teachers faced a minor dilemma as they weighed the pros and cons of joining the Philippines or Carlisle experiments—as Ralph Taylor, cited in the opening paragraph of this chapter, did before deciding to board the USS *Thomas*—the journey to their new work assignments was more or less straightforward. Whether inspired by friends, opportunity, or circumstance, for most teachers (except, perhaps, those of Native American descent), the act of joining one or both of these US imperial missions suggests their buy-in to the project and their belief that education could assimilate or even "save" peoples deemed inferior. Thus, besides perhaps some hiccups along the way, the literal or figurative journey itself to Carlisle and to the Philippines did not *yet* place teachers in an awkward, sometimes even untenable position. As will be seen in the next chapters, the journeys that often began with such high hopes and idealistic visions of the educational mission did not always fulfill teachers' expectations as they moved from the excitement of gaining an appointment and arriving in Carlisle or the Philippines to the day-to-day work of implementing government policy on the ground. Teaching empire from the bottom-up among peoples often resistant to imperial authority and within environments largely unconducive to such ambition will be explored over the next several chapters. Examining the details of teachers' efforts and negotiations, beginning with Carlisle in chapters 2 and 3 and following with the Philippines in chapter 4, exposes both the intimacy and vulnerability of building American empire via education at the turn of the twentieth century.

CHAPTER TWO

LIFE AT CARLISLE, 1879–1918

In 1901, over twenty years after the civilizing efforts at Carlisle had begun, the commissioner of Indian affairs, William Jones, wrote in his annual report:

> The qualifications that bring success in a white school are not an absolute criterion of the success a public school-teacher will have in this branch.
>
> Employees are required to look carefully after the culture and morality of the pupils in the class rooms, dormitories, and at the workbenches. The Indian's education does not comprise the circle of classroom duties alone, but the wider one of home life in all its features.
>
> The term at Indian schools is practically twelve months. During all this time the watchful eye of the employee must be upon the pupils committed to his charge.[1]

Here, Commissioner Jones used race to rationalize the demanding and unique work required of employees at Indian schools, and he was not alone in assuming that white children did not need as much guidance in terms of "culture and morality" as indigenous children. In addition to fulfilling classroom duties, he suggested that teachers must also serve as general stewards of all that shaped mainstream "white" culture and civilization. Of course, at an off-reservation boarding school, work proved more strenuous than in public schools since employees lived with students and served as their caretakers inside and outside of the classroom. Like parents in a household, teachers at Carlisle were responsible for the constant care of the children—around the clock, every day of the year—and expected to keep an ever "watchful eye." Unlike parents, Indian school teachers were instructed not to trust the children and hired to correct the children's perceived flaws—that of "being Indian."[2]

During Carlisle's existence, from 1879 to 1918, "being Indian" was considered problematic for reasons that changed over time. In the school's earliest years, founder and superintendent Richard Henry Pratt strongly believed that Indians could and should be "saved" and only needed a new environment—away from "uncivilized" tribal lifestyles. In this way, Pratt hoped to change what it meant to "be Indian" by taking children east to Carlisle where they could quickly learn and adopt new cultural norms, thus becoming "less" Indian within a generation. By the turn of the century, education leaders in Washington, DC, who had gained increasing control over Carlisle, believed that Indian assimilation would take many generations and constructed "being Indian" as a permanent racial category, whereby "progress" or "uplift" could not be rushed.[3] Still, while white reformers' visions for transforming "Indianness" changed, their goal of complete assimilation remained. Part of this work, of course, involved ignoring the diversity of North American indigenous peoples, purposefully lumping them into one identity: Indian. In this way, Carlisle and all Indian schools worked simultaneously to create and destroy an "Indian" identity, ultimately relying upon teachers to do the dirty work.[4]

Of course, since most teachers featured here eagerly adhered to and promoted US government policies regarding Indian education, perhaps they would have characterized their work differently, in more practical terms. For example, the endless workdays, meager supplies and resources, remedial status and "immoral" tendencies of students, among other obstacles, encumbered teachers' work. Such challenges will be discussed here, followed by attention to discipline, disease, and scandal in the next chapter. Despite such worldly challenges, most teachers remained steadfast, citing divine inspiration as motivation enough in this difficult but, in their minds, worthwhile endeavor. Thus, the challenge was not *whether* to educate Indian children to assimilate to white society but *how* to go about doing so effectively, with little to no value given to Native American opinions on such matters.

Although many aspects of life at Carlisle changed over time, the school consistently demanded that its staff and students work hard for long hours, suggesting that complete assimilation required the full commitment of everyone involved, as Commissioner Jones argued in his 1901 report. Those hired as classroom teachers were, with few exceptions, single white women without children; and they were expected to do much more than teach reading, writing, and other subjects, as they were foremost tasked with the "moral uplift" of indigenous children. Vocational education also played an important role in the school's assimilation efforts, as it aimed to prepare students to be productive citizens in a "civilized" white society, and men were often hired to educate students in trades as varied as bakers, band leaders, and coaches. But these male teachers were usually married with children and were not necessarily expected to spend time with Indian students outside their classes.[5] The focus of this chapter is on the mostly white female classroom teachers at Carlisle, although Native American teachers—women and men—as well as white male academic leaders are also discussed.

The story of Carlisle and the roles teachers played in actualizing its imperial mission is complex and, as mentioned above, will be told over two chapters. First, a broader historical context regarding white intervention in Indian education, and Carlisle specifically, provides a framework for chapter 2 before moving into details about the swiftness of the school's opening. Curricular decisions, particularly its infamous English-only policy, extracurricular activities, as well as the pressures teachers and students experienced both inside and outside the classroom then begin to paint a picture of life at Carlisle. For many Indian children separated from their families, Carlisle became an imperfect surrogate family, filled both with love and discipline. As will be seen, teachers oversaw a culture marked by constant surveillance of their indigenous wards, including regular reinforcement of Christian teachings. In these and other ways, teaching empire was all-encompassing, requiring constant maintenance of one's own respectability as well as that of superiors, colleagues, and students.

The staff and students at Carlisle left many types of sources through which we can track teachers' lives, including personal letters, interviews, student and superintendent memoirs, institutional reports, personnel files, and school publications. Although the intended audience for most of these sources is clear, it is important to clarify the readership and purpose of the school's newspapers. These publications, of which there were several different versions over the years, were intended for Indian students and school staff as well as people interested in Indian education across the nation. Serving in part as propaganda, these publications reported on school events and achievements while reminding readers about the importance of the school's mission.[6]

Carlisle was, of course, part of a much longer history of Indian education in North America. Christian missionaries founded schools to "save" Indian souls soon after white settlers came to North America and continued to do so through the nineteenth century. In order to effectively spread Christianity, missionaries taught English and developed a curriculum that emphasized both basic academic skills and hard physical labor. By the early nineteenth century, for example, Protestant missionaries across the continent (mirroring efforts in foreign countries) instituted a "half-and-half" pattern, where students spent part of each day in a classroom and the rest of their time tending the fields or learning domestic skills, depending upon their sex. Thus, the combination of vocational and academic training associated with Armstrong's Hampton Institute and Pratt's Carlisle had its roots in missionary work. And while Carlisle was the first federally funded off-reservation Indian boarding school, the US government had been subsidizing educational missionary work—including half-and-half programs—throughout the nineteenth century.[7]

By the 1870s the government had shifted its funding from missionary schools to their own Indian education operations, and the number of government-run Indian schools rose dramatically. Between 1870 and 1900, government appropriations for Indian schooling increased from approximately $20,000 to almost $3 million. One hundred fifty government schools targeted 3,000 Indian students in 1877; by 1900, over 300 schools enrolled more than 21,000 Indian pupils.[8] The difference, of course, between government schools and their Christian predecessors was that whereas missionary schools aimed to mold Indians into "good Christians," government schools sought to prepare them to be "good citizens." Of course, for most schoolteachers and educational leaders, these two goals were practically equivalent. Although the Indian School Service, and Carlisle in particular, did not formally endorse a specific Christian creed, the majority of Indian Service and Carlisle employees were overtly encouraged to draw inspiration from their own, mostly Protestant, religious heritage and to encourage students to follow suit. Intentionally blurring the line between church and state, the US government invested in Carlisle at a critical time, hoping the school would create a generation of morally upright—in their eyes, "Christian"—Indian youth loyal to the United States.

This long history of white Christian intervention in Indian education was part of a broader process of Anglo-American subjugation of native peoples. As white settlement and westward expansion increasingly took indigenous people's lands, missionaries and reformers sought to influence native people's way of thinking. Historian Cathleen Cahill explains, "The process of conquest and dispossession had a long history, [and] it accelerated and intensified in the decades after the Civil War," when the federal government strove to sever native people's "emotional and legal claims to land," in part by breaking treaties and implementing assimilation policies.[9] In this way, settler colonialism continually redefined the US borders as white Americans endeavored to occupy native people's lands *and* minds. Pratt's experiment at Carlisle played a key role in this project of conquest and dispossession, working to break Indian children's ties to their cultural heritage. Its apparent success ultimately spawned more than twenty-five other off-reservation boarding schools by the turn of the twentieth century.[10]

Somewhat ironically, Pratt and his successors at Carlisle who endeavored to "save" the Indian were largely intertwined with the same institution formally charged with killing indigenous peoples for over a century: the military.[11] Recounting his life and work in his memoir, *Battlefield and Classroom*, Pratt's earliest encounters with indigenous peoples was as a soldier, responsible for enforcing the will of the US government.[12] In addition to perpetrating violence himself, he witnessed the devastation western tribes suffered when white settlers continued to demand access to western lands and the US government went to war to ensure their success. And he felt redeemed when he successfully "civilized" Indian prisoners at Fort Marion, Florida. Still, Pratt's professional background, the site chosen for the school, and the government department that approved the project were fundamentally inseparable from the US military, the force behind Indian removal and imperial desire. In fact, four of the five superintendents who oversaw the school during its forty-year existence, including Pratt, were military men, and the one exception had direct experience with the US conquest of the Philippines. Thus, all of Carlisle's leaders maintained strong ties to the US military or government, and they all symbolized US imperial power.

With approval from the War Department in August 1879, imperial education began at the old army barracks in rural Pennsylvania under the direction of eager army Captain Pratt, who looked to experienced teachers to help him in his mission. Sixty-three-year-old Sarah A. Mather wrote to Captain Pratt on August 21, 1879:

> Your trip has been constantly in my mind . . . and the more I think of it the more I think I should like to go *anywhere* you go. I know I should be taken good care of and as for the fatigue I could stand that. . . . I hope no old fogy will say I can't go. Why I'll help you make good selections! You know I have been studying children all my life.[13]

When Pratt invited Mather to assist him in recruiting the first class of students for the school, she jumped at the chance to travel through Indian territory and was thrilled to use her expertise as an educator to help select students for the first off-reservation Indian boarding school. Reminiscent of the Thomasites (discussed in chapters 1 and 4)—most of whom were eager at the prospect of adventure and committed to the US mission in the Philippines—Mather had become an enthusiastic supporter of Pratt's work educating Indians, having taught English to the prisoners under his charge at Fort Marion a few years earlier.[14]

Still, Mather and Pratt faced many obstacles throughout their westward journey, and their perseverance serves as one of the earliest examples of the commitment and dedication Carlisle's teachers exhibited to help the school—and US imperial aims—thrive. Demonstrative of some of the physical challenges they faced, Pratt recalled that Mather became "wretchedly seasick" as she traveled overland by wagon. At night, she slept on the floor of the wagon with a few blankets, while Pratt scared away wolves with his revolver. Upon arrival in mid-September 1879, Mather accompanied Pratt and an interpreter to the council house to convince the Indian chief, Spotted Tail, and other Sioux to allow their children to return to Carlisle, Pennsylvania, with them—not an easy task. At first, Spotted Tail fervently resisted Pratt's pitch and declared, "'The white people are all thieves and liars. We do not want our children to learn such things.'" Mather, whom Pratt introduced as the "good lady [who would] . . . look after the girls," spoke next and softened Pratt's proposal, helping to secure five of Spotted Tail's dozen children and several other children from the tribe. In all, Pratt and Mather recruited over eighty children from three reservations to bring back to Carlisle, overcoming parents' resistance.[15] Together, they persuaded American Indian mothers and fathers—who felt profound personal and historic distrust of whites—to entrust their children's lives with them, and thus the first class of Indian students was successfully enrolled at Carlisle.

Of course, that was Pratt's account of his and Mather's westward journey to attract the first cohort of indigenous children to Carlisle's classrooms. Native American stories of Pratt and Mather's arrival would not likely highlight such adventure or triumph but might instead point to the white man and woman's perhaps gentle but frightening threats, or perhaps, their ancestors' broken promises. Writing his autobiography, *My People the Sioux*, years later, former Carlisle student Luther Standing Bear claimed to have been the "first Indian boy to step inside the Carlisle Indian School grounds." He recounts his childhood journey from the reservation eastward, describing the crying children surrounding him, all consumed by the sadness of leaving home but not yet understanding the significance of the moment. He recalls:

It did not occur to me at that time that I was going away to learn the ways of the white man. My idea was that I was leaving the reservation and going to stay away long enough to do some brave deed, and then come home again alive. If I could just do that, then I knew my father would be so proud of me.[16]

In contrast to the pride captured by Pratt, Standing Bear remembers his innocence. Fixated on his youthful bravery and his father's ensuing admiration, young Standing Bear did not know what was to come, or yet, what would be lost.

Although Zitkala-Sa did not arrive on Carlisle's campus until adulthood, when she joined the teaching faculty in 1899, she recorded her memories about having left her South Dakota reservation as a child in the 1880s, and, like Luther Standing Bear, similarly depicts her youthful innocence, contrasting this with her mother's pained insights. She recalls how missionaries lured her and other children east with stories of boundless red apple orchards and a chance to ride "the iron horse." She describes her mother as skeptical but hopeful, and captures such conflicted sentiment, recounting that her mother reasoned, "'This tearing her [daughter] away, so young from her mother is necessary, if I would have her an educated woman. The pale-faces, who owe us a large debt for stolen lands, have begun to pay a tardy justice in offering some education to our children. But I know my daughter must suffer keenly in this experiment.'"[17] Of course, like Pratt's and Standing Bear's memoirs, Zitkala-Sa's autobiographical vignette uses poetic license in telling her story. Still, she, too, depicts some of the devastating truths of her own life, and likely that of other American Indians persuaded and pushed away from home by white missionaries' tales of better things off the reservation: childhood desires to see and experience such richness as well as a mother's wisdom and sacrifice, drawing from years of personal and historic loss but still somewhat hopeful for a daughter's future.

Of course, considering such different perspectives complicates the historical narrative, but the fact remains that in the fall of 1879 Pratt headed east in charge of over eighty Indian children. The degree to which these Sioux children "in blankets" heading to Carlisle were filled with dread, awe, or something in-between is certainly debatable. Luther Standing Bear's memoir recounts the excitement, fear, and anxiety that he and other Indian children faced as they traveled east, particularly as they encountered throngs of people gathered at railroad stations along the route, described by one Indian boy as being as numerous as "'ants . . . all over—everywhere.'"[18] Standing

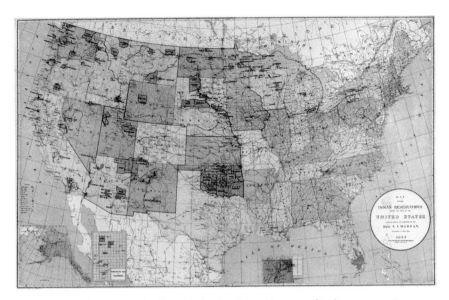

Published by the Office of Indian Affairs in 1892, this map of Indian reservations shows the vast distance between remote western Indian reservations and a boarding school established in an eastern location like Pennsylvania. Richard Henry Pratt and other reformers believed that Carlisle's location in the East, far removed from the "backward" influence of Indian home life, would facilitate Indian assimilation into white society. (Map by T. J. Morgan, Library of Congress Geography and Map Division, Washington, DC.)

Bear also wrote of such white crowds gathered at train stations "making a great noise" and "throw[ing] money at us," and remembered "the whites who acted so wild at seeing us. They tried to give the war-woop and mimic the Indian and in other ways got us all wrought up and excited, and we did not like this sort of treatment."[19] In his own memoir, Pratt recalled that the numbers of onlookers were even greater than when he chaperoned Indian prisoners to Florida in 1875 or Indian students to the Hampton Institute in 1878. Regarding the journey to Carlisle, he recalled "crowds of people assembled at the railroad stations" who craned their necks to glimpse the Indian children. It seemed that they hoped to witness these "others" moving from west to east, the children dressed in tribal garb as they approached "civilization." To limit the number of ogling eyes, Pratt arranged to arrive in the children's new hometown of Carlisle at midnight on October 6, 1879. Even then, scores of people met them at the train station and walked alongside them to their new "home."[20] Thus, Standing Bear, other Indian children, Pratt, and white crowds participated in a journey—willingly or not—from

west to east that served as a spectacle, creating imagined and real significance marked by the arrival of students to the nation's first Indian boarding
school established outside of a reservation.

Like the crowds who gathered, Pratt and other reformers saw the journey east—or at least the school's location—as exceptional and critically
important for quick assimilation. In fact, one of the most radical elements
of the Carlisle experiment was its location. A year into the experiment, Pratt
remained optimistic about the speed at which Indian children could imbibe
the lessons of civilization in their new eastern home. In January 1881 Pratt
wrote to US Representative Thaddeaus C. Pound:

> I am sure that if we could bring to bear such training as this upon all
> our Indian children for only three years that savagery among the Indi-
> ans in this country would be at an end. This bringing their children east
> among the whites is to many of them now, and would be to all in time,
> an open door by which they can migrate into civilization.[21]

In Pratt's view, Carlisle served as a vital step in the Indian's journey from
barbarity to civilization, and from living by Indian custom to adopting the
ways of white men and women. Other individuals of Indian heritage had
made such migrations before, but an eastern boarding school ensured their
distance from reservation life for an extended period, which, it was thought,
would allow masses of Indian children to enter civilization and give them a
chance to fit into the dominant white culture. For Pratt and other reformers,
the removal of Indian children from the "corrupting" influences of reservation life was believed to be the only way to "save" the Indian race.

Underscoring rhetoric about the contrast of civilization versus savagery,
Carlisle emerged from and was part of a larger culture whose dominant
voices heralded and naturalized such racial inequality, and some whites
recognized their complicity, at least in part. An August 1879 letter from a
US Indian agent in the Dakota Territory, republished in Carlisle's school
newspaper the next May, recognized this disparity: "The reason that Indians
are not educated and civilized is not because they do not want to be, but
because we do not want them to be."[22] Rather than placing blame solely on
the Indian, the agent boldly declared his own role, and that of the larger
white society, in preventing native populations from assimilating into an
educated, civilized life. Of course, this agent still upheld the false dichotomy
that Western education equaled civilization, assuming both to be universally desirable, and this helps to explain why it was republished in a Carlisle

school newspaper. Still, while the agent did not recognize the inaccuracies of such an absolutist framework, he at least partially recognized the role that whites played, from his perspective, in keeping the Indian down, and he was not alone in such thinking. Printing this letter in the school newspaper was also a way for leaders at Carlisle to acknowledge early in the school's endeavors the role that white society played in exacerbating, and even perpetuating, Indian isolation and "backwardness."

Eighteen years later when Pratt was asked in a *New York Sun* interview to describe the biggest obstacle he faced in his work, he echoed the Indian agent's sentiment: "Well, I think I should say it is the prejudice of the Anglo-Saxon race, and the unwillingness to give the man a chance, or to believe that he can be educated."[23] Although it is easy from a twenty-first-century perspective to demonize both Pratt and white society for their profound and destructive prejudice, it is significant that Pratt recognized how Carlisle was constrained by the biases of the dominant society. Modern scholars often condemn Pratt and the work at Carlisle simply as racist and degrading to Indian cultures.[24] Yet, in the late nineteenth and early twentieth centuries, Carlisle and its work represented a rather radical and benevolent, if problematic and yes, racist, means of "saving" the Indian. Historian David Adams recognizes Pratt's oversimplification of the "Indian problem" in which the choice seemed to be "education or extinction." Nevertheless, he also gives some credence to the belief that for reformers like Pratt and perhaps the agent quoted above, education *seemed* the best means to help the Indian within a society seemingly driven to destroy "others."[25]

Certainly, whites' beliefs regarding the inviolability of an essentially white-supremacist, racialized hierarchy continued to guide Carlisle's mission into the twentieth century. For example, a March 2, 1900, school newspaper article described the recent visit of a "civilized" Indian, Mr. Richard Heyl, as "an educated Apache Indian who knows more about the white man than he does about his own people."[26] This made him "a perfect exemplification of the Carlisle idea although he never saw Carlisle before." Clearly, the ideal Carlisle student would forever abandon his Indian heritage and assimilate into white culture as fully as possible. The article continued: "There is only one way to bring the Indian up to the superior race and that is to give him all the advantages of the superior race in the midst of the people of the superior race. No race distinction can be traced between Mr. Heyl and any cultivated gentleman you may meet anywhere, except the dark complexion."[27] These words hammer away at the idea of whites being a "superior race," repeating this phrase *three times* within one sentence. A relentless reminder

Written on the image: "Sioux Girls as they appeared on their arrival at Carlisle Barracks on the 5th of October 1879." Photographer John N. Choate captured Carlisle's first female students wearing blankets and traditional hairstyles and shows how children were often separated by gender at the school. The girls are flanked by Miss Mather, who helped to recruit them, and an interpreter. Such images were used as propaganda to show the dramatic transformation that students embodied, from traditional blankets to Western-style dress, suggesting students' apparent "rise" to civilized life. (Photo by John N. Choate, courtesy of Richard Henry Pratt Papers, Beinecke Rare Book and Manuscript Library, Yale University.)

of the goal at Carlisle—"to bring the Indian up" to a particular standard of cultivation and refinement as displayed by Heyl—the visitor's success came despite his "dark complexion," hinting at his supposed inferior heritage. Furthermore, the article credits Heyl's "cultivated" achievement to his immersion in white culture, suggesting that students at Carlisle, similarly saturated in white societal norms, had a unique opportunity that enabled them to reach similar "greatness." Such racialized "reasoning" was not intimated delicately here but rather declared quite boldly. The article assumed that its readership—of students, staff, reformers, and interested "friends" of the Indian—would *or should* be sympathetic to such ideas, since the fundamental mission of Carlisle, to save Indians through complete assimilation in white culture, was never hidden but rather proudly celebrated.

Carlisle's solution, then, to the so-called Indian problem lay in the possibility of one-way cultural transformation. As remembered by founding

Written on the image: "Sioux Boys as they appeared on their arrival at Carlisle Barracks on the 5th of October 1879." Similar to the preceding photo, photographer John N. Choate captured Carlisle's first male students wearing mostly traditional clothes and hairstyles. The boys range in age and are flanked by Superintendent Richard Henry Pratt and an interpreter. (Photo by John N. Choate, courtesy of Richard Henry Pratt Papers, Beinecke Rare Book and Manuscript Library, Yale University.)

teacher Emma Cutter, Pratt insisted on a dualistic purpose at Carlisle: "The aim of Gen. R. H. Pratt in establishing the school at Carlisle, Pennsylvania, was to give the Indians a chance to show that they are human and capable of receiving an education. He also wished to educate the people of the East and of the West to believe in the despised race."[28] Having worked with Pratt for over two decades at Carlisle, Cutter was intimately familiar with the founder's purpose. Sympathetic with his ideals, she recognized how white society demeaned the Indian—even dismissing their humanity—and trusted that the school was established to correct such notions. By implementing and enforcing cultural change among the school's Indian students—including dramatic reeducation efforts regarding dress, language, and gender norms—Carlisle aimed to prove native people's adaptability, and at the same time, counter biases held by the dominant society, an agenda that suited Pratt's personal goals as well as that of a burgeoning imperial power. The school, like the nation, relied on teachers to facilitate this conversion.

Even before Carlisle opened its doors to the first students in October 1879, a distinct school culture was already in the making: that of separating children by sex. On their journey to the school that fall, Pratt and Mather had already divided the first cohort of over eighty schoolchildren into "boy" and "girl" groups, and when they arrived at the school, these gendered divisions continued. Pratt recalled, "The matron who was to take charge of the girls was on hand to camp them in the unfurnished north tier of officer quarters, while the boys went into the north barracks under Interpreter Tackett's care."[29] With only Pratt, Mather, the matron, two interpreters, and Pratt's wife, Laura, in charge of the students, a fundamental component of the school culture had already been instituted before most of the teachers arrived on campus: the deliberate division of labor and living according to sex in order to set "appropriate" boundaries between boys and girls. Such gendered separations were mirrored in mainstream public schools as well, with girls and boys provided different academic opportunities and tracked for distinct occupations, despite coeducation becoming the norm around the turn of the twentieth century.[30] Establishing these separate spheres for the children came to be a central component of the work in "civilizing" the Indian. For the children themselves, these divisions must have escalated their anxiety as they were separated from siblings on their journey east and as such divisions were further cemented upon arrival at Carlisle. Of course, these separations were an intentional part of Carlisle's plan to erase children's cultural and familial heritage, ironically as a means of "saving" the race.[31]

Staff members learned early on that they would have to "make do" with less, creating a culture that admired frugality and hard work. When Pratt and Mather brought a second group of over fifty Indian children to Carlisle in November 1879, the school had still not received the food, clothing, and school supplies requested from the Indian Bureau. Thus, for the first several weeks at the school, staff members utilized the sparse material provisions as best they could and came to rely upon the children's labor as well as local volunteers and philanthropists to meet the school's basic needs.[32] In this way, students, teachers, and others built the school from the ground up, together creating an institution intended to produce profound cultural change, although some participated more eagerly than others.

One of the earliest, most dramatic and infamous acts of cultural transformation involved renaming students, and this task fell to teachers. Teachers approached this in different ways, and as with most of the cultural changes imposed on children at the school, students accepted these new names to varying degrees. In fact, several students vividly recalled their renaming, suggesting the significance of the experience: for some, it proved traumatic, while for others it was less so. Luther Standing Bear recounted how his teacher, Miss Marianna Burgess, helped him "choose" a new name, revealing both the careful planning on the part of his teacher as well as the great meaning he associated with his new name:

> The teacher had a long pointed stick in her hand, and the interpreter told the boy in the front seat to come up. . . . Finally he pointed out one of the names written on the blackboard. Then the teacher took a piece of white tape and wrote the name on it. Then she cut off the length of the tape and sewed it on the back of the boy's shirt. Then that name was erased from the board. . . . Soon we all had the names of white men sewn on our backs. . . . I had selected the name "Luther."[33]

Here, Luther painted a powerful image of Indian children wearing shirts whose backs literally bore "the names of white men" at the behest of their teacher. Yet, he also reveals that Burgess, whom he came to admire, allowed her students to "choose" their Americanized names, although students, of course, had no real choice as to whether they could instead maintain their Indian names. Nevertheless, Luther suggested that such naming could not rid the boys of their heritage even as he suggested how this ritual supposedly helped transform young Indian boys into white men.[34] Another student, Jason Betzinez, explained in plainer language how his teacher modified his name, "Batsinas," and gave him a first name as well. He explained, "Miss Low . . . changed the spelling . . . to Betzinez . . . [and] selected for me the name of Jason. She said that Jason was some man who hunted the golden fleece but never found it."[35] Unlike Miss Burgess, who at least may have conveyed a sense of choice, Miss Low reportedly bestowed a name upon her student, one that she, rather than he, found meaningful. Still, another student resented his renaming and "always hated that name forced on me by white people." Apache student Asa Daklugie explained of his Americanized name, "It was forced on me as though I had been an animal."[36] Ultimately, the teachers' responsibility to rename students served both symbolic and practical purposes. It enabled white teachers to create names that they could easily pronounce and spell while also suggesting to students and whites alike that new "civilized" identities would be created at Carlisle.

In addition to new names, students were given Western-style clothes and hairstyles, changes admired by Pratt and his staff and used to further the cause of Indian assimilation. As Pratt had done at Hampton, he arranged for Carlisle students to have their photographs taken in their traditional garb with long hair and then as "civilized" young men and women, wearing school uniforms with boys' hair cut short and girls' pulled back. Pratt used these photographs as propaganda, to prove that Indians could be civilized. As anthropologist Genevieve Bell argues, "At the time, these photographs were seen and sold as irrefutable proof that it was possible to raise Indians out of savagery and transform them into model pupils and citizens. A century later, those same photographs seem shocking, serving as an enduring reminder of the power and brutality of the American State."[37] Bell's observation points to a critical question concerning the extent to which teachers and other whites viewed their work as part of something larger. Evidence suggests that some teachers cared deeply about "saving" the Indian race and thought broadly about the "Indian problem," with most believing that their efforts to "civilize" Indian students were fundamentally benevolent. They eagerly fulfilled the school's mission of "killing the Indian but saving the man," a goal that they thought would help students participate more fully in society.[38] Still, this does not make teachers', reformers', or imperialists' efforts any less cruel.

White teachers and others also believed that transforming students' physical appearance was essential to enabling their full participation at the school. As declared in the first issue of Carlisle's school's newspaper: "All [students] were eager to learn, but it was soon evident that the barber and tailor must take precedence in the work of civilization. The daily sessions were short, and not much was effected until blankets had disappeared."[39] Thus, changing the hairstyles and clothing of the students was believed to enable better learning. Perhaps with fewer distractions and visible reminders of their heritage, it was believed that students, and teachers for that matter, could remain more focused on the lessons.

Of course, students themselves did not necessarily appreciate their new appearance. Mrs. Pratt explained how pupils wailed after having their hair cut. Asa Daklugie likened getting his braids cut off to torture. Luther Standing Bear explained how he felt ashamed, less Indian, "an imitation of a white man" after having his hair cut, though he was eager to receive "white man's clothes." Whatever the effect on the students, white teachers and other white staff members at Carlisle most likely felt more comfortable and perhaps in more control of their students as the "Indian" appearance was shorn away. As Luther remembers it, "Our teachers and the other white people were greatly pleased at our new appearance."[40]

Once students appeared "civilized" to "White Eyes," teachers' primary academic task involved teaching English.[41] Over time, methods of teaching English at Carlisle changed, although one constant remained throughout almost the entirety of the school's existence: a prohibition on speaking native languages. This rule did not exist in early October 1879, however, when the first cohort of Sioux girls and boys arrived at the school accompanied by interpreters, a luxury not available for most successive groups of students. The next group, who arrived a month later, were from various Oklahoma tribes, and they could not communicate well with one another, let alone with the students and staff members already at the school. Not surprisingly, one teacher remembered this latter group of children as "very timid." Moreover, she recalled that these children, along with the school's earliest teachers, learned a bit of the Sioux language.[42] Thus, in the school's nascent stages, teachers and students *both* learned some foreign languages to facilitate understanding in their everyday lives. However, soon after this short grace period in which multiple languages were tolerated, students were forbidden from using any language except English, and teachers were encouraged to do the same. This English-only policy endured until the school closed in 1918. As remembered by Luther Standing Bear, within his first couple of months at the school, children arrived "from various tribes in other States and from other reservations. We were not allowed to converse in the Indian tongue, and we knew so little English that we had a hard time to get along."[43] Even if Sioux words and phrases were sometimes used to facilitate communication, the overarching English-only policy limited the use of most native languages throughout the school's forty years.

Perhaps Pratt rationalized the English-only policy in order to more quickly homogenize students' diversity of languages and backgrounds, thus speeding up the process of assimilation, despite facing criticism. In 1896 when asked, "Why is it necessary to make these children forget their mother tongue?" Pratt defended himself: "It is not the policy to make them forget their mother tongue. But we make them learn English. . . . English is the language of this country. The wall that separates the Indian from the other population of the country is the wall of language to begin with."[44] Thus, Pratt justified the English-only policy as a means of better integrating his students into the larger society, denying that it was intended to make them "forget" their native language. This inability to admit the policy's faults is, in part, an example of the blindness that Pratt and many of his supporters suffered: the inability to see or even entertain the damage that their work incurred, including its almost complete decimation of indigenous language and culture. Of course, for Pratt and many white teachers who bought into such imperial reasoning, displacing the "barbaric" culture—including its language—was intentional, perhaps considered a small sacrifice necessary to "save" the Indian. Such efforts at Carlisle preceded, and perhaps facilitated, similar trends in late nineteenth-century Indian education reform.

Although not all reformers agreed, English-only policies became the norm as the end of the nineteenth century approached. In 1887, US government officials forbade teachers at Indian schools from teaching any language besides English. This reportedly upset some missionaries who had used both English and indigenous languages in their work.[45] With this decree, the Bureau of Indian Affairs sided with Pratt and other boarding school leaders who privileged English above all other languages. By 1889, ten years into Carlisle's efforts, the annual report of the commissioner of Indian affairs lauded boarding schools where, "They hear and use only the English language, are removed from the contaminating influences of camp life, become accustomed to the usages of civilization, and are trained to habits of industry, thrift, and self-reliance."[46] In this way, authorities in Indian education considered English-only policies as part of a broader curriculum designed to impart lessons of "civilization" to its pupils. From the top down, education officials believed such immersive policies to be the best way to uplift the Indian to white standards of citizenship.

At least one Carlisle student echoed this sentiment. In an 1887 essay contest that proclaimed Carlisle a place where "every opportunity is given for free and independent thought," students were asked to analyze the English-only teaching policy from their own personal experiences:

You have been home, some of you, after studying nothing but English at Carlisle. How did you succeed? Did you wish you knew less English and more Indian? Some of you have tried the other way studying English with the Indian. Did you get along any faster? YOU know whether the work among your people by the native missionaries who were taught in Indian is good work or not.[47]

The winning essay, itself evidence of the school's lack of "free and independent thought"—or, perhaps, its realization of assimilation—celebrated student Dennison Wheelock's largely unoriginal proclamation: "The Indian language . . . is . . . the cord that pulls down the race who have been bound by the same cord to ignorance and barbarism for centuries."[48] Though the essay's authenticity is suspect, Wheelock's winning words do reflect the culture of living and learning at Carlisle. Both the assignment and his "winning" response suggest that Carlisle, perhaps successfully, convinced its students that reservation life and Indian cultural traditions prevented them from succeeding in American society. Or, that some students astutely learned how to fake it.

Years later Wheelock continued to grapple with questions regarding the extent to which indigenous people needed to be removed from the influences of "ignorance and barbarism" to advance, indeed to survive. A member of the Oneida, Wheelock had been a serious music student at Carlisle. He graduated in 1890 and returned to the school as bandleader several years later, having become a world-renowned musician. He later became an attorney and an active member of the Society of American Indians, founded in 1911 for "the purpose and protection and advancement of [the] race." Ultimately, Wheelock committed himself to Indian advancement through both music and legal work and continued to praise the promise of Carlisle while remaining an Indian rights activist for the rest of his life.[49] Whatever his true childhood or adult beliefs were regarding English-only language policies, his life testifies to the transformative culture at Carlisle, perhaps for better *and* worse.

Yet, for at least one teacher who worked at Carlisle in its final years, enforcing an English-only policy seemed cruel. Verna Dunagan, who taught music at Carlisle from 1915 to 1918, explained that teachers were supposed to "report" students every time they spoke in their native tongues. However, she admitted, "I closed my ears—every time. I never squealed on them, I just couldn't do it. . . . They'd feel so badly because they couldn't speak their language and there's where *I* think they made a mistake at the school."[50] Dunagan believed in the mission of Carlisle, but she did not support—or abide by—all of its rules, particularly its English-only policy. She resisted simply by refusing to enforce the policy outside the classroom, a tactic that other teachers also must have used to grant students more freedom than the official Carlisle rules allowed. Such actions expose some vulnerability in the imperial mission, as it depended upon teachers' adherence to its policies. At the same time, however, Dunagan remained at the school from 1915 until the school's closing in 1918, and there is little evidence to suggest that she otherwise resisted the school's rules during her tenure. Still, even teachers' small transgressions—coupled with students' much greater and more consistent forms of resistance—undermined the imperial mission, although not enough to derail it.

Regardless of the extent of such resistance, for some students and teachers, learning and teaching a new language proved laborious. Nevertheless, their diligence and dedication sometimes paid off, as evident by students' recollections.[51] Student Jason Betzinez remembered:

It was extremely difficult for me to learn to speak English. . . . I progressed very slowly, so slowly, in fact, that for the first three years it didn't seem that I would ever learn. . . . I was helped by my teachers, who patiently went over with me again and again the words and phrases I was trying to say. Finally I was pleased to have my teacher, a Miss F. G. Paull, of Blairsville, Pennsylvania, compliment me by saying, "Jason, you have made quite an advance. You are beginning to show improvement in your English." Thus encouraged I began to make better progress not only in English but in my other subjects.[52]

For Betzinez, learning English took years of repetition, and only then was he able to advance in other subject areas. His teachers' patience and encouragement made a strong impact on him, and he attributed his learning to their painstaking efforts and guidance, undoubtedly helped by his own tenacity as well. Although other teachers certainly helped Betzinez as he struggled with the new language, he credited Miss Paull with giving him confidence. Like many teachers at Carlisle during its early years, she demonstrated great dedication to her students and the school, facilitating extracurricular performances, advising literary societies, and hosting Sunday School events.[53] Thus, it is not surprising that Betzinez identified Miss Paull for helping him learn English, as she tended students' academic and moral interests inside and outside of the classroom.

Other students also appreciated an individual teacher's commitment, even if they otherwise resented or resisted Carlisle's forced assimilation methods. Although Asa Daklugie likened the school's imposition of an Anglo name and haircut to being treated like an animal or torture, learning came more easily to him than to Betzinez, including English. He described his teacher fondly, despite his negative view of other white women:

Learning English wasn't too bad. There was a necessity for memorizing everything because we could neither read nor write. Before the winter was over I was learning to read. My teacher was a white lady and she was very patient and kind to us. She taught us to write, too, and she was not bossy as most white ladies are. She was polite. She seemed to know without being told that I wanted desperately to be able to read and she helped me.[54]

Eager to learn, Daklugie picked up English rather quickly and particularly appreciated his teacher's work, manners, and insights. Distinguishing

One of many staged photographs of classroom activities. Dated March 25, 1901, the photograph is titled, "Conversation lesson, subject—the chair"; the same words are written on the chalkboard, and it was likely taken to illustrate how everyday objects were used to teach English. The image also makes light of such learning as well as the students and teacher involved. Like other photographs of Carlisle classrooms, this otherwise typical schoolroom includes desks in rows, chalkboard with letters and instructions, an American flag, and photographs of American leaders as well as other artwork. (Photo by Frances Benjamin Johnston, courtesy Library of Congress, Prints and Photographs Division, Washington, DC.)

his teacher from other Carlisle teachers, whom he suggested were among Carlisle's "bossy . . . white ladies," Daklugie demonstrated his fundamental resistance to the educational experiment at Carlisle. Unwilling to be a keen participant in all respects, he accepted lessons or teachers he found interesting or worthwhile but resisted other demands of assimilation. Moreover, much like Betzinez, Daklugie believed that this teacher instinctually knew his academic desires and appreciated her guidance.

Like Betzinez and Daklugie, Luther Standing Bear admired his teacher, Marianna Burgess, even keeping in touch with her many years later. As an adult, Standing Bear sought his childhood teacher's advice to "ask her any question which may come up in my mind." Back when Standing Bear was a new, young student, Miss Burgess—who had sewn the name "Luther" onto the back of his shirt—taught him to write the alphabet, initially communicating through a translator and facial expressions. When he became frustrated and overwhelmed, she adjusted his assignments accordingly.[55]

Overall, some students—including Asa Daklugie, who largely resisted Carlisle's assimilation measures—appreciated the efforts of individual teachers and their commitment to student learning, even if they resented some of the white customs and norms forced upon them. Of course, these accounts are not necessarily representative of the larger student body at Carlisle, the majority of whom did not publish memoirs and were perhaps not as fluent or eager to learn English as Betzinez, Daklugie, and Standing Bear. Still, their voices help to tell stories of some of the struggles and "successes" that Carlisle's students and teachers experienced in English education.

Part of this English-only instruction, anathema to some but accessible to others, followed a broader, progressive teaching pedagogy common at the turn of the century. [56] Teacher Emma Cutter described the early teaching method at Carlisle as the "natural or conversational one," whereby teachers showed students an object and had students recite the English word before teaching them to write it in script on the blackboard. According to Cutter, "When about twenty or thirty words had been learned, verbs were introduced, at first only such as could be illustrated by action and could follow the nouns already known. We walked, we ran, we jumped." Cutter explained how other words and adjectives, the easiest of which to teach were colors, were then taught to aid students in helping to pronounce, write, and read simple sentences.[57] While the repetitive recitation served to teach correct pronunciation, spelling, and writing, the use of objects and of everyday activities to familiarize students with English vocabulary drew on progressive pedagogy. Beyond rote memorization, Carlisle faculty relied upon objects and the immediate surroundings to aid student learning. Similar "objective" or "natural" lessons were used to teach numbers and counting, where faculty relied upon objects and the senses to teach basic skills that catered to students' learning needs.[58]

Other subjects exposed students to what must have seemed to be radical ideas, although to a certain extent this new knowledge alternatively undermined or enhanced former beliefs. Subjects like science and geography could transform the way students viewed the world in which they lived, generating both skepticism and wonder, and ultimately earning teachers greater respect. For example, Luther Standing Bear did not believe the globe that his teacher shared with the class accurately represented the Earth until a guest speaker, an astronomer, correctly predicted an upcoming lunar eclipse. Standing Bear remembered, "After that, we readily believed everything our teacher told us about geography and astronomy."[59] Presumably the expert astronomer was a man, and thus he likely held more authority in the children's minds than their teacher, especially if they had begun to buy into Western norms of gendered power dynamics. Whatever the case, for Standing Bear, the astronomer's authority transferred over to his teacher in apparent perpetuity.

Just as Standing Bear came to understand what appeared to him to be miracles of science, Daklugie became enthralled with geography. He explained:

> One day she [his teacher] opened a big book to show me Arizona, and for the first time in my life I saw a map. I was fascinated. When she showed me mountains and rivers I could tell their names in my language. I knew the Spanish for some of them and a few in English. She let me take that geography book to the dormitory and Frank Mangus and I almost wore it out.[60]

Daklugie and his friend relished seeing maps of their homeland and poured over visual representations of a region with which they were intimately familiar. Perhaps Daklugie's teacher appreciated her eager students' prior knowledge of the landscape, although this cannot be known for sure. Certainly, Daklugie reimagined his own life, using memories of his experiences to understand maps in geography books more fully. In either case, Western education privileged standard geography, astronomy, and knowledge held in books over firsthand accounts of life on Earth and beyond, and from the school's earliest days the curriculum utilized teacher-driven lessons, mapping, and drawing exercises to better understand the world.[61] This likely contrasted with how indigenous children were accustomed to learning, as according to historian Jacqueline Fear-Segal, "in no native community was education a discrete endeavor conducted in a separate institution. It was woven into everyday patterns of living and took place informally in daily interactions between children and their elders."[62] Reconstituted as members of an institutional community, Carlisle's teachers substituted as children's "elders" and formally, as well as informally, instructed indigenous children in what they believed to be a more civilized worldview, both within and outside the confines of the classroom.

Reflecting transformations in the school's student body as well as broader educational trends, Carlisle's curriculum changed over time as did the needs of the institution. Over Carlisle's first two decades the student population grew steadily, reaching its height in 1904—the same year Pratt left—and not declining significantly until the school's last few years (see Table 2.1).[63]

Miss Emma Cutter's physics class, 1901. Carlisle's upper-level students pose with various technological devices, showcasing the school's modernity and student advancement. (Photo by Frances Benjamin Johnston, courtesy Library of Congress, Prints and Photographs Division, Washington, DC.)

Early on, teachers mixed primary skills—speaking, reading, and writing in English in addition to arithmetic—with a few other subjects, like geography, and an industrial training program.[64] This curriculum was intended to target students' basic needs since most of them—including Standing Bear, Betzinez, and Daklugie—did not know English and had not had much experience with Western-style schooling. In contrast, by the 1910s many Carlisle students, often the children of the school's alumni, had attended day schools close to their reservation before heading east to boarding school. These students were better prepared for an academic program that emphasized specialized subjects, and the school accommodated this growing need as well as national education trends by shifting its focus from elementary to high school coursework, reflecting the already decreasing enrollment of younger students.[65] To meet higher-achieving students' needs, from as early as the 1890s until the school closed in 1918, teachers advanced their professional development and energized their teaching by attending sum-

Table 2.1: Student Attendance at Carlisle

Year	Average Number of Students	Average Age of Students (Male)	Average Age of Students (Female)	Number of Students Who Graduated	Number of Student Deaths
1879	158	16.44	14.6		1
1880	239	13.35	11.76		6
1881	295	14.21	12.33		8
1882	393	14.73	12.48		10
1883	368	16.71	14.91		8
1884	421	15.25	13.33		4
1885	494	16.11	14.37		9
1886	484	15.24	13.87		8
1887	547	15.1	15.12		11
1888	563	16.12	13.92		21
1889	595	16.43	14.52	14	13
1890	702	15.7	13.59	18	10
1891	754	15.57	14.84	11	8
1892	779	16.32	16.13	3	5
1893	731	17.47	15.48	6	5
1894	656	15.75	14.94	19	4
1895	668	17.01	14.52	20	11
1896	741	16.38	14.12	25	6
1897	790	15.81	14.42	26	3
1898	851	16.32	14.88	24	3
1899	878	16.83	15.49	31	6
1900	981	14.91	15.40	37	7
1901	970	17.1	14.93	29	3
1902	1,023	16.67	15.8	42	0
1903	963	16.3	14.73	47	5
1904	1025	16.68	14.51	43	6
1905	898	16.44	14.58	43	7
1906	981	15.7	15.08	30	4
1907	984	18.46	15.47	23	3
1908	970	17.62	16.75	27	3
1909	967	18.02	15.81	25	2
1910	N/A	17.85	17.04	23	6
1911	932	17.75	16.7	23	3
1912	792	17.51	16.56	21	4
1913	N/A	17.48	15.97	15	4
1914	668	17.5	16.49	18	2
1915	~661	17.95	17.02	30	1
1916	~661	17.39	16.24		4
1917	~246	16.74	15.87	56	2

(continued on the next page)

Table 2.1 (*continued*)

Year	Average Number of Students	Average Age of Students (Male)	Average Age of Students (Female)	Number of Students Who Graduated	Number of Student Deaths
1918	~246	16.4	16.6	25	1
TOTAL				758	220

Note: ~ refers to numbers that are averaged according to superintendent administrations; see Bell's figure 2, "Total Number of Students Who Attended Carlisle, Organized by Tenure of Superintendents," page 77.

Source: Adapted from Bell, "Telling Stories out of School": 45, 77, 333, 400, 402.

mer training programs, enabling them to bring their new expertise into the classroom and helping both students and faculty to sustain their commitment to Carlisle and its mission.[66] However, not all students were able to meet Carlisle's higher standards of learning. In fact, low graduation rates throughout Carlisle's forty-year history suggests, among other things, that most students did not demonstrate mastery in key subjects, further burdening teachers' daily classroom work and overall mission.[67]

Several teachers felt this increased pressure, particularly in the school's final decade. As discussed in the introduction, in 1914 Emma Lovewell, who had taught fourth grade for two years, was moved up to seventh grade. She noted that seventh grade "has always been considered undesirable because one has to promote to please four department teachers. Therefore, one has to be doubly conscientious. As the pupils are weak in both language and arithmetic when they come to me a great deal devolves on me."[68] For Lovewell and teachers in similar situations, the challenge of preparing students who lacked basic skills for more advanced level classes proved almost impossible.

In 1912 Mattie Lane left Carlisle after teaching for one year, in part because she felt overwhelmed by students' lack of preparedness, disinterest in studying, and a learning environment she found lacked rigor. She noted:

> I had sixth room work and there were pupils in my room that could not subtract to save their souls nor divide, in arithmetic. They had simply been put there by the former teacher I supposed to look like she had "done something." I complained of this fact to the Principal but he seemed to think it was "all right." No pupil was required to study, and even come into school . . . without even having looked at his or her

lessons and with only half a day in school I could not see any chance for much advancement.[69]

For Lane and perhaps other teachers, particularly those accustomed to working outside of the Indian Service, teaching at Carlisle proved over-whelming. Ultimately, cultivating an academic culture, whether geared toward low- or high-achieving students, created a trying task for many Carlisle teachers throughout the school's history.[70] It is also important to consider that students' "poor" performance may have been intentional. Although fewer students may have resisted Carlisle's methods in its later years—including those whose own parents had gone to and likely bought into the school's mission than of, say, students like Asa Daklugie, who felt dehumanized—perhaps inadequate student performance was a form of protest. Unwillingness to study or progress could have been a way to dem-onstrate opposition, or perhaps apathy, toward white Western education.

Whether poor academic performance was a form of student protest or not, teachers were also assessed on their level of "success" in the classroom. A Progressive era reform more formally introduced in Carlisle's later years involved "Efficiency Reports," used to measure teachers' overall fitness for their positions by tracking employees and their work over time.[71] More than demonstrating teachers' actual productivity, close readings of these reports reveal the qualities that Indian education officials valued. For example, monitoring employees' age and overall physical condition reassured school officials that teachers would be physically fit to meet what was deemed to be the particularly demanding work of Indian education.

A closer look at Emma Lovewell's evaluations show that she was largely described as an asset to the school, though her advancing age was charac-terized as somewhat of a liability. Such bureaucratic "Efficiency Reports" described her as "a good instructor, pleasant in the school room and [one who] tries to see that her pupils thoroughly understand a lesson before it is passed."[72] But in February 1911, Supervisor of Indian Schools Chas F. Peirce reported, "Mrs. Lovewell has no doubt been a very good teacher in years gone by, but her age is beginning to tell against her as a first class teacher at present. She uses good methods, is patient and kind to pupils, but her work lacks the life and spirit necessary for complete success as a teacher."[73] A year later, Acting Commissioner of Indian Affairs F. H. Abbot also insinu-ated that Lovewell's age was a hindrance.[74] Yet, a December 1914 Efficiency Report modified this critique, describing her as "a diligent teacher and plenty of energy and interest" but chastising her for "overdoing herself in

Table 2.2: Categories from Indian Service "Efficiency Reports" Used at
Carlisle, Sorted by Category, 1909–1918

Identifiers	Personal	Work
Position	Habits as to appearance	Native ability
Salary	Courtesy to others	Acquired ability
Race	Manners and speech	Initiative
Sex	Kindness to pupils	Openness to suggestion
Age	Loyalty	Adaptability
Years in service		Interest in work
Married or single		Industry
Physical condition		Musical ability (vocal, instrumental)
		General efficiency

Source: Based on teachers' individual files held at the National Personnel Record Center.

her efforts at being affable—a thing which does not add anything to her standing among either the students or her fellow-employees."[75] Critiqued for her age, energy level, or poor social skills, such reports provide a window into how the growing bureaucracy tried to measure a teacher's effectiveness.

Perhaps even more subjective, such Efficiency Reports also attempted to assess teachers' "loyalty." Though a vague and subjective category, its inclusion in the reports intimates a certain anxiety among education officials concerning teachers' allegiance to Indian education, administrative policies, or the specific school. Of course, most of the categories were similarly subjective, and assessments thus likely reflected administrators' preferences and prejudices (see Table 2.2). Overall, then, these reports tell more about Indian officials' beliefs regarding an ideal working culture—one that valued progress and improvement—than about teachers' actual skills and effectiveness. At the same time, these documents reveal how such officials believed that teachers should model respectability to best cultivate "civilization" among its Indian charges. Despite intentions, these annual or biannual evaluations underscore that the Indian bureaucracy fundamentally relied upon its teachers to do the day-to-day work, often with little oversight.[76]

Something not reflected on such Efficiency Reports is the extent to which Carlisle teachers were expected to do much more than tend to students' academic needs, even serving as parental figures. Students had been taken away from their own family structures and norms, which were devalued by "civilized" authorities at Carlisle. To make up for this, Pratt described one of

Carlisle's unique roles: "An Indian school differs from most others in that there is so much to teach in regard to manners that with others come naturally in the course of family life. One of these necessary features is that of association of the sexes on a proper footing."[77] However, most of the school's teachers lived outside of the idealized roles that the dominant society held for women. The majority of teachers at Carlisle were single women who had neither children nor a household to run. In fact, in 1885 all twelve teachers were single women between the ages of twenty-two and fifty-five. By 1904, seventeen of the twenty-one teachers were women, all white, of whom one had been at the school since its opening.[78] Some married couples did teach at Carlisle—including Elizabeth and John DeHuff and Fernando and Katharine Tranbarger—as the broader Indian Service sought by the late 1890s to hire married couples to model traditional gender roles for students and limit teacher turnover.[79] However, within a couple of decades, the service found this to be problematic in terms of hiring spouses of superintendents, as explained in a 1925 letter: "It was found that there was no one feature of the Service which caused more trouble than the employment of the wives of superintendents and other administrative officials, and for sometime past it has been the policy of the Office to discontinue the practice and to eliminate from time to time as occasion demands the services of those who are yet fulfilling positions in the Indian Field Service."[80] Regardless of the benefits or problems associated with a superintendent and wife officially working together, the Pratts both worked at Carlisle, Richard as superintendent, supported by his wife, Laura, although she was not officially a school employee. The rest of the Carlisle teaching staff was composed mostly of single white women, which made it more difficult for them to model ideal behaviors related to domestic life and the proper "association of the sexes" (see Table 2.3).

Even with large numbers of single employees, boarding school staff served as a substitute family for Indian children, demonstrating the intimacy involved in this imperial education project. Indian boarding school superintendents, usually male, served as a father figure for the children while his wife, matrons, or other female employees took on a maternal role.[81] At Carlisle, Pratt assumed the role of school father with pride and viewed his wife as the school's mother, but several other Carlisle teachers also played maternal roles. Complicating this scenario, teachers—like many students—also looked up to Pratt like a father figure. Upon Pratt's dismissal in June 1904, twenty-two Carlisle employees—most of whom were teachers—signed the following:

Table 2.3: Marital Status by Gender/Year Hired (Carlisle)

Year Hired	1880s	1890s	1900s	1910s	Total
Female single	9	6	9	14	38
Female married	0	0	1	1	2
Female widow	1	1	2	0	4
Male single	0	0	0	2	2
Male married	0	0	3	1	4

Source: Based primarily on teachers' individual files held at the National Personnel Record Center; also drawn from Carlisle Indian Industrial School Collection, Cumberland County Historical Society, Carlisle, Pennsylvania (CCHS); National Archives, Washington, DC (NADC), Preliminary Inventory of the Records of the Bureau of Indian Affairs, Carlisle Indian Industrial School, Record Group 75, Entry 1331, 1344, and 1344A; Richard Henry Pratt Papers, Beinecke Rare Book and Manuscript Library, Yale University, New Haven, Connecticut (BRBML).

> Dear General Pratt,
>
> We, the employes [sic] of the Carlisle school wish to express our deep regret and heartfelt sorrow in parting with you as our leader.
>
> We feel that we are better for having known you intimately, and are proud to have been associated with you. You have been like a kind father to us—taking us into your confidence—guiding us in our daily work. These thoughts of our relations with you will ever be glad memories to us.[82]

Among the teachers who signed the letter were Marianna Burgess, Ann Ely, and Fannie Paull. More than losing a supervisor, these and other teachers felt that they were losing the guidance of a parent, and Pratt likely reciprocated such sentiment. More than a decade later, a school newspaper reported on the visit of the founding superintendent and his wife: "General Pratt presented a picture of himself and his wife to the girls for their new reception room. He said, 'If I am the father of Carlisle, Mrs. Pratt is the mother.'"[83] The extent to which students imagined the Pratts in these roles is harder to gauge, although historical evidence provides clues.

Some pupils came to love and respect Carlisle staff members as they would family members, including teacher Marianna Burgess and Superintendent Pratt.[84] Luther Standing Bear recalled being one of a handful of students selected to return to the reservation in 1882 under Miss Burgess's care to serve as her interpreter and "in order to show the Indians there that we were really learning the white man's ways." In describing this trip, Standing Bear wrote, "Although we knew but little of the English language, we were ready to do anything for Miss Burgess."[85] He claimed here and elsewhere in his memoir the great love and respect he felt for Miss Burgess, expressing a sense of devotion that children might show toward their parents. Similarly, Louis Paul of the class of 1906 thought of Pratt as a father figure even years after he left Carlisle. Upon Pratt's death in 1924, Paul wrote a letter to his wife expressing his profound appreciation for having been one of Pratt's "boys." He wrote of his "School Father": "He is gone? Yes, but he will ever be with his children." Although not a devoted "son" while at Carlisle, when Louis thought white education was "wasted time," years later he came to value the lessons learned there and to admire Pratt's "unswerving effort . . . the Father who encountered more opposition than we have ever had to meet."[86] Paul clearly came to respect Pratt as a paternal figure and a man with deep convictions.

In fact, teachers took on parental roles in several ways. They regularly offered advice, cared for sick students, scolded children when they acted out, and served as role models, all as real mothers would have.[87] In a rare instance, one teacher became a student's adoptive mother. Recall Sarah Mather, who helped Pratt recruit Carlisle's very first students. She formed a special bond with a Carlisle student, "Jack," ultimately adopting him as her own son and taking him to live with her in Florida when she retired.[88] In lieu of formal adoption, most teachers simply thought of themselves as mothers or "motherly." As Emma Lovewell boasted in 1914, "The motherly talks which I have given the children have been appreciated by them and I trust have been helpful."[89] Of course, the extent to which her students truly welcomed or valued her "motherly talks" is less known, though Lovewell herself clearly felt confident assuming a maternal role in her students' lives.

Other teachers also took their unofficial parental roles very seriously, including Marianna Burgess. As noted earlier, Marianna Burgess was a founding teacher, known for her forthright manner and strong will, and admired by former student Luther Standing Bear. Soon after she began work at the school, she extended her reach beyond the classroom and took charge of the printing press, helping to publish the school newspapers for the next twenty years. In this capacity Burgess had an even greater influence than most classroom teachers.[90] By 1889, a decade after joining the staff, Burgess wrote a story, *Stiya, A Carlisle Indian Girl at Home: Founded on the Author's Actual Observations*. It was published in one of the school's publications, the *Indian Helper*, as a serial and later as a book. Her story depicted a young Pueblo girl, "Stiya," educated in the East, who returned "home" to her reservation, only to feel disgusted at her people's customs. Ostensibly based on

Burgess's observations while visiting several reservations to recruit students for Carlisle, the story's protagonist ultimately triumphs, leading her family to embrace a "civilized" lifestyle fit with tablecloths and silverware despite opposition from her tribe. Toward the end of the story, Stiya describes her teachers' satisfaction having witnessed the proper home she had helped to create, filled with Western foods, dress, and decorations. She then proclaims, "They [her teachers] seemed so delighted that I felt more than repaid for the hard times I had passed through. And, indeed, I have never regretted having braved the first hard steps that led me out of the accursed home slavery and made me a free woman."[91] Thus, according to Burgess's tale, Stiya was glad to have been able to escape a life of almost certain servitude on the reservation, despite the difficulties she faced along the way, as she was ostensibly freed by her boarding school education. Moreover, the story cast Stiya as a learned child who craved the approval of her teachers more than that of her own parents and in this way reaffirmed the boarding school as a place of superior morality, family values, and even love.

According to an 1891 article in the *Indian Helper*, also likely penned by Burgess, Stiya served both as "encouragement" to Indian students to stand fast against the pressures to "return to the blanket" by their families and as "an apology" for "a system of Indian training, which does not and cannot guarantee" protection from the "circumstances and conditions of savage life."[92] Of course, Stiya represented much more than encouragement or an apology. It spoke to the centrality that Burgess believed teachers *should* hold in students' lives. Rather than working to please their parents, who the story suggested were disgusting and filthy, *Stiya* reflected the belief of Burgess and no doubt other teachers: that students *should* maintain a "civilized" lifestyle, one that would impress their Carlisle teachers and eventually grant students' freedom. Despite such a rigid perspective, one that demonized indigenous life but heralded Western norms, Burgess—and other teachers like her—managed to earn her students' respect, as evident in Standing Bear's lifelong devotion to her. Although Burgess's methods likely terrorized some students who fought to hold onto their own cultural identities, her strength, influence, and steadfast commitment to the imperial mission of assimilation demonstrate the extent to which some teachers lived, breathed, and propagated a "civilized" lifestyle.

Burgess and others sought to imbue Carlisle students with white "American" family and lifestyle norms because, as has been stated, they sincerely believed that they were helping to save the Indian race from extinction. In their view, part of raising respectable Indian children involved impressing upon them the importance of following Victorian gender roles, including interacting appropriately with the opposite sex. As mentioned earlier, such norms were instituted prior to students' arrival at Carlisle, with some children having already been separated along the journey from the only other people they knew: their siblings, adding to the trauma of leaving home.[93] Divisions between the sexes became more firmly entrenched once they entered the school's gates, with boys and girls living in separate quarters and learning different industrial trades. Like other schoolchildren of the time, boys learned trades like carpentry, blacksmithing, and farming while girls practiced domestic skills like sewing, laundry, and cooking.[94]

Although girls and boys attended the same academic classes and dined together, Carlisle employees made deliberate efforts to separate the sexes whenever possible and maintained close surveillance of their behavior. Teachers monitored hallways, watching students as they came to or from class or returned to their room, purportedly for their own protection. Perhaps teachers considered the constant surveillance normal, as they largely did not mention it explicitly in their personal papers, except for more oblique complaints regarding the consuming or exhausting nature of working in an Indian boarding school. Or, perhaps they, like their students, had little space to make their ideas known. Yet such seemingly constant surveillance could only reach so far, even for an imperial project reliant upon its intimate relationships to effect cultural change.[95]

Authority figures could not fully control student behaviors, particularly when it came to love and attraction. Some students passed notes or "exchang[ed] a silent greeting," as Asa Daklugie described his flirting with his beloved, Ramona.[96] Other students met behind closed doors to have sex. Such behavior convinced some teachers and administrators that vigilant surveillance was necessary to keep students in line. In November 1912, Superintendent Moses Friedman expressed shock and disappointment when he learned that two well-regarded Carlisle students had "illicit intercourse." To prevent other students from making such grave errors, Friedman expelled the two students and ordered that "the boys and girls of this school should take heed of the miserable ending in this case."[97] A few weeks later, Friedman detailed another account of a sexual relationship between students that resulted in pregnancy, marriage, and their leaving Carlisle.[98] In September 1913 Friedman admonished principal teacher John Whitwell, strongly advising that he watch the halls more carefully for the "safety of the girls" and to stop the boys from lingering around waiting for them.[99] By January 1914 a former Carlisle nurse was "said to have knowledge of a number of girls being sent home from Carlisle on account of being in a delicate condition."[100]

Such "alleged immorality" among students, that reportedly led to their being locked up or sent home to "become mothers," became more public once revealed by school employees at the 1914 congressional hearings investigating the corruption and apparent inadequacy of Carlisle's leadership.[101] As discussed in the Introduction, at the hearings Lovewell publicly condemned Superintendent Friedman for his lack of control over such wayward students, despite sometimes harsh punishment. To better control students' illicit relationships, Lovewell proposed hiring a guard to watch over the girls' school building, intimating that male students' sexual prowess could not otherwise be fully controlled. Although she disapproved of sexual relationships among the youth—particularly outside the institution of marriage—she also condemned the superintendent's usage of imprisonment to punish male students suspected of sexual indiscretions.[102] Yet, she supported sending pregnant students home, believing that having such a student in the classroom "was contaminating."[103] Ultimately, Lovewell revealed her personal distaste for Friedman's leadership, casting blame at him for what she saw as the school's moral and cultural deterioration. At the same time, she cast Indian students as shrewd enough to recognize the immorality at the top but unfit to properly manage their own relationships with the opposite sex. Ultimately, Lovewell's comments and proposed remedies regarding students' sexual lives demonstrate that she saw herself as a bastion of morality and that the school should similarly not tolerate or allow such behavior. Still, other unreported or unnoticed instances of sexual intercourse undoubtedly took place, revealing both the existence of students' romantic activity and teachers' inability to monitor all of their actions.

In part to counter such transgressions and promote "decent" behavior, teachers oversaw extracurricular activities to occupy students' downtime and model proper etiquette for young men and women.[104] The goal was to enable them to interact in a respectable manner, also deemed increasingly important in public schools in this period. Still, at Carlisle, teachers and staff had more control over students' free time than in most public schools. Throughout much of the school's history, Friday nights were reserved as "society night," referring to the literary and debating societies that formed and met from the 1880s through the 1910s. These groups, like much student life at Carlisle, were segregated by sex. In 1896 the boys had two debating societies while the girls were involved with the Susan Longstreth

Literary Society, "under the direction of some of the ladies, but they keep themselves in the background."[105] By 1898, two teachers were required to visit meetings of the school's three literary societies and provide "helpful criticisms" to these student-managed groups.[106] The *Indian Helper* reported that the responsibility imposed "no strain upon faculty" and was even enjoyable when the discussions were lively.[107]

One debate focused on women's rights and occurred more than once over the years. In January 1890 the Girls' Literary Society and the Standard Debating Club, open only to boys, sparred on "the question of the privilege which should be granted to women." The *Indian Helper* reported that it was a "masterly effort on the part of both societies . . . [and the] judges decided that the girls advanced the best argument" in favor of expanding women's rights.[108] Many years later, in December 1914, the literary society known as "The Mercers" debated a similar question: "That woman suffrage should be granted throughout the United States," and "the negative side won."[109] Acknowledging Marianna Burgess's control over the campus newspapers over the school's first decades, it is likely that she is the voice behind the support for the "masterly" winnings of the girls' literary society in 1890, although this is speculation. Still, it is otherwise unknown what teachers felt about the outcomes of such debates, although they likely had firm beliefs regarding their own access to voting. With teachers' oversight, these sex-segregated, student-run societies sometimes grappled with issues concerning the place women should hold in society, all while reinforcing dominant cultural norms concerning male and female respectability.

Whereas Friday nights were reserved as society night, Saturday nights often involved a sociable or other entertainment that helped underscore the importance of proper behavior while letting the students have some fun. At the monthly sociable, teachers supervised the students during the "two hours . . . spent in social visiting, games, etc.," and students looked forward to such entertainment.[110] In September 1898, the *Indian Helper* reported:

> The sociable on Saturday night seemed like old times. It was the first
> of the season and there were many happy comings-together of brothers
> and sisters, and sisters of other peoples' brothers with brothers of other
> peoples' sisters. The band played its best pieces, while the throng prom-
> enaded or played games. It was a good time for the new students to get
> acquainted. There were very few "wall flowers," for the entertainment
> committee kept things lively.[111]

Making light of the "sisters and brothers" who enjoyed each other's company, a vague reference perhaps to playful but well-monitored flirting between the sexes, this first sociable of the year was reported as a resounding success. However, rules regarding respectability were not enforced equally under all of the school's administrations, with rules particularly relaxed under Superintendent Mercer's leadership, discussed in greater detail in the next chapter. After Mercer, the next several superintendents instituted greater surveillance over students at social events, achieving varying degrees of success at controlling their behavior.[112] Ultimately, while public school teachers might be expected to help students prepare for musical or other performances, those at Carlisle guided students' behavior and performance inside and outside of the classroom essentially twenty-four hours a day, seven days a week.

Beyond reinforcing dominant cultural norms around sex and respectability at weekend gatherings, teachers helped to guide students' moral compass toward Christianity, sometimes in very overt ways. As a government-sponsored school, Carlisle did not have an official religious affiliation nor did it include religious education classes as part of its curriculum. Nevertheless, even more than public schools in the late nineteenth century that promoted Protestant ideals while claiming to be secular, Carlisle openly embraced and promoted Christianity. In January 1880, only a couple of months after the school opened its doors, its newspaper, *Eadle Keatah Toh,* declared, "God Helps Those Who Help Themselves," and a front-page article described students' daily gatherings in the chapel, weekday singing, and prayer sessions, as well as Sunday services. The writer then proclaimed, "The pupils . . . are beginning to respond to the earnest and kindly efforts of the teachers to instill into their darkened minds Christian truths, and a desire to seek God and to know His world."[113] Thus, from the school's inception, teachers were responsible for "saving" Indian "heathens" by making them "good Christians." Years later government officials, including Superintendent of Indian Schools Estelle Reel, publicly claimed that the course of study designed for Indian students should lead to "better morals, a more patriotic and Christian citizenship, and ability for self-support."[114] While the extent of teachers' overt proselytizing undoubtedly changed over time and differed depending upon the individual, Carlisle relied upon its teachers to influence students' beliefs, and the behaviors that reflected those beliefs. In this way, work at the Pennsylvania boarding school mimicked that of Christian missionaries in its reliance upon an intimate network to spread the gospels, or in the case of imperial education, in replacing indigenous norms with those of the dominant culture.

Tasked with "saving" Indian children or simply serving as models of Christian behavior, teachers' religious convictions and way of life certainly shaped their work and the lives of many of their students. Teachers chaperoned students who "chose" to leave campus and attend church in town and encouraged other students to "voluntarily" attend nondenominational services held at school.[115] Whether church attendance was mandated, coerced, or encouraged, teachers clearly influenced students' religious inclinations through their own example and leadership. They led Sunday School small group discussions, read Bible verses at or advised the school's YWCA group, took students to YMCA meetings, and demonstrated their personal Christian devotion. They both directly and indirectly demonstrated to students what it meant to "be a good Christian."[116]

Of course, outsiders did not always praise overt evangelizing, particularly in the decades after Carlisle closed its doors. Into the 1920s, reformers continued to promote Christianity in Indian schools, although by the end of the decade the US government began to reconsider this and other assimilationist practices after an influential 1928 report blamed the government and missionaries for failing "to study, understand, and take a sympathetic attitude toward Indian ways, Indian ethics, and Indian religion."[117] By 1933, Commissioner John Collier ordered all superintendents to forbid "interference with Indian religious life or ceremonial expression."[118] Likely referring to this shift in Indian reform, Elaine Goodale Eastman published *Pratt: The Red Man's Moses* in 1935, in which she defended the founding superintendent and Carlisle against accusations of obligatory conversions. She argued, "In reference to recent charges of forcible proselyting . . . the main factors of spiritual growth were to be found in the unconscious influence and example of a devoted group of high-minded teachers, and that such young people as formally accepted Christianity . . . did so quite voluntarily."[119] Although Eastman agreed with some reformers—believing that Indian schools should be closer to reservations and that students should interact with their families and communities—she still valued the means of persuasion embodied by Carlisle.[120]

Despite Eastman's claims concerning students' "voluntary" conversions—and, looking beyond the guidance of government leaders like that of Superintendent of Indian Schools Estelle Reel's call for raising indigenous students' "patriotic and Christian citizenship" in 1901—evidence demonstrates that evangelizing was very much a conscious decision made by Carlisle's teachers. For example, in contemplating a promotion, teacher Katherine Bowersox wrote a series of letters in 1902 to Superintendent Pratt in which she admitted feeling "in entire sympathy in the religious and moral life of the school."[121] She explained, "I regard the work of teaching the boys and girls directly as just as deserving of honor—in fact more so. After all—we serve the Lord God in any position."[122] Bowersox was one of the majority of teachers who believed that Indian education had holy, as well as a practical, purpose. In June 1904 she and almost twenty other teachers wrote to Pratt upon his dismissal from the superintendency:

> The idea which God entrusted to your care twenty five years ago has carried conviction into the hearts of all thinking men and women. . . . Long after you shall have passed away, our red brother will bless the man who made the "Brotherhood of Man" a reality . . . out of our momentary defeats God brings eternal victory. . . . We are confident that the spirit which has so nobly striven to overcome ignorance and oppression will continue to be the guiding star that shall lead the Indian into noble self-support and citizenship.[123]

In addition to revealing their thanks and praise of Pratt's godly devotion, teachers believed that their work to uplift Indians was mandated by God and, therefore, destined to succeed, a belief that continued well after Pratt left. This sense of divine purpose enhanced the imperial education mission, inspiring many teachers to fully commit to their work, and justified these intimate yet expansive efforts.

Teachers further helped to reinforce the importance of Christianity by hosting elaborate Christian holiday celebrations, notably Christmas. Luther Standing Bear fondly remembered his first Christmas at Carlisle. Having arrived at the school just over two months earlier, he recollected being "marched down to the chapel" in December 1879 and was surprised to find it filled with a big decorated tree and presents for all of the students. His presents included gifts from teacher Marianna Burgess as well as his Sunday School teacher, Miss Eggee.[124] Christmas celebrations, often held over several days, regularly included grand feasts, a church service, and a sociable. Teachers facilitated these festivities, providing food for the turkey dinner, attending the holiday service, and chaperoning social gatherings.[125] They handed out gifts, encouraged students to make gifts for one another, prepared the children for Santa's visit, received presents from their students, and enjoyed a festive meal with their colleagues.[126] Of course, not all teachers remained on school grounds during the holidays; some returned home to celebrate with their own families for a few days.[127] Still, whether Carlisle teachers were on campus or visiting relatives, they showed Indian students both the joy and solemnity of the holiday.

For many Carlisle students, Christianity had a profound influence on their lives and they attributed their conversions to the school's culture and teachers' Christian spirit. Former student Paul Good Bear wrote to his teacher, Ann Ely, on April 4, 1894, sending her seventy-five cents that he had borrowed four years earlier, and suggested that, as a Quaker, he wanted to repay her.[128] A more obvious example of the significance of Christian conversion, Jason Betzinez recalled in his memoir: "The most powerful influence on my life at this or any other time was my introduction to the teachings of Christianity. . . . It changed my whole life."[129] He attributed his conversion, in part, to the powerful influence of the superintendent and his teachers:

> Pratt had the wisdom to select teachers who were mature, experienced, and possessed of firm religious convictions. Although he intended for disciplinary and other reasons to make the school military in its outward appearance, at the core it was to be strongly religious in character. Pratt believed that discipline, kindness, and religion were the three foremost elements in rehabilitating these primitive children.[130]

Although other Carlisle graduates may not have remembered the religious influence with such fondness, Betzinez highlighted the profound impact that it played at the boarding school, particularly among the many teachers who held "firm religious convictions." Indeed, it is hard to imagine Pratt or the Indian Service hiring teachers who did not embrace Christianity with fervor.[131] Carlisle teachers' "mission" to help assimilate and prepare Indian students for responsible citizenship was both subtly and overtly affected by their faith. Indeed, Betzinez suggested that religion, softened by kindness, served in a sense as a form of discipline—even more than the military structure of the school. Thus, while military drilling "outwardly appeared" to control students' behavior, according to Betzinez, Christianity made a deeper impression on students' conduct by teaching them the importance of internal control. The extent to which this proved true for other students, of course, was variable. Still, Christianity played a critical role at Carlisle, in large part due to teachers' efforts to influence students' spiritually as they taught them largely middle-class, white Protestant norms and rules.[132]

Despite the comforts that religion may have provided for teachers and at least some students, life at Carlisle was difficult. Children entered an institution that brutally devalued their heritage: cutting their hair, changing their clothes, forbidding their native languages. The trauma of being separated from all they had known must have been deepened by the further separation of brothers, sisters, and tribe members under the almost constant surveillance of teachers and staff.[133] For teachers, the work could be overwhelming—consuming their lives—but for many, such work was affirming. Most were fundamentally dedicated to "saving" the Indian, believing that their work of Christianizing and Westernizing Native American youth fulfilled divine purpose with earthly rewards, not yet admitting the cultural violence wreaked by Indian schooling. Exacerbating the schooling's attack on indigenous customs and family life were the physical and psychological cruelties perpetrated against American Indian children, which in the school's last decades were worsened by political and sexual scandal. Such trying topics are explored further in the next chapter, as well as the "fun" and friendships which also formed at the Indian institution despite it all.

CHAPTER THREE

DISCIPLINE AT CARLISLE, 1879–1918

In April 1880 the Carlisle school newspaper *Eadle Keatah Toh* reprinted a letter that Sioux chief White Thunder had written to his son:

> You did not listen to the school teacher, and for that reason you were schooled. . . . I send you there to be like a white man and I want you to do what the teacher tells you. . . . I hope you will listen to your teachers for it makes me feel bad when I hear you do not. . . . When you get this letter take it to Capt. Pratt and have him read it and I hope he will rite [*sic*] to me. That is all. Your father, WHITE THUNDER.[1]

By publishing the letter, school officials used the voice of the Sioux chief to remind *all* students that they must listen to their teachers, as they were there to assimilate, "to be like a white man." The letter shamed White Thunder's son and threated to shame other students if they disrespected school authorities while at the same time encouraging them to keep an alert eye on one another. Beyond utilizing the newspaper as a watchdog of student behavior, Carlisle employed multiple public humiliation or shaming tactics—some more egregious than others—to further emphasize student conformity to white expectations.[2] Pratt reported, "Walking in the band stand for one or two or three hours, in sight of all the other pupils, is excellent punishment."[3] Other times students wore a sign that pointed to their offense, for example, "Drunk," as was determined by the student-run court in one particular case.[4] Ultimately, students' adherence to Carlisle's rules and expectations was monitored and meted out in multiple ways, with teachers on the front lines making split-second decisions and reinforcing the chain of command. This burden of ensuring proper student behavior to more closely align to white norms and mores was central to teaching empire.

This chapter begins by examining the range of disciplinary methods used at the Indian boarding school—including some quite severe punishments—with all measures relying upon students to keep one another in line. Even more than the prior chapter suggests, indigenous pupils resisted Carlisle's authority over their lives in big ways and small. Still, some could not escape what was an even greater threat to hundreds of students' (and fewer teachers') lives: disease. Despite such dangers, those living and working at Carlisle also found time for fun and friendship, even in its all-consuming work culture in which some teachers thrived. And, although the school experiment saw relative stability under the founding superintendent's more than two decades of control, its last fifteen years were marked by almost constant scandal. Ultimately, Carlisle closed its doors almost as abruptly as they had opened, somewhat stained by incompetent leadership. Despite teachers' profound commitment throughout its forty years, they could not "save" the Indian—nor could they save the Indian school they had helped to create.

Beyond the methods discussed in the previous chapter that were used to control indigenous students—including the creation of cultural and curricular mandates, surveillance, fictive kinship ties, and Christianity—Carlisle instituted other disciplinary systems to maintain order, some of which were quite severe. Teachers employed a wide range of measures to maintain authority over student learning and behavior, including at times corporal punishment. To redress mild insubordination, some ordered students to repetitively write a phrase on the chalkboard, stand in a corner, or scrub the floors. When their authority and tactics were not enough to redirect an unruly student, they often sought the help of a supervising teacher or, if violations were severe, the superintendent. Thus, teachers relied upon the hierarchy of power within the school to ensure student compliance, but sometimes even this was not enough. Although some pupils thrived in the structures imposed at Carlisle, others did not, resulting in extra disciplinary measures. For some teachers, at least, particular forms of discipline must have tested their Christian principles. Others clearly believed that the ends justified the means, even if those means seemed cruel in practice.[5]

Within the broader context of the Indian School Service, scholars have cited diverse methods of punishment and rightly emphasized their harshness. In *Boarding School Blues,* for example, historian Clifford Trafzer details the many options teachers and staff had to discipline pupils they considered unruly:

> When students spoke their own languages, lied, used obscene language, fought, stole, destroyed property, acted stubbornly, or misbehaved, teachers, disciplinarians, matrons, and superintendents could inflict corporal punishment or imprison the child. School officials withheld food, restricted student privileges, or forced children to march, mop floors,

paint walls, clean filthy bathrooms, and perform other distasteful jobs. Teachers slapped the palms of students' hands, made students stand in the corner, lie on the floor in front of classmates, wear dunce hats, stand on one foot, and clean the mortar between bricks with a toothbrush.[6]

The varied nature of the punishments, as well as the punishments themselves, suggest the severe, violent, even sadistic nature of discipline implemented at Indian schools. Trafzer points to the ubiquity of such punishments, reinforced by all individuals at the schools—administrators, teachers, even students. Regardless of the specific disciplinary methods used at Carlisle, which changed over time, the school's mission, "to take the Indian out," suggests a culture that tolerated, and sometimes encouraged, physical violence—in addition to cultural violence—demanding that Indians conform to white societal norms.

From its earliest years Carlisle promoted a culture that valued self-discipline. Although not officially a military school, Pratt implemented military-style drilling and marching and grouped students into squads soon after they arrived at the school.[7] The founding superintendent explained that upon establishing the school, "I concluded I would relieve myself and my faculty of the responsibility of determining punishments so far as I could, and inaugurated a system of courts composed of the pupils themselves, and throughout the whole period of the School we have managed our punishments in that way with greatest success."[8] Such student-run courts were used at only "some more advanced schools" where it was deemed "practical and advisable to have material offenses arbitrated by a school court composed of advanced students, with school employés added to such court in very aggravated cases." The federal government advised that while these courts could rule on a student's guilt and determine the punishment, "the approval of the superintendent shall be necessary before the punishment is inflicted, and the superintendent may modify or remit but may not increase the sentence."[9] Used at Carlisle and other "advanced schools," this measure of self-discipline—where students were responsible for moderating one another's behavior—gave the appearance of a less hierarchical disciplinary system than those used at other schools. However, overseen by Pratt and other employees, these courts worked within a larger structure of discipline and behavior expectations. Although the superintendent could not increase a sentence, his oversight suggests that these courts were not as autonomous as they appeared. Still, sometimes student sentences were harsher than those employed by Pratt.

In addition to Carlisle's student-run courts, pupils watched over one another, serving as guards responsible for fellow classmates in confinement, or, at least in some Indian schools, ordering students to directly employ corporal punishment against classmates. Jason Betzinez recalled, "I myself was on guard duty on many occasions and had the job of guarding some of my fellow Indians who had gotten drunk or committed offenses of a more serious nature."[10] Like Betzinez, some Indian students took pride in their role reinforcing school policies. Writing more broadly about discipline at Indian schools, historian Clifford Trafzer claims, "Teachers and administrators sometimes ordered older students to perform the punishment of their classmates. This included whipping the backs, buttocks, and thighs of boys and girls."[11] In this and other ways, the Indian School Service as a whole employed a system of extreme punishment and coerced students to reproduce such violence. Ultimately, the success of imperial education relied upon students' internalization and reinforcement of behaviors admired by the dominant culture, even those that promoted terror.

Still, some students invariably broke the rules, and infractions deemed serious led to solitary confinement and corporal punishment, reinforcing a school culture based on fear. Although teachers did not usually mete out such punishments themselves—though, as was mentioned, in some schools such violent reinforcement was expected of students—they likely relied upon it as a threat to counter serious misbehavior. Over time corporal punishment fell out of favor, at least systemically. In 1890 corporal punishment was banned at on-reservation schools, except for severe rule violations, and by 1895 the federal government banned corporal punishment at Indian schools altogether. However, ensuring adherence to such policies was difficult, and the practice continued at Indian schools throughout the country, including at Carlisle.[12]

Policies and incidents of corporal punishment at Carlisle were rationalized, but they were not always understood or effectively meted out. Asa Daklugie tells of a time when his teacher sent him to see Pratt for insolence, and the superintendent threatened him with a whip. According to Daklugie, he grabbed the whip from and threatened Pratt, but was later cajoled into returning to class, agreeing that this was his first disagreement with his teacher. Still, Daklugie expressed outrage at white norms as Pratt purportedly explained, "'You know that men must be courteous to ladies and indulge them in their whims,'" upon which Daklugie reflected in his autobiography, "White Eyes! Their men spoil women. . . . No wonder all white women are bossy."[13] Although Daklugie escaped corporal punishment in this case, he was

not convinced that white mores led to upright or acceptable behavior, including among white women. In other cases, Pratt admitted to sometimes using
Carlisle's facilities particular to an army barracks, including the two light and
four dark cells "for the confinement for the young men to a limited extent.
. . . It is one of the best methods that can be administered to a criminal to
let him have only his own company."[14] Casting students who broke the rules
akin to "criminals," as well as the actual punishment of confinement, reveals
the severity with which Pratt treated insubordinate students. Elaine Goodale
Eastman recalled that although Pratt "approved of corporal punishment on
occasion," he judged each case individually.[15] She thus defended him against
"enemies [that] called him a 'martinet, harsh, arrogant, arbitrary.'" Admitting that even some of Pratt's supporters considered such methods "severe,"
Eastman concluded that the disciplinary system ultimately worked, earning
the respect of many students.[16] Even Asa Daklugie ultimately concluded: "I
was at Carlisle for eight years. During that time I had no further trouble with
Captain Pratt. I began to realize that some of the things he required of us
were beneficial. It was his intention that all decisions be for our good, regardless of our dislike for them."[17] In retrospect, Daklugie saw some of Pratt's
methods and objectives as largely helpful, even if he did not appreciate them.
Of course, not all students came to such conclusions, and incidents of strict
punishment continued after Pratt's term.

Because school leaders defined the severity of punishment meted out for
particular infractions, changes in school leadership and personnel shifted
these norms, perhaps making students further wary of the seemingly arbitrary rules. In the years after Superintendent Pratt left Carlisle, methods of
confinement continued to be used to punish wayward students, evident in
accounts where students accused of sexual indiscretions were "locked up,"
sometimes for "several days."[18] Another example of perhaps unwarranted,
or, at least overly severe punishment, involved four students who stole and
ate twenty pies from the bakery in 1906. Three of the four accused were
subsequently locked in the guardhouse with "privileges taken away and
. . . given extra work" while the ringleader was given unspecified "special
punishment or dismissal" from the school.[19] Considering that Indian students were reportedly undernourished may explain why these four students
would have stolen twenty pies in the first place, although this is simply speculation. Whatever the reasoning, the offense of stealing food led to severe
consequences, suggesting that the reign of discipline and punishment continued, perhaps even heightened by later superintendents.

Another aspect that shaped the types of punishment school authorities imposed involved gender norms. The case of Mary Gray sheds some light on this and also shows how teachers instituted their own forms of punishment to maintain classroom control. In 1914 under Superintendent Friedman's administration, student Mary Gray complained that the principal teacher John Whitwell had treated her too harshly. Whitwell defended himself against accusations of slapping Gray "as hard as I could in the face," claiming that he may have "slapped her lightly in the face" as he had done a couple of times to other impudent girls over the course of his thirty-year teaching career.[20] However, he claimed that otherwise he was "unqualifiedly opposed to corporal punishment for girls under any circumstances, aside from the fact that I know it is a violation of the regulations."[21] Although the Indian Service had outlawed corporal punishment at its schools in 1895, Whitwell apparently believed it was only unacceptable "for girls" and did not consider slapping on the face to meet the definition.[22] Moreover, he seems to have disagreed with the larger ban in cases of boys' insubordination. Whitwell also admitted to standing Gray in a corner while denying that he treated her roughly on this or other occasions. To justify his own behavior, he noted Gray's history of troublemaking and reported that other teachers had made her "get down on her knees" for being "so bad."[23]

Emma Lovewell, who had taught Gray three years earlier, testified that:

> When gentle reprimands and good motherly talks proved to be of no avail, I resorted to putting her in the bookroom. . . . I made her do scrubbing which seemed to work well for a few days, but her bad nature would assert itself. However, the attacks were less frequent, for she had the scrubbing hanging over her which she very much disliked.
>
> When asked about her conduct she would state positively that she did not do a thing when it was done right before my eyes. She was so much improved that I had hopes of her but my heart was made sad when I learned from the next teacher that the reform was not lasting.[24]

While a boy who displayed such insolence likely would have received more severe punishment, Lovewell listed what she clearly considered more "acceptable" methods employed to corral Gray's behavior—kneeling, separation from the class, "motherly talks," and scrubbing. All of these were apparently intended to maintain the girl's feminine dignity while punishing her insolence. As with most cases of discipline at the school, when questions arose it was often one person's word against another, usually teacher versus student. Not surprisingly, teachers' authority generally won out.

While Whitwell clearly pushed the boundaries of physical punishment and Lovewell used methods she hoped would persuade the students to improve his or her behavior, at least one teacher believed the culture of punishment at Carlisle did not go far enough. In July 1912, again under Friedman's administration, teacher Mattie Lane abruptly left Carlisle and justified her actions by arguing, "It is supposed to be a military school, yet there is no such thing as discipline."[25] Lane expected Carlisle to have a much stricter code of conduct because of its reputation as a military school, although, of course, it was in actuality simply an Indian boarding school. When students refused to do work or were otherwise insolent to teachers, Lane believed the "punishment" to "scrub some floor or else give such 'light diet'" only encouraged other acts of insubordination.[26] Here, "light diet" likely refers to withholding food as a form of punishment, listed as one of many forms of discipline utilized at Carlisle and other Indian schools.[27] Rather than tolerating a work environment that to her mind was not strict enough, Lane left the school without any notice, in part to reinforce her absolute disapproval of what she viewed as the school's leniency against student unruliness. Overall, decisions regarding what type and degree of punishment often fell to teachers, as is evident in the case of Mary Gray, but without institutional support, such disciplinary measures could only go so far.

Over the school's forty-year history, administrations enforced discipline to different degrees. Drawing from his military background, Pratt founded a school environment that mimicked the structures and expectations held by the armed services, including its reliance upon students, like soldiers, to reinforce the rules. Less is known about Mercer's administration, although historical evidence suggests that his oversight was much less strict than his predecessor's, leading to several years where students became more accustomed to slightly greater freedoms and less risk of punishment. In 1908 Superintendent Friedman inherited a school that had experienced great decline. He spent his six years at the school working to reinstitute some of the structures known under the school's founder, including strict rules regarding drinking and socializing; however, he ultimately faced great resistance from students, teachers, and the Indian Office. Carlisle's last two superintendents, like Friedman, attempted to bring more order to the school but ultimately struggled to return the school to its former ways. Much of the change in discipline can be attributed to the individuals in charge and the expectations they set for students and staff members.

However, Carlisle functioned within a society that experienced great change over forty years, including beliefs regarding the speed at which Indians could be assimilated. Perhaps the school's lax discipline in later years drew, in part, from the racially held beliefs regarding Indian capabilities. Whereas Pratt worked under the assumption that with a change of environment Indians could adapt to white culture within a generation, later superintendents, including Mercer, reflected beliefs held by the twentieth-century Indian bureaucracy: that Indians' progress toward "civilization" would be slow because of their racial inferiority. Moreover, Pratt was personally and professionally invested in Carlisle; it was his school, design, and vision, and his successors did not have the same level of commitment or stake in its success. Thus, for various reasons, Carlisle's disciplinary methods changed over time. Still, throughout the school's history, students, teachers, and administrators created a school culture that reflected norms held by the dominant society, including disciplinary actions. Placing such disciplinary methods into a broader historical context—including those used at non-Indian boarding, public, and parochial schools—suggests that Indian students, like other students throughout the country, experienced a range of punishments, some harsher than others; some, perhaps, were racially or culturally motivated, and others were intended to align student behavior to school and societal expectations.[28] At Carlisle these methods demonstrated the power of US imperial ambition, used to assimilate Indian youth to white, middle-class, Protestant norms.

Within the confines of such a system, many Carlisle students resisted, and when overt or covert defiance was not enough, they fled. Anthropologist Genevieve Bell writes that over the course of the school's forty-year history, over 1,800 students deserted, of whom one-third, she estimates, were successful. Ninety-seven percent of these were male, and they left alone or in groups: by foot, bicycle, bus, and train. Some plotted to flee the moment they left home, including Old Elk, who simply wanted to return home. Others sought to escape the school with no set destination. Reasons for flight included "poor food, poor conditions, boredom, abuse, and homesickness." The first student deserter, Josiah Wolf of the Ottawa, reportedly ran in 1883. Over time, the number of students who fled dramatically increased, with the greatest number of runaway students within a year reaching 140 students in 1913 under Superintendent Friedman's watch. In reflecting on the increasing numbers of students rising over time, Bell aptly notes that "not only different administrative styles and policies but also changing conditions at Carlisle and the changing profile of the student body" impacted rising numbers of deserters.[29] Local awareness of Carlisle desertions was on par with the school's sports achievements, with little else published in area newspapers. This molded public awareness of American Indian students as either heroes on the football field or juvenile delinquents, both wrong-headed and both reinforced by racist assumptions. For student deserters who were caught, punishment for running away included taking away food or privileges, lock-up, or sometimes, quite ironically, expulsion. Besides such punishments, Bell asserts that all students knew of the great risks involved, including the racial violence of the time period as well as hunger, thirst, injury, and survival.[30]

Although discipline and desertion rates were largely distinct from another harsh reality Carlisle faced—disease—one article in the *Indian Helper* con-flated these threats. In January 1900 an article reported the following:

> The state of Pennsylvania, and the West are full of small pox, so it is reported. A runaway boy who was brought back to the school was the first to come down with it, and he was noticed before he came down. We are safer here than almost any place in the state or country, for we have a systematic watch, and a suspicious pimple is at once spotted.[31]

Although a burgeoning smallpox outbreak threatened the nation, infect-ing almost fifty thousand and killing 1,528 people between 1901 and 1904, Carlisle authorities suggested that the school could protect students from such disease.[32] Perhaps this is, to at least a certain extent, true, for records of a smallpox outbreak are not evident in the school records during those years. However, such records are hardly complete. A decade earlier, Pratt reported ten student deaths out of a student population of four hundred, about three times the national average. Over the course of the school's his-tory, 220 student deaths at Carlisle are confirmed—roughly 3 percent of the student population—although some scholars believe these records were "sanitized" and that there were likely many more. Thus, the school's invest-ment in "a fully staffed hospital—the first dedicated exclusively to the care of Native Americans," was not enough to prevent student deaths.[33] Moreover, the school's strict discipline and punishment, including that which pushed students to run away and condemned those who were found—never mind its assault on indigenous cultures—belies the claim that students would be "safer" if they remained at the school. Although running away posed its own risks, as discussed earlier, remaining at Carlisle presented others. Ultimately, the January 1900 *Indian Helper* minimized the threat posed by disease on campus and heightened the risks to students who tried to escape. However, both posed real dangers to students' lives.

Diseases such as consumption, measles, tuberculosis, and trachoma plagued all Indian schools, including Carlisle, with tuberculosis and trachoma as the most common.[34] By 1908 the Bureau of Indian Affairs took measures to address health and sanitation conditions of its schools, but disease continued to take its toll.[35] Some estimates suggest that "Carlisle reported an average of nine to ten deaths a year," although the actual number of deaths was higher since "all of the Industrial Schools engaged in a policy of returning sick and dying students to their reservations so that they would not die at school and thus increase the perception of health risks."[36] Whether Carlisle officials sent students back to the reservation to protect the school's reputation, to prevent contagious diseases from spreading, or to reunite sick children with their families, the fact is that it—like other Indian schools—suffered from disease. Dealing with death and disease thus became part of the Carlisle culture.[37]

Students died of disease beginning in Carlisle's earliest days, often devastating students and faculty alike. In January 1880, Cheyenne student Abraham Lincoln died of pneumonia complicated by meningitis; and that March, Iowan Henry Jones died less than three weeks after arriving at the school. After Jones's death, *Eadle Keatah Toh* reported, "Although here so short a time he had won the love of both teachers and scholars, and his death cast a gloom over our usually happy community."[38] Pratt reported that a total of six boys had died over the course of the school's first year, with four more dying after returning to their reservation homes.[39] In December 1880 he wrote a series of heartfelt letters to Chief Swift Bear and Chief White Thunder, both of the Rosebud Agency in Dakota, about the death of their children. In addition to relaying his own grief, Pratt detailed how the deaths affected the entire school community. He reassured Chief Swift Bear that "lady teachers" visited his daughter, Maud, and brought her gifts while she was in the hospital. Upon her death, the teachers were "full of grief" and "the ladies put a new shawl around her and she had many flowers . . . about her" for her burial. He made a point of adding, "Maud's teacher says to tell you she loved your daughter because she was so good in school, and because she was gentle in her ways."[40] Relating to Chief White Thunder as the father of an only son, Pratt described how sorry and sad the teachers and children felt upon Ernest's illness and death, noting that they "cried a great deal."[41] Recounting both deaths, Pratt wrote, "My heart is sad because my children are dead."[42] For Pratt and Carlisle's earliest teachers, student deaths felt like a personal, even parental loss, further cementing the solemn duty held in raising an assimilated generation of Native Americans for purposes of salvation.

A decade later, disease continued to ravage the school, although it seems that Pratt had, at least to a certain extent, come to expect it. He wrote in the 1889 annual school report, "With the exception of a number of chronic cases of scrofula and consumption . . . the sanitary conditions of the school has been good." He then stated that over the course of the preceding school year, "There were 18 deaths; of these, 14 were Apaches who arrived here tainted with hereditary consumption."[43] Though writing for a different audience—the Bureau of Indian Affairs—by that time, Pratt may have become more accustomed to death at the school or more hesitant to reveal too much about health conditions at Carlisle.

Not only Pratt's students but also his employees fell ill, as was the case with a measles outbreak in 1891 that burdened teachers with a heavier workload as well as threat of sickness. That December Pratt wrote to his daughter, Nana Hawkings, and admitted that forty students had the measles and listed several teachers—Misses Botsford, Paull, and Merritt—who "have been in bed and off duty." To manage the outbreak, one teacher took the boys to the gymnasium and another took the girls to the old chapel, where they watched closely for others becoming sick.[44] When Pratt sent his letter, "the worst of the measles epidemic" was thought to be over and the gymnasium was "cleared of patients"; but ten days later, six new cases were identified.[45] Teachers filled in for their coworkers while also nursing the afflicted. To recover from illness and overwork, some employees went "to the mountains for a few days' rest."[46]

When teachers could not tend to their classes, their colleagues covered for them. Indeed, teachers regularly served as substitutes, often while still maintaining their regular responsibilities.[47] This sense of mutual responsibility and obligation no doubt helped to forge tighter bonds among the teachers who spent lengthy terms at Carlisle, although it could also engender ill will if a teacher was seen taking advantage of others' largesse. Clearly the demands on teachers to be available to students twenty-four hours a day, seven days a week reflected the distinctive role they played at Indian boarding schools. Such an intimate yet intense atmosphere reflected the immersive nature of imperial education in action, often magnified in times of difficulty.

In addition to frequent and prolonged outbreaks of disease, Carlisle students faced other illnesses and injuries. In 1896 Pratt identified "chronic troubles of . . . consumption and scrofula" as "the two great health enemies of the Indians" both on the reservations and at the school.[48] In 1898, a year described as exhibiting "unusual good health among our pupils," only four of the 1,080 students sent to Carlisle died, although Pratt reported that "a number of students sent to us in bad health have had to be returned to their homes."[49] Varioloid, a mild type of smallpox, infected a few boys in 1900, who were quickly "quarantined in a comfortable house at a remote corner of the farm."[50] In later years, students were operated upon for trachoma and other eye troubles. Unfortunately, students also suffered accidents like severed fingers, problems that were witnessed and tended to by teachers.[51] All of these problems—from incidents of injury to widespread illness—challenged educators in the business of teaching empire.

Disease, injury, and death—combined with the range of punishments, the ever-watchful eyes, and the school's fundamental attack against indigenous culture—create a sense that Indian boarding schools were solely sites of violence. Still, most teachers and students highlighted moments of leisure and fun during their tenure at Carlisle. In addition to the Friday- and Saturday-evening entertainments discussed in the previous chapter, scholars have documented "day-to-day humorous moments that served to lighten students' hearts and spirits" as well as the opportunity "to create a social world of their own making."[52] Students played pranks on their teachers, and school newspapers sometimes noted the humor in such acts. For example, in January 1888, the *Indian Helper* reported, "One of the teachers found a dead mouse on her school-room desk. It is very evident that the pupils of that room would like to study natural history."[53] Pratt described another incident where boys tricked a matron into holding a string attached to a rat before explaining that such pranks "constitute a great deal of the life and fun of the place. If you will ask any of the teachers they can tell you instances."[54] In addition to practical jokes, students formed close friendships with one another. Bell writes of several such relationships including two girls who regularly locked themselves in a closet to speak in their own language, boys who snuck out of their dormitories to steal apples from the orchard, and friends missing one another when no longer together at the school. In fact, several students formed lifelong friendships, exchanging letters years after attending Carlisle, and such alumni were likely among those who chose to send their own children to the Indian boarding school in the East.[55]

Of course, teachers had much more freedom of movement and opportunities to socialize than their students, although they, too, were limited by time and space. With little time off from work, teachers had to find ways to have fun on or close to school grounds. For recreation, they played tennis, went on sleigh rides, and enjoyed short hikes into the mountains.[56] They also attended lectures and exhibitions held at the school and elsewhere.[57] A

Emma Foster reading for pleasure or work, circa 1902, in an elaborately decorated room. Wall hangings depict religious and secular maternal images. Books are on display throughout the room, among other decorative items. Though posed, the image conveys an intimate view of the life of an Indian boarding school teacher. (Photo by Frances Benjamin Johnston, courtesy Library of Congress, Prints and Photographs Division, Washington, DC.)

tradition established in 1888 gave teachers a chance to socialize each Thursday night in the teachers' club parlor. Here employees provided one another with entertainment and enjoyed "social games and free discussion of matters outside of Indian affairs."[58] A year later the teachers' club became a place where members enjoyed pleasant meals and "spicy conversations."[59] Employees took other breaks from their regular routines to build relationships with their colleagues. School newspapers detail teachers' comings and goings, listing the people who teachers visited or where they journeyed for a day excursion or a short trip. Oftentimes teachers visited family close by or spent weekends visiting with guests at the school.[60] Although work at Carlisle was serious business, teachers found some reprieve from the school's tightly controlled schedule, fulfilling some of their own needs and desires while meeting the school's strict expectations. Even this moderate level of flexibility helped to reinvigorate teachers' work ethic, effectively reinforcing the momentum and structures of imperial education policy.

Still, teachers' everyday lives consisted mostly of working, eating, and sleeping on school grounds, a lifestyle that some found fulfilling. Indeed, several teachers prided themselves on the consuming nature of their work. After teaching at Carlisle for nine years, Katherine Bowersox explained, "My reputation and success as a teacher are of *first* importance to me. It is my life work." She continued, "Your unbounded faith in the Indian and your courageous fight against the degrading conditions have inspired me many times to do the little I am able to do to help redeem a few of them. Carlisle has done much for me and the school deserves my whole-souled devotion to its interests."[61] Humbled by Pratt's commitment to uplifting the Indian, Bowersox proclaimed her deep dedication to his school, however small her contribution might be. By exemplifying such total commitment to her work, she reflected her understanding of both the practical and moral obligations that teachers and reformers believed were inherent in Indian education. For most Carlisle teachers, the "extra work" was simply part of the job, an expectation as well as a duty.[62]

Ultimately, many teachers embraced a culture of "life work" that did not differentiate between one's personal or professional time. Of course, some exceptions existed, such as one employee, Marianne Moore, who lived off-campus during her three years at Carlisle, where she taught business and clerical classes. While she taught at Carlisle, Superintendent Friedman sought to make sure Moore recognized that she would still "be guided by the same regulations governing other teachers" and advised her, "While it is not absolutely essential that you live on the grounds, you will take your turn regularly in all matters such as study hour, acting as chaperone at various times, etc."[63] Thus, Friedman made clear that the teachers' duties went well beyond the classroom, regardless of their residence. Still, even with additional responsibilities to classroom work, Moore likely had more time to herself than she otherwise might have if she had lived on campus. Perhaps this living arrangement accelerated her writing career, as she published her first poem during her final year at Carlisle, later becoming a world-renowned poet. Even with such exceptions, the vast majority of teachers lived on school property and devoted much of their time to their "life work." Some withstood the intense work and living environment while others thrived in it, but all contributed to the making of imperial education.

With so much time and energy devoted to working at Carlisle, it is not surprising that many teachers cemented lifelong friendships, particularly those who remained at the school for several years. Founding teachers Marianna Burgess and Ann Ely worked together, traveled together, and sustained a strong bond long after their twenty-plus years at the school. Having met before arriving at Carlisle, they were "constant companions" during their tenure there, rooming next door to one another and vacationing and visiting family and friends together in their free time. Although some might assume that Burgess and Ely were lovers, in the late nineteenth century, intimate bonds between female friends were not necessarily viewed from this perspective, and teachers were particularly likely to form domestic attachments that may or may not have included sexual relations.[64] Of course, Burgess and Ely also fostered friendships with other teachers while at Carlisle. Emma Cutter considered Burgess a longtime "intimate friend."[65] And other Carlisle teachers also forged strong bonds as they committed themselves to shared work and helped one another achieve their best.

Some teachers also formed close ties with other Carlisle employees. Katherine Bowersox pleaded to have the laundress, Miss Hill, move with her to a new building, having spent "seven happy years together." Bowersox wrote to Pratt, "I *need* Miss Hill. She is like a mother to me in many ways. She looks after my health and comfort since I was sick, five years ago, thus relieving me in my ways and enabling me to give my *whole time* to my work and study."[66] Other employees must certainly have relied upon one another as friends and companions. As the Bureau of Indian Affairs gained control over hiring in the school's last decades, fewer staff members may have formed lifelong friendships since they were transferred among schools with greater frequency. Still, even then, friendships helped teachers perform their best and enjoy their time at the school. Such personal bonds between workers likely strengthened the school's mission, helping them withstand the rigors of work and fulfill their roles as cultural translators.

Of course, teachers were not always enamored with their fellow employees or employers. One of the few male academic teachers at Carlisle over the course of its forty-year history (and the only male teacher in 1914 besides the principal teacher, John Whitwell), Royal Mann, requested a transfer "because of no co-operation among employees."[67] The supervisor in charge, O. H. Lipps, handwrote on Mann's application that "being a young man he does not find his associates as congenial as he would like."[68] It is difficult to assess the extent to which Mann was treated unfairly or just differently by his mainly female coworkers due to his sex or age, as he was in his early twenties. Certainly, it is possible that his older female colleagues considered it unfair that Mann received a higher salary than many of them, particularly since Carlisle was his first teaching job in the Indian Service.[69]

At least some women also found the atmosphere at Carlisle challenging.

In 1912 Mattie Lane, who found the discipline lacking and quit after a year, complained that many of her fellow teachers had given up on their work. She wrote that some of them had "'gone to seed' mentally years ago" and indicated that they gave her a hard time.[70] Although the validity of such charges are unknown—and perhaps untenable, considering that charges of senility are not found elsewhere—other teachers likely did not fit in and may have simply left Carlisle soon after arrival, taking advantage of the high rates of movement between schools in the Indian School Service. For those who remained at Carlisle, teachers had to earn respect from one another at least to a certain degree, proving their dedication—even loyalty—to their work, one another, and the school, all while adapting to the specific social norms of the Indian boarding school.

While other teachers likely experienced strained relationships with one another, some of the most destructive relationships developed between teachers and two of Pratt's successors, superintendents Mercer and Friedman. During their tenures, according to historian David Adams, "Carlisle entered a period of general decline."[71] Whereas records indicate that the school's first two decades were reasonably free of scandal, the two administrations following Pratt were not. Under the troubled leadership of Mercer and Friedman, teachers continued to demonstrate their agency by speaking out against and resisting what they considered unjust policies and practices, ultimately helping to carry the work of imperial education forward.

In June 1904 the Bureau of Indian Affairs abruptly relieved Pratt of his duties at Carlisle and appointed Captain William A. Mercer superintendent.[72] Mercer had worked as an Indian agent and, like Pratt, was an army man. Many teachers, loyal to Pratt, resented Mercer, leading to high staff turnover in his first year. Yet, Mercer pleased Indian Office authorities as he aligned the school's curriculum with federal standards, something Pratt had resisted.[73]

However, in April 1907 Mercer was discovered having an affair with a Carlisle student, Dora Shongo. Mrs. Anna Hoffman, likely an employee or spouse of an employee, was sitting quietly in her room embroidering as her baby slept when she heard the superintendent and Shongo next door. She recalled, "I heard them on the bed and I know they had Sexual Intercourse and I heard him rattle money-coins, and she said, Don't be so stingy and I know he gave her money."[74] Dora's friend, Marie MacCloud, also knew of the relationship. In a confrontation with Mercer in December 1907, MacCloud told the superintendent that other staff members knew of the affair, including the school nurse, Lucretia Ross. According to sworn statements, Mercer then exclaimed, "My God! I am a ruined man. She [Nurse Lucretia Ross] is the one woman on the post I wouldn't want to know it. She is my enemy and the enemy of my family."[75] Soon after, Mercer transferred Ross to the Haskell Institute, another Indian boarding school, and wrote her, "I trust that you will like your new field of work, and regret exceedingly that untoward events and unfortunate conditions should have caused Carlisle the loss of your services."[76] Under his signature, Mercer wrote, "*In Haste—so excuse imperfections*," admitting at least some wrongdoing and level of guilt.[77] Although it is not clear why Mercer otherwise considered Ross his "enemy," her removal did not save the superintendent's job. By the end of December, Mercer wrote to the commissioner of Indian affairs asking to be "relieved from duty." He explained:

Though in good physical health, I have, for several months past, experienced at frequent intervals severe loss of brain power, and I find the daily annoying responsibilities all more than I can stand and am advised by my physicians that I should have relief from them, and take a few months leave of absence. Such a course, followed by a change back to the more out of door military life, I am convinced is a necessity, and that relief as above all will best suit the conditions.[78]

Feeling stifled in Carlisle's confined quarters, which he may have believed weakened his mental capacities and compelled him into the sexual relationship with a student, Mercer left Carlisle in January 1908, never to return.

However, a year later, rumors surfaced that Washington officials were considering reinstating Mercer as Carlisle's superintendent or appointing him elsewhere in the Indian Service. At that point, former teacher Ann Ely spoke up. Although retired, she pleaded with Lucretia Ross, still serving as a nurse at Haskell, to use "any ammunition left" to prevent Mercer's return. Ely wrote, "What a calamity it would be to the School. The School that so many of us are interested in."[79] Soon after, Ross wrote a letter to the Indian Rights Association divulging some of the evidence of Mercer's sexual affair and threatening that she would "publish the whole story," as per an agreement she had made with the former superintendent if he attempted to reenter the Indian Service.[80] The Indian Rights Association subsequently wrote a letter to the secretary of the interior claiming to be "in possession of charges of a very serious nature reflecting upon Major Mercer, which, if true, show him to be absolutely unfit for the position named, or any other position in the Indian Service."[81] Although the Mercer sex scandal did surface during a 1914 congressional investigation of deplorable medical conditions at Indian schools, it was buried in this much larger investigation.[82] Working largely behind the scenes, teachers and other staff members ultimately wielded tremendous power over their superior, helping to prevent his reinstatement.

Clearly Ann Ely and Lucretia Ross did not respect Mercer, nor did many other Carlisle staff members. In the context of revelations about the scandal, Marie MacCloud noted that Mercer intended to fire several employees, including Misses Cutter, Bowersox, Hill, and Robertson, and Mr. Thompson.[83] Several of these were veteran teachers of Carlisle, and Mercer may have viewed them as obstructing his vision for the school. Certainly some teachers were dissatisfied with Mercer's leadership who did not know about the sex scandal. For example, teacher Emma Hetrick pointed to shady dealings under Mercer's administration, reporting that money had been illegally exchanged while he was in charge.[84] Clearly, Mercer's corrupt leadership frustrated many of his employees and appears to have poisoned the work environment at Carlisle. Such dishonorable behavior at the level of school leadership weakened the moral cause or "benevolence" of assimilation, though teachers' intolerance of such depravity demonstrated their commitment to respectability at all levels.

Unfortunately, the next superintendent fared even worse, though evidence against him was less damning than that held against his predecessor, with some scholars speculating that Superintendent Moses Friedman was predominantly victimized by anti-Semitism.[85] Friedman served as Carlisle's superintendent from 1908 to 1914 and had a vastly different background from his predecessors, having worked as a teacher in the Indian and Philippine Services before becoming an administrator at the Haskell Institute in Kansas.[86] After Mercer's dismissal, Friedman assumed leadership at Carlisle but was largely unable to prevent the school from further decline.

In particular, several teachers clashed with Friedman. For example, in 1909 Superintendent Friedman transferred teacher Mariette Wood elsewhere, claiming she was "not in sympathy with his policies, and . . . a disturbing element."[87] Yet, other teachers knew Wood in her almost ten years at the school and never considered her a "disturber."[88] When Emma Hetrick substituted as a temporary clerk beginning in 1909, she witnessed and refused to participate in corrupt bookkeeping under Friedman's watch, ultimately characterizing work at the school as poisoned by favoritism. She resigned in 1910 and spent the next several years writing to the commissioner of Indian affairs in an effort to clear her name, believing that Friedman was "downing me all around."[89] As noted in chapter 1, Katherine and Fernando Tranbarger accused Friedman of threatening them and believed that the superintendent purposefully withheld their full salary as well as sick and vacation time and also attributed their inadequate living space to Friedman's antipathy. After exchanging a "wordy war" with Friedman, Fernando accused the superintendent of displaying "conduct unbecoming an officer and *gentleman*."[90] In 1911, the couple resigned from Carlisle, followed a year later by the rushed departure of teacher Mattie Lane, who, as noted earlier, was disgusted by the lack of discipline at the school.[91]

Tensions between the superintendent and his staff worsened over time, as illustrated by Friedman's relationship with John Whitwell. Whitwell initially supported his superior's authority and decision making. Claiming to be compelled by "duty . . . [and an] interest in the general welfare of the school," the principal teacher notified Friedman in September 1909 of employees who he believed purposefully thwarted the superintendent's rules. A year later, he continued to support the superintendent, although by the summer of 1911 their relationship started to deteriorate.[92] Whitwell believed that Friedman was asking too much of him, as the superintendent continued to add more and more duties to his workload, a trend that Whitwell noted hampered other teachers as well.[93] Finally, in October 1913 the principal teacher engaged in a heated exchange with his superior where he admitted calling him a "dirty skunk," leading Friedman to formally charge Whitwell with being "incompetent" and "disloyal."[94] Whitwell was immediately notified that he would be transferred to another school, but he did not leave for six more months. Due, in part, to his "long service" (and probably Friedman's imperfect record), Whitwell was even given a promotion and raise, proving that his transfer could hardly be considered punishment.[95] In at least some cases of insubordination, teachers demonstrated power over their supervisors and were able to move within the service to find more agreeable work environments. In this way, teachers demonstrated their agency within the hierarchical structure. For Whitwell, he lashed back at and in a sense had the final word against Friedman when he testified against the former superintendent in the 1914 congressional investigation of Carlisle.

As noted in the Introduction, testimony at the February and March 1914 congressional hearings revealed a profound level of discord among Carlisle faculty members as well as a long list of complaints against the superintendent. Of the ten teachers who testified at the hearings, seven spoke against Friedman, including John Whitwell, and three defended him.[96] Those who opposed his leadership accused Friedman of neglecting the school's "moral standing," citing cases of student pregnancies and drunkenness, creating an unpleasant, divisive work environment, and enabling the misappropriation of funds.[97] The three teachers who defended the superintendent claimed that the school environment had been stable until a few months prior, when it seemed, perhaps, that the personal disagreement between Whitwell and Friedman had spilled over to the student body and staff.[98] After the first three days of testimony, the commissioner of Indian affairs suspended Friedman's superintendency at Carlisle, and his formal resignation was accepted a few months later.[99]

Anthropologist Alice Kehoe contends that Friedman was largely a victim of anti-Semitism, and some teacher and student testimonies suggest that this as well as other reasons may have motivated school community members to condemn the superintendent.[100] Genevieve Bell describes student testimony that supports Kehoe's position:

> When asked how students treated Friedman, one Lakota student replied: "Well about the boys throwing shoes at Mr. Friedman. They told him to get out, and 'Who let him loose?' and everything. They called him 'Christ-killer' and 'Pork-Dodger' and 'Jew.'" . . . This anti-Semitism provoked no response from the senators who went on with their questions about dietary inadequacies and accommodations. They seemed more concerned that students did not respect authority than with the form that such disrespect took.[101]

Clearly, Friedman encountered severe discrimination at various levels—from students all the way up to the senators conducting the hearings. In addition to such anti-Semitism, Bell suggests that the investigation may have been "about finding a scapegoat for the Jim Thorpe medal debacle," in which the former Carlisle student was stripped of his gold medals once it was discovered that he had earned money as a semi-professional baseball player before competing in the 1912 Olympics.[102] Most likely, there is some truth in both theories, but there were also serious problems at Carlisle during Friedman's tenure.

Overall, after Pratt's departure, Carlisle's school leadership was never quite the same. The material or physical challenges that had hampered teachers' work—from inadequate materials to disciplinary problems and disease—were thus exacerbated by ill-advised or corrupt school leadership. Pratt had helped to instill a certain stability as well as admiration for the school's goals among its teachers and even many students, despite the institution's fundamental threats against indigenous culture and life. As discussed, the Mercer administration that took over after Pratt was plagued by sex and financial scandal, and the Friedman administration led to further institutional decline and mistrust among staff and students that played out on the national stage. Teachers at Carlisle were forced to navigate their way through such uncertain and troublesome times. The institution as a whole experienced a decade of unprecedented upheaval and anxiety. Still, the work of assimilation continued through it all.

Over the next four years, before Carlisle's closing in 1918, two new superintendents somewhat stabilized the situation of Carlisle, but their short tenures ultimately undermined efforts to reestablish the school's reputation. During its final years, the school returned to many of the policies familiar under Pratt.[103] Oscar Lipps filled in as Carlisle's temporary superintendent beginning in February 1914 and was made the school's permanent superintendent in May 1915, credited with bringing "the institution up to a high standard of efficiency."[104] However, he only served a couple of years before John Francis Jr. replaced him in 1917.[105]

Soon after Francis's appointment, former student Dennison Wheelock (who had won the 1887 student essay contest for praising Western over indigenous education), by then an accomplished attorney, commended the commissioner of Indian affairs for promoting Lipps to supervisor of education and selecting Francis as superintendent. Wheelock wrote, "With a man like Mr. Lipps to devise educational methods and prescribe courses of study, and with a militray [sic]-trained man like Mr. Francis to compel obedience [sic] to the demands and requirements of such methods and courses of study so prescribed, I can see a bright future for the Carlisle Indian School."[106] Interestingly, the personnel records indicate that Francis did not serve in the military prior to Carlisle, though he did attend St. John's Military School in Manlius, New York, whereas Lipps served as a private in the US Army for two years before teaching at Indian schools beginning in 1890.[107] Nevertheless, Wheelock's sentiment is clear. By 1917, this school alumnus believed Carlisle needed greater discipline, perhaps similar to what he had experienced under Pratt years before.

In spite of such confidence, Superintendent Francis admitted that he was not as assured in his position. In January 1918 Francis wrote to Commissioner of Indian Affairs Cato Sells explaining, "I have been at Carlisle for almost a year now. The complete change of work and point of view naturally made it a very strenuous time for me. The war has brought difficulties to us too. . . . I now understand my difficulties here and there are several matters regarding the school about which I would be glad to have your advice if you would feel justified in permitting me to come to Washington."[108] Prior to his appointment at Carlisle, Francis had been a Washington bureaucrat, not a school administrator.[109] Although it is not known if Francis and Sells ever met in Washington, six months after writing to the commissioner, Francis was relieved of his duties at Carlisle, and the first off-reservation Indian boarding school soon after closed its doors.[110]

Ultimately, World War I determined Carlisle's fate, returning the old army barracks to their original owner, the US military, as a hospital for returning veterans, and scattering Carlisle teachers all over the country. By then, Carlisle's student population had dwindled, from a peak of over one thousand to around two hundred fifty, and the staff had been reduced from its maximum of ninety employees to around sixty.[111] Of the remaining teachers, none had been founding members of the school, and few retained any firsthand memory of its first superintendent, Richard Henry Pratt. Still, several were committed to Indian education, choosing to remain in the Indian Service and teach at other schools. Other teachers went to work for the Indian Bureau in Washington, DC, and still others left Indian education altogether.

Although few teachers were as invested in Carlisle as its founder, the vast majority of those who spent some time at the school believed in their work. Most of those who worked there for several years or more cared about their students even as they sought to replace native customs with the ways and means of the dominant culture. They taught English and other academic subjects, enforced certain gender roles, and promoted Christian values all in an effort to "uplift" the Indian. Their endeavors fundamentally reflected the race-based Indian education movement that attempted to "civilize" the "uncivilized." Yet, unlike the bureaucracy they represented, teachers interacted with students at a personal level and strove to create an environment they believed would improve lives. Unfortunately, whites' profound mistrust of purportedly "backward" and "misguided" Indian morality resulted in a school culture dominated by constant surveillance and severe punishment. Not all teachers were suited for such work. At the same time, not all teachers earned a reputation for being unkind. In fact, sometimes even the most committed assimilationists earned their students' lifelong trust. Many teachers formed close bonds with their students and with one another. Yet, despite even those who held the purest intentions, or who may have managed to create sincere respect for their Indian children, the work was not benevolent.

Significantly, the Carlisle experiment had both national and imperial implications, as it was part of a larger system that privileged the few, concentrating power among the already powerful at the expense of those living on the margins. Teachers were critical to carrying out this work. Ultimately, the Carlisle and Indian Service model were reproduced in other US imperial operations outside of the continental United States, and in one case, at an ambitious scale: when, beginning in 1901, the government sent hundreds of teachers overseas on the heels of military servicemen to indoctrinate the newest wards of the state—Filipinos.

CHAPTER FOUR

LIFE AND DEATH ON THE ISLANDS, 1901–1918

In July 1901 Mary Fee waited aboard the USS *Buford* in Manila Harbor watching her friends, including other teachers and US soldiers, head to shore. Years later she recalled, "They had gone out of our lives after a few brief days of idleness, but they would take up, as we should, the work of building a nation in a strange land and out of a reluctant people."[1] This work, "building a nation" in the Philippines, fell to American soldiers and teachers alike, both tasked with using their unique expertise to pacify a "reluctant" Filipino people and cultivate a Western civilization in the archipelago. US policymakers were certain that such a society could be built if the government established an American-styled public school system on the islands. This project would effectively turn US President William McKinley's mission of "benevolent assimilation" into reality. Focused on such a grand educational goal—and believing their purpose to be exceptional, altruistic, and morally grounded—most teachers who joined the venture did not anticipate the extent to which the US military presence would impact their work and their very survival. Nor were they fully cognizant of other threats and obstacles, such as disease, corruption, and environmental disaster, or the threat they, too, posed to Filipino culture and lives as they embarked on the mission of teaching empire.

In December 1898 the United States gained the Philippines from Spain, which had occupied the archipelago since the mid-sixteenth century. During Spanish rule, colonial authorities instituted a schooling system backed by the Roman Catholic Church. When American teachers arrived hundreds of years later, they found that students were accustomed to a form of education that valued recitation based on biblical teachings, usually under the direction of priests. US authorities largely considered these schools as an extension of the church and deemed them of little educational merit, and thus tasked teachers to replace the existing school structure with one that reflected more American values. As teachers reached their posts scattered throughout the vast archipelago, they encountered various types of schools and traditions, and sometimes none at all—at least nothing akin to what

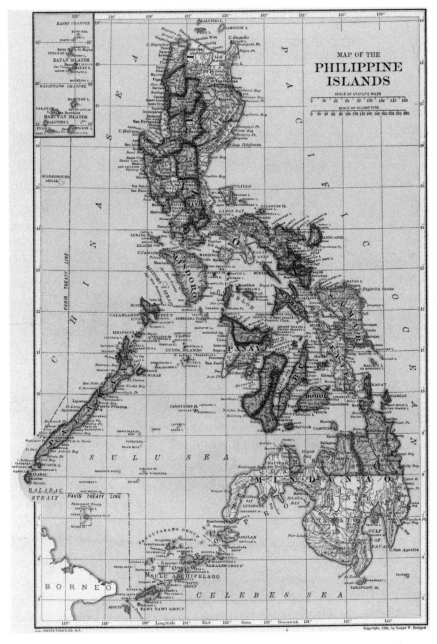

Map of the Philippine Islands, LL Poates Engraving Company, 1906. (Library of Congress.)

they considered to be education. Ultimately, their work involved replacing the norms of the former colonial power with those of the United States.[2]

Scholars have recently argued that missions like the US government's educational project in the Philippines should be seen as part of a century-long tradition, including those that depict such schooling as strengthening the elite and reinforcing a hierarchical and racist power structure in conquered lands. Although some researchers specifically address teachers' involvement in such schooling endeavors, their wide lens does not allow for a deep interrogation of Thomasites' experiences. Moreover, much of this compelling work on imperial education focuses generally on educational institutions and their relationship with government sponsors and agendas.[3] A deeper understanding of educators' work to implement grand policy on the ground illuminates a more complex story in which teachers, imperialism, and Filipinos were all transformed.

Voluminous first-person accounts of experiences in the Philippines, along with other rich sources, allow us to trace teachers' journeys throughout the islands and examine some of the profound challenges they faced as they set up schools. Drawing primarily from the records of thirty-three Thomasites, this chapter explores teachers' varied and sometimes shifting ideas regarding race, sex, and civilization over the course of their tenure in the Philippines. It begins with the spectacle of their arrival in the archipelago and their stay in Manila, as they awaited their teaching assignments and prepared for the next leg of their journey. Once settled in their teaching posts—which often involved arduous treks to remote locations—many teachers faced significant obstacles in setting up functional classrooms. Beliefs regarding American versus Filipino "civilization" and norms regarding respectability influenced, to a certain extent, their tenacity under such strenuous conditions, and otherwise guided (or condemned) teachers' behavior in this new foreign environment. Many adjusted their expectations and behaviors as they settled into their new way of life. Significantly, several Thomasites steadfastly believed in racial hierarchies and rationalized their self-proclaimed biological and intellectual superiority as reason for their own, and the larger US, intervention in the archipelago, sometimes blaming Filipinos for being unteachable. Regardless of their perspectives on race or civilization, virtually all teachers were exposed to a level of violence that was unexpected, and the profound effects of the ongoing military conflict, which threatened their lives, inspired some to take up arms against, or sometimes with, Filipino rebels. Beyond such man-made brutality, teachers and the communities in which they lived confronted the biological violence of disease—turning teachers into de facto doctors, sanitation workers, and patients. At the same time, environmental crises in the region, such as famine, intensified as a result of widespread political corruption. Teachers captured all of these experiences in their diaries, letters, interviews, and memoirs. Whatever particular experiences individuals faced on the islands, they all struggled to make sense of their surroundings and ultimately exposed the fragility of the "benevolent" empire.

On August 23, 1901, the first contingent of over five hundred teachers arrived in Manila, and their disembarkation from the USS *Thomas* caused quite a spectacle; soon all American teachers in the Philippines were known as "Thomasites." As teacher Norman Cameron recorded in his diary, "The Filipinos gazed at us with much curiosity, wondering, I suppose, what is our purpose here in so large numbers."[4] His colleague Ralph Taylor similarly commented on the scene caused by the arrival of hundreds of US civilians: "At the wharf there were a great many soldiers and citizens who were apparently amused as they watched the fresh pedagogues advance."[5] The Thomasites' speculation as to what their onlookers were thinking indicates, if nothing else, that they felt the gravity and novelty of the situation.

For others, including Elizabeth Mitchell, the welcome from US soldiers in Manila was more memorable than that of Filipinos, or in her words, "the brown skinned natives." Writing a long letter to the ladies of the La Crosse, Wisconsin, Twentieth Century Club, she revealed her own desires, some with racist underpinnings: "I shall never forget that landing, when on the dock the soldiers crowded for just a glimpse . . . of more white women than they had seen in three years, nor shall I forget the courtesy with which they made room for us to pass through this their midst."[6] Appealing to her white countrywomen at home, Mitchell differentiated the American soldiers from Filipinos and likely exaggerated her reception among the white men in uniform. Highlighting the "courtesy" with which the US soldiers gave herself and other white women, she intimated that these men felt a racialized form of desire, perhaps revealing more about her own longings than those of the troops. Although it is reasonable to think that some (or many) soldiers felt aroused at the rare sight of white women, Mitchell's observation indicates that in that moment, she felt more excited or anxious about her relations with white soldiers than her future work with Filipinos, or at least that is what she emphasized to the Wisconsin clubwomen.

Of course, as scholars suggest, racialized beliefs were dynamic, both at an individual and systemic level. An individual's racist perspectives were subject to change depending upon context: on when, where, and with whom one might be surrounded. Still, calling out moments of racist intent, as well as the duration of racist perspectives, can add up, helping to paint a picture of how Americans viewed their place in the archipelago and within American society more broadly. Moreover, such analysis can help to parse out the systems of power promoted by American imperialism, acknowledging that those who helped to transport or resist such systems shaped them, even as they continued to reinterpret the meaning or significance of race for themselves and others.[7]

As discussed in the Introduction and throughout the book, by the early twentieth century beliefs regarding racial hierarchies had been entrenched in law, policy, practice, and now-debunked "science." Centuries of rationalizing and codifying systemic racism had enabled slavery, citizenship restrictions, scientific inquiry that purportedly "proved" racial supremacy, and cultural mores that dehumanized people of color, as well as projects of imperial education, including that in the Philippines. Thus, teachers' racist thought was not anomalous but rather reflective of the dominant culture that strove to protect, idealize, and equate whiteness with Americanness at the expense of "others." Although it took many forms and was dynamic, racism had been so seamlessly woven into the fabric of early twentieth-century America that beliefs regarding white supremacy had been normalized. Thus, many teachers consciously and unconsciously brought such ideologies with them to the archipelago, where they reshaped, redefined, and reconstituted modes of power accordingly.[8]

US educational leaders in the Philippines similarly tried to make sense of the mission and the peoples it aimed to uplift, sometimes drawing from their expertise based on what is today recognized as dubious racial "science." Trained as an anthropologist who studied and felt an affinity for indigenous American peoples, David P. Barrows had tremendous interest in the racial origins of Filipinos. Appointed as the superintendent of Manila schools in 1900, the following year he served as the chief of the Bureau of Non-Christian Tribes of the Philippine Islands. As chief, Barrows published a circular in 1901 that instructed American and Filipino volunteers to observe and measure Filipinos' physical characteristics (from eye shape and skin color to breast shape and nose dimensions) as a means of recording ethnological data, part of the research deemed necessary to understand the "little known pagan and Mohammedan tribes of the Archipelago."[9] A couple of years later Barrows was appointed the superintendent of education for the Philippines, a position he held until 1909. During that time he published a book, *A History of the Philippines*—which is less a history

"Races and Tribes of the Philippines." (David P. Barrows, *A History of the Philippines* [New York: American Book Co., 1905], 30.)

of the archipelago and more an anthropological account of its people. In chapter 2, "The Peoples of the Philippines," he investigates "ethnology, or the science of the races," to determine "how and where different races of mankind originated" and evaluates Filipinos' physical bodies—skin color, height, hair, shape—as well as cultural norms, classifying some peoples as more civilized than others in an effort to determine their historic migratory patterns and geographic origins (see the map "Races and Tribes of the Philippines").[10] Clearly, Barrows brought this "expertise" in ethnology to his role as head of the US educational mission in the Philippines, thus further elevating the significance and meaning of race—and the aim of "civilization"—within the imperial project.[11]

Even as race affected Americans' thought and behavior—and shaped the mission itself—more tangible or practical experiences and expectations occupied the forefront of teachers' minds as they disembarked from their ships and eagerly awaited settlement into their new homes. Whether they arrived in 1901 or a decade later, once in Manila it usually took over a week to receive specific assignments within the vast archipelago, and several more weeks before they began the journey to their posts. During the lull, the Thomasites went sightseeing, visited with one another, and, on many evenings, gathered at the Luneta, a seashore park where the army band played concerts, always ending with "The Star-Spangled Banner."[12] Teachers also gathered supplies for their impending assignment—including food, tailored suits, and whatever else was rumored to be useful. They attended lectures given by US education experts to prepare for their assignment and heard tales, sometimes contradictory to information they had earlier received, from American soldiers about life in the Philippines.[13] They also adjusted to simple living, such as sleeping on cots covered in mosquito netting in the army barracks on the Exposition Grounds. As Harrie Cole described this period, "It is lots of fun, especially when we are paid for it, and . . . like a camping expedition."[14]

For some, including Elizabeth Mitchell, the city also provided an opportunity to express notions of racial, gender, and class exceptionalism. She quickly separated herself from local people who hurried along the streets of Manila, observing, "As one watches the crowd as it jostles along the narrow sidewalks—Filipinos, Chinese, Japanese, Spanish, East Indian—old and young, clad and half clad—all chattering in strange exciting gibberish—one is thankful it is not the custom of ladies to walk along the streets of Manila."[15] Mitchell's audience, the Wisconsin clubwomen, engaged in community service as part of a national women's club movement that emerged in the late nineteenth and early twentieth centuries.[16] Although critically important in US women's political and social activism, most clubs reinforced sometimes racialized middle-class cultural and social norms as they sought to uplift and improve their local communities.[17] Thus, Mitchell's letter reassured the ladies of La Crosse that even in the foreign city of Manila, white American women embodied a level of refinement and privilege that separated them from people of other cultures, even when they simply walked on the city streets.

Of course, Mitchell was not the only Thomasite whose personal writings suggested their unfamiliarity with people different from themselves. In fact, many other teachers wrote about brown bodies, Chinese business owners, and numerous "others," indicating that they had spent most of their lives in fairly homogenous white communities. For these teachers, whiteness had defined their cultural norms and expectations and bolstered their beliefs regarding the righteousness of a race-based hierarchy. For example, in August 1901, soon after arriving in Manila, Mary Cole, Harrie's wife, used race to help describe her work to family back home. Making clear distinctions among nonwhite races, she wrote: "Our business will be to establish schools and teach the native teachers English. . . . The teacher (American) will be the power behind the throne, so to speak. I think we are going to like it very much. The people are a very bright intelligent race and nothing like the negro race."[18] In this short passage Mary clearly revels in the power she will have as a white teacher in a foreign land. Given the casual way in which she discusses her prospective work coupled with her ready assumption of racial differences, she was clearly comfortable with understanding herself and the world in terms of a racial order. While Mary privileged white over black, she also made clear distinctions among people of color. At the same time, by writing in this way to the folks at home, she assumed that they shared her racist views and likely her beliefs regarding "the negro race." For Mary and other Thomasites, skin color connoted significant meaning and induced race-based judgments about her work well before she entered a classroom.[19]

As Mary and other Thomasites awaited their assignments in Manila—sometimes for several weeks—they experienced various types and levels of anxiety. Mary and Harrie Cole had been given a few false leads as to when they would be leaving for their final destination. Of the over five hundred original Thomasites, they were among the few teachers left in the barracks by mid-September 1901—over a month after having arrived in the Philippines. They enjoyed their time in the city but were ready to move on. Mary was particularly eager to leave Manila and explore other ports in the archipelago, explaining, "that's one of the things we came for."[20] Norman Cameron also likely felt some apprehension during his weeks of waiting in the capital city, particularly since he encountered violence soon after his arrival. Like the Coles, Cameron was one of the last teachers sent to his station, although unlike the Coles he learned early on that he would be sent to the island of Bohol, "reported to be in insurrection."[21] Although he did not dwell on the island's conflict in his diary while in Manila, Cameron wrote about several violent incidents in the city: a "scrap in Barrack B" between teachers because one man would not stop talking, a story he heard of a town where American soldiers advised a teacher to leave for his own safety, and the murder of an American soldier at the Luneta apparently by a Filipino weapon, a bolo. Thus, almost immediately upon his arrival, Cameron felt the presence of violence.[22] Most other teachers would not realize their close proximity to bloodshed until they left the capital city and began settling into their new homes, where the extent, depth, and ubiquity of violence deepened.

Of course, violence well preceded Cameron and the other Thomasites' arrival and continued throughout the teachers' early years on the islands. As discussed earlier, the United States occupied the archipelago as a result of a war against Spain in 1898, only to have to continue fighting to retain control of the territory in the Philippine-American War. Filipino rebels resisted the transfer of the islands from Spanish to American authority almost as soon as the two imperial powers signed their treaty, insisting instead on complete independence. By early 1899, US soldiers were battling the people they had recently freed from Spanish occupation. While the Americans were well armed and had other important military advantages, Filipinos relied upon their knowledge of the land and skill at guerilla warfare to gain the upper hand in some parts of the archipelago. To crush the Filipino resistance, American soldiers resorted to brutal military tactics. They implemented torture, burned entire towns, and corralled civilians into concentration camps. At the same time, the US government's belief in the power of education to win over Filipinos was so great that it sent American civilians into known combat zones. Thomasites thus entered an occupied Philippines in the summer of 1901 as fighting continued and as the US military increased its harsh treatment against rebel fighters. Although the war was declared officially over a year later, insurgent uprisings erupted for several more years.[23]

American newspapers had detailed reasons for and against occupying the islands in 1898, with imperial-minded editors emphasizing the military necessity and inevitably of US power in the region while anti-imperial editors pressed for a "moral course" and general goodwill in deciding how to

treat the islands. Still, even though the press covered the wars in the Philippines, the American public was not privy to the atrocious details of US
military methods since censorship forbade any such reports. Then, just as
teachers were recruited for the educational experiment in the archipelago,
the ferocity of US military methods intensified and again remained largely
unreported. By this point Americans had become tired of the war, which
was reflected in newspaper editorials, low army enrollment, and government debates over military appropriations.[24] Thus, the Thomasites were
cognizant of the larger war but generally unaware of the harsh realities on
the ground until their arrival in specific outposts scattered around the vast
archipelago. As Harrie Cole wrote to his brother on October 21, 1901, soon
after arriving on the island of Leyte, "This country is not what it is reported
to be in the papers at home. Only the bright side of things is put forward
in reports there. The truth is, one is not entirely safe in many of the towns,
and it is out of the question to attempt to make an excursion out into the
country alone."[25] Teachers new to the islands often noted the fragility of US
occupation soon after their arrival, with many commenting on their own
vulnerability to violence. Later, some noted the tenuous nature of the education mission itself.

For the most part, unless teachers volunteered for an undesirable location, they had little say about where they might be stationed. Urged to write
a memoir after more than twenty-five years of service on the islands, John
Early recalled that back in 1906 he "received a round of applause" from his
colleagues when he volunteered to work with "the Kalingas, then reputed
the worst head-hunters in Northern Luzon."[26] Though the danger may have
been exaggerated, many places and peoples in the Philippines remained
far removed from the American occupation—even five years into the US
educational experiment. Early was among those eager to venture into a faraway and perhaps dangerous post. In contrast, in 1909 George Carrothers
thought he would be teaching chemistry in Manila but upon his arrival was
ordered to go to "the far north in Samar . . . the wildest part of that wild,
undeveloped island."[27] Not pleased with this new assignment, he attempted
to return to the States, submitting his resignation multiple times to educational authorities. However, his resignations were rejected. Finally, feeling
that he had little choice in the matter, he packed up and prepared to go
to Samar.[28] Though teachers could make their preferences known, more
often than not, bureaucrats assigned them where they thought the need was
greatest.

In making their decisions, US authorities assumed that teachers' potential for success rested, in part, upon their sex. The issue of gender loomed large in the world of education at the turn of the twentieth century. By then, most schoolteachers in the United States were women, a shift that had been commented on and justified in multiple ways. However, US government recruiters imagined male teachers better suited for the more rustic conditions of island living and for supervisory positions.[29] Recall the 1904 publication issued by the Philippine Bureau of Education and discussed in chapter 1: single women were assigned in locations where they might have "advantages of American society and an American home" whereas officials assumed that remote teaching stations could "obviously only be done by a man," unless, perhaps, a couple was married.[30] While such assumptions regarding the gendered nature of work largely guided teachers' job assignments—and resulted in more men gaining teaching appointments in the Philippines than women—exceptions certainly existed.[31]

All four of the originally single female Thomasites featured in this book—Mary Fee, Alice Hollister, Clara Donaldson, and Elizabeth Mitchell—initially taught in remote parts of the archipelago, and for all of them race and racial difference as well as gender isolation loomed large. Fee, sent to the village of Capiz on the island of Panay, explained in her memoir that she "was willing to go anywhere" and preferred to be assigned alone, hoping to avoid any unnecessary social quarrels, which she attributed as natural to the female sex. Not the only white woman in Capiz upon arrival—as several white American soldiers and their wives already lived there, in addition to one white American male teacher—Fee openly wrote about the role of race in her memoir. She recounted how her use of the term "poor white trash" was appropriated by a Filipina friend who was upset to see "poor Filipino trash" children—barefooted and unkempt—depicted in a text book. In another case she described her interactions with an African American soldier she described as a "coal-black African" whom, due to her upbringing in Missouri, she assumed to "know enough of the colored race" to judge his trustworthiness. She also likened working-class Filipinos indebted to wealthier Filipinos as reminiscent of enslaved African Americans to their masters, recalling that these relationships mirrored "the feeling [that] used to be between Southerners and their negroes. The lower-class man is proud of his connection with the great family."[32] Collectively, these examples illustrate the degree to which race and racial hierarchies shaped Fee's understanding of life in the Philippines as well as in her home country. At other times defensive of the Filipino people, her memoir, perhaps not surprisingly, praised the US experiment on the islands in purpose and practice, ultimately underscoring her belief—and that of the mission itself—in white supremacy.

The other three female teachers point to varying degrees of racially informed ideologies, noting the significance of being a single, white female in the US-occupied archipelago. Alice Maude Hollister was reportedly the first white woman to visit the remote town of Dagami, on Leyte island, in seven years. According to her future husband's account, her arrival caused great interest among the Filipinos, and even six weeks later the natives still "flocked out to see her." Indeed, an American lieutenant "finally detailed two soldiers to chase them away from the house."[33] Similarly, Clara Donaldson (who later taught at the Carlisle Indian School) was originally assigned to a remote province on the island of Luzon and "for many months was the only white woman in a population of many thousand." Only years later did she teach at a high school in Manila, which her sister categorized as more "civilized."[34] Finally, Elizabeth Mitchell taught for two years in the village Nueva Caceres, on the island of Mindanao, before returning to Manila to teach art. Recalling Mitchell's own accounts of her racialized reception in Manila via her letter to the ladies of Wisconsin's Twentieth Century Club, it is not surprising that she wrote about having "learn[ed] to distinguish by their appearance between the pure Filipino type, the Spanish type, and the Spanish Mestiso" as well as the "Chinese Mestiso" and "Chinamen." And, like the other white American women "exceptions" who worked virtually alone in remote outposts, Mitchell commented on the gendered and racial isolation that she experienced, marveling at the relatively large number of white women (mostly officers' wives and some teachers) able to join the frequent social gatherings held in such otherwise inaccessible provinces.[35]

Significantly, for all four women, racial and gendered isolation are conflated with geographic isolation, indicating the prominence that skin color and sex played in their and loved ones' minds. Of course, other cases of single women assigned to remote locations undoubtedly exist, and with it further presumptions regarding race and gender. However, the archival records of such placements are harder to find than those of their male counterparts. Still, the historical record suggests that American women were not appointed as supervisors, even when they acted as such, and there were many men who served only as barrio (village) teachers rather than as supervisors, adding inconsistencies and complexity to policymakers' visions.

For many Thomasites, whether men or women, reaching their posts in isolated parts of the archipelago proved arduous, although some considered this all part of the adventure. Unless stationed in Manila, most teachers had to utilize several modes of transportation to reach their destinations: small and large boats, pony or carabao (water buffalo) rides, significant hiking up hillsides and through rivers, and, for a lucky few, a train. Teachers usually traveled with their American colleagues for at least part of the journey: some seemed to thrive in the chaos they encountered, or at least remembered their arrival as particularly spectacular. John Early, who reportedly volunteered to work in a village of headhunters, provides perhaps the most extreme story of a teacher's journey to his village. He recalled traveling aboard a small boat in which a drunken man broke his paddle over another man's head and the boat filled with water, forcing him to swim ashore.[36] The village that he reached put him to work while the incumbent teacher was absent on a six-week vacation. On the next leg of his journey, Early rode a runaway carabao through thorny bamboo and was covered with scratches before he spent another day climbing up a mountain. There he encountered a Bontoc man in little clothing, who after a time, "lowered his lance and came forward with a grin on his face and his hand extended."[37] Although the outlandishness of such an account raises questions about its veracity, placed in the context of other teachers' journeys to their stations it is likely that Early endured a great adventure to reach his post. Perhaps teachers embellished their accounts to create livelier stories or emphasize the significance of their trips. For example, Mary Fee recalled that as her boat approached the town of Capiz, she heard "cries of La Maestra!" as a crowd eagerly waited to meet the new woman teacher.[38] It is hard to imagine that Filipinos were so excited about their teacher's arrival that they chanted her title, literally cheering her on as she came to town. Whether exaggerated or not, such stories make clear that teachers viewed their journeys to island villages as exciting and, for Early and Fee at least, worthwhile adventures. Oftentimes these rigorous journeys exposed Thomasites to danger and symbolized the vulnerability of the entire imperial education venture. Accounts of teachers like Early and Fee perhaps unintentionally served to counter such vulnerability by highlighting their purported heroism, and thus the valor of the US mission itself. Still, the US occupation of the Philippines and its educational endeavors were more fragile than American authorities—and even some teachers—admitted.

As suggested earlier, many Thomasites first encountered the risks of living in a war-torn country when they left Manila. Several traveled to their posts under guard for protection, with some appearing unfazed by such challenges. On his way to Bonton, on the island of Negros, in September 1901, Frederick Behner initially traveled with twenty other teachers, including two

Frederick Behner with shotgun and servant carrying ducks, Marinduque Isle, Philippines, 1903. Proud of his hunting expedition, Behner was among many American male teachers who hunted for sport, part of the adventure of living in the archipelago. (Frederick G. Behner Papers, Bentley Image Bank, Bentley Historical Library, University of Michigan.)

women, and reported that they had a "delightful" eighteen-hour journey together aboard a small boat. He wrote, "The sea was exceptionally calm and last evening's sunset was the prettiest I have ever witnessed."[39] He seemed equally enamored with his new home in the mountains, which had a view of the sea, and was only slightly concerned that upon his arrival in the village he and his American colleague, Mr. Blakeslee, had to be ushered out under guard until Bonton was deemed safe enough for them to return. Behner exclaimed, "Such experiences truly seems like pioneering."[40] A couple of days later, the two Americans, escorted by soldiers, returned to Bonton and settled into the convent, which was to be their home and school. There, Behner and Blakeslee remained under the protection of ten constabulary men, assigned to "insure us of our safety."[41] For Behner, traveling to unknown and unstable environments at least initially seemed exciting and new.

For Harvey Bordner, traveling through the bush became particularly arduous as he had three different teaching assignments in one year, each requiring a difficult journey. To reach his first post at Nueva Vizcaya, Bordner initially traveled with seven other teachers about eighty miles by railroad from Manila and then alone for 140 miles by foot, pony, and carabao, under guard of one hundred native soldiers for protection from insurgents.[42] Six months later, having been reassigned to Nueva Eciha Province, Bordner noted, "My trip across the mountain was certainly very interesting and one I shall not soon forget, because I was water-bound for about five days . . . had to ford no less than 30 rivers. . . . Of course I had plenty to eat and 5 soldiers for a body guard so that I felt very comfortably at all times."[43] Uncertain as to the reason for his transfer, Bordner learned shortly after arriving at his new post that he would probably be moved again.

Considering the strenuous nature of the journey between posts, it is difficult to imagine why educational authorities ordered such transfers as often as they did. Of the thirty-three Thomasites surveyed in this book, only a few remained in the same post for more than one or two years, with a few, like Bordner, transferred several times in one year. Perhaps authorities were eager to reach remote areas on the islands and purposefully looked to teachers experienced in arduous travel to extend the mission's reach. It is likely that they believed men like Bordner were best prepared to withstand the taxing treks and resettlement. Or, perhaps the authorities making these decisions had little sense of the practical difficulties such reassignments involved. In either case, the teachers themselves quickly tired of the transfers; Bordner certainly hoped to settle down somewhere more permanently.

Of course, teachers' arrival at their posts was merely the beginning of their ventures, and for most there was little risk of losing touch with American norms and sentiments, even as they adjusted to new customs. The vast majority of Thomasites maintained a respectable distance between their lives and those of their students and neighbors. While most made the best of their housing, they often noted that it was not up to the standard they were accustomed to back in the States. H. O. Whiting wrote to his parents regarding the antiquated technology and claimed sarcastically that "Arkansas is very modern and up to date compared to Siquifor. Thousands of people [have] never seen a stove, fire place, or any thing of the kind."[44] Mary Fee seemed a bit more adaptable. Soon after arriving in the fall of 1901, she described the crude showering system of using a coconut shell to pour water over herself and resolved that she was "beginning to look upon a bath from the native standpoint as a means of coolness, and incidentally of cleanliness."[45] She and others wrote also about the pigs that often rooted below the house and elsewhere in the streets, eating the refuse and serving as a makeshift sewage system. Similar conditions persisted decades later, as Laura Gibson Smith described the town of Iloilo, where "chickens and pigs are the sewer system."[46]

Although the teachers did their best to maintain a certain level of hygiene—including boiling their drinking water—they also had to adjust their expectations, especially in more remote barrios. George Carrothers complained in an interview years later, "One of the crimes that Uncle Sam committed against American teachers was to send them off into some primitive barrio where there were no conveniences. Americans didn't know anything about what they would need. A little medicine, useful clothing, a few cooking utensils—these things would have been of very great help to me."[47] Carrothers, who was stationed in the Philippines eight years after the first Thomasites had arrived, suggested that American authorities had still not adequately prepared teachers venturing abroad. Perhaps the educational mission in the islands was too ambitious, even eight years into the project. Or educational leaders in the Philippines were unable (or unwilling) to build on teachers' practical insights or suggestions for improving teachers' prospects. Alternatively, Carrothers's experiences may have been anomalous, though evidence suggests that many teachers—particularly over the first decade of US involvement in the archipelago—were unprepared on several fronts for the work and cultural adjustments that lay ahead. Such teachers represent both the tangible and symbolized vulnerabilities of American empire: from simple things—like teachers not knowing what supplies or medicines to pack—to bigger, more fundamental questions, like America's blinded "benevolence" that led it to attempt acquisition and uplift of a vast, diverse, rich land before fully considering the obstacles, methods, or consequences of such bold action.

Even so, in teachers' day-to-day lives, some Filipino norms were appealing. One such enticing Filipino practice involved the hiring of servants. Even before landing in Manila, the Coles bragged in a letter addressed to family at home that "unless we have servants to wait upon us, that the natives will not respect us, so servants we must have."[48] Similarly, H. O. Whiting realized the importance of this custom early on. He hired a cook soon after arriving in the village of Larena on the island of Siquifor and explained to his mother that the act of hiring a servant was more a matter of respecting local expectations than gaining help with household chores: "I dare not live alone and do my work for work is considered disgraceful."[49]

However, living with servants proved to be more difficult than the Coles or Whiting had anticipated. A few months into her tenure, Mary Cole wrote home:

> I got sick of my dirty servants and *"fired"* them. . . . Lieut. Eames told us when we first came that we couldn't teach them to do anything our way but I said we could . . . but I thoroughly agree with him now. The habits of 500 yrs cannot be over come in a day and especially when they don't care to over come them. Some times I get disgusted with the whole race and think it is useless to try to teach them any thing. But I suppose with patience and perseverance they will progress little by little until within 2 or 300 years they maybe quite Americanistic.[50]

Clearly, Mary was frustrated by more than just her servants' inability to keep house "our way." Here, she conflated her servants' housekeeping shortcomings with problems she considered endemic to the "whole race," perhaps as a result of the little progress she felt she was making with her students. Moreover, her reference to "dirty" servants, particularly in the context of condemning an entire race, demonstrates how her own racism—and perhaps that of others who had already given up, notably Lieutenant Eames—fueled despair. By February 1902—six months into her venture—Mary came to believe, at least in her worst moments, that building US-style civilization in a place as ostensibly uncivilized as the Philippines would take hundreds of years. Lieutenant Eames had warned her of the impossibility of enacting quick cultural change, suggesting that at least some military personnel believed the "benevolent" US mission was futile.

Although some Thomasites at times came to agree with such sentiments, others felt differently. Whiting, for example, almost lost his job for refusing to conform to Philippine expectations of a "civilized" life, in part by refusing to hire more help. Although he hired a cook upon his arrival in 1906 to keep up appearances, a year later he wrote his mother that he was being transferred, in part, for not having servants. He insisted, "I will not be a slave to fashion nor will I depend on servants for every thing. I must be independent and being dependent on servants, is worse than serving."[51] Whiting valued doing good work and saving money above upholding appearances. He believed it was not the natives who disrespected him but white officials who disapproved of his "'Strict economy in small matters' and 'Peculiar habits.'" Upon meeting with the director of education, Whiting understood this to mean that he did not spend enough money on servants or accommodations since he chose "living with natives at Normal [training school for Filipino teachers] instead of paying more than four times as much to live with the 'mess.'" He also did not present a sufficiently civilized appearance, eschewing white suits and a shaven face for more comfortable clothes and whiskers.[52] But for education officials who sought to maintain borders between what they considered "civilized" and "uncivilized," Thomasites who did not draw a strict enough line between themselves and their subjects undermined the entire experiment and thus risked losing their jobs.

Of course, the stakes were not always so high, particularly for Thomasites who continued to wear clothes befitting white middle-class American norms despite the islands' tropical weather. In some cases, teachers risked the scorn of their colleagues or local people rather than US authorities. For example, in August 1903 Blaine Moore privately censured white American women for not wearing hats or corsets, finding them "careless in dress" and dismissing one woman's explanation that in the islands "'women had to sacrifice looks for comfort.'"[53] Several years later, in September 1918, Harvey Bordner, who had risen through the ranks in his many years on the islands, gave a speech on "Teacher Qualifications Sought by Superintendents." He explained, "A teacher's personal appearance is . . . [a] tremendous moment. A teacher may not be beautiful, but he or she should look beautiful to the children."[54] Thus, regardless of personal comfort, teachers were to exhibit a beautiful, "civilized" posture in order to earn their colleagues' and students' respect.

In addition to some concerns over appearance, several teachers became frustrated with the crude school accommodations they confronted and modified their expectations. Some of the more committed Thomasites decided to acclimate themselves to the school environment and work to improve conditions gradually. Particularly in the experiment's earliest years, teachers found schools to be in an appalling state. Most village school buildings, if they existed at all, did not have adequate space or seating to accommodate all of the students, evidence of the material fragility of this imperial endeavor. Some villages had buildings with dirt floors and a few benches while others had no building designated for a schoolhouse. Having received a promotion to division superintendent of a province of forty thousand Filipinos, in April 1903 Harvey Bordner felt overwhelmed yet optimistic regarding the present and future educational work, declaring that his first order of business would be to "build a schoolhouse." In most cases, teachers worked with local officials to build suitable accommodations, though some complained that such construction was too slow.[55]

Other teachers described overcrowded classrooms, off-putting habits, and environmental hazards or inconveniences and adjusted to these new norms to differing degrees. Many classrooms had few or no desks, forcing teachers to use whatever materials they had available to organize their classrooms—which, as Mary Cole described, sometimes left children sitting on a classroom's dirt floor.[56] Other teachers were forced to turn students away, as was the case for Glen Evans when over four hundred students showed up for class at once.[57] On February 4, 1902, Frederick Behner recorded a detailed account of overcrowding in his diary:

> School filled up to about fifty girls and which gives me about 75 on roll with 82 boys. Presidente [the mayor] still aids us as much as possible but we need seats very badly. Every box on the premise, all our room chairs etc. are in use now. Still there are many boys and girls so I do not know what will do if all come.
>
> The work is interesting with those who have room, and seats but certainly confusing when all are packed together like we get them.[58]

Unlike some other teachers, even when describing the difficult conditions caused by overflowing classrooms—like the lack of furniture that might hamper learning—Behner remained optimistic. He was pleased with his students' attendance, thankful for the local official's support, and noted students' interest despite the chaos.

Other Thomasites, including Harrie Cole, were often less enthusiastic. Concerned about the unruliness of an overcrowded classroom—allegedly packed with over 235 students—Harrie complained of an unhealthy environment and described how dirt from the room above his fell through the cracked ceiling, creating dusty air in the overpacked room.[59] Other potential health hazards involved students spitting on the floor or blowing their noses without handkerchiefs, a habit described by several teachers. As Glen Evans wrote in August 1904, only a few days into the term, "Am trying to teach kids to stop spitting and blowing their noses out the windows."[60] Further distractions in the classroom involved animals. Fee recalled, "The school was popular not only with boys but with goats," and she soon learned that it would cause fewer disruptions in class to allow the goats to wander in and out than try to keep them outside.[61] Clearly, the school facilities and norms that Thomasites faced in the archipelago were vastly different than those most had been accustomed to stateside. For some this was overwhelming, and for others this was all part of the adventure.[62]

Mary Cole and students, Palo, Leyte, Philippines, circa 1902. Mary presides over
an orderly all-female Western-style classroom, equipped with desks in rows and
textbooks on students' desks. Contrasting with the educational structures and
resources many American teachers found inadequate, this photograph depicts
Filipina students under the direction of a white American teacher, underscoring US
authority and purported "benevolence" on the islands. (Harry Newton Cole Papers,
Bentley Image Bank, Bentley Historical Library, University of Michigan.)

Perhaps more challenging than the physical space of the schoolhouse
was breaking students' prior learning habits. Some teachers' biggest pedagogical complaint was generally related to students' practice of studying "out
loud"—reciting passages and thoughts orally, but not in unison—although
other teachers seemed relatively unphased by such conduct.[63] Mary Fee
noted quick progress, writing that after "repeated admonition and practice
. . . the habit of studying aloud was overcome."[64] Others, including Mary
Cole, predicted in October 1901 that "it will be a long time" before such habits could be broken, although by February 1902 she boasted to family back
home, "You remember I always was fortunate enough to have good order at
school and now I have as quiet and orderly a school as I ever had at home
and have done no whipping either."[65] Here, Mary was likely referring to the
priests who had formerly served as teachers and who allegedly whipped students into submission, a practice that she condemned and apparently did
not continue. Still, other teachers, including Blaine Moore, were not as suc-

cessful. Having been in the Philippines for almost two years, Moore settled into a new teaching station in 1903 at Moncada, a village that reportedly had a "good school" the year before. Yet, in describing it to his parents he wrote:

> Unless you have seen a newly organized Filipino school you can have no idea of the lack of discipline. The scholars will get up, run around the room or out doors, laugh, talk, in fact everything contrary to discipline. They are inveterate talkers and this habit is the hardest of all to control. They will talk to their neighbors, study "out loud" and think the same way.[66]

Moore had faced such chaos before and was not thrilled to be burdened by yet another unruly classroom. Intimating that American classrooms might have a certain level of confusion, he suggested that none of these were comparable to the "lack of discipline" found in a "newly organized Filipino school." Considering the lack of seating and proper equipment, overcrowded classrooms, noise, and even goats, the chaos of teachers' first encounters with schooling in the Philippines cannot be underestimated. In a sense, the performance of empire within the colonial space of the classroom exhibited, at times, the ridiculousness of Americans' attempts to gain full authority in this vibrant foreign environment.

In addition to changing students' habits inside the classroom, the Thomasites struggled with altering village norms regarding attendance. Although some teachers initially grappled with overcrowded classrooms, maintaining students' participation over time proved difficult. Compounding this problem was the fact that American teachers were instructed to respect the Filipinos' many feast and religious holidays. Thomasites noted the high number of holidays, not fully understanding the meaning of these celebrations but ultimately respecting the natives' traditions by not holding school. However, the real problem was attrition, and several teachers resorted to engaging local law enforcement authorities to round up students or sought the mayor's help in fining families who did not send their children to school.[67]

For teachers assigned to work in one barrio, work and life in the small village sometimes became monotonous. Their days included anywhere from two to five hours of teaching, with some choosing to teach night school two or three nights a week to make extra money.[68] Despite their exotic location, several found that the days blurred from one to the next. Only five weeks into his first assignment on the islands, Harrie Cole wrote, "I find this work very monotonous trying to teach these monkeys to talk."[69] Likely frustrated with the little progress his students were making, Harrie resorted to racist name-calling, in part blaming the students for their slow English acquisition and revealing his own prejudice. Not surprisingly, he found the work uninteresting. Others found vacation days to be more tedious. Frederick Behner claimed during one holiday that "Day after day without work is truly monotonous and the only bearable thing is that our pay continues."[70] Blaine Moore felt similarly and advised his brother to stay in college back in the States rather than venture to the Philippines, in part arguing:

> This country soon becomes a most monotonous place to live in. Absolutely no entertainments or amusements of any kind. Shut up in a little 2x4 nipa shack town with no communication & no means of transportation the novelty wears off after a time and then it is what the soldiers call hell. . . . You have no reference books, no leading people of your own profession to come in contact with and you are doing well if you stand still and do not go backward. This last is especially true![71]

In addition to viewing everyday life as boring and isolating, Moore admitted that after having taught basic skills on the islands, he felt incapable of doing much else and even struggled at this. He believed his work in the Philippines to be beneath the skills of a college-educated man, and without any contact with a larger intellectual or professional community, he felt his own capabilities were greatly hampered. Like Cole, Moore revealed feeling a certain amount of superiority over his students and, more generally, to work and life on the islands. Behner, in comparison, found free time overwhelming. For all of them, the novelty of life on the islands wore off at least to a certain extent, sometimes leaving them bored.

Supervising teachers had more varied experiences, although they, too, sometimes became tired. They spent much of their time traveling between schools, trekking several hours at a minimum to visit or establish a new school in a barrio. Before being demoted back to a classroom teacher (resulting from his clash with educational authorities over his dress and seemingly overeager adaption to Filipino ways of life), Whiting traveled extensively:

> We are having rain almost every day. Sometimes I have to ride 6 or 8 kilometers (to my furthest school) and back thru the rain. I have three barrio schools and a central one. Employ 13 teachers. Have about 900 children enrolled. The clay is so slick and the mountains so steep that

the horse can hardly climb them. I can go (on horse) only about 2 miles an hour. I make one visit to each school each week.[72]

The physical rigor and independence required to hike or ride between barrios proved exhausting. Other supervising teachers had even larger territories and greater numbers of teachers and schools to manage. Harvey A. Bordner wrote to his siblings on October 15, 1905:

> To look after the schools of a province with a population of more than 223000 people with cities of 30000 people is no small job. . . . I have at present close to 200 teachers who must all be examined and licensed, hired and paid by the month. . . . To visit all the schools requires not less than two months during the year. I have already visited more than half of the schools this year but the half that are still to be visited are those situated in the more out-of-the-way places and will require more time.[73]

For those with similar responsibilities, the scope of the work was enormous and the expectations almost impossible to fulfill. Overseeing hundreds of employees and multiple schools scattered around the province required constant vigilance, leaving little time for anything but work. Needless to say, both local and supervising teachers had profound responsibilities as they worked to establish a US-style school system on the islands. For many, the concept of civilizing the Philippines by educating young people must have seemed increasingly utopian, if not hopeless.

Those teachers who lived and taught in Manila were often more optimistic about the potential for American education to transform the nation. And for some, who regularly taught in rugged outposts, the city came to represent a modest bastion of civilization, filled with white bodies and more familiar activities. Upon returning to Manila after teaching for a year on the remote island of Banton, Frederick Behner noted that the city "looked as natural as ever and it seems like civilization again to get back into a place where white faces are common and noise and bustle are all about."[74] Other Americans echoed his sentiments. After spending just over half a year working in a small village on Masbate Island, Blaine Moore visited the capital and wrote to his parents in April 1902, "I've enjoyed this week in Manila. Been resting around in all sorts of deals & things & it seems like doing something instead of being shut up with a lot of little brown kids. . . . Also saw a couple of baseball games between the army & marines & it seemed a little like civilization

Frederick Behner with Filipina teacher in Tayabas, Luzon, Philippines, circa 1904.
(Frederick G. Behner Papers, Bentley Image Bank, Bentley Historical Library,
University of Michigan.)

again."[75] Of course, a friendly game of baseball between the US Army and Marines may have mocked the idea of "civilization" for some Filipinos, who had been terrorized by their forces for the past several years, or who may have experienced racist taunts by American teachers. Significantly, for both Behner and Moore, civilization was equated to whiteness, suggesting that for them and other Thomasites, life among "brown bodies," particularly outside of the city, constituted barbarism.[76]

In addition, some Americans violated the unwritten rules prescribed by a so-called civilized life, and this plagued teachers' consciences. George Carrothers remembered:

> Gambling, drinking to excess, promiscuity everywhere and other vicious practices were so generally accepted that it was distinctly difficult not to indulge a bit occasionally. . . . Passions and emotions of white foreigners seemed to carry them to depths into which natives seldom descended. As one man put it: "When a white man goes down he goes lower than the native."[77]

No longer under watchful eyes at home, some Thomasites engaged in behaviors they would not have dreamed of doing back home, perhaps including Carrothers, having practically admitted some indulgences, at least "occasionally." Such pressures or enticements may have complicated the teachers' educational mission, as early twentieth-century American norms reinforced Victorian ideals of respectability where upholding "traditional" family and values was paramount. Such standards required a male breadwinner to oversee the household, with his wife responsible for childrearing and moral leadership.[78] In such a construct, "gambling, drinking to excess, [and] promiscuity" had no place. Years earlier, Carrothers—after being the first in his family to graduate from high school and become a teacher in rural Indiana—recalled in June 1900 that "Christianity became real and personal," as he was baptized into the First Methodist Episcopal Church in Kentland, Indiana.[79] Single when he joined the US mission in the Philippines in 1909, Carrothers was largely guided by Christian, small-town American teachings, and he held certain standards for himself and other (white) Americans. In the Philippines—outside of what he saw as the strict moral code maintained in the States—he essentially blamed the Filipino environment for causing American foreigners to stoop even "lower" than the "natives." In this way, Carrothers practically forgave "white foreigners'" indiscretions on the islands while upholding the Christian values that defined his own worldview—separating right from wrong, morality from immorality—and effectively defended the (perverse) rationale for white supremacy.

Significantly, teachers' beliefs regarding race and respectability also affected their choices regarding the extent to which they engaged in or avoided intimate relationships with Filipinos. In April 1908, J. W. Cheesborough, then living in Manila, received a letter from former teaching colleague Isaac Adams, then an assistant attorney in the Philippines Bureau of Justice, who had recently visited their "old district" in Batangas. Adams wrote:

> Your friend Señora Catalina and her two tall daughters are still in waiting, and when you come back I think you had better go down there and enjoy some of the good things of life that you are missing on account of your present abstemious habits. . . . It is a confounded pity that you have so much race prejudice and are so high-toned; otherwise you could come back and dance your life away with one of Catalina's tall daughters, and you would have the best mother in law in the world.[80]

Although the letter's playful tone suggests that Adams was only half serious, it suggests that some teachers held to certain standards of respectability—including not dancing, particularly with people of color—while others, including perhaps Adams himself, bent such rules. While most American teachers ultimately blamed the negative influences of Filipinos for their own or their colleagues' uncivilized behavior, Adams's letter, together with Carrothers's reminiscences, suggests that racist views of Filipinos perhaps had as much to do with some teachers' choices as their concerns with maintaining respectability.[81]

Although racist beliefs certainly clouded many American teachers' views of morality, some admitted more freely to being burdened by preconceptions of proper behavior, including whether they should participate in local social events like Filipino dances, or *bailes*. Some teachers rarely gave in to temptation or altogether resisted it. Several described these dances held in the local barrios, and some chose to participate. John Early remembered that in the town of Old Cervantes, "Nearly every week there was a baile in the Provincial Building, at which many Ilocanos [local people] and Americans assembled," although he recalled a group of US teachers choosing not to partake in the fun.[82] Yet for many teachers, life in the Philippines offered opportunities unavailable or seen as improper at home. On December 13, 1902, Frederick Behner wrote in his diary about a big dance with over one hundred people, including Americans from other villages, where he "danced for the first time in my life. First trial a failure but second, with Bacilia, went a little better."[83] Back in the States, Behner had never set foot on a dance floor, but in the Philippines he felt freer to participate in such festivities.[84]

Beyond dancing, most teachers avoided confessing what were considered much graver missteps: sexual indiscretions. Instead, like Carrothers and Adams, several teachers reported the promiscuity of others or the temptations they resisted. One teacher, Jules T. Frelin, sometimes used code in his diary or wrote with purposefully vague language in detailing relations with local women. On September 10, 1901, he asked, "Will God forgive a man whose repentance is brought about only by a corporal fear of hell.—In tropical countries a girl becomes a woman at thirteen, like a plant which buds at night and blooms the following morning." Three months later he pondered, "Do you think your daughter can change lovers as easily as she changes dresses—Gross hand were playing with her heart ignorant of the delicacy of its fibers."[85] Whether Frelin was referring to his own or other Americans' sexual exploits, US teachers clearly did engage in improprieties.[86] In fact, some reportedly had families with Filipino women despite having wives and families back in the States. As recorded by Behner in June 1904, "Just the other day Mr. Molvor told me his story of how a teacher in whom he had confidence, and whom his daughter tho't single had outraged his daughter only to tell her that since he already had a wife in America it would be impossible for him to allay or soothe her troubles by a wedding."[87] Some teachers held contempt for fellow countrymen who violated norms of "civilization," although they often viewed these as isolated events—not representative of broader US cultural failings.

In contrast, some teachers pointed to examples of Filipino sexual indiscretions as indicative of a largely backward culture, condemning Filipino men, women, and in at least one case, the Catholic clergy. Writing to his brother in May 1902, Harvey Bordner noted, "Talking about the catholic priests, they are certainly a lot of fakes," and then went on to list complaints regarding their purportedly tenuous loyalty to the US mission. He then elaborated:

> and if the bride is good looking or if the bride arouses the passions of the priest, he tells the groom that the first child should have a spiritual parentage or in other words should be a child of a priest the groom

submits with pride and lets the priest sleep with the bride for the first night. Again the priests usually has two or sometimes half a dozen women living in the same house to furnish satisfaction for his beastly passions. When any of these women become pregnant they are sent to their homes and the father of the woman raises the child as a child of God. I know that these stories are so base and sound so vile that no American is willing to believe them, however I have seen enough and saw enough of these Godly children that I know what I am saying when I write these things.[88]

For Bordner, all parties involved in alleged illicit cases of sexual relations were to blame. He condemned priests and their polygamous cohorts, Filipino brides and grooms, and Filipino fathers, as well as the resultant "Godly children," all to underscore what he saw as evidence of Filipino—particularly Catholic—depravity. Whether coerced, compliant, or somewhere in-between, Bordner criticized Filipino women and men for their ignorant participation in such relations, though he held priests chiefly accountable, vilifying them for abusing power to purportedly satisfy their own "beastly" pleasure. Although no other teachers recount such detailed condemnations of the priesthood, several suggest either mistrust of priests or the Catholic Church more generally, reflecting broader white Protestant distrust of Catholicism, a belief that predominated well into the twentieth century.[89] And, as noted earlier, other Thomasites alluded to the apparent promiscuity and allure of Filipino "natives," blaming white American men to varying degrees. Ultimately, for those Americans who believed that a traditional family structure grounded in monogamous marriage was sacred and foundational to society, Filipinos' indiscretions—whether with a priest or those living in an unsanctified relationship—indicated that the possibilities for developing a robust civilization on the islands were fraught.

In fact, teachers' writings abound with accounts that they thought proved Filipino incivility and backwardness, sometimes rationalizing accusations with vehement, racially charged language. Their charges included laziness, thievery, uncleanliness, and promiscuity.[90] For example, toward the end of her three years in the Philippines, Mary Cole fumed in a letter to her mother, "Our cook was such an old thief. . . . But these people are just like the niggers. They got to steal for some how it seems to [be] born in 'em. I knew he was stealing a little all along but tho't we'd just put up with it if he didn't go too far and get to stealing commissaries again."[91] Here, Mary extended her charges of thievery against her servant to the entire Filipino population—and simultaneously condemned all African Americans—believing that race somehow explained depraved actions like stealing. Moreover, she admitted to expecting deceitful behavior from people whom she considered to be lower on a racial hierarchy, presuming her mother to be of a like mind. Although Mary's words might simply reflect a fit of rage or extreme frustration, her racist intent is undeniable. Similarly hate-filled rants fill several pages of her letters home and personal diary, exhibiting what seems to be an almost constant flow of racist thoughts as she largely struggled through her years in the Philippines.

In fact, several teachers' racist beliefs intensified over the course of their work on the islands, though for some, such race-based fears may have subsided decades later. Although Norman Cameron noted the lessening of civilized behavior as early as his cross-country trip to meet the USS *Thomas* in July 1901, diary entries during his time in the Philippines increasingly referred to Filipinos with racial epithets, including "googoo" and "nigger."[92] His earliest usage of the term "googoo" described Filipino rebels who attacked or killed American soldiers, but later on Cameron employed the racial slur to describe Filipino civilians as well.[93] He used "nigger" more sparingly in his diaries, in one instance resorting to the term to describe the individual who killed his supervisor.[94] Other Thomasites similarly used hateful language in situations where they felt afraid or to emphasize what they perceived as fundamental differences between themselves and others, including Mary and Harrie Cole, whose racist language will be further discussed below. Another example involved Thomasite Walter Marquardt, who by 1934 may have had a change of heart. Upon discovering a 1902–1903 diary, he acknowledged that in the intervening decades his "view point on a number of things mentioned" had dramatically changed. Still, he chose to preserve his decades-old thoughts by transcribing some diary extracts "verbatim." In a September 30, 1902, entry, Marquardt wrote that US soldiers on the island of Samar "found dead googoos in every shape, one trench had them four deep covered with canvas cots," before suggesting that Filipino insurgents who fought back were largely incapable of inflicting damage upon the American troops. In the transcription, the word "googoo" is crossed out in pencil and written above it the word, "Filipinos." Though it is unclear who or when such revisions were attempted, perhaps it was Marquardt himself, who years later was shocked by his own account. Whatever the case, his and other Thomasites' racism undoubtedly shaped their everyday interactions with Filipinos as well as the larger US educational mission. In these and other cases, teachers rationalized their anger and anxiety concerning both real and imagined threats of Filipino attacks or to explain what they viewed as the backward ways of Filipinos.[95]

Other teachers wrote more directly about a racial hierarchy, contrasting white superiority with Filipino inferiority. For example, in March 1903, Blaine Moore questioned the effectiveness of policies that sought to govern a "half civilized Oriental race" in the same ways as "an American or European white race," believing Filipinos not yet ready for a "civilized" rule of law.[96] A few months later, Moore wrote to his parents how he and his white colleagues had to demonstrate "an endless amount of patience and shrewdness" to determine whether a Filipino's actions or words were sincere, as he, like others, attributed a certain level of deceitfulness to the entire race.[97]

Having taught just over a year in the islands, Harrie Cole had also come to believe that Filipinos' intellectual capacity was inferior to whites. Exposing his frustrations, Harrie rationalized in a letter to his mother:

Anglo-Saxons have, with the greater capacity, struggled for hundreds and thousands of years to attain the present imperfect standard of government. How can we expect a colored race with the baser natures and the natural tendencies to evil, to attain without years and years, or even generations, of training, even to a crude imitation of a good form of government?[98]

Here, Harrie naturalized Filipinos' abilities, placing this "colored race" well below the standard that he argued Anglo-Saxons had achieved, however "imperfectly." With this bias in mind, he questioned the entire policy of "benevolent assimilation" as an effective way of transforming a people, at least within a reasonable amount of time. Yet, the same prejudice ironically justified imperial expansion. Such debased people as Filipinos, Harrie assumed, desperately needed a more experienced, superior hand to guide the way to civility. His belief in white superiority only strengthened over the course of his term in the Philippines.[99] In October 1903 he wrote to his mother, "When I get home, I want to forget about this country and people about as soon as possible. I shall probably hate the sight of anything but a white man the rest of my life (and some of these are none too lovable)."[100] By the following April he explained how he thought he had changed since he had last seen his mother, admitting without any remorse, "I guess there is not much change only in my pride for our own race as compared with others—and I really do not think that is *bad* in itself."[101]

Of course, exacerbating teachers' racial bias was the fact that they had been deployed in a war zone. Over their years in the Philippines, teachers felt threatened by the violence around them, particularly in remote parts of the archipelago. They largely worked within an extremely hostile environment, as US military and civilian authorities both instituted and rationalized the violence that plagued the islands. For example, in September 1901, just as the majority of Thomasites were settling into their new homes, a particularly gruesome massacre occurred on the island of Samar when Filipino insurgents attacked US soldiers mourning the recent assassination of President McKinley. But US military retaliation proved extreme: American soldiers were authorized to kill without orders, shoot Filipino boys over ten years of age, kill wounded Filipinos, and attack Filipinos even as they surrendered. US soldiers plundered towns, established concentration camps, and confined prisoners to overcrowded jails. Scattered reports of such violence reached Washington, DC, and by January 1902 Congress launched hearings to investigate the ongoing war in the Philippines. Soon after, military tribunals tried officers accused of operating outside the rules of war. The hearings and trials revealed further horrors on the islands and the general acceptance of such brutality by nonmilitary personnel. Significantly, the education director in the Philippines, David Barrows, testified at the hearings. He defended use of the "water cure" to elicit information from prisoners of war, minimized the inhumanity of concentration camps, and suggested that Filipinos ultimately benefited from the war.[102] Barrows was not alone in making such justifications; missionaries on the islands similarly defended the morality of torture. Unfortunately, the hearings did not lead to the end of fighting or acts of inhumanity in the archipelago. Even as President Theodore Roosevelt declared the war officially over on July 4, 1902, the US military was planning an offensive on the island of Mindanao. Indeed, the violence continued for several more years.[103]

For many teachers, the responsibilities of educating students and supervising schools was often overshadowed by the reality of ongoing, brutal military violence. The majority of the thirty-three teachers examined here discussed the threat of violence in diary entries and in letters home to loved ones. A third of the teachers wrote extensively about the violence while several others discussed it briefly, perhaps so as not to worry friends and family members back home. For some, especially those in volatile areas, the violence consumed their lives. While others did not seem as concerned, everyone was aware of the ongoing conflict.

US-Philippine hostilities greatly hampered the Thomasites' work, affecting their lives and sense of well-being. Among the pioneer teachers, the

Coles certainly faced one of the most frightening situations. Early on, Mary Cole found the military conflict overwhelming, likely worsening her racial opinions. Within a few weeks after arriving in Palo on the island of Leyte, Mary recorded in her diary that she heard that ten American soldiers had been killed on the nearby island of Samar. The next day, she reported that officers' wives had been ordered to leave the islands of Leyte and Samar and to seek safety in Manila, including the only other white woman in her town, the wife of Lieutenant Eames. On October 28 Mary admitted, "We are very much worried to day about the state of affairs here," and two weeks later she noted her concerns yet again. Her husband had returned home late from a walk to the seashore, and she "tho't the bolomen had found him maybe."[104] When US soldiers left for another station on December 9, the Coles were the only Americans who remained in Palo. Writing in her diary three weeks later, Mary confessed, "I do feel sorry for the home folks, not knowing but any time we may be killed but it seems very peaceable about here now."[105] Not knowing where the next violent outbreak would occur, Mary lived in almost constant fear that she or her husband would be among the targets.

Although Mary's husband Harrie experienced similar threats of violence, he reacted very differently to the instability of their surroundings. Whereas Mary frequently expressed her anxiety and fear, an almost relentless sense of worry, Harrie positioned himself offensively. In June 1902—less than a year into his three-year teaching contract in the archipelago—he unapologetically confessed in a letter to his mother and brother, "And I guess it is a good thing I am not a soldier, for I am afraid I should shoot every 'dirty nigger' I should come across if I were out on a 'hike.' Too many American lives have already been sacrificed to the treachery of these people."[106] Revealing the immense stress that living amid such omnipresent violence brought, Harrie expressed his absolute terror using racially charged, hateful language. While Mary repeatedly confessed to feeling afraid, she did not suggest she developed any fantasies about participating in violence herself. Harrie, however, imagined that if he were more directly involved in the warfare, he would kill Filipinos indiscriminately. A year into his contract, his letters increasingly disclosed his anxiety as he tried to deal with his own emotions in a severely unstable foreign environment. He coped through fantasies of manly strength where he aggressively protected himself and his wife through brute force.

While Harrie only imagined taking up arms, Norman Cameron ultimately engaged in military-style missions to kill insurgents. As early as October 15,

1901—just over a week after his first day of teaching in the Philippines—Cameron wrote, "I find that a gun and one man has been able to go—almost anywhere in the islands. But beware of these people at night,—at least for the present."[107] A month later, Cameron recounted, "Went to Dauis loaded to kill, one Ives-Johnson and one Colts Model 96 and 60 rounds of ammunition or more."[108] Two days before Christmas, he rejoiced that the *insurrectos* had surrendered, and it was "a red-letter day."[109] Yet, at the end of January 1902 he lamented, "Well, if I go by the board, I want to empty my gun into the carcass of some Filipinos. . . . If I am killed here, I shall feel contented that I have not died in vain, but that I have fallen trying to do my duty."[110] Certainly American teachers in the Philippines were not expected to engage in armed conflict, which had the potential to undermine the goal of using education to pacify and civilize Filipinos. Yet Cameron believed that arming himself was necessary for survival. Feeling his life threatened, he not only visualized himself brutally killing Filipinos as a measure of self-defense but also carried the weapons to do so.

Like Cameron, Glen Evans armed himself and joined the fight against the Filipino rebels. Years after the 1901 bloodshed on Samar, the island continued to experience great violence, ultimately overwhelming Evans's tenure from August 1904 through May 1905. On the same day that Evans reported opening his school in the town of Barongau—August 1, 1904—he also noted the killing of twenty-seven men, women, and children by the insurgents a week earlier in a nearby town. Thus, from his first day teaching in the Philippines, he was on guard, aware of the violence surrounding him as Filipino rebels threatened the village. He recorded other accounts of violence in his diary during his first month in Barongau and on August 30 received word from then head superintendent for schools in the Philippines, David P. Barrows, that "No more teachers will be sent out till the trouble is over."[111]

Feeling further isolated and increasingly at risk of losing his life, Evans took up arms less than a month after his arrival. On September 22 he desperately reported: "Three bands riflemen burning coast towns north and south. . . . Many natives killed & prisoners. Entire barrios deserting to poulahaus [Filipino insurgent groups]. Situation grave & alarming. Immediate assistance urgent."[112] That evening Evans armed himself and joined fifty bolomen volunteers to intercept the approaching rebels. Over the next several months he recorded several incidents where he participated in fighting, capturing, and sometimes killing men, women, and children. In one such incident on October 1, he wrote that he and a friend saw a boat with five people approaching them in the river. He loaded his Winchester shotgun, the people in the boat jumped overboard, and, "We opened up on them and got them all. 2 boys 3 men."[113] While the US military had been ordered to kill boys as young as age ten, teachers were not soldiers. Glen Evans expressed no regret for having helped shoot and kill two boys and three men. He lasted less than a year at his post, likely traumatized by the violence of his surroundings and the practical abandonment of US education authorities. The US government's stated policy of "benevolent assimilation" did not intend for Thomasites to engage in military combat. Still, some teachers—like Cameron and Evans—used guns to defend themselves or their villages, and only books when conditions permitted.

Other teachers armed themselves but did not engage directly in fighting. Throughout his tenure in the islands, Blaine Moore noted the proximity of military violence to where he lived and considered it a necessity to have guns. Stationed on the island of Catangan in January 1902, Moore wrote to his parents, "Scarcely a day goes by now but we can hear the gun boats throwing shells into Samar."[114] In August 1902 he specified the guns he procured for self-defense in a letter to his brother: "I have two revolvers now. One is a handy .38 double action Colt's used by the army officers. The other is a .45 Colt's and is an old gun. Believe us I guess we can protect ourselves."[115] Reading Moore's tone here is difficult; it is not clear whether he believed that he could effectively defend himself given his dismissive "I guess," but it is clear that he felt the need to arm himself as a measure of protection. Among items Moore believed essential in the Philippines, he listed a shotgun and ammunition as well as a revolver, "almost a necessity here," in a January 1903 letter to his brother.[116] A month later Moore wrote to his parents and explained why he felt the need to be armed, detailing a story of insurgents raiding a nearby town. Although he recognized the real threat of violence, he also poked fun at some Americans' overreaction given the presence of local police, US soldiers, and guns in every American household in the town:

> It's rather peculiar and amusing too to note the effect of this [the recent raid] on the Americans. Lamb the treasurer got a rifle from the military and always carries a big six shooter stuffed in his pants. Leperd the provincial doctor won't go out of the house without a six shooter strapped on him. This is all nonsense here in town for with the American soldiers, the constabulary, and every civilian American in town with two or three guns in his house there will be no ladrone [insurgent] attack here.

A man that carries a gun in sight in town in the day time only invites ridicule from the natives.[117]

After laughing at the nervous Americans in his village, Moore then reconsidered his audience and assured his parents, "Don't worry about this Ladrone business, I'm safe enough."[118] While Moore saw at least some humor in living with other civilians amid a military conflict, he, too, chose to arm himself, although perhaps not as ostentatiously.

Other teachers dealt with threats of violence without arming themselves. Female Thomasites seem to have remained largely unarmed: whereas their male counterparts usually owned a gun—whether for protection or sport—women teachers never suggested in their letters and diaries that they did.[119] Instead, they largely relied upon native or US guards for protection. Writing from Tanauan, a town close to Alice Hollister's station at Dagami, Walter Marquardt reported on the violence that threatened both himself and Hollister. On July 20, 1901, he wrote, "NO American goes from town to town without an armed escort. The towns are safe but these bolo men are unknown quantities."[120] As the only American woman in a remote outpost, Hollister faced dangers similar to those of her colleagues elsewhere. Indeed, she may have been more vulnerable given rebel outrage at US soldiers who killed women and children. A couple of years later, Marquardt and Hollister married, and violence continued to affect their lives, in one case frightening Alice in particular. On February 17, 1903, Walter Marquardt reported that an unknown person rang the "church bell at 9 P.M. [and] [s]ix police jumped out of tribunal tore across plaza like mad, (yelling) and . . . Alice thought pulahans had entered sure."[121] Thus, a year and a half into her tenure, Alice remained on guard, still fearful of the possibility of attack even with the presence of local law enforcement, not to mention her husband. Although Walter Marquardt sometimes carried a gun, he learned through the experiences of colleagues that it could increase the danger since Filipinos might attack you to capture the weapons.[122] Carrothers learned the same lesson. In an interview, he discussed the violence that continued to rampage the island of Samar in 1909 and explained, "One day to a Filipino teacher way up in the mountains in Mugton, I said: 'The constabulary think I ought to carry a gun. What do you think about it?' He said, 'If I were you, I wouldn't. The Filipinos are not allowed to have guns. They'd see you with the gun and they might kill you to get your gun.'"[123] For his own safety, Carrothers took this local teacher's advice and decided never to carry a weapon.

Whether or not teachers chose to arm themselves against the threat of

Filipino insurgents, several Thomasites came to regret the brutality perpe-trated by US soldiers. Even teachers who had directly engaged in or imag-ined combat criticized their country's use of torture to defeat the Filipino insurgency. Over time, teachers became increasingly aware that certain US military officers were known for their expertise in extracting information from Filipinos by using unsavory methods and taught others how to do the same. Desperate to obtain hints of the next attack, American soldiers used the "water-cure" and other forms of abuse on Filipino insurgents and civilians alike. While some US soldiers disapproved of and reported such heinous acts themselves, officers and soldiers were rarely held accountable for such actions.[124]

The US military's practice of torturing Filipino prisoners sickened many teachers, causing some to doubt whether any Americans on the islands could appear "civilized" in light of such barbaric behavior. In January 1902 the Coles spoke at length with a Filipino priest who had endured five days of torture. Harrie, who often used racist language to describe the Filipinos, nonetheless wrote, "The prisoners of Samar, and especially the padres, were given the 'water cure'—and this term ought to bring the blush of shame to the face of every American. . . . I have seen the terrible mutilations with my own eyes, as has Mary."[125] In separate accounts, Harrie and Mary described the terrible sores on the priest's neck and wrists, the awful bruises on his body, and the steps of the "water-cure" in detail. They also recounted how soldiers had cut the cord under the priest's tongue and refused him food. Mary wrote in her diary, "It isn't civilized warfare when the[y] act like sav-ages. If they were to judge the American people as a race from the soldiers, they must surely think we are their inferiors. . . . It makes my blood boil when I think that any American would do such a thing. It is a disgrace to the Nation."[126] Seeing the bruises and cuts of torture firsthand disturbed the Coles, who certainly had no idea when they left US soil that they would become witnesses to such brutality. To know that such cruelty was wrought by American hands shook their worldview and pointed to profound imper-fections and, at times, the desperation of imperial authority.

Later that year, Norman Cameron also questioned the efficacy of such vicious methods. In October 1902 he wrote in detail about techniques of torture and reported, "Learned the 'water-cure' as applied to Googoos to force their secrets from them. . . . I would not put much dependence in the information thus extracted. . . . The ways of extracting information are vari-ous and severe."[127] Although Cameron had used guns in self-defense, dem-onstrating that he was hardly a pacifist, he doubted that American methods of torture were necessary or worthwhile. Even as he readily adopted racist terminology in referring to the native population, his negative views about Filipinos did not lead him to believe that they deserved such abuse or that it would be productive. He, too, recognized the flaws of such tactics, if not the entire "benevolent" endeavor.

Beyond the devastation wrought by man-made violence, disease further threatened teachers' lives and their work, adding yet another layer to the fragility of empire. Prior to arriving on the islands, the Thomasites were aware of the risks that foreign viruses might pose. In fact, the idea that tropical places were ridden with disease and that white people were more susceptible to such illnesses was, in part, the reason that members of the Philippine Commission investigated the mountain region of Baguio as early as August 1900 to consider "the possibility of establishing a 'summer resort' for people living in the lowlands."[128] A retreat was soon built there and attended by many Americans, including teachers, throughout the US occupation of the islands. Many visited Baguio for respite from the oppressive heat and to attend teacher conferences.[129] While hysteria caused some whites to fear the tropics in general, disease proved to be a devastating reality in the Philippine Islands, killing Filipinos and Americans alike.[130] Moreover, the prevalence of a wide variety of illnesses required teachers to engage in work well outside of their educational expertise. During the worst of the epidemics, US authorities officially recruited teachers to engage in sanitation work. At other times, teachers tended their sick colleagues and Filipino neighbors, while others faced disease alone.

As with military violence, teachers faced the threat of disease from the very beginning of their stay in the Philippines.[131] For Mary and Harrie Cole, the onslaught of disease seemed relentless and became almost commonplace, yet they did not accept it as a given but blamed education authorities for their slow and inadequate response. Only a few weeks after their arrival in Palo in fall 1901, Mary wrote home that "funerals occur every day or so."[132] By January, Mary was losing count. In writing about the low attendance at school in a letter home late that month, she explained, "Our attendance is not so large now as there is so much sickness in town. There were 7 funerals Fri; a half doz or more Sat., and 10 yesterday. I don't know how many to day [sic]."[133] While Mary initially blamed consumption for the high mortality, by January 1902 smallpox had invaded the region, perhaps brought by Americans. By mid-February, the scourge seemed so ordinary that even after one of Mary's students told her that she would no longer be able to attend school because her entire family was infected with smallpox, Mary wrote, "At home I would have been scared to death to have had such a thing happen but here we seem to think nothing about it."[134] With the death toll from smallpox sharply rising—a priest in Palo having counted eighty dead from smallpox, and forty-five more from other maladies in the month of January alone—the provincial governor of Leyte had ordered the local mayor to quarantine those exposed to the disease.[135] Yet, to Harrie and Mary's dismay, Superintendent Sherman ordered schools in Palo to remain open into March even though elsewhere—including in Tanauan, where Alice Hollister taught—schools were closed on account of smallpox.[136] This irresponsible decision astounded Harrie, who expressed his rage at the carelessness with which American civilian leaders in the Philippines treated the needs of teachers, ignoring the most basic precautions for their safety.[137] In early March, Harrie's fears were realized when he fell ill with a fever and general aches and pains. Fortunately, he recovered, only to hear by the end of the month that cholera had made its way into Manila and killed thirteen people.[138]

Although the smallpox epidemic closed some schools and not others, the spread of cholera in the spring of 1902 forced more widespread school closures, quarantines, and rigorous sanitation efforts. As with smallpox, cholera devastated the Filipino community and caused great stress among teachers, even taking some lives. By May 1902 both Tanauan and Palo had been quarantined to help prevent the spread of the disease.[139] In June Harrie revealed a sense of despair in a letter to his family, writing, "If we all keep well, and Mary and I return with good health and our pockets full of money, we may not be sorry that we came, at least I hope that all will be well."[140] A few days later, he tried to reassure them, explaining how they disinfected the house, boiled water, and regularly saw a visiting doctor to be sure that the town was following orders to keep things sanitary.[141] For the Coles, their first year in the Philippines proved extremely challenging, with the threat of death very real to them, and from multiple sources. And while they longed to keep in close contact with loved ones at home, they did not want to cause them unnecessary anxiety. As for so many teachers in the Philippines, figuring out how to communicate honestly about the threat of disease without creating panic back home was difficult.

Some Thomasites seemed genuinely less fearful of cholera and other diseases and were careful to reassure family members of their safety, some more delicately than others. In May 1902 Blaine Moore wrote to his parents from Manila:

There is but little or any danger from cholera here to an American who lives right. There have only been about a half dozen Americans die and these were either disreputable fellows living with the natives or else become [sick] while working for the sanitation Dept. in the dirty infected districts. Of course I wouldn't go on the Sanitary force unless I had a clean district to work in. Hardly think I shall any way though I would like something to help pay expenses.[142]

Here, Moore claimed to be living "right," away from the filth of disease and sin. Unlike his "disreputable" counterparts whom, he implied, succumbed to the disease for living too closely, even intimately, with Filipinos, Moore presented himself as a more moral, careful, clean man. In this way he conflated disease and morality, refusing to admit that cholera could infect anyone. He also refused to risk his life by joining other teachers who worked for the sanitation department in regions contaminated by the disease, despite the additional pay. In spite of Moore's seemingly cavalier stance on disease, he still took precautions and tried to minimize his exposure.

Ralph Taylor, living in the town of San Fernando on the island of Union in August of 1902, also took special care to not worry his mother about disease on the islands. Indeed, he voiced a rather optimistic perspective. Rather than focusing on the deaths from cholera that he had witnessed in his own pueblo and neighboring barrios—which came "as close as our second door neighbor"—Taylor emphasized the "very social time" he and his colleagues were having on account of the schools being closed. They played games, sang college songs, engaged in "general rough house," and had great discussions.[143] Taylor opened a subsequent letter, "I hope you are not worrying about what I said as to cholera someweeks [sic] ago: if I haven't mentioned it in a later letter it is because there was nothing doing."[144] A year later, in April 1903, Taylor explained that a smallpox epidemic prevented the American teachers from being able to hold their classes for native teachers.[145] Although the extent of the disease in his experience was probably similar to that of other teachers in the Philippines, he seems to have deliberately limited candor on this issue in his letters home. In sharp contrast to the Coles's fear and Moore's cynicism, Taylor's letters consistently reflected his love for the islands, work, and life in general—in spite of risks like disease.[146]

Not surprisingly, some teachers were personally afflicted by disease and wrote about it extensively. Frederick Behner suffered from bouts of "Breakbone Fever" (dengue fever), terrible headaches, and dysentery during his first year on the islands.[147] Sometimes illness forced him to stay home from teaching, though other times he managed to work through his aches and pains and was recruited to help limit the spread of disease while tending many other duties. In September 1902, just into his second year of teaching, Behner declared, "To be Dr., teacher, Sanitary officer, and do the work of insp of cargo and papers of boats is too much."[148] Still, having witnessed almost one hundred deaths in his small village due to cholera that fall, he accepted the increased responsibilities. One of two Americans in town, he had been asked to take on tasks akin to a health official—deciding which boats to quarantine, how best to promote good hygiene, how to assist local villagers suffering illness and injury—all while continuing his official obligations to the school. By mid-December, Behner wrote in his diary, "Am getting as strong as I was before I had the cholera and enjoy my food again."[149] Apparently, having worked to protect his Philippine village from the worst that an outbreak of cholera could bring, he had succumbed to the disease himself.

Harvey Bordner also suffered personally from profound illness. Although he claimed perfect health for his first six months on the islands, Bordner wrote home to his brother in February 1903, "Yes the holiday season is passed and mine were spent in the hospital under strict quarantine. . . . Of course I am out now and am perfectly well and sound. I was in the hospital about 49 days but at present I weigh 190 lbs so you can imagine that I must be feeling rather well."[150] A couple of months later, he clarified the nature of his illness: "While I was in Nampicuan or in Anao I was exposed to smallpox, which kept me off duty for forty-eight [sic] days, beginning with the 12th of December 1902."[151] While most American teachers in the Philippines did not contract serious illnesses like cholera or smallpox, some did. Most of these teachers survived, some were sent home, and others died. Yet, even if they were not directly afflicted, teachers felt suffocated at times by the omnipresence of such diseases.

When not ill themselves, Thomasites also spent much of their time nursing one another back to health, sometimes at great risk. As the only two Americans in the region, Behner and Blakeslee regularly tended to one another's health needs. They sat by one another's bedside and procured medicines, until a serious illness forced Blakeslee to head back to the States in the fall of 1902. Other friends and loved ones also assisted one another. In May 1902, Alice Hollister's fiancée, Walter Marquardt, had been hospitalized for a high fever due to dengue fever before she, too, contracted the disease.[152] By July, Alice was the fifth American teacher that the Coles knew who was taken ill with dengue. Harrie and Mary were reluctant to visit

Alice while she was ill, afraid that they would be at greater risk of infection, though they ultimately heeded her request and went to Tanauan to assist her.[153] Six months later Walter was hospitalized again, and after returning home he experienced a high fever—perhaps another bout of dengue.[154] Thus, for some teachers, the onset of disease seemed relentless, requiring constant vigilance and care.

Other Thomasites lived too remotely to receive help from their colleagues. Carrothers recalled suffering alone from severe illnesses like dengue fever or amoebic dysentery: "I had to 'doctor' myself and suffer the excruciating pains alone. . . . Occasionally in those days I wrote in my diary, 'This may be the last.' . . . 'If I die now as young as I am I will have accomplished very little in life.'"[155] For those serving alone in very rural parts of the islands, illness clearly threatened teachers' emotional as well as physical well-being.

In addition to doctoring themselves, American teachers helped Filipinos who suffered from illness and injury, sometimes at a significant cost. As Carrothers recounted regarding Samar, "About 400,000 people and no doctor anywhere. The primitive conditions were worse than anybody can conceive unless they've been through such themselves. . . . When children were injured or got hurt in some way, they called on the American teacher to doctor them."[156] Other teachers, including Behner and Blakeslee, also discussed the high level of medical assistance that they were unofficially asked to undertake. In January 1902, Behner recounted, they "were called to the side of a young man who had dropped from a mountain and whose head was badly broken besides internal injuries. We dressed his wounds as best we could but chances are he is not long for this world."[157] A few weeks later he wrote, "All this month we have had from 2 to 6 calls to help the sick, each day. We charge nothing for tis God's cause, but it costs us quite a little."[158] Though teachers did not charge for their medical services, the cost of procuring medicines and treatment added up, both economically and emotionally. To some, it seemed that the same people who sought their help at other times wished them gone. In many ways, teachers were both feared and revered: feared, as they resembled US soldiers who ravaged their country and represented an occupying force, and revered for their knowledge, skills, and access to greater resources.

Even less predictable than an outbreak of military violence or disease, environmental crises, too, wreaked havoc on the islands, further demonstrating the education mission's vulnerabilities. Although several teachers reported mild earthquakes—that they either slept through or that barely shook the ground—the greater threat was the typhoon. Several teachers described a particularly bad storm in September 1905, characterized by Harvey Bordner as a "terrible typhoon which caused a great loss of life and wrought considerable damage to property and the crops."[159] Another time, Walter Marquardt recalled that when transporting Filipino teachers to the Normal Institute during "typhoon season, a severe storm came up and a number of teachers were so frightened they ran from one side of the boat to the other. . . . In spite of their fear they obeyed me and the boat weathered the typhoon."[160] Perhaps Marquardt exaggerated his heroism, as Filipinos would have been more accustomed to weathering such storms. Still, American teachers had witnessed destructive weather back in the United States, although few had experienced a storm of this type and severity. Moreover, they felt particularly vulnerable in the Philippines—isolated and far from modern conveniences to help in a recovery.

Mary Fee suggested that worse than any storm, disease, or war was famine. This chapter began with Fee's characterization of teachers' work as "building a nation in a strange land."[161] Thus, it is fitting to return to her account of the many obstacles that she and other teachers faced in the islands. She wrote:

> If we lived in a slightly hysterical state as concerns the possibilities of war and bloodshed, we soon learned to be phlegmatic enough about disease and pestilence. Nearly five hundred starving people had gathered in Capiz, and their emaciated bodies and cavernous eyes mocked all talk of the brotherhood of man. . . . A certain Capiz politician with his eyes on the future caused word to be sent out through the province that if the needy would come into Capiz he would see that they were fed. Of course he did no such thing. They came and starved to death; but meanwhile the report of his generosity was spread abroad.[162]

Acknowledging the profound fear she and her countrymen felt due to war and disease, Fee found it even more devastating to live among people suffering from extreme hunger, especially one that seemed preventable. Alleging that a politician used people's desperation to his own advantage at the expense of human lives outraged Fee, an otherwise intrepid Thomasite. She was not the only teacher who witnessed cruelty that "mocked all talk of the brotherhood of man." In March 1902, Behner reported, "Town has been destitute of rice for a month. . . . Have learned that the Constabulary, or four of them have been forcing the country people to give them food at the point of the gun."[163] In a country where corrupt politicians ruled in the worst of times, the devastation wrought by environmental crises was too often worsened by human greed. American teachers bore witness to this and other instances of Filipino suffering and death, sometimes by the hands of their own countrymen. While they certainly realized that corruption existed in the United States and some may have wondered whether US intervention had only worsened the problem in the Philippines, they did not directly connect the US mission and Filipino corruption, at least in their memoirs and diaries.

In order to carry on, teachers like Fee emotionally detached themselves from their surroundings. To a certain extent, they allowed themselves to fear bullets and "bolos," which they could, at least theoretically, try to evade. However, the misery of such things as disease and famine, further exacerbated by inhumane acts of cruelty, at times seemed ubiquitous and overwhelming, causing American teachers to protect themselves with a kind of numbness to ease the pain. At times, the idea of teachers "building a nation" simply became impossible.

The making or breaking of empires is often discussed in terms of state actions and policies, but people are central to building and destroying them. In the case of turn-of-the-century Philippines, US officials appointed teachers to construct a Western-educated Filipino polity, re-creating an American schooling system in a land that had not fully accepted US authority. In their haste to extend the American empire into the Pacific, US decision makers underestimated the extent to which military, biological, and environmental violence continued to wreak havoc throughout the islands, not to mention the mission's own cultural and racialized violence. Thomasites witnessed this multi-tiered violence; they created, exacerbated, or remade this violence. Most of them survived it, perhaps some with emotional scars. Yet, as they faced the harsh realities of armed conflict, torture, disease, and disaster, some struggled to make their work meaningful at both a personal and political level. For others, their experiences abroad deepened their commitment to the US mission and their belief in (white) American supremacy, with several rationalizing the need for a strong hand among peoples deemed "backward." Still, some teachers managed to remain focused on their educational mission; others, understandably overwhelmed, did not. Most teachers remained in the archipelago for only a few years—or even less time—although a few spent several decades there.

In the end, the Thomasites did help to build an educational structure in the Philippines modeled on the US system, however fragile; and, in doing so, they helped extend and create the American empire. But few felt the same way about that goal at the end of their tenure as they had at the beginning. While many voiced concerns and anxieties during their time in the Philippines, it was only after they returned home that they could begin to make meaning of their time abroad, or, at the least, move on with their lives.

CHAPTER FIVE

AFTER THE(IR) SERVICE
Reflections on Imperial Education

In July 1930 former teacher and superintendent John DeHuff wrote to the commissioner of Indian affairs in hopes of returning to the Indian Service:

> I feel that there are some good special reasons why I should be considered for reinstatement. I have had twenty-five years of experience in educational work among the so-called "primitive peoples," twelve years in the Philippines and thirteen among the Indians. I feel that I have a knowledge of the Indian people and their problems. . . . It was my life work that I left; and now . . . I sincerely want to resume it and go on to the finish. I can be of real assistance to the Indian Service and the Indian people.[1]

John DeHuff and his wife, Elizabeth, had taught in the Philippines for several years before working at the Carlisle Indian Industrial School from 1914 to 1916 and then relocating to the Santa Fe Indian School, where John served as superintendent and Elizabeth likely worked as a teacher in addition to hosting painting lessons for students at their home.[2] During her time in the Southwest, Elizabeth's interest in Indian art continued, and she published several books about her students and other Indian artists' work throughout the 1920s.[3] By 1927, John left the Indian Service, in his words, "not because I wanted to, but because I felt that it was the correct thing for me to do," as he and one of the school's teachers were reported to have been in "almost constant friction."[4] After the Indian Service, John worked for the Santa Fe Chamber of Commerce and Elizabeth worked as a lecturer and instructor for Harvey Detours, teaching the couriers—in charge of driving tourists around the Santa Fe area—about the local culture, including that of the Pueblo Indians.[5] Despite John's personal and professional investment in Indian education—which he considered his "life work"—he was not reappointed to the service. In 1934 Elizabeth declined a teaching position at the Santa Fe Indian School, though she hoped to fill a new position of her own creation: as a "Supervisor of Domestic and Commercial Indian Arts and Crafts."[6] The historical record suggests that Elizabeth, like her husband, never rejoined the Indian Service.

Over the course of their careers, both John and Elizabeth claimed a deep commitment to Filipino and American Indian peoples and the US educational mission, considering themselves uniquely qualified for such work. In their letters to Indian education administrators in the 1930s, they positioned themselves as professionals equipped with an intimate understanding of their own culture's flaws and that of the Indian Service as well as Indians' needs. When John sought reinstatement in the Indian Service in 1930, he qualified the term "primitive peoples" with the phrase "so-called," so as to distance himself from such a derogatory classification, one generally promoted by white Americans.

Elizabeth similarly presented herself as different from other whites in a November 1934 letter. In it she explained her particular "interest in working with" Indians in the region and envisioned herself acting as a mediator between Indians and whites:

> It seems to me that one of the most distressing features connected with the Indians' contact with the so-called "civilization" of the White man is his lack of judgment as to what of our "culture" to adopt for himself and what to avoid. . . . I believe it is generally felt that we of the White race have made our lives too complex. . . . It seems too bad to allow these Pueblo Indians to change from a simple, happy life to one that is unhappily complicated and governed by greed of material things. . . . I would like to have frequent visits in the Indians' homes as a simple caller and friend, to become acquainted and to advise. . . . Finding out, unobtrusively, at these times their ambitions and desires, I would try indirectly and thus most effectively to convince them of what is best for them to adopt from us.[7]

Like John before her, Elizabeth expressed ambivalence about the assumptions held by most white Americans and conveyed skepticism about their attainment of "civilization." However, at the same time, she essentialized white and Indian customs, declaring her own to be overly complex and the Pueblo's as, perhaps, too simple. Moreover, while she viewed the two cultures as more different than alike—"them" and "us"—she saw herself as capable of preserving the best in both. Ultimately, both John and Elizabeth DeHuff presented themselves as experienced educators invested in the welfare of Indian peoples, likely reflecting the shift in public discourse, as the assimilationist movement fell out of favor in the late 1920s and into the 1930s.[8] As insider-outsiders to the clash of cultures between whites and Indians, the DeHuffs believed that they were peculiarly suited to continue working in the Indian Service. They sought to disrupt some of the norms and assumptions of the dominant society while improving the lives of the Pueblo, although neither was given the chance to resume such work.[9]

Teachers who worked both in the Philippines and at Carlisle often gained new perspectives on their own culture and that of others. Serving as cultural translators and mediators, many developed a unique expertise or under-standing of the world and redefined their personal and professional mis-sions. Most of these crossover teachers apparently thrived in the difficult and demanding work environments, committing their careers to the educa-tion of "conquered" or colonial peoples. Other teachers, who only served in one of these experiments, could not wait until their contract ended or another opportunity arose. Still other teachers fell somewhere in-between, with such experiences having adjusted their perspectives or career goals but otherwise not having been permanently transformed. Ultimately, whether teachers eagerly or reluctantly left the Philippine or Indian Service to pur-sue alternate vocations, most were undoubtedly influenced by their experi-ences on the islands and at Carlisle one way or the other.

Focusing on teachers' lives after they left Carlisle and the Philippines, this chapter demonstrates the significance of imperial education from the perspective of the intimate to the structural. Examining the experi-ences of crossover teachers—those who, like John and Elizabeth DeHuff, worked in both locations—reveals that despite various challenges, all five of those studied here committed their "life work" to education or Indian affairs. Other teachers committed several years to the Indian or Philippine service. Marriage also seems to have sustained several Thomasites in their efforts abroad as some couples made lifelong careers in imperial education, remaining in the Philippines for over twenty years. Others who left after their initial commitment in the archipelago made substantial contributions to their communities back home, with several pursuing higher degrees, some choosing careers inspired by their time overseas, and others, thriving in wartime situations. Former Carlisle teachers were also affected by war—especially World War I—exhibiting their patriotism and ongoing activism at home. Yet, several Carlisle faculty agitated against the Indian bureau-cracy and Indian Service authorities, while others secured alternative "for-eign" teaching positions. Whatever occupations or activities they pursued once they left the Philippine or Indian Service, many teachers—especially women—remained close friends with their former colleagues, carried their experiences into their later careers, and left behind rich if complicated legacies. Tracing these stories beyond teachers' experiences in the Philippines and Carlisle reveals their part in a much larger story of American education and empire in the early twentieth century and complicates any simple concept of these ventures as either "benevolent assimilation" or "cultural imperialism." Moreover, such an analysis depicts teaching empire as dynamic, one that changes over time and space, and a process dependent upon its many constituents who alternately expose and reinforce its strengths and vulnerabilities.

Working on multiple fronts of American empire, crossover teachers largely thought of themselves as specially qualified education experts, often glossing over the differences between the Carlisle and Philippines missions. Like John and Elizabeth DeHuff, Moses Friedman claimed to have a critically distinct perspective on Indian and Filipino education, whether in spite of or because of the scandal he endured during his last couple of years at the Pennsylvania Indian boarding school. Aware that his position as Carlisle superintendent was insecure in the months leading up to his suspension in February 1914, Friedman wrote to the Bureau of Insular Affairs seeking reappointment to the Philippine Civil Service, where he hoped to fill the vacancy left by the death of Frank White, the Philippines director of education. However, the position had already been filled.[10] Perhaps he wrote to the bureau that January because he yearned to flee the controversy at Carlisle or to escape the anti-Semitism he experienced while working there.[11] Or, perhaps he longed to return to the Philippines, genuinely missing his work in the foreign service. Whether his outreach to the bureau came out of despair, desperation, dedication, or even nostalgia, his interest in becoming the director of education in the Philippines suggests that he felt confident in his own abilities as an administrator, despite the scandal in which he was embroiled and the several years that had passed since his time in the islands.

After Friedman left Carlisle, rumors abounded regarding what happened to him. Teacher Verna Dunagan claimed that a friend of hers who taught English at Carlisle kept in touch with the Friedman family and thought they had escaped to the "Southwest someplace and established a private school for boys [from] . . . wealthy families and he made a lot of money."[12] Although Friedman did move with his wife and two daughters to New Mexico, he did not become wealthy by setting up a private school. Rather, he served as superintendent at the Anchor Ranch School for Defective Boys near Valdez until 1921 and then moved to Pocono Pines, Pennsylvania, to serve as

that town's vocational school superintendent.[13] In spite of the federal investigation into Friedman's superintendency at Carlisle, the damage done to
his career was limited. Effectively banned from the Philippine and Indian
Service, Friedman remained a school administrator. Still, the personal and
professional insults he endured undoubtedly haunted him and tainted his
legacy, as well as that of the broader experiment of imperial education.
His dismissal left teachers like Dunagan happy to avoid working under
his authority. Moreover, Friedman's disgraced leadership symbolized and
perhaps foreshadowed problems inherent in methods of assimilation as a
means of uplifting the Indian. In 1928, Lewis Meriam submitted a report
titled "The Problem of Indian Administration" to the secretary of the interior. It largely condemned the bureaucracy and "frankly and unequivocally
[noted] that the provisions for the care of the Indian children in boarding
schools are grossly inadequate."[14]

Although Friedman found some success at two schools following Carlisle, his former employees did not fare as well, at least initially. Fernando
Tranbarger, who had also taught in the Philippines, and his wife, Katharine, left Carlisle in large part due to their mistrust of Superintendent Friedman. They believed he held a personal grudge against them, but Katharine's
health might also have been a factor, perhaps related to her pregnancy, since
she gave birth to a daughter around that time.[15] It is not clear where the
Tranbargers went immediately following their resignations in August 1911,
but the family moved at least three more times between 1913 and 1918,
and, for at least part of this period, faced financial instability.[16] As of August
1913, Fernando was teaching at the Chilocco Indian School in Oklahoma
while his wife unsuccessfully sought reinstatement in the Indian Service.[17]
However, they found the accommodations at Chilocco too small. Katharine
described the one room as "neither ample nor healthful for my husband,
little daughter and myself," a complaint that echoed those that the couple
had made during their time at Carlisle.[18] By that December they moved to
Albuquerque, New Mexico, in anticipation of work there. For some teachers
the expansiveness of the Indian Service offered welcome alternative work
opportunities, although sometimes even these new environments were
deemed inadequate.

Upon the Tranbargers' arrival in New Mexico, a position was only available for Fernando, and the family's financial problems continued. Still, they
were reassured by the Albuquerque Indian School superintendent that a
position would be available to Katharine "in due time." She explained, "As
the Honorable Commissioner surely realizes that a man cannot support a

family on $660 a year, especially in the West, I trust that the 'due time' will be in the very near future."[19] While Fernando knew he would face salary reductions as he moved from the Philippine Service to the Indian Service, he and his growing family were not prepared for a further cut following Carlisle. Nor was Katharine ready to give up her own career. Prior to marriage, Katharine Bingley had supported herself for over a decade, earning an income at least since 1896. Nevertheless, the couple was forced to manage on one salary for several years. By 1918 Fernando was earning the same salary he had received at Carlisle—$720 per annum—although then teaching at the Birdtown Day School in North Carolina.[20] In spite of Fernando's frequent moves and temporary pay reduction at Albuquerque, he taught for a total of eighteen years. By 1931 he was employed as an associate attorney in the Interior Department's Indian Office in Washington, DC, a move driven perhaps by financial circumstances, where he continued to work for the next decade.[21] Whether Katharine ever worked again is unknown, although it is clear that she never returned to the Indian Service. Their experiences reflect their personal vulnerabilities as well as those of the larger system, one that often did not pay its employees a proper living wage, causing it to rely upon a somewhat unstable or dissatisfied workforce.

Clara Donaldson, who also served in the Philippines before working at Carlisle, similarly tried to commit the remainder of her career to the Indian, although the Pennsylvania boarding school's closure, her financial circumstances, and systemic discrimination ultimately determined her career. Prior to Carlisle's official takeover by the Department of War in September 1918, government officials scrambled to reassign teachers to new positions within the Indian Service. According to a July 22, 1918, article in the *Carlisle Evening Sentinel*, Indian Commissioner Cato Sells visited the school and interviewed employees to ascertain their preferences, most of whom would be sent to work at Indian schools out West.[22] Having been on leave from her teaching duties at Carlisle since April due to a severe case of pneumonia, Donaldson did not have a chance to meet with Sells. But upon reading the *Sentinel* article, she immediately wrote to the commissioner, outlining her preferences. Confident in her teaching, Donaldson explained: "I trust that my work at Carlisle has been of such character as to merit transfer to a similar position elsewhere. . . . I wish work in the advanced grade of the Vocational classes, and the subjects I prefer and therefore, teach the most successfully, are chemistry, physics, botany, and child study."[23] A few weeks later Sells transferred the experienced Donaldson to a position at the Chilocco Indian School in Oklahoma.[24]

Although Donaldson consistently received glowing work evaluations—as she had in both the Philippines and at Carlisle—age discrimination and wages limited her employment options. As noted earlier, Donaldson was almost refused a job in the Indian Service in 1914 due to her "advanced" age of fifty-two despite over a decade of experience in the Philippines.[25] After four successful years at Carlisle, she transferred to the Chilocco Indian School without incident in 1918. Two years later, however, she reluctantly resigned her position to teach in her native Ohio to ensure her eligibility for retirement.[26] Responding to her decision, the assistant superintendent-in-charge at Chilocco, C. M. Blair, wrote to the commissioner of Indian affairs, "I regard Miss Donaldson as one of the best, if not the best teacher I have known in the Indian Service, and regret exceedingly that she is leaving us, yet, under all the circumstances I can appreciate her situation, and recommend that her resignation be accepted."[27] Having left Chilocco reluctantly—and despite receiving almost a 50 percent pay raise in relocating to Greenwich, Ohio—after one year in the public school and at sixty years of age, Donaldson sought reinstatement in the Indian Service.[28] Her request to return to Chilocco suggests that in spite of lower pay she was deeply committed to Indian education or at least felt more confident in her work there, as she was consistently valued as an expert and an asset to the Indian Service. But no positions were then available at Chilocco.[29]

Commissioner E. B. Meritt then looked to the Haskell Institute, whose superintendent, H. B. Peairs, replied:

> I respectfully state that while I know that Miss Clara R. Donaldson is an exceptionally well-qualified teacher, I doubt the advisability of bringing persons of her age back into the Service. The fact is that we have too many teachers in the Service who have passed the half-century mark. I realize that Miss Donaldson is an exceptionally strong teacher and, as a teacher of chemistry, she certainly would be very valuable. It happens that we do not need her for that particular work.[30]

Thus, despite recognizing Donaldson's expertise and glowing reputation, Peairs focused more on the fact that she was well over "the half-century mark." The Indian Service had instituted a policy by the 1910s that prevented teachers over age fifty from joining the Indian Service; but by the early 1920s, the issue seems to have become more about how many older teachers continued to work in Indian schools, which clearly some superintendents considered a problem. Unable to secure Donaldson a position anywhere in the Indian Service, Commissioner Meritt informed her in September 1921, "You are advised that owing to age limitations . . . and in the absence of a suitable teacher vacancy which specializes in chemistry, etc., no encouragement can be given you regarding re-appointment in the Indian Service."[31] Thus, one of the most lauded teachers in the Philippine and Indian school programs was ultimately refused a job. In spite of her prior success and preference to teach Indians, Donaldson remained in the Ohio public school system until her retirement. Her story reveals some of the vulnerabilities teachers faced working for a system that had, by then, become a large, established bureaucracy with rigid rules that advantaged young teachers. In spite of her personal connections, she was unable to return to the Indian Service. At the same time, such an account reflects a weakness of a system unable to reap the benefits of an experienced employee due to inflexible policies and its impersonal structure.

While the five teachers featured here who taught both in the Philippines and at Carlisle faced challenges in their careers, all of them continued in the field of education upon leaving Carlisle, and a few tried to return to the classroom after pursuing other opportunities. John DeHuff and Clara Donaldson sought reinstatement in the Indian Service but were denied positions while Elizabeth DeHuff was willing to return, though only in a supervisory role. Moses Friedman remained in education, although not on behalf of Filipinos or Indians as he, at least briefly, had hoped. And, after a long teaching career, Fernando Tranbarger continued to work for the Office of Indian Affairs, although as an attorney rather than an educator. Overall, the trajectory of these crossover teachers' careers suggests either their long-term dedication to education—perhaps a genuine interest in working on behalf of "so-called primitive peoples"—or their entrenchment in vocations that, due to personal and structural barriers, were difficult to change. The degree to which they fully embraced the system's imperial mission or strove to empower their students through a US-style education system is less clear. Perhaps, some of them, like the DeHuffs, came to see real value in Filipino or Indian ways and hoped to merge the "best" of such "'primitive cultures'" with the "best" that white society had to offer, rather than simply replacing "uncivilized" with "civilized" customs. Whatever the case, their paths demonstrate the complexity of teaching empire, the profound effect imperial education had on their own careers and lives, and, of course, begin to shed further light on the systems that fundamentally sought to disrupt peoples from "being Indian," "being Filipino," being themselves.

Beyond these five individuals, the majority of the eighty-eight teach-

Table 5.1: Teachers' Work Experiences in Years Immediately Following Carlisle

Work Immediately After Carlisle	Number of Teachers
Elsewhere in Indian Service	18
Washington, DC (Indian Office, War Department)	10
Unknown	11
Teaching service outside continental United States	4
Other	4
Education outside of Indian Service	3
Retired	2
Other work with/on behalf of American Indians	2
Died	1
Total	55

Source: Based primarily on teachers' individual files held at the National Personnel Record Center; also drawn from Carlisle Indian Industrial School Collection, Cumberland County Historical Society, Carlisle, Pennsylvania (CCHS); National Archives, Washington, DC (NADC), Preliminary Inventory of the Records of the Bureau of Indian Affairs, Carlisle Indian Industrial School, Record Group 75, Entry 1331, 1344, and 1344A; Richard Henry Pratt Papers, Beinecke Rare Book and Manuscript Library, Yale University, New Haven, Connecticut (BRBML).

ers examined for this book taught for several years on behalf of the growing American empire or remained in complementary fields, with several dedicating the majority of their careers to imperial education outright. For example, after their years at Carlisle, thirty-four of the fifty-five teachers studied here continued to work on behalf of the imperial experiment, with three more in education outside of the Indian Service (see Table 5.1).[32] Of the thirty-three Thomasites, nineteen remained in the field of education, including seven who sought higher education degrees, six who remained in the archipelago for the remainder of their careers, and five who transferred to the Indian Service, with one more serving as a teacher outside of these experiments (see Table 5.2).[33] Thus, almost two-thirds of the teachers in this study (56 of 88, or 64 percent) remained committed to these imperial experiments, including a few who pursued other educational endeavors. Moreover, both Carlisle and the Philippines produced some teachers that spent the majority of their careers in Indian and Filipino education. Four of the Carlisle teachers worked at the school for over twenty years, including founding teachers Marianna Burgess, Emma Cutter, and Ann Ely, as well as student-turned-teacher Nellie Robertson Denny. Others worked for as many years in the broader Indian Service, including Emma Foster, who began in 1891 and retired in 1929 at the age of seventy-one, after thirty-eight years

Table 5.2: Teachers' Work Experiences in Years Immediately Following the Philippine Civil Service

Work Immediately After the Philippines	Number of Teachers
Pursued higher education degree	7
Field outside of education	7
Remained in the Philippines for career	6
Unknown	6
Joined Indian Service	5
Other education work	1
Other	1
Total	33

Source: Compiled by author from multiple archives and papers identified in the bibliography.

of government service. Similarly, Jessie Cook was forced to retire when she reached seventy after teaching for thirty-two years in the Indian Service.[34] Other teachers, including Mariette Wood and Margaret Sweeney, worked for the Indian Service for over a decade. Similarly, several Thomasites made work in the islands their career, including Alice and Walter Marquardt, Harvey and Maude Bordner, and John and Willa Early, all of whom worked in the islands for twenty-five years or more. Several others spent over a decade teaching in the Philippines, including John DeHuff, Clara Donaldson, John Evans, Mary Fee, and Frank Cheney. Altogether, this record suggests that the majority of teachers studied here had strong, sometimes decades-long, ties to the work of American empire, whether due to personal interest, necessity, or structural causes.

Interestingly, of those teachers who remained in the Philippines for virtually their entire careers, *all* were married. It is likely that marriage provided a support system that enabled Thomasites to endure the many hardships they faced while on the islands, even though other married couples left when their initial contracts expired. The Coles, for example, eagerly returned to the States after three years of service, and the DeHuffs left because they wanted to begin a family closer to home. Nevertheless, it is telling that of the thirty-three Thomasites in this study, those who remained the longest were not only married but wed either just before venturing to the Philippines or shortly after their arrival.[35]

Of the married couples who spent the bulk of their careers in the Philippines, Alice Hollister and Walter Marquardt remained the longest: forty years. Alice and Walter met sometime in 1901 while teaching in the islands.

They married in December 1902 at the home of Mary and Harrie Cole and celebrated the day with sixteen American friends.[36] When their first son was born in 1904, Alice continued to teach though her husband helped by taking on some of her classes.[37] They spent their first nine years in various towns on the island of Leyte and the next nine in Manila, where in 1916 Walter began a three-year term as director of education of the Philippine school system.[38] By 1919 Walter oversaw Filipino students sent to the United States for college under the "pensianado system," and in 1923 he became a representative of the American Book Company in the Philippines, helping to prepare textbooks for use in island schools. After forty years of service, the Marquardts permanently returned to the United States in 1941. Walter retired in 1948, and the couple traveled around the United States and Mexico for three years before settling in California.[39]

Although ample records exist of Walter's career in the Philippines, Alice's story is more difficult to trace, particularly beyond the early years. This difficulty, coupled with other evidence, indicates a gendered bias in the archives. Walter's voluminous records detail his professional achievements, while accounts of Alice's life and work are revealed only through careful reading of other teachers' personal papers, including her husband's and the Coles'. Absent of any letters, diaries, or other personal writing, Alice's voice is almost silenced in the historical record. While having a family interrupted Alice's professional career, even details regarding her arrival and first year on the islands can only be gleaned through other teachers' files.[40] Her records are not the only ones missing or buried in the historical record. Of the four married couples discussed in this book, the archives of only one of the wives—Mary Cole—have been preserved, and even Mary's letters and diaries are housed in her husband's file. This bias in record keeping clearly shapes the histories we can tell and the conclusions we can draw, raising questions about other ways that gender informed the experiences of teachers in the Philippines and Indian Services. Still, it is clear that long careers in the Philippines, at least, depended on the mutual support of husbands and wives.

Like the Marquardts' many years on the islands, Harvey and Maude Bordner lived and worked there for thirty-four years, during which time they relied upon one another for comfort and support. Although, as in the Marquardts' case, only Harvey's personal papers are archived, his letters suggest the importance of their companionship.[41] Writing to family members during their first few years in the Philippines, Harvey regularly complained about threats of disease and insurrection, detailing some of the less pleasant aspects of his work. After three years on the islands—in October

1905—Harvey intimated that he and his wife might "go to the United States for good or for a visit."[42] Yet, the Bordners stayed for thirty more years, and Harvey made it clear that Maude was crucial to their long-term service there. Commenting to his brother and sister in 1907 on his wife's temporary return to the States, Harvey noted, "Men cannot manage a house without a wife even though there is a cook and a house servant besides."[43] For Harvey and likely other men in his position, servants maintained the house but a wife made it a home and offered irreplaceable companionship. A decade later, the tables turned. In September 1918 Harvey was serving as the superintendent of the city schools of Manila, and it was Maude who complained of his absence, at least according to Harvey's recollections. Detailing his increasing responsibilities, Harvey noted:

> Maude often complains that all I do is to eat, sleep, attend to my office duties, and read. She says I have no time for calls, for recreation, for cines, or for other social affairs. . . . You see with 715 teachers, 35 principals, 68 school buildings, more than 30,000 pupils, 12 special supervisors . . . I have enough to keep me busy all of the time, in fact I have so much going on all of the time that I never get all of things accomplished which I think ought to be done. However, the more fully one keeps occupied, the less time one has for brooding and for lonesomeness and usually this keeps a person happy and contented.[44]

Developing and overseeing such a large school system proved to be all-consuming for Harvey, whose efforts and vision were widely praised. Yet such devotion to his work also led to criticism from his wife. Although Maude was teaching at the time, and had been for several years, her work apparently did not keep her as busy or contented as her husband, and it is unclear whether the couple had any children of their own.[45] Nonetheless, the Bordners remained in the Philippines until 1936, when Harvey's failing health forced them to return to the United States.[46] Clearly, Harvey and Maude Bordner both participated in building a school system in the Philippines, though to varying degrees and with distinct successes and sacrifices.

John and Willa Early also committed their lives to the Philippines, spending almost thirty years on the islands, although the historical records again leave little information as to Willa's life or work there. However, a potential mistake in the employment records raises an interesting question concerning Willa's service. According to John's personal papers (and verified by employment records), he began teaching in the Philippines in 1906 and

Willa joined him in 1912 upon their marriage. But Willa's employment record indicates that she resigned from a teaching position in the Philippines a decade earlier—in November 1902—due to "ill health," although no other records discuss her earlier work in the Philippines.[47] While this reference may be in error, noting the high rates of illness recorded in 1901 and 1902, it is quite likely that Willa had worked on the islands well before John ever set foot there but was forced to leave after becoming sick.[48] Whatever the case in 1902, Willa served as a temporary teacher beginning in 1917, was appointed a probational teacher in 1923, and resigned in 1932 after her husband's death.[49] Like Alice Marquardt and Maude Bordner, information concerning Willa's life and work in the Philippines is incomplete, with only scant evidence embedded in her husband's files.[50]

In contrast, John Early's varied career is well documented. John worked in the Philippines until the day he died, with only a few trips home. Although the Earlys intended to move back to the States permanently on a couple of occasions—in 1922 and again in 1929—they returned to the Philippines when John received promotions he could not refuse.[51] Beginning as a teacher in 1906, by 1909 he was raised to the position of lieutenant governor of the Mountain Province and a year later in Bontoc, where he was given permission to conduct his "experiment in extending education to the nearby barrios."[52] Over the next two decades, John received other promotions, including division superintendent, governor of the Mountain Province, and finally, governor-general of non-Christian affairs, a position that he described gave him "a wider scope of work than previously because I now have not only the Mountain Province but also the Special Provinces in Mindanao and Sulu in my wards."[53]

In addition to teaching and establishing schools, John Early's work included mapping unexplored terrain, molding bricks and building solid structures, and, as an administrator, overseeing schools, towns, and provinces.[54] As a leader in the "warring" Mountain Province, he earned the reputation of being "not a chieftan [sic] of war, but of peace," at least among fellow American officials on the islands.[55] Sadly, in January 1932, John died of cancer in Baguio after suffering several years from the disease.[56] In a grand memorial service, he was remembered fondly for his dedication to his work among the Filipino people.[57] Six months after John's death, Willa left the Philippine Service, although little is known about the rest of her life.[58]

The experiences of these six individuals who worked in the Philippines for decades suggests the importance of intimate relationships in sustaining

John C. Early seated with two American women in a Western-style living room in the "warring" mountainous region of Bontoc, Philippines, circa 1910. Early's work with brickmaking was instrumental for creating such a Western structure in the region. (John C. Early Papers, Bentley Image Bank, Bentley Historical Library, University of Michigan.)

their work, and thus, the work of imperial education. Similarly, as discussed in chapter 3, strong bonds and intimate friendships sustained several teachers' tenure at Carlisle, particularly in the school's earliest years. Although the broader movement of imperial education relied on hundreds of employees to implement policy, the long-term endurance of such schooling experiments also rested upon the commitment of a few individuals who provided at least a modicum of stability to an ever-changing and often fragile endeavor. In the Philippines, the three aforementioned couples were among the most committed enthusiasts. At Carlisle, such individuals included Superintendent Richard Pratt as well as two of his founding teachers, Marianna Burgess and Ann Ely, who dedicated themselves to one another and their work to Indian education. In both locations, teachers' work responsibilities changed over time, reflecting the dynamic character of imperial education, a process that embodied change at both structural and individual levels. For example, the education ventures themselves adapted somewhat to accommodate environmental, personnel, and myriad other challenges and opportunities that emerged over the years. At the individual level, the husbands of the three married couples in the Philippines particularly benefited from various career opportunities that arose, demonstrating their own and their family's flexibility, as well as that of the larger mission. As for Carlisle's Burgess and Ely, Burgess moved from the classroom to taking charge of the school newspapers while Ely left the schoolhouse to head the boarding school's infamous Outing Program. In these and other ways, the success of imperial education balanced, at least in part, on the dedication, flexibility, and competence of its workers who gained immeasurable encouragement from their partners. Yet, for some individuals, particularly those in the archipelago, intimacy did not sustain their work abroad but perhaps reinforced desires to return to a more familiar environment.

Unlike the other married couples in the Philippines featured here, Harrie and Mary Cole served on the islands for just three years. Although they supported one another throughout their time in the Philippines, they were eager to return to the States almost as soon as they reached their first teaching post. By the end of their initial contract, the Coles felt desperate to leave, unable to cope with the uncertain and often dangerous conditions that defined their experiences. Considering the profound violence that they faced (discussed in chapter 4), their longing for home and stability is not surprising. Still, noting that the Marquardts, Bordners, and Earlys faced similarly severe challenges, the Coles stand out. Perhaps more than the other married couples, the Coles harbored particularly intense racial animosity toward "others," people who did not look like themselves, and this may have been enough to undermine their longevity in the Philippines. It likely did not help that as everyday companions to one another, Harrie and Mary regularly reinforced one another's racist inclinations. So, just as Alice and Walter Marquardt, Harvey and Maude Bordner, and John and Willa Early may have encouraged one another's stamina, Harrie and Mary Cole likely heightened one another's bigoted sensibilities. Of course, they did stay the full three-year term despite almost consistent complaint. Two years into their contract, in May 1903, they took a rejuvenating trip to Japan, which enabled Mary to recover from a "break down" due to overwork.[59] But when they returned to teaching that September, she and Harrie resumed their countdown of the number of days remaining in the Philippines.[60] Two weeks before their departure, Harrie wondered if he could last any longer, but he wrote with profound relief on July 12, 1904, from Victoria, Canada, "Expect to leave for Seattle this Eve. . . . It seems *mighty* good to get a glimpse of America."[61]

Although Mary Cole became a mother after returning to the States, little else is known about her. We do know that Harrie shifted his professional interests back to those he had nurtured prior to his departure for the Philippines in 1901. The couple moved back to their native Michigan in 1904 and had at least one child, Margaret Cole.[62] Many years later, Margaret remembered her mother telling her when she was a child, "I just finished the dishes—but I was really climbing Mt. Fuji again."[63] Although much of Mary's writing during her stay in the Philippines suggested her contempt for the Filipino people and the islands—apparent in her many racially charged rants and desperate pleas to return to "civilization"—years later she remembered her travels abroad more fondly, at least the part of her journey that took her outside of the Philippines. While Mary reminisced over dishes, her husband went on to have a prestigious career. In 1904 Harrie returned to graduate school at the University of Michigan, studying chemical engineering and physics. By 1907 he was hired as an instructor in analytical chemistry, remaining in the University of Michigan's chemistry department until 1935.[64] For him, teaching in the Philippines served mostly as a brief interruption of his life's work as a scientist. Although the couple had ventured to the islands voluntarily, they preferred home, taking comfort in early twentieth-century norms of segregation manifest in both their personal and professional lives.[65]

Like Harrie Cole, several other Thomasites sought degrees in higher education after working in the Philippines, many becoming leaders in their chosen fields. In a sense, this is not surprising considering that the vast majority of Thomasites had already graduated from college, an achievement attained only by the most privileged young adults living in the United States at the time. One Thomasite, John Muerman, relied in part on his experiences teaching on the islands to write his doctoral dissertation, "The Philippine School Under the Americans," completed at George Washington University in 1922.[66] Other Philippine coworkers who attained higher degrees included George Carrothers, Norman Cameron, Herman Hespelt, Jules Frelin, Blaine Moore, and Frederick Behner. Their experiences after their island postings illustrate how their time abroad influenced their scholarly interests. Moreover, their pursuit of higher education reinforces the idea that the structures of empire in part relied upon and shaped the paths of the elite, at least for several educators involved in the Philippines.[67]

Like Harrie Cole, George Carrothers had studied and taught chemistry prior to joining the Thomasites, but he shifted his academic interests to education after his experiences in the Philippines. Carrothers had been hired to teach chemistry in the College of Education in Manila, but upon his arrival in 1909 he was instead sent to teach high school science on the remote island of Samar.[68] Rising to assistant superintendent of Samar in 1913, he briefly served as the academic assistant to the director of education for the Philippine Islands, where he worked on curriculum and education administration. Later that year, he returned to the States to attend graduate school at Columbia University's Teachers College, receiving a masters in 1915.[69] Ultimately, Carrothers earned a PhD and worked in higher education for thirty-five years. Working at several universities, he specialized in school administration and spent the majority of his career, 1928–1950, at the University of Michigan.[70] His professional experiences in the Philippines and his growing belief in the effectiveness of US-style schooling on the islands led him to become an authority on education administration in the United States.[71]

Like Carrothers, Norman Cameron dedicated his career to education after teaching in the Philippines and also sought a higher degree. As discussed earlier, Cameron recorded ample evidence of the violence and disease that he faced on the islands, yet he remained committed to the mission. Still, after fulfilling his three-year contract with the US government, he concluded, "I believe there is little use of my returning."[72] Cameron moved back to the United States confident that he had completed his personal and professional mission abroad and ready to advance education within US borders. In the spring of 1904, Cameron was hired to teach at Western State Teachers College in Kalamazoo, Michigan, later earning his doctorate from the University of Pennsylvania. He served as principal of the Baltimore Teachers Training School in the 1920s and then as president of Pennsylvania's West Chester Normal School from 1927 to 1935. From there, he was appointed superintendent of schools in Cecil County, Maryland, and then in Garfield, New Jersey, from which he retired in 1941.[73] Ultimately, teaching in the Philippines helped prepare Cameron for a lifetime devoted to American education.

Other Thomasites became academics outside the field of education, including Jules Frelin and Herman Hespelt, both of whom also served in the military prior to becoming professors of foreign language. Frelin served as a soldier in the Philippines during the War of 1898 before returning to the islands as a teacher, where he worked from 1901 to 1904. After this unusual transition from wartime to peacetime service on the islands, he devoted his life to academia. He became a professor of romance languages at the University of Minnesota, where he worked until retirement in 1938.[74] Hespelt taught in the Philippines for five years, from 1911 to 1916, before taking a leave of absence. The outbreak of World War I extended his leave, although he was not drafted until fall 1918. During this period of limbo, Hespelt earned his master's degree at Cornell University. With the end of the war in November 1918, his military service ended shortly after it began, and over the next several years he earned his doctoral degree from Cornell, graduating in 1925.[75] Hespelt devoted his scholarly career to Spanish literature and spent the majority of his career at New York University.[76] For both Frelin and Hespelt, it is likely that their earlier teaching experience in a foreign environment fostered their interest in languages but did not otherwise appear to shape their later careers.

Thomasites Blaine Moore and Frederick Behner were also likely inspired, at least in part, by their time overseas and pursued higher degrees that reflected their broadened interests. After having taught in the Philippines from 1901 to 1906, during which time Moore could be quite critical of his colleagues and Filipinos alike, he studied political science, writing on topics as varied as the US Supreme Court, commerce in the Netherlands, voting in Illinois, trade in Japan, and international banking. A professor at George Washington University, Moore's interests in foreign affairs remained central to his professional identity, although he never published on the political or economic situation of the Philippines.[77] For Behner, his exposure to other cultures and worldviews as a Thomasite helped him find his calling. In addition to teaching in the Philippines, Behner spent three summers in Japan and China studying their educational systems and became increasingly interested in mission schools. Drawn to religion, in the spring of 1905 Behner left the Philippines and visited thirty countries on his way home. He then attended seminary in Ohio and dedicated more than fifty years to the Presbyterian ministry, serving as pastor in several states including Ohio, North Dakota, Missouri, West Virginia, and Michigan. Upon his retirement, Behner continued to study Christianity while again traveling the world.[78] Moved by more than the US geopolitical mission in the Philippines, Behner embraced a Christian mission to spread the gospels.

Of course, several Thomasites chose career paths that did not include graduate school or "higher" callings, although they were otherwise inspired by their time in the Philippines. As discussed earlier, some teachers joined the Indian Service while others remained on the islands and made Filipino education their career. Still other Thomasites also remained abroad, including one drawn by the desire to travel and others whose decisions were shaped by the outbreak of war. Although teachers pursued various vocations after the Philippines, their intense yet (for at least some) monotonous experiences on the islands influenced subsequent work ventures.

For Frank Cheney, teaching in the Philippines was his first experience overseas and led him to yearn for further work in foreign environments. He spent twelve years teaching and then served as a superintendent in the Philippines—the longest time he spent anywhere during his fifty-six-year teaching career. While in the Philippines, he traveled to "nearly all the outports in the islands."[79] Perhaps the vastness and diversity of the archipelago, with the possibilities of always seeing new things, lured him to remain longer on the islands. After the Philippines, Cheney taught in California before requesting in 1927 to teach in South America, which he explained "is not made thru curiosity to see what foreign service is like but because I have had a lot of it and want to go back for more."[80] Although Cheney never did teach in South America, he ventured abroad again by 1931, teaching in Turkey, China, and India. In China during World War II, Cheney was held in a Japanese internment camp (1941–1945), yet even this horrific experience did not inspire him to return home immediately. Instead, after the war he taught in India for a year. He did, however, return to the States in 1947, spending the last nine years of his career teaching in Tennessee and Kentucky.[81] Cheney's frequent moves suggest a certain restlessness and a desire to travel and see the world, in spite of the risks sometimes entailed. Overall, teaching enabled him to embrace a sense of autonomy and catered to his whimsical side, as he once explained, partly in jest, "The chief reason that impelled me to stick with the teaching profession was the long vacations which enabled me to change the subject annually."[82]

Whether or not Cheney ultimately returned stateside because he suffered during the war, other Thomasites felt compelled to be closer to battlefields, one as a journalist and another a soldier, and both worked for a time on behalf of the Red Cross. Mary Fee arrived in the Philippines in 1901 to teach, and within a few years she proved to be a leader in the curricular and literary worlds. She helped create textbooks specifically geared toward Filipinos and published two memoirs about her experiences on the islands.[83] Fee retired from the Philippine Service in 1916 and chose to head to France as a volunteer with the Red Cross in 1917, having been unable to find suitable work in the United States.[84] In Europe, Fee continued her writing career by covering the war and published an article, "Night Raids from the Air," which described her experiences in Northern France during World War I. Claiming that "I would not for anything leave the war zone," Fee lived through bombings and served in many roles as she helped to house, feed, and nurse the injured.[85] A few years later she declined an offer to return to the Philippine Service, eventually taking a position in the Indian Service in Oregon before finishing up her teaching career at an Indian day school near San Diego, California.[86] Throughout her career, Fee embodied an adventurous spirit, living and working in new and challenging environments abroad before returning to the schoolhouse, this time among the colonized subjects of her homeland.

Like Fee, Reece Oliver followed military action, though in World War II where he engaged in combat. Originally from Indiana, Oliver taught in the Philippines from 1914 to the 1930s. When Japan invaded the Philippines in the early 1940s, he became an army officer and fought alongside Filipinos. Armed with personal knowledge of the islands and invested in the lives and livelihoods of his fellow soldiers, Oliver defended his adopted homeland, exhibiting his dual patriotism. Following the war, he remained abroad for almost his entire career, working at one time for the American Red Cross in its China Famine Relief Operation.[87] Thus, for Oliver, teaching in the Philippines led to a life devoted to US missions abroad, ostensibly helping and uplifting others in times of war and peace.

Of course, war also affected teachers at Carlisle, although not as intimately as their Philippine counterparts. Most significantly, as the United States became increasingly embroiled in World War I, the Carlisle school was forced to close its doors. Injured soldiers returning to the States needed rehabilitation, and the then secretary of war, N. C. Baker, invoked the department's right to repossess the facilities at Carlisle for this purpose. On September 1, 1918, the US Department of War reabsorbed the Carlisle Indian Industrial School buildings and property, it having only been leased to the Department of the Interior in 1879.[88] With the school's closure, many Carlisle teachers were sent to teach in other Indian schools or to work in the Indian Bureau and other government offices in Washington, DC. In a sense, the closure of the first federally funded off-reservation Indian boarding school symbolized the changing needs of the US empire, suggesting that the devastation posed by the war in Europe threatened its power more than the persistence of the "Indian problem." Moreover, by 1918 some government officials had tired of the growing and increasingly unmanageable Indian bureaucracy, and at the same time, reformers reconsidered the "Indian problem," casting it as less critical than it had been in the nineteenth century; almost four decades into the Carlisle experiment, white settlers had successfully populated many formerly Indian lands, the bloodshed wrought by Indian wars had ended years earlier, and the demise of the entire race had not proved imminent. Still, other Indian Service schools continued to function well into the next several decades, indicating both the entrenchment of the system and the continued value held in separate schools for those living outside of white middle-class culture.[89]

In addition to forcing Carlisle teachers to relocate or retire, World War I inspired some to express their patriotism, including two individuals firmly committed to Indian affairs. For example, in 1917 John Whitwell was eager to participate in the US war efforts. Whitwell had served as the principal teacher at Carlisle for seven years, and that April he was working as the assistant superintendent and principal at the Cushman Indian School when he asked the commissioner of Indian affairs to transfer him to the Department of Justice for the purpose of "procuring and preparing . . . confidential reports, e.g. I know the general feeling (good and bad) of foreigners towards this Government."[90] Although denied this position, Whitwell apparently considered his work with Native Americans to be similar to engaging with "foreigners," sensitizing him to better understanding patriotic or unpatriotic sentiments. Instead, he was transferred to the Phoenix Indian School as principal, where he worked until he retired in 1929.[91]

Similar to Whitwell, Marianna Burgess—who had dedicated twenty-five years to Carlisle—volunteered her expertise to aid the war effort. In the spring of 1918 she applied to join fellow Quakers who volunteered to aid in European reconstruction, emphasizing her skills which defied gender and age stereotypes. She wrote Pratt, whom she was sure could testify to her fitness for such work, that she was accustomed to "office work such as men usually perform" but "was not altogether helpless in occupations usual to my sex."[92] Clearly, Burgess hoped that Pratt would help her secure a position alongside men, although she was also willing to do "women's work." At the same time, she hoped that testimony regarding her youthful energy and moral leadership would counteract any doubts about her capacity to fill such a role at the advanced age of sixty-five. Vincent Nicholson, chairman of the committee responsible for recommending Quakers fit for reconstruction work in Europe, described Burgess in the following way: "Now I don't know Marianna Burgess' age but I know she is very young in spirit . . . entirely free from family ties . . . very healthy and strong. . . . She is bright, breezy, vigorous, strong, tough and motherly, and her moral and social influence would be a great adjunct to the Friends' Service Work, and a good deal more."[93] Nicholson described her as a candidate who defied age and gender stereotypes, emphasizing instead her independence, good health, and strength as well as her maternal and moral sensibility. Nevertheless, such confident recommendations were not enough to enable Burgess to gain a place abroad.

Instead, Burgess remained very active at home as she continued to advocate on behalf of Native Americans. Working alongside other Quakers, Burgess lamented the continued failure of white society, particularly her fellow

Friends, to recognize its own role in ignoring the problems of American Indians and allowing inequities to persist. In a survey that she had been assigned to conduct, Burgess found a profound difference between the Quaker community's commitment to the uplift of African Americans and "our Brother-in-Red," finding the relative inactivity and indifference regarding the latter inexcusable. In an August 9, 1917 letter to a fellow Quaker activist, Burgess recounted:

> The [Quaker] membership . . . are not aware of the appalling conditions of poverty, disease, crime, filth and other disheartening and hopeless situations now prevalent on most of the Indian reservations. . . . Yet a Friend, a Friend, I repeat, said the other day, "They do nothing to help themselves, let them rot." . . . My heart bleeds for these people whom I had arduously served for three decades, and under favorable environment and incentive, away from the tribes, with the hopes that are found in civilization, succeeded in arousing hundreds to desire to be and to do, but who under the present iniquitous system are powerless to change conditions for the better.[94]

Fueled in part by an encounter with a Quaker unsympathetic to the hardships faced by American Indians, Burgess recalled Carlisle as a place where hopes and dreams of civilization were instilled in students. However, after decades of service, she recognized that this was not enough. The "iniquitous system" continued to prevent Native Americans from attaining dignity and access to adequate resources. By the 1910s, Burgess recognized the structural inequalities constraining Indians, particularly on reservations, despite what she saw as the positive influence of schools like Carlisle. She pleaded for attention from more sympathetic Quakers while continuing to value the Indian boarding school model of assimilation through immersion.

Burgess's activism was not limited to arousing fellow Quakers to action but also pointed to flaws within the federal Indian bureaucracy, earning her further support from many elite Native Americans. In 1919 she felt honored to be considered for the position of editor of the *Magazine of the Society of American Indians*. Once again seeking advice from Pratt, she recounted how members of the magazine's advisory board felt "there is no other person as free as I, who knows as much of real Indian characteristics and the full Indian situation and at the same time on the right side of the fence as far as the Bureau is concerned. . . . They also feel that I am better able to reflect General's [Pratt's] ideas than any other person, and they know I'm not afraid to do so."[95] Although she did not accept the position, the fact that the Society of American Indians (SAI) approached her to become editor is very significant since the organization was organized by and for Native Americans. In 1911 Indians from various tribes had formed SAI "to promote a positive image of Indianness to white Americans and address a variety of concerns shared by Native people, especially federal policy."[96] Most of SAI's leaders nurtured their support for the organization's pan-Indian perspective when they had studied at Indian schools, including Carlisle, and believed that the diverse indigenous peoples of North America needed to work together in strength and solidarity to achieve positive change and counter the negative stereotypes that both fueled and were reinforced by Indian Bureau policies. Reaching out to Burgess—the former editor of Carlisle's slew of newspapers, and right-hand woman of Pratt—seemed a logical choice within the historical context, noting that she, along with the school's founding superintendent, reviled the Bureau of Indian Affairs for celebrating "efficiency" and "progress" instead of adequately funding or otherwise supporting Indian education or reservation life.

Although it might be difficult to understand how Burgess's seemingly brutal methods at Carlisle did not alienate her from future leaders of the Indian rights organization, many of SAI's elites knew her personally from their childhood days at the Indian boarding school and admired her. In fact, soon after rejecting the SAI offer, Burgess joined former student Luther Standing Bear on stage in 1919 at a conference of a new Indian organization in Riverside, California. Here, she underscored Luther's claims regarding the limits of the Indian Bureau and its employees by speaking honestly about the needs and conditions of American Indians.[97] Alongside Native American leaders like Standing Bear and the Society for American Indians as well as Pratt and other activists, Burgess had come to believe that the bureau—with all its excesses—should be abolished.

As noted earlier, Pratt had parted ways with leaders in the Indian Bureau prior to his forced retirement in 1904, and some of his most loyal teachers, including Burgess, harbored similar negative sentiments, particularly as the bureau's leaders implemented increasingly invasive or otherwise flawed policies. By the 1910s they had instituted reforms typical of the Progressive era, intended to increase professionalism and efficiency. These included regular reports regarding teachers' performance and other forms, among them one that surveyed teachers' reading habits. In this, as in other areas, historian Catherine Cahill notes, "Progressive Era thinking also had a darker side, from which flowed lowered expectations of Indian people's capacity."[98]

Pointing to popular beliefs that emerged after Reconstruction regarding the need for a permanent working class and to expanded white settlement in the West, Cahill argues, "Beginning with Commissioner Jones (1897–1905) and gathering strength under his successor, Commissioner Leupp, policy makers began to move the Indian Office away from its goal of rapid and full assimilation and toward a racialized vision of a people destined by heredity for permanent manual labor."[99] To meet these new goals, Indian schools increasingly stressed vocational education at the expense of liberal arts learning. At the same time, federal policies continued to change requirements needed for American Indians to qualify for citizenship, which was not granted for all Native peoples until 1924.[100] Thus, during this time of profound change in federal Indian policy and leadership, Carlisle founding members, including Superintendent Pratt and Marianna Burgess, consistently pushed back.

Of course, Pratt and Burgess were not the only two Carlisle personnel who sought change within the Indian Bureau or Indian Service. Beyond teacher Emma Lovewell's complaints against the bureau and Carlisle leadership, detailed in the introduction and chapter 2, several teachers who remained in the Indian Service after working at Carlisle were noted as agitators in other ways, with some able to take advantage of larger problems in the bureaucracy. As discussed earlier, high rates of turnover and frequent transfers were common in the Indian Service, giving teachers a certain level of freedom to stand their ground or act in ways that would otherwise not be tolerated.[101] Although similar problems faced public schools at the time, the Indian Service included fewer schools and teachers, creating particularly high rates of turnover within individual schools.[102] Some of the high teacher turnover in education more broadly can be explained by the strenuous work conditions and low pay, exacerbated by teachers' youth and gender, as women were not permitted to continue working once married. Similar conditions were true in the Indian Service, although transferring within the system was a unique characteristic. For many years, the service faced the problem of finding and keeping quality teachers, which may have added to teacher unrest, intentionally or not. Among those who clashed with supervisors and colleagues or who otherwise agitated for change were Emma Lovewell (already discussed in the introduction and chapters 2 and 3), Lucy Case, Margaret Sweeney, and Gwen Williams. Of the latter three, Sweeney and Williams nonetheless remained in the Indian Service for the remainder of their careers.[103]

Lucy Case worked in the Indian Service for three years prior to her time at Carlisle, from 1913 to 1915, during which time she received mediocre teacher evaluations. Deemed a "diligent worker" with "plenty of energy and interest," Principal Teacher John DeHuff described that her "services approach . . . being very satisfactory," having demonstrated improvement, but not yet having reached acceptable, let alone excellent, appraisal. He elaborated that she had been "somewhat lacking in tact" although again had shown improvement. Her biggest strike against her at Carlisle was her ability to control the classroom, particularly among older students. Therefore, when Carlisle eliminated its elementary programming in 1915, she was transferred elsewhere.[104]

Case's subsequent job assignments proved less successful, at least according to administrators. She moved from Carlisle to the Fort Apache Agency in Arizona, where Superintendent Peterson's initial evaluation described her as "very peculiar in her personal appearance" and evaluated her work ethic as limited as "she takes no part in the social development of the pupils, in short, she does nothing outside of the classroom."[105] A few years later, Case apparently admitted to displaying "disloyal activity against Superintendent Peterson," helping to justify her transfer to the Tulalip Indian Agency, where she allegedly antagonized fellow workers at the Swinomish Day School.[106] Superintendent Charles Buchanan blamed Case for the school's deterioration, describing her manner as "extremely queer and odd" and alleging that she "destroyed" the Indian Women's Improvement Club.[107] Despite her bad reputation, the vastness of the Indian Service and its continued demand for teachers enabled individuals like Case to remain in its employ. Finally, after eight years of problematic service, Case left to teach at a boys' school in Vermont.[108] Whether she was any more successful there is unknown.

Similar to Case, Margaret Sweeney was characterized as being discontented, unenergetic, and uncooperative over several years in the Indian Service, although she was sometimes unaware of this, and ultimately worked for the system for her entire career. Allegedly "dissatisfied" while teaching at the Mt. Pleasant Indian School in Michigan and eager to be closer to family in Pennsylvania, Sweeney transferred to Carlisle in November 1909, where she remained until the school closed nine years later.[109] Her formal teacher evaluations during her time at Carlisle reflect a range of opinions, including one from January 1909 where her supervisor, Chas. F. Peirce, deemed her as "doing very good work" and "thorough in her work" although "not [as] energetic as some teachers."[110] Perhaps Sweeney's lack of energy stemmed from the fact that she had two dependent sisters, including one "invalid," and struggled to provide for them.[111] In the months leading up to the US congressional hearings of Indian schools in February and March 1914, Superintendent Friedman described her as having "a rather pessimistic turn of mind, and does not show the interest in the school and its work."[112] In February 1914, Sweeney then testified against Friedman, saying that he lacked discipline and further speculated that Carlisle had "the worst class of pupils; a class of pupils that can not be controlled in other schools," requiring, in her opinion, that the school leader needed to be a "very strong man," which, she surmised, Friedman categorically was not.[113] Ten months later, Principal Teacher John DeHuff assessed Sweeney's teaching as falling below average in "energy, erudition, or knowledge of pedagogical procedure," classifying her as "somewhat less than 'very satisfactory.'"[114] Despite such negative evaluations, she remained at Carlisle for its remaining four years.

After Carlisle closed in 1918, Sweeney moved to Washington, DC, and worked in various offices within the War Department, but was laid off in June 1920 due to "a reduction in force."[115] She was then reinstated in the Indian Service and transferred to teach at the Sherman Institute.[116] Three years into her time there, Sweeney was in the midst of being transferred elsewhere when she discovered that she had been accused of causing a "lack of harmony" between the principal and other employees, prompting her to request an investigation into the matter.[117] In the meantime, Sweeney asked to be sent to a school close enough to a Catholic Church to "attend to my religious duties" and soon after transferred to the Carson Indian School in Nevada.[118] Most teachers within the Indian Service were Protestant, and differences between Protestants and Catholics often seemed irreconcilable well into the mid-twentieth century. In fact, at the 1914 congressional hearings, Sweeney had testified that Friedman had purposefully prevented students from continuing to attend Catholic confession and communion, breaking tradition and stoking animosity with a local priest, though the veracity of her claim is unknown.[119] Still, perhaps some of Sweeney's apparent conflicts at various Indian schools related to her religious difference. Whatever the case, Sweeney faced further difficulties at Carson, at least initially. After three years at this Nevada Indian school, she was described as "not tak[ing] suggestions and instructions from the principal as well as she should. She likes to argue."[120] However, several months later an evaluation reported that Sweeney's "attitude toward the principal has changed, and she appears to be getting along better in her school work."[121] In spite of some setbacks, which may have been in part due to religious quarrels, Sweeney worked at the Carson Indian School as a fourth grade teacher for nine more years. Although she had clashed with her supervisors at several schools, she remained in the service for many years without further incident. In March 1935 she died at the age of fifty-eight, having worked in the Indian Service for nearly three decades.[122]

Sent to Washington, DC, alongside Sweeney, former Carlisle teacher Gwen Williams agitated for change on her own behalf, something to which she was unaccustomed as a teacher in the Indian Service.[123] Years earlier when she taught at the Mt. Pleasant Indian School in Michigan, Williams was rated the second best teacher, choosing to transfer to Carlisle in July 1914, likely to be closer to relatives.[124] At Carlisle, she continued to receive positive evaluations and was recommended for a raise within six months, having covered for a sick colleague, requiring her to do "double work" for an extended period of time.[125] A November 1917 teacher evaluation described Williams as a "very earnest and hard working instructor . . . loyal and sincere in her endeavor to be helpful to the Indian boys and girls."[126] Thus, she was largely praised and rewarded for her work, apparently not needing to advocate for herself or her paycheck.

This changed once Williams entered the Washington, DC, Indian Office bureaucracy. As early as 1919, Williams demanded higher wages to match those of her colleagues in the Indian Office.[127] Persistent in her request for an increased salary, she wrote to her superior officers in April 1922, "I have lived here in Washington under conditions other women, as old as I am, have not been required to live, because their salaries were increased regularly."[128] Responsible for taking care of her sister as well as herself, Williams ran a "rooming house" to supplement her income.[129] She had intended to return to teaching in the Indian Service, but without giving specific details, refused a teaching appointment due to a traumatic experience in the DC government office during the winter of 1918 and 1919. She explained, "I have kept silence not because I am too dull to talk. I am not in the Field to day because my spirit is not dead, nor do I intend it shall die while my body is stalking on earth."[130] Although the historical record does not clarify the nature of Williams's trauma, considering her coded language and documented problems of sexual improprieties in the Indian Service more broadly, she may have been referring to an unwanted advance by a male peer. Sexual harassment was a significant problem in the Indian Service, although women who presented accusations were generally ignored or otherwise penalized. Historian David Adams cites several other examples of teachers who complained to the Indian Office and the Indian Rights Association of supervisors who made unwanted sexual advances.[131] In addition to these cases, of course, is Superintendent Mercer's sex scandal. Yet another Indian school superintendent, Charles Davis—who married Lydia Dittes after her time at Carlisle—was accused of "immoral conduct" for having taken "improper liberties" with at least three employees at different schools, one of whom "died of an abortion," and the charges found "substantially proved."[132] Ultimately, whatever the cause of Williams's unease, she remained in the Office of Indian Affairs for twenty more years, perhaps reluctantly but responsible for providing for herself and her dependents, until her retirement in February 1939, at which point she was commended for her work.[133]

Whether or not these agitators and others remained working for the Indian bureaucracy or moved on, their noncompliance reflected their individual agency and, in some cases, their intention to make change. Although they disrupted institutional norms for personal reasons, their individual actions threatened the status quo and cautioned greater consequences. Some of the Indian Service's greatest strengths lay in its vastness, its large number of employees who ostensibly worked toward complementary goals and likely reinforced one another's conformity. Yet, the size of such a network also guaranteed that in certain moments people would defy its rules and norms, while others would simply leave.

Other Carlisle teachers left the Indian Service for more promising teaching opportunities abroad, including places like Alaska and Puerto Rico, both part of the growing American empire. As evident by the American occupation of the Philippines, US expansion around the turn of the twentieth century opened up opportunities beyond continental borders that still offered some of the reassurances associated with working for the US government, even though conditions on the ground could be quite challenging, if not insurmountable. One draw of such places was significantly higher pay. And, at a time when women teachers were paid well below their male colleagues, some could not resist higher salaries. Still, other teachers sought less stressful work conditions, believing at least in the case of Puerto Rico that an island lifestyle was more suited to their desires.[134]

Committed to and valued by the Indian Service, Carlisle teacher Dora LeCrone was unable to resist the higher salary offered to teachers in Alaska and jumped at the opportunity. LeCrone expressed enthusiasm for Indian education and taught at Carlisle for seven years, beginning at age twenty-one in 1904. She resigned in 1911 to tend to "conditions at my home" but soon after sought reinstatement in the Indian Service, explaining, "I am much interested in the cause of Indian education and I feel that the opportunities for usefulness are greatest in an Indian school."[135] She was hired at Oregon's Salem Indian Training School in 1912, where she received high accolades, but resigned after one year to teach in the public schools in Unga, Alaska, unwilling to turn down the significant raise from $600 a year to about triple the salary: $175 a month.[136] As explained by the Salem school's superintendent, "She regrets exceedingly her leaving this school but in justice to herself could not decline the position offered to her."[137] Purchased from Russia in 1867 and incorporated as a US territory in 1912, Alaska was part of the burgeoning US empire that offered high pay to lure American teachers. Somewhat similar to their counterparts in the Philippines and Indian School Service, these teachers were tasked with spreading mainstream American norms to assimilate native peoples.[138] In addition to higher compensation, LeCrone likely believed that teaching in Alaskan schools would offer similar "opportunities for usefulness." Whether they did is, unfortunately, unknown.[139]

Another teacher who ventured abroad into the growing American empire was Miss Ericson, who left Carlisle for Puerto Rico in 1899. Like the Philippines, this Caribbean island had been transferred from Spanish to US authority as a bounty of the War of 1898, although Puerto Rico took a different trajectory. Noting that Filipinos fought for independence from the United States only to receive it after almost half a century of US occupation, still today Puerto Rico remains an unincorporated territory. In 1917 Puerto Ricans were made US citizens, enabling its men to be drafted into the US armed forces in time to fight on behalf of American empire during World War I. In contrast, Filipinos were never granted US citizenship, although the archipelago was recognized as an independent nation in 1946. At this critical time after World War II as Filipinos gained independence, measures were taken in Puerto Rico to limit the island's sovereignty, although some concessions were made, including allowing a democratically elected governor in 1947. While the Philippines has been an independent nation for over seven decades, Puerto Rico remains part of the US empire, seen as dependent on the mainland but lacking a voice in US government and markedly under-resourced.

Back in 1899 when Miss Ericson reached Puerto Rico, she corresponded regularly with her former colleagues and students at Carlisle about her experiences in the Caribbean. In a letter published in the *Indian Helper* in January 1900, she reported enjoying her new work, even though the pupils gave her "a good deal more to do as far as discipline is concerned than the Indians." Nevertheless, she explained, "I am very happy here. I like the new life exceedingly. I do not know what homesickness is, and hope never to learn it."[140] Ensuring her readers that she had adapted well to her new position, Ericson also tried to reinforce continued good behavior among the Indians. For example, she described how she kept tabs on a Carlisle student who was now a US soldier stationed in Puerto Rico:

> Russell Whitebear has been to see me several times. He is a nice, gentlemanly, sober boy, with the best reputation. Such a name means a great deal here where the soldiers so often disgrace themselves in one way or another. I am proud of Russell and find from my talks with him that he is making good use of what he learned at Carlisle, and that he is very fond of his old school. He looks well and it has done him good to be out and to have seen the world a little.[141]

Praising Whitebear for his upstanding behavior in contrast to other US soldiers' apparent depravity, Ericson emphasized how important the Carlisle experience proved for him. Acknowledging the advantages that Carlisle offered students—helping to create upstanding, well-adapted citizens like Whitebear—the publication of the letter in the school newspaper encouraged current students to explore "the world a little" beyond the school and the reservation.[142] Significantly, the fact that Whitebear was serving as a US soldier in an imperial war although American Indians were not granted US citizenship until 1924 reveals the imbalance of power and service within American empire.

A decade after Ericson's move from Carlisle to the Caribbean, Emma Hetrick made a similar move, leaving Carlisle for the "Porto Rican Service" in 1910. However, she left the States under unfavorable circumstances—amid accusations concerning her unfitness for work within the Indian Service—though she soon longed for home.[143] Hetrick reportedly enjoyed teaching in Puerto Rico but within a month requested to be transferred back to Carlisle or Washington, DC, as a clerk. In a series of letters to the commissioner of Indian affairs, Hetrick defended her conduct while clerking at Carlisle and sought to clear her name against any charges against her.[144] Meanwhile, the acting principal of schools in Toa Alta, Puerto Rico, praised Hetrick, who taught the fifth and sixth grades: "Her great activity, her kindness to the pupils, her valuable disciplinary power and loyal behaviour to her fellow teachers make her worthy of esteem."[145] Despite such high regard, Hetrick continued to seek clerical work back in the Indian Service. Perhaps she felt homesick, missing her family or the more familiar work environment.

In November 1911 she explained that she and her sister "should like to be together somewhere among the civilized tribes," perhaps referring to indigenous peoples designated part of the "Five Civilized Tribes," or otherwise classifying American Indians as superior to Puerto Ricans.[146] Whatever the case, Hetrick's request was not met, and she remained in Puerto Rico, where she continued to receive praise for adapting to the local conditions, being "a loyal, faithful and conscientious teacher," and deemed able to thrive even "under difficulties."[147] The "difficulties" Hetrick faced may have included poor student behavior, as experienced by Ericson, or may have involved serious problems with disease. For in July 1912, Hetrick expressed fear of an outbreak of bubonic plague on the island and finally secured a Washington, DC, clerkship in the Pension Bureau that August.[148] Happy to leave the "difficulties" she faced in Puerto Rico, Hetrick returned to the United States, having managed to successfully defend her reputation at home. Certainly other Carlisle (or at least broader Indian Service) teachers ventured to Puerto Rico, Alaska, or other US territories in the early twentieth century and experienced various degrees of success, satisfaction, and homesickness.

The Indian Service adequately prepared some Carlisle teachers for the unique challenges that they would face working for similar institutions overseas, although not in all cases. The existence of these parallel teaching services suggests that US government officials continued to attribute great power to education's potential for effecting positive change as the nation occupied new territory. Though education as panacea offered an attractive tool for expanding empire, its effectiveness varied and prospects worsened as grave problems including disease impacted individuals on the ground.

While illness did not end Hetrick's career, it did have that effect on a number of other teachers. This was especially true in the Philippines. Cholera, smallpox, and other diseases devastated local Filipino populations and burdened US teachers on the islands with more work and additional anxieties. Not surprisingly, sickness also cut some Thomasites' careers short, as it did for B.N. Blakeslee, Frederick Behner's colleague who was sent home. Other teachers were also forced to leave the Philippines after contracting diseases, including John Evans and Edward Sharp. Evans, who arrived in the Philippines aboard the *Thomas* in July 1901, rose from teacher to governor-general of the Mountain Province by the 1910s. But a few years later, tuberculosis sent him home. He relocated to New Mexico due to the drier climate, working there as a postmaster for many years, and spent his last years living with family in Coldwater, Michigan.[149] Sharp taught in Bohol from 1902 to 1904 but was forced to return to the States after contracting malaria. He soon moved to the capital of the Cherokee Nation in Tahlequah, Indian Territory (Oklahoma), where he opened a business, married, and remained for sixty years, until his death in 1965.[150] In returning to the United States, both Evans and Sharp took up new careers, severing their ties with education, but, interestingly, continuing to work among colonized peoples.

Of course, exposure to disease was also a risk in the United States, and a career working among peoples afflicted by communicable diseases, including tuberculosis, increased that risk and ended the careers of a number of teachers. For example, after thirty-two years in the Indian Service, John Whitwell was forced to retire in 1929, aged sixty-one, due to illness likely contracted on the job. Whitwell, who worked at Carlisle from 1907 to 1914 and then at the Cushman Indian School, was finally transferred to the Phoenix Indian school, where he spent the remainder of his career as principal. By 1929 Whitwell suffered from heart disease, a tremor, and fibrosis in his chest. As explained in his June 1929 application for retirement: "The cause probably dates back to the years 1897 to 1903 when as teacher and Superintendent I was in almost daily contact with both young and old Indians suffering from Tuberculosis.... Twenty six more years as Principal in the large boarding schools of the Service has completed the physical breakdown."[151] Thus, Whitwell believed that a career dedicated to Indian education had led to his physical debilitation. Other Carlisle teachers, too, contracted tuberculosis, forcing them to leave the school and relocate to drier climates.[152]

Still others found the work itself debilitating. For example, Idilla Wilson joined the Indian Service in 1912 and held her first and only position as a teacher at Carlisle until 1918. During her final year there, however, Wilson took a yearlong unpaid leave of absence due to a "physical breakdown."[153] In June 1918, Carlisle Superintendent Francis expressed his respect for Wilson after she requested a transfer to a nonteaching position: "She is a most kind, conscientious teacher who has the respect and love of her student [sic]. She is capable and valuable to the school and I regret exceedingly to see her go, both from personal reasons and for the welfare of the school."[154]

Unlike some teachers whose difficulties to sustain their work were met by condemnation from their superiors, Wilson continued to have her superintendent's support. In her own words, Wilson explained:

It has been a rule of my life to put my very best and most earnest effort into my work and that has its effect on physical strength.... You well know there is not the mental and nervous strain in clerical work that there is in teaching and the realization of this fact was the reason why our generous hearted Supt., Mr. Francis, so heartily approved of my request. . . . Pardon me for persisting in this matter but it vitally concerns me for [I] have to earn my living and want to secure the employment best suited to my physical ability.[155]

Due in part, perhaps, to Wilson's work ethic, she found teaching too stressful, both physically and mentally. Perhaps Wilson found clerking in the US War Department and later in the Department of the Interior, which oversaw Indian affairs, less taxing to her health than teaching at an Indian boarding school.[156] At a basic level, the strength of the empire rested upon that of its workers, and the straining demands that such work often placed on individuals contributed to their fragility and thus, the empire's. Yet, for Wilson and others who relied upon the Indian Service for a paycheck, their personal vulnerabilities contributed to the power of the bureaucracy, as they were bound to a job in order to earn a living, sometimes despite working conditions or debility.

Even when not afflicted with illness themselves, several Carlisle teachers resigned temporarily or permanently from the Indian Service to help loved ones who needed care. Some had responsibilities for aging, ailing, or otherwise dependent relatives, including those who could not manage work and familial obligations, so they sometimes left the service.[157] These included Dora LeCrone (who left Carlisle to assist an ill relative before eventually moving to Alaska) as well as Frances Scales, Clara Snoddy, and Hattie McDowell. A teacher in the service since 1894, Scales worked at Carlisle from 1902 to 1908, at which point she was transferred to the Phoenix Indian School. However, she soon requested "to be located as near home as possible on account of the precarious condition of my father's health" and was subsequently given the opportunity to teach at the Cherokee Indian School in North Carolina, much closer to her parents. However, she did not initially accept this position, preferring to return to Carlisle. Unable to do so and having resigned in August 1909, Scales apparently never again worked in the Indian Service.[158] Like Scales, Clara Snoddy's career in the Indian Service ended abruptly due to familial obligations, although she managed to continue teaching outside of the service. Snoddy dedicated fourteen years to teaching in the Indian Service, moving to the Haskell Institute following Carlisle's closing in 1918. Three years later she transferred to the public schools in Topeka, Kansas, to be closer to her recently widowed mother. There she taught English and social studies in the Topeka Kansas Junior High School for two decades. "Seeking a change" after her mother's death in 1941, Snoddy sought reinstatement in the Indian Service, having enjoyed her work years earlier and learning of a "shortage of teachers in the Indian Schools." She was denied a position, perhaps due to her advanced age.[159] Another Carlisle teacher, Hattie McDowell, also made career decisions to best suit her family's needs but was able to remain in the service. McDowell was responsible for caring for her fifty-three-year-old brother, who suffered from a weak heart. She worked at Carlisle from 1904 to 1918, at which point she was transferred to the Chemawa Indian School in Oregon. However, by 1924 McDowell realized that her brother would have to move in with her and requested a transfer to a day school in southern California so that he could live more comfortably at a lower altitude. She moved to the Pala Mission School in California, working there until she retired in 1928 at the age of sixty-seven.[160] While these three women had very different experiences regarding their ability to help family members and remain in the Indian Service, they all seemed to value their familial obligations above their work, or at least felt compelled to make it their priority.

Other teachers, including Margaret Sweeney, Emma Hetrick, and Gwen Williams, also gave up work for family members. Although their specific familial circumstances are unknown, it is likely that as women—particularly single, wage-earning women—they adhered to societal norms that assumed that they, rather than their brothers or other male kin, should sacrifice their careers to minister to family members. Although these women worked outside the home, they were assumed to be more nurturing and "maternal" because of their sex. Of course, these and other women may have felt a personal obligation to tend to family members regardless of their sex. Nevertheless, it is significant to note that it was mainly women who altered their careers to help their ailing relatives.

Gender norms affected Carlisle teachers in other important ways, including promotions and salaries within the Indian School Service. Transferred to teach at the Wahpeton Indian School in North Dakota following budget cuts at Carlisle in 1916, Margaret Roberts was then recommended to become principal teacher at the Lake Leech Boarding School in Minnesota.[161] She was nominated for the latter position due to her presumed ability to "direct the home care of the children" as well as her "experience in the Indian School Service which could not be secured in a male appointee at the salary now available and while there is so great a demand for good men."[162] Thus, Roberts's sex rendered her more capable of guiding children's development and, at the same time, allowed the Indian Service to pay her a lower salary. In spite (or perhaps because) of such a recommendation, Roberts did not accept the position.[163] Her situation was typical in that she was presumed to need less money than a man, and at the same time, that she was more capable of tending to domestic duties because of her sex. Most women apparently accepted that they would earn lower wages for the same work as men in the Indian Service as they did in other situations and professions, although they were not always prepared to tend to domestic tasks.[164]

Whereas Roberts rejected a promotion to principal teacher, Mariette Wood's poor performance in such a position led that school superintendent to prefer male principals in the future. Having taught at Carlisle from 1897 to 1909, Wood intended to retire after a year at her next school, the Santa Fe Indian School. Suffering from altitude sickness, she in fact resigned only a couple of months into the school year. Without further explanation, when the Santa Fe superintendent sought to replace Wood, he noted his preference for "a man teacher to a woman for principal."[165] In a subsequent letter, he explained that Wood had never truly embraced the principal teacher position and "found the work arduous and difficult." Perhaps, the superintendent believed that a man would be better able to handle the responsibilities.[166]

Of course, being a man did not guarantee that one would be successful in a particular position. Having left Carlisle due, in part, to his inability to get along with other teachers, Royal Mann became a principal teacher at the Southern Ute Boarding School, where in December 1915 he was criticized for being "without tact" and having "a way of irritating employees."[167] Mann found more success as a teacher at the Rosebud Agency in South Dakota, where he later became a clerk. He was then promoted to chief clerk at the Seneca Agency in Oklahoma, a position that might have required fewer interpersonal skills.[168]

While Mann's social awkwardness affected his success as a teacher and prevented him from making friends with his colleagues, for many other teachers, friendships proved to be invaluable, and many lasted a lifetime. As Fannie Peter wrote after leaving Carlisle for Washington, DC, in 1904, "I have more friends at the school than anywhere else that being my home for so long."[169] Teachers like her who remained at Carlisle for several years often developed deep and lasting bonds. Other Carlisle teachers reunited years later and reminisced about the "good ole days," creating new memories. For teachers sent to Washington, DC, social gatherings were far easier than for their counterparts scattered across the country. Peter maintained friendships with her fellow teachers, occasionally socializing with Emma Cutter, Della Botsford, Anna Luckenback, and Bessie Harper in DC.[170] Cutter, having begun her work at the school's inception, wrote over fifty-five years later of recent visits and conversations with old Carlisle friends such as Miss Bowersox and Miss Hill. They talked "all about Carlisle" and the many school employees with whom she had kept in touch over the years.[171] Even teachers sent to other schools in the Indian Service oftentimes found themselves working alongside former Carlisle colleagues and were able to maintain relationships, though evidence of such friendships is scarcer. Thus, a certain level of intimacy developed among many workers at Carlisle, drawing friends to remain in touch years after they left. Moreover, employees' unique experiences at the school ultimately reinforced these friendships, and for many, strengthened their belief in Carlisle's righteous mission well after their tenure and even following the school's closure.

Among the strongest friendships cemented at Carlisle, and one that continued for the rest of their lives, was that between Marianna Burgess and Ann Ely. As discussed earlier, Ely and Burgess were friends for decades, having met before their twenty years together at Carlisle. A unique friendship, Burgess and Ely respected one another as colleagues, friends, and constant companions, and their love and devotion to one another lasted well beyond their years teaching. When eighty-one-year-old Ely suffered a stroke, she "rallied sufficiently to travel alone to New York State to spend six weeks at a summer resort with her long-time friend, Miss Burgess."[172] She died on July 27, 1914, after which Burgess penned a long, loving obituary published in the *Carlisle Arrow*. In it she explained the depth and breadth of Ely's influence at Carlisle and beyond: "To hundreds of co-workers in the Indian Service, and to thousands of ex-students of Carlisle scattered throughout the Indian reservations of our country, the name of Miss Ely is a synonym for repose and readiness to serve as a cup of strength in distress, and is ever uttered with emotions of esteem and grateful remembrance."[173] More than reflecting what others may have thought of Ely, the obituary revealed Burgess's deep pain and continued admiration for her friend. In a heartfelt letter to Richard and Laura Pratt soon after her friend's death, Burgess wrote, "I'm nearly prostrate with grief. Never was devotion more unselfish, more persistent, more beautiful and pure than she gave to unworthy me."[174] Four years later, Burgess wrote to Superintendent Pratt again, noting that Ely appeared in a dream, "And I shall never get over missing her."[175] Although others probably did not feel the personal devastation that Burgess suffered, years later, Ely was fondly remembered along with the institution she helped to create. In 1982, over one hundred years after Ely began her work at the Carlisle Indian Industrial School and almost seventy years since her death, a building at the Carlisle Barracks was named "Ann Ely Hall." Noted as "the first building on Carlisle Barracks to be named after a civilian and a woman," the hall's renaming symbolized the work of all the teachers who dedicated their lives to teaching Indians on the barrack grounds.[176]

Similar to Ely's recognition, in 1987 a Thomasite was posthumously recognized for his service to the islands for both his own life's work and that of all American teachers who helped to establish a public school system in the Philippines. Described as the "first memorial to a foreigner, an early American school teacher," a bust and plaque of Walter Marquardt was erected in front of an old schoolhouse to honor all Thomasites' work and dedication to the archipelago over eighty years earlier.[177] Revered years after their service at Carlisle and the Philippines, Carlisle teacher Ann Ely and Thomasite Walter Marquardt represented the presumed benevolence of US imperial ambitions and those who worked on its behalf. However, as with many historical markers, these memorials say more about the time in which they were erected and the process of historical memory and amnesia than they do about the people commemorated. Ely and Marquardt should not be blindly valorized as individuals—or on behalf of the larger experiments they represent—without also acknowledging both the devastating faults of the larger system in which they worked, as well as, in some cases, their own shortsightedness.

At the risk of oversimplifying these imperial missions' "positive" contributions, Western education undoubtedly provided several colonized individuals opportunities that they otherwise would not have had. For example, some recipients of forced assimilation rose to be leaders within their communities and beyond and used the tools of Western education to fight back against those in power. Still, such schooling stripped away indigenous knowledge, privileging modern, "civilized" norms and values. Individual teachers like Ely and Marquardt made daily decisions in the classroom and beyond that impacted their students, sometimes for better and others for worse. Guided by their own biases, they, like their students, worked within a system perverted by structural inequalities. Serving on the front lines of this educational experiment, teachers ultimately determined much about the successes and failures of US imperial policies. Clearly, many teachers embraced the racist or elitist views embedded in the educational mission of the Indian and Philippines Services. Still, in these and other cases, their professional choices during and after working at Carlisle and the Philippines overwhelmingly suggest a collective investment in education as a means of improving the lives of Filipinos and Indians, rather than simply their dependence upon a system they helped to create. While most teachers seem to have supported the US government's mission to assimilate colonized populations, some came to criticize the larger bureaucracy or flaws of the dominant culture. And, even those who fully embraced imperial education likely provided their students with the skills and means that allowed them to increase their own, their family's, and their communities' autonomy.

Regardless of the extent to which teachers intentionally promoted imperial education or empowered indigenous students, they, in turn, navigated and reproduced the systems that sought to indoctrinate Indian and Filipino subjects to follow "civilized" American mores. Purposefully or not, they normalized white supremacist ideas at the expense of indigenous autonomy, even as a few individuals sought to preserve what they saw as the "good" in the Indian or Filipino cultures. Ultimately, the extent to which teachers' behaviors or written reflections exhibited their "being civilized" is debatable, and their actions—benevolent or not—reinforced power at the center of empire rather than the periphery.

CONCLUSION

LEGACIES OF IMPERIAL EDUCATION

On June 7, 1924, former Carlisle teacher Jessie Cook wrote to the commissioner of Indian affairs:

> Before severing my connection with the Indian service I want to thank you for your heartening letter, commending my working during more than thirty years of teaching in Indian schools.
>
> The highways and byways of the service are not thickly sprinkled with words of praise, and, while I have not missed them, finding ample reward in the love of the girls and boys with whom I have come in contact, your letter makes me realize that it is very pleasant to be commended.
>
> I leave the service with regret, and shall watch with keenest interest the progress of the Indians, towards understanding citizenship, which, though slow, I believe to be sure.[1]

Cook's enthusiasm regarding her work and her confidence in American Indians' "progress . . . towards understanding citizenship" can partially be explained by the fact that just five days before she wrote to the commissioner of Indian affairs, President Calvin Coolidge signed the Indian Citizenship Act of 1924. It guaranteed that "all non citizen Indians born within the territorial limits of the United States be . . . declared . . . citizens of the United States."[2] Of course, not all people shared Cook's apparent excitement about the new legislation, nor were all Indians actually given the full rights of citizenship until decades later.[3] Nevertheless, Cook's optimism regarding Indian advancement appears genuine, as she credited Indian youth's "love" with having sustained her thirty-two year career in an otherwise thankless job.

Years before retirement, Cook expressed her particular commitment to Carlisle, writing to Superintendent Friedman in 1912 that she hoped to return to the school to teach because she "believe[d] in Carlisle," where she thought Indian students could "acquire a broader outlook and more power from their fuller life there."[4] Although she never returned to the Pennsylvania Indian school, where she had taught between 1898 and 1903, Cook remained in the Indian Service for twelve more years, ultimately expressing her faith in Indian "progress," however "slow."

Like Cook, some of the most committed teachers in the Philippines believed in their work, enabling them to bear the multiple challenges that threatened their success. In 1909, eight years into his three-decade-long career in the Philippines, then superintendent Walter Marquardt explained that teachers new to the islands must be confident in their long-term ability to make positive change in order to withstand the stresses they would encounter. Addressing teachers recently appointed under his supervision, he advised:

> In order to prevent despondency and fear of imaginary ills, he [the teacher] must throw himself body and soul into his work so that each night he can retire ready for a night's repose and each morning arise ready for the day's problem and work. He must have sufficient faith in the ultimate outcome of his efforts and sufficient enthusiasm in his work to meet all obstacles cheerfully. He must learn to consider broken promises, cholera, dysentery, and typhoons as part of the regular work. . . . He must do a certain amount of reading in order to retain his vocabulary and to maintain his mental balance . . . keep himself well informed on school affairs both here and current events at home.[5]

Marquardt instructed new teachers to dedicate themselves wholeheartedly to their work but to expect multiple problems that would test their physical and mental health. He suggested that teachers maintain ties to home and pursue intellectual activities to counterbalance the chaos and mental anguish that they would inevitably have to manage while in the Philippines. For Marquardt, maintaining a certain distance between "us" and "them" and preserving a sense of self and purpose would make the work bearable, even enjoyable and worthwhile. The job of the teacher abroad, then, was not to overly accommodate or learn from local customs—it was not to view the educational venture as a two-way learning opportunity—but instead to remain steadfastly committed to the imperial mission. Clearly, teachers in the Philippines experienced severe hardships, sometimes making their work impossible. Still, some, at least from an imperialist's perspective, found success perhaps because they, like Marquardt, maintained their faith and enthusiasm in their work, even in the face of grave adversity.

Acknowledging that indigenous and Western cultures are dynamic and diverse is critical: that they change over time and space, interact with, adapt, and influence one another, and, on their own, represent multiple peoples and customs, ultimately enhancing the understanding that, even outside of discussions of these imperial education experiments, "Filipino," "Indian," and "Western" cultures were (and are) not monolithic. However peoples and cultures are classified, they are all part of a larger world, and they, too, have moved through history, changed due to internal as well as external forces. Thus, to view the Filipino and Indian education experiments as simply being forced upon unwilling participants is an oversimplification, as Native American and Filipino peoples saw some benefits that such schooling might offer but also struggled to maintain certain autonomy. Of course, indigenous people's reactions and accommodations to such educational intervention must be considered within a broader historical context, as powers vied for control and as individuals sought what was best for themselves, their loved ones, and their communities within a particular moment.

Still, both at Carlisle and in the Philippines, structural inequities shaped students' and teachers' experiences. Such power imbalances often advantaged teachers, whose cultural assumptions and prejudices reinforced their commitment to the work, even as they faced challenges. At times, educators worked with pupils unable or unwilling to adapt to new norms. They had flawed, even abusive, leaders incapable of providing support or guidance. Moreover, they encountered profound threats, including disease and violence, as well as personal crises and traumas—death or illness of loved ones, sexual harassment, financial hardship—all while enduring what some of them saw as the monotonous yet all-consuming lifestyle that characterized imperial education. Ultimately, the US government's charge to teachers—to acculturate peoples who, in various ways, resisted federal authority—suggests that policymakers and educators alike believed in the power of schooling to affect profound change. Thus, teaching empire arose not as a choice regarding whether Western education was benevolent or just but rather, having already bought into its perceived promise, it became the method of effectively transferring such knowledge and ideology in the face of challenging circumstances on the ground.

In many ways, Indian and Philippine Service teachers transformed indigenous cultures and structures. They introduced new ways of living and communicating, disrupting familial and social norms, and put into place a schooling system that represented US power, sometimes inflaming anti-US sentiments in the populations they claimed to serve. Yet they also gave Indians and Filipinos knowledge and skills to develop powerful responses to colonial and imperial ventures, whether they sought to assimilate or resist government efforts. In these and other ways, schoolhouses served as micro sites of empire; teachers—representing US interests and Western ideals of civilization—passed along knowledge in an attempt to assimilate students to the dominant culture, reproducing gendered and raced hierarchies of power. They taught boys and girls skills according to their gender and how to embody norms of respectability, all while emphasizing white superiority and native inferiority. Yet, in other ways, teachers challenged norms of the larger society, provided students the means to reshape their own futures, and demanded respect from their superiors, shaping their own and their students' experiences.

Although many teachers reflected upon their work—their successes, failures, strengths, and weaknesses—only a few set their efforts in a broader context, at least in their writings. Some considered teaching, particularly education of native peoples, their life's work, while many others likely deemed it just a job, and others fell somewhere in-between. Most teachers came to recognize—willingly or not—that their vocation involved at least a minimal amount of reciprocal learning and that they, as well as their students, demonstrated agency. Even in situations where, as philosopher Paulo Freire describes, teachers only attempted to "pour in" knowledge and dismiss students' contributions, they still learned about native cultures, of whom some came to respect.[6] Indeed, a few romanticized indigenous ways of life in ways that ultimately challenged their mission. Still, most teachers dedicated to Indian or Filipino "uplift" often did not see much value in the cultures that their work sought to replace or destroy. Indeed, many of the most ardent education activists continued to devalue their colonial subjects' autonomy and way of life. Even so, many genuinely believed that their work would ultimately help native peoples and prepare them to be productive citizens. Others learned that without full societal investment, education was not a panacea; it could not counter the devastation wrought by social ills like poverty or racism. Moreover, while some of these teachers were committed to Indian and Filipino "rights," they did not always understand those rights in the same ways as did their students or the communities from which they came.

Ultimately, the business of imperial education was serious. After leaving the Philippines Service and before working at Carlisle, Clara Donaldson pledged on September 8, 1914:

I *Clara R. Donaldson* do solemnly swear that I will support and defend the Constitution of the United States against all enemies, foreign and domestic; that I will bear true faith and allegiance to the same; that I take this obligation freely, without any mental reservation or purpose of evasion; and that I will well and faithfully discharge the duties of the office on which I am about to enter: So help me GOD.[7]

In joining the Indian School Service, Donaldson—and hundreds of other teachers—were required to declare their loyalty to the US rule of law as represented by the Constitution. Teachers headed to the Philippines took similar oaths. Largely a symbolic gesture, taking such an oath did not, in fact, ensure teachers' patriotism. However, writing and mandating such an oath suggests that policymakers envisioned these individuals' work as critical to the security of the United States. It bound civil service teachers together, at least in the realm of imagination, even when reality—such as the horror some teachers felt at the US use of torture in the Philippines—undercut such unity.[8]

Still, many teachers did embrace a sense of national purpose, and most felt that they represented a force larger than themselves, even as on-the-ground work of imperial education was sometimes fragile. In reminiscing about her venture to the Philippines, recall that Thomasite Mary Fee characterized herself as "one of an army of enthusiasts enlisted to instruct our little brown brother."[9] In many ways, such a description can also apply to Carlisle teachers who were hired, in a sense, to "pass the torch of Occidental knowledge" to American Indians within the borders of the continental United States rather than, as Fee described, "several degrees east of the international date-line."[10] Although not organized as part of official military operations, the Carlisle and Philippines projects were authorized by the US Department of War and sought to take over where soldiers left off. In the nineteenth-century American West, US soldiers decimated Indian peoples and lands, forcing them onto reservations before the Indian wars moved into classrooms. In the Philippines, US soldiers continued to suppress Filipino resistance as teachers established schools to quell unrest and disseminate American culture, again shifting the war for people's hearts and minds into the schoolhouse. Yet such work was vulnerable to both material and more elusive threats: from violence, disease, and initial lack of infrastructure to poor or stressful working conditions, teachers' agitation, and outside criticism. Further complicating our understanding of how empires work, some of these same hazards, at times, strengthened the broader mission—for example, bolstering teachers' and education leaders' resolve—while at the same time revealing its weakness, including the overgrowth of bureaucracy.

While the history of teachers involved in building US empire has largely gone untold, the legacy of their labor remains. Within the continental United States, American Indian boarding schools continue to exist a century after Carlisle's demise. As of 2019, the oldest boarding school still standing is the Riverside Indian School in Oklahoma; founded in 1871, it continues to teach Native American children. The 2019–2020 school application requests guardians to complete a "Social Summary" for their child and explains, "The enrollment of your child in a federal government boarding school should be a shared and continuous responsibility with you as parent(s) and/or guardian(s) or responsible relative—particularly, in reference to your child's social and educational development while he/she is in attendance at a boarding school." The prior year's application also included a "Parent-Student-School Compact" whereby each party was asked to sign an agreement that listed "respect" of "cultural differences" and one's own culture as responsibilities of all participants.[11] In many ways, these modern applications seem anathema to Carlisle's nineteenth-century slogan: "To civilize the Indian, get him into civilization. To keep him civilized, let him stay."[12] Like Carlisle of a century ago, Riverside originally sought to "take the Indian out" of its students, although today the school honors students' heritage. In many ways, Indian schools are a product of their time, reflecting the biases and ideals of the broader society. Carlisle marked the beginning of a new era in Indian assimilation, one that still makes efforts to integrate American Indians into US society but that today also respects cultural difference. Of course, without addressing larger structural and policy inequities plaguing Native communities today, even the most enlightened education programs can only do so much to alleviate the poverty, lack of resources, and lack of opportunity that continue to haunt indigenous lives and well-being.

Twenty years after Carlisle opened, the Thomasites' departure for the Philippines signaled a similar strategy overseas. The year 2001 marked the centennial celebration of their arrival on the islands. The US Embassy, the American Studies Association, and the Phil-Am Educational Foundation held events throughout the year, including a memorial ceremony, art exhibition, and academic conference.[13] Such commemorations honored the original Thomasites, attributing much of the Philippines's modern school system to their hard work. In some ways, the Indian and Philippine school systems of today—with all of their achievements and flaws—can be attributed to teachers' labors of a century past. Of course, American Indians and Filipinos shaped these structures as well, supporting and resisting US intervention in their children's education. Many other actors—from government leaders to students—also played key roles. Ultimately, it was teachers who implemented, negotiated, and mediated US government education policies with Native Americans and Filipinos, helping to make meaning of imperial experiments and ambitions.

A decade into the US education experiment in the Philippines, Mary Fee wrote, "Twenty or thirty years from now, when the American school system will have aided certain sons of the people, men of elemental strength, to bully and fight their way to the front, and they will have become the evidence that we were telling the truth—then the results will be visible in more things than in annual school commencements and in an increase in the output of stenographers and bookkeepers."[14] Although Fee supported US intervention in Filipino schooling, she believed that progress would take time. More than statistics, she believed that full success lay in Filipinos benefiting from and buying into American schooling, ultimately joining the fight to become its leaders. She believed in the "truth" of the mission but also recognized at least some of its limitations. In the Philippines as in Carlisle, policymakers hoped that teachers would be able to effect rapid and "benevolent" cultural transformation and force colonized peoples to accept a new way of thinking and being. Perhaps a few teachers learned from their experiences that true change was not as simple: it required careful negotiation and time; was messy, chaotic, and complex; and ultimately was dependent upon and shaped by the will and agency of colonized peoples. Instilling and inspiring such transformation defined teaching empire.

Although I knew from the outset of this project ten years ago that the stories recounted in in this book were critical to understanding the structures and systems of power that continue today, I did not imagine that the US government would, in 2018, implement and defend a policy that purposefully separated mothers and fathers from their children as a purported deterrent to US migration, as a means of bolstering the nation, one that echoed the separation of indigenous families more than a century before.

Around the turn of the twentieth century, white reformers' efforts to resolve the "Indian problem"—the persistence of indigenous life and culture despite centuries of physical and cultural genocide—latched onto the family as the site of cultural change, sending thousands of American Indian children to boarding schools far removed from the "barbaric" influences of natal mothers, fathers, and communities, and this book recounts part of this devastating history and legacy. This practice of family separation as a measure of building nationhood had a long, devastating historical precedent, having begun centuries earlier as peoples were brutally ripped from their homelands and sent across an ocean to labor on behalf of a nation ultimately built on their blood and sacrifice, only to be further separated across generations as enslaved children and kin were sold to faraway homes and plantations. The Indian boarding school movement, too, is but one chapter in a much larger story of family separation among indigenous communities, rationalized by US government officials and reformers as a necessary measure toward building a stronger, more unified America.

Writing in 2011, sociologist Julian Go asserted that the American empire was already in decline, arguing that "falling empires, like rising ones, do not behave well. As the American empire falls, it will not go down without a fight."[15] In the spring of 2018, Donald Trump's administration asserted power in line with its America First ideology in one of the most inhumane ways possible: separating asylum-seeking parents and children from one another. Media outlets told stories of infants and toddlers sent to faraway institutions without their parents' consent or knowledge. The US government deported fathers and mothers with promises of reunification, though bringing families back together was not only unlikely but perhaps impossible; other parents were detained in immigration detention centers indefinitely. Protesters took to the streets. Immigration rights activists lobbied Congress. Lawyers volunteered to represent desperate guardians and locate children scattered across the nation. Ordinary citizens volunteered to serve as foster parents, and American mothers raised money to drive cross-country to reunite separated families one by one. If ever an empire behaved poorly, 2018 witnessed an American empire in tumultuous decline, a power whose moral compass had failed.

Of course, Trump's election and his actions did not signal the beginning of the end of American empire; instead, his rise to power is a symptom of an empire that, as suggested by Go, was already falling. Still, just as turn-of-the-twentieth-century policies of imperial education illustrate how a growing empire does "not behave well," the 2018 policy—created to defend American citizens and the nation from the apparent threat posed by asylum-seeking children, mothers, fathers, aunts, uncles, and grandparents—epitomizes how an empire in decline misbehaves. One of the central facets of this book is to put the people into empire, to show that empire is not an amorphous thing that acts alone but rather something that depends upon the will and actions of human beings. While everyday folks around the turn of the twentieth century largely bought into and drove the nation's imperial desires, in 2018 a critical mass of Americans resisted family separation that had been declared necessary on their behalf, giving at least a modicum of hope for the most vulnerable and for the nation.

APPENDIX ONE

CARLISLE TEACHERS, INCLUDING
WORK IMMEDIATELY AFTER CARLISLE

Alphabetical List of Carlisle Teachers	Sex	Marital Status at Carlisle	Race	Years at Carlisle	Work after Carlisle
Elizabeth Bender	F	Single	American Indian	1915–1916	Nurse
Della Botsford	F	Single	White	1890s	US government, DC
Katharine Bowersox	F	Single	White	1890s–1910s	Unknown
Marianna Burgess	F	Single	White	1879–1904	Activist/other
Lucy Case	F	Single	White	1910/ 1913–1915	Indian Service
Jessie Cook	F	Widow	White	1898–1903	Indian Service
Mabel Curtis	F	Single	White	1910–1911	Indian Service
Emma Cutter	F	Single	White	1879–1907	US government, DC
Elizabeth DeHuff	F	Married	White	1914	Other
John DeHuff	M	Married	White	1914–1916	Indian Service
Nellie Robertson Denny	F	Married	American Indian	1894–1918 (as teacher/ clerk)	Other
Lydia Dittes	F	Single/ Married	White	1885–1886 1890–1892 (matron)	Indian Service
Clara Donaldson	F	Single	White	1914–1918	Indian Service
Verna Dunagan	F	Single	White	1915–1918	US government, DC
Clara May Ellis	F	Single	White	1908	Unknown
Ann Ely	F	Single	White	1879–1903	Retired
Hazel Emery	F	Single	White	1911–1914	Indian Service
Miss Ericson	F	Single	White	1890s–1899	Puerto Rico Service
Emma Foster	F	Widow	White	1902–1918	US government, DC
Moses Friedman	M	Married	White	1908–1914	Education
Lottie Georgenson	F	Single	White	1910–1914	Indian Service

(continued on the next page)

Alphabetical List of Carlisle Teachers	Sex	Marital Status at Carlisle	Race	Years at Carlisle	Work after Carlisle
J. W. Gibbs	F	Widow	White	1880s	Unknown
Sallie Hagan	F	Single	White	1911–1914	Unknown
Annie Hamilton	F	Single	White	1889–1896	Unknown
Miss Haskins	F	Single	White	1879	Unknown
Rey Heagy	M	N/A	White	1918	Indian Service
Emma Hetrick	F	Single	White	1905–1910	Puerto Rico Service
Mary Hyde	F	Single	White	1879	Unknown
Lida Johnston	F	Single	White	1907–1912	US government, DC
Elizabeth Jones	F	Single	White	1913–1914	Education
Mattie Lane	F	Single	White	1911–1912	Education
Dora LeCrone	F	Single	White	1904–1911	Alaska Service
Jerome Lilly	M	Single	White	1916	Unknown
Emma Lovewell	F	Widow	White	1909–1914	Unknown
Anna Luckenback	F	Single	White	1890s	US government, DC
Sarah Mather	F	Single	White	1879	Retired
Royal Mann	M	Single/ Married	White	1913–1915	Indian Service
Hattie McDowell	F	Single	White	1904–1918	Indian Service
Amelia McMichael	F	Single	White	1906–1909	Alaska Service
Marianna Moore	F	Single	White	1911–1914	Writer
Fannie Peter	F	Single	White	1890s–1904	US government, DC
Adelaide Reichel	F	Single	White	1907–1918	Unknown
Margaret Roberts	F	Single	White	1900–1904; 1914–1916	Indian Service
Sadie Robertson	F	Single	White	1918	Indian Service
Frances Scales	F	N/A	White	1902–1908	Indian Service
Miss Semple	F	Single	White	1879	Unknown
Clara Snoddy	F	Single	White	1914–1918	Indian Service
Laura Spencer	F	Single	White	1879 (soon became matron)	Unknown
Margaret Sweeney	F	Single	White	1909–1918	Indian Service
Fernando Tranbarger	M	Single/ Married	White	1909–1911	Indian Service
Katherine Bingley Tranbarger	F	Single/ Married	White	1908–1911	Other
John Whitwell	M	Married	White	1907–1914	Indian Service

Gwen Williams	F	Single	White	1914–1918	US government, DC
Idilla Wilson	F	Single	White	1912–1918	US government, DC
Mariette Wood	F	Single	White	1889–1891; 1897–1909	US government, DC

PHILIPPINES TEACHERS (THOMASITES), INCLUDING WORK IMMEDIATELY AFTER PHILIPPINES

Alphabetical List of Thomasites	Sex	Birthplace/ Year	Marital Status, in Philippines	Race	Years in Philippines	Work after Philippines
Frederick G. Behner	M	Ohio, 1874	Single	W	1901–1905	Minister
B. N. Blakeslee	M	Unknown	Single	W	1901–1902	Unknown
Harvey A. Bordner	M	Pennsylvania, 1872	Married	W	1902–1936	Philippines
Maude Ethel Martin Bordner	F	Pennsylvania, 1876	Married	W	1902–1936	Philippines
Norman W. Cameron	M	Maryland, 1876	Single	W	1901–1904	Higher ed.
George E. Carrothers	M	Indiana, 1880	Single	W	1909–1913	Higher ed.
J. W. Cheesborough	M	North Carolina, 1879	Single	W	1903–1908	Unknown
Frank W. Cheney	M	New York, 1881	Single	W	1908–1920	Education
Harrie Newton Cole	M	New York, 1870	Married	W	1901–1904	Higher ed.
Mary Cole	F	Iowa, 1871	Married	W	1901–1904	Homemaker
John DeHuff	M	Indiana, 1872	Single	W	1901–1913	Indian Service
Elizabeth Willis DeHuff	F	Georgia, 1886	Single	W	1910–1913	Indian Service
Clara R. Donaldson	F	Ohio, 1861	Single	W	1901–1914	Indian Service
John C. Early	M	Missouri, 1876	Single/ Married	W	1906–1931	Philippines
Willa Rhodes Early	F	Montana, 1883	Single/ Married	W	1902; 1912–1932	Philippines
Glen Evans	M	Michigan (after 1873)	Single	W	1904–1905	Unknown
John Evans	M	Michigan, 1873	Single/ Married	W	1901–1915	Postmaster
Mary H. Fee	F	Missouri or Illinois, 1872	Single	W	1901–1917	Writer
Jules Theophile Frelin	M	Ohio, 1877	Single	W	1901–1904	Higher ed.
Moses Friedman	M	Ohio, 1875	Single	W	1904–1906	Indian Service

Herman Hespelt	M	New York, 1886	Single	W	1911–1916	Higher ed.
Alice Hollister	F	Michigan, 1872	Single/ Married	W	1901–1941	Philippines
Walter W. Marquardt	M	Ohio, 1878	Single/ Married	W	1901–1941	Philippines
Elizabeth Winifred Mitchell (Campbell)	F	Unknown	Single	W	1901–	Unknown
Blaine Free Moore	M	Ohio, 1879	Single	W	1901–1906	Higher ed.
John Muerman	M	Ohio, 1865	Single	W	1901–1915	Higher ed.
Reece A. Oliver	M	Indiana, 1889	Single	W	1914–1930s	War/relief
Edward Sharp	M	Tennessee	Single	W	1902–1904	Business
Earl Smith	M	Iowa, 1890	Married	W	1917–1920	Lawyer
Laura Gibson Smith	F	Iowa, 1891	Married	W	1917–1920; 1923–1925	Writer
Ralph Wendell Taylor	M	Michigan	Single	W	1901–1908	Unknown
Fernando G. Tranbarger	M	Indiana, 1876	Single	W	1906–1909	Indian Service
H. O. Whiting	M	Missouri, 1881	Single	W	1906–1908	Unknown

APPENDIX THREE

STUDENT ATTENDANCE AT CARLISLE

Year	Average Number of Students	Average Age of Students (Male)	Average Age of Students (Female)	Number of Students Who Graduated	Number of Student Deaths
1879	158	16.44	14.6		1
1880	239	13.35	11.76		6
1881	295	14.21	12.33		8
1882	393	14.73	12.48		10
1883	368	16.71	14.91		8
1884	421	15.25	13.33		4
1885	494	16.11	14.37		9
1886	484	15.24	13.87		8
1887	547	15.1	15.12		11
1888	563	16.12	13.92		21
1889	595	16.43	14.52	14	13
1890	702	15.7	13.59	18	10
1891	754	15.57	14.84	11	8
1892	779	16.32	16.13	3	5
1893	731	17.47	15.48	6	5
1894	656	15.75	14.94	19	4
1895	668	17.01	14.52	20	11
1896	741	16.38	14.12	25	6
1897	790	15.81	14.42	26	3
1898	851	16.32	14.88	24	3
1899	878	16.83	15.49	31	6
1900	981	14.91	15.40	37	7
1901	970	17.1	14.93	29	3
1902	1,023	16.67	15.8	42	0
1903	963	16.3	14.73	47	5
1904	1,025	16.68	14.51	43	6
1905	898	16.44	14.58	43	7
1906	981	15.7	15.08	30	4
1907	984	18.46	15.47	23	3
1908	970	17.62	16.75	27	3
1909	967	18.02	15.81	25	2
1910	N/A	17.85	17.04	23	6
1911	932	17.75	16.7	23	3

1912	792	17.51	16.56	21	4
1913	N/A	17.48	15.97	15	4
1914	668	17.5	16.49	18	2
1915	~661	17.95	17.02	30	1
1916	~661	17.39	16.24		4
1917	~246	16.74	15.87	56	2
1918	~246	16.4	16.6	25	1
Total				758	220

Note: ~ refers to numbers that are averaged according to superintendent administrations. See Bell's figure 2: Total Number of Students Who Attended Carlisle, Organized by Tenure of Superintendents, page 77.

Source: Genevieve Bell, "Telling Stories out of School: Remembering the Carlisle Indian Industrial School, 1879–1918," PhD dissertation, Stanford University, 1998, 45, 77, 333, 400, 402.

NOTES

INTRODUCTION: AN INTIMATE AND FRAGILE EMPIRE

1. Six weeks earlier, on December 10, 1898, the United States and Spain signed the Treaty of Paris after months of negotiations, ending the War of 1898 and resulting in the transfer of the Spanish empire's control over Puerto Rico, Guam, and the Philippines to the United States, with Cuba established as a US protectorate. The United States annexed Hawaii as a territory in 1898, after decades of economic, military, and political dealings in the islands.

2. Although Uncle Sam's attention seems particularly focused upon the front-row students, his gaze looks toward a prospective student standing in the doorway, a caricature of "China," evident by the stereotypical ponytail hairstyle. The Native American student's gaze is also directed toward this newcomer, China. On the periphery of empire, in the back of the classroom, a caricature of an African American man stands on a ladder, washing windows. He looks toward the center of the classroom showing his interest in Uncle Sam's lesson but stares blankly and ultimately is not welcome at the table. The second tier of desks are occupied by white-skinned pupils studying books on Texas, California, Arizona, New Mexico, with one darker-skinned pupil concentrating on Alaska, representing its indigenous community. The United States purchased Alaska from Russia in 1867, and it became a US territory in 1912. For more on Alaskan history including its colonial legacy, see Stephen W. Haycox, *Alaska: An American Colony* (Seattle: University of Washington Press, 2002).

3. See Gail Bederman, *Manliness and Civilization: A Cultural History of Gender and Race in the United States, 1880–1917* (Chicago: University of Chicago Press, 1995). Bederman complicates the meaning of "civilization," illustrating how its use changed over time, was wielded for different purposes by various individuals, and had particular implications for gender and race. For a discussion of "civilization," education, and the so-called Indian problem, see David Wallace Adams, *Education for Extinction: American Indians and the Boarding School Experience, 1875–1928* (Lawrence: University of Kansas, 1995), especially part I. Also see David Wallace Adams, "Fundamental Considerations: The Deep Meaning of Native American Schooling, 1880–1900," *Harvard Educational Review* 58, 1 (February 1988): 1–28; Genevieve Bell, "Telling Stories out of School: Remembering the Carlisle Indian Industrial School, 1879–1918" (PhD dissertation, Stanford University, 1998); Brenda J. Child, *Boarding School Seasons: American Indian Families, 1900–1940* (Lincoln: University of Nebraska Press, 1998); Margaret L. Archuleta, Brenda Child, and K. Tsianina Lomawaima, eds., *Away from Home: American Indian Boarding School Experiences, 1879–2000* (Phoenix: Heard Museum, 2000); Cathleen D. Cahill, *Federal Fathers and Mothers: A Social History of the United States Indian Service, 1869–1933* (Chapel Hill: University of North Carolina Press, 2011); Mi-

chael C. Coleman, *American Indian Children at School, 1850–1930* (Jackson: University Press of Mississippi, 1993); Jon Reyhner and Jeanne Eder, *A History of Indian Education* (Billings: Eastern Montana College, 1989); Jacqueline Fear-Segal, *White Man's Club: Schools, Race, and the Struggle of Indian Acculturation* (Lincoln: University of Nebraska, 2007); Jacqueline Fear-Segal and Susan D. Rose, eds., *Carlisle Indian Industrial School: Indigenous Histories, Memories, and Reclamations* (Lincoln: University of Nebraska Press, 2016); Frederick E. Hoxie, *A Final Promise: The Campaign to Assimilate the Indians, 1880–1920* (Lincoln: University of Nebraska Press, 1984), 53–54; Margaret D. Jacobs, *White Mother to a Dark Race: Settler Colonialism, Maternalism, and the Removal of Indigenous Children in the American West and Australia, 1880–1910* (Lincoln: University of Nebraska Press, 2009); Anne Paulet, "To Change the World: The Use of American Indian Education in the Philippines," *History of Education Quarterly* 47, 2 (May 2007): 173–202; Clifford E. Trafzer, Jean A. Keller, and Lorene Sisquoc, *Boarding School Blues: Revisiting American Indian Educational Experiences* (Lincoln: University of Nebraska Press, 2006); Andrew Woolford, *This Benevolent Experiment: Indigenous Boarding Schools, Genocide, and Redress in Canada and the United States* (Lincoln: University of Nebraska Press, 2015). For more on "Anglo" identity in the context of empire, see Julian Go, *Patterns of Empire: The British and American Empires, 1688 to the Present* (New York: Cambridge University Press, 2011). For a discussion of citizenship, education, and empire in other American contexts, see Clif Stratton, *Education for Empire: American Schools, Race, and the Paths of Good Citizenship* (Oakland: University of California Press, 2016).

4. A. J. Angulo, *Empire and Education: A History of Greed and Goodwill from the War of 1898 to the War on Terror* (New York: Palgrave MacMillan, 2012); Benjamin Justice, "Education at the End of a Gun: The Origins of American Imperial Education and the Case of the Philippines," in Noah W. Sobe, ed., *American Post-Conflict Educational Reform: From the Spanish-American War to Iraq* (New York: Palgrave Macmillan, 2009), 19–52; Glenn Anthony May, *Social Engineering in the Philippines: The Aims, Execution, and Impact of American Colonial Policy, 1900–1913* (Westport, CT: Greenwood Press, 1980); Paulet, "To Change the World"; Peter Tarr, "The Education of the Thomasites: American School Teachers in Philippine Colonial Society, 1901–1913" (PhD dissertation, Cornell University, 2006); Jonathan Zimmerman, *Innocents Abroad: American Teachers in the American Century* (Cambridge, MA: Harvard University Press, 2006).

5. Cahill, *Federal Fathers and Mothers*, 44–45, 55–56. The Indian School Service was established in 1882 to focus on American Indian children's education.

6. Noting the diversity of the US population in the late nineteenth century—considering indigenous peoples, the legacy of slavery, and immigration trends—I use the term "American" here mindfully, acknowledging its multiple meanings but noting the power that white, Anglo, Protestant authorities claimed in defining "American" culture.

7. This book contends that "empire" is not simply made by states but by the people on the ground doing the everyday intimate work of empire. This focus on "the intimate" is inspired by Ann Laura Stoler's foundational work; see Ann Laura Stoler,

Carnal Knowledge and Imperial Power: Race and the Intimate in Colonial Rule (Berkeley: University of California Press, 2002). Also see Jane A. Margold, "Egalitarian Ideals and Exclusionary Practices: U.S. Pedagogy in the Colonial Philippines, *Journal of Historical Sociology* 8, 4 (December 1995): 375–394. Margold focuses on US teachers in the archipelago and examines "local sites and ordinary, everyday practices of social regulation," and comes to different conclusions, 375. Also see Tarr, "The Education of Thomasites," 565–695.

8. Paulo Freire, *Pedagogy of the Oppressed* (1971; repr., New York: Continuum Press, 2001).

9. For commentary on the makeup of the Indian School Service teaching force being largely white middle-class women, see Adams, *Education for Extinction*, 82–86; and Cahill, *Federal Fathers and Mothers*, 63–81. For commentary on teachers sent overseas in the twentieth century (including those who ventured to the Philippines) being largely white and middle-class as well as a discussion on the meaning of "middle class" in this time period, see Zimmerman, *Innocents Abroad*, 13–14 and Tarr, "The Education of Thomasites," 198–199.

10. "Lovewell" became Emma's married name in 1890, but it is used here because only the first letter of her maiden name is known.

11. Memorandum: Emma C. Lovewell, 19 November 1915, Emma C. Lovewell Folder, National Personnel Records Center (NPRC), Saint Louis, MO; Personal Record of Emma C. Lovewell, 11 May 1911, Emma C. Lovewell Folder, NPRC.

12. Assistant Commissioner of Indian Affairs E. B. Merritt to Emma Lovewell, 6 May 1922, Emma Lovewell Folder, NPRC.

13. Emma Lovewell to Commissioner of Indian Affairs Francis Leupp, 28 February 1908, Emma Lovewell Folder, NPRC.

14. Memorandum: Emma C. Lovewell, 19 November 1915, Emma Lovewell Folder, NPRC; Bell, "Telling Stories out of School," 46, 158; Cahill, *Federal Fathers and Mothers*, 89.

15. Emma Lovewell to Inspector of the Office of Indian Affairs E. B. Linnen, 5 September 1914, Emma Lovewell Folder, NPRC.

16. Ibid.

17. Emma Lovewell to Mr. J. Whitwell, 23 October 1912, John Whitwell Folder 2, NPRC.

18. United States Congressional Inquiry, *Carlisle Indian School, Hearings before the Joint Commission of the Congress of the United States to Investigate Indian Affairs, Feb. 6–8 and March 25, 1914*, 63rd Congress, 2nd Session, Part II (Washington, DC: Government Printing Office, 1914), 935–1390: Testimony from teachers Mrs. Bertha D. Canfield, Mrs. Angel Dietz, Mrs. Lydia E. Kaup, Miss Emma C. Lovewell, Miss Hattie M. McDowell, Miss Margaret M. Sweeney, Mrs. Emma H. Foster, Miss Lelah Burns, Miss Adelaide B. Reichel, and Principal Teacher Mr. John Whitwell.

19. See Adams, *Education for Extinction;* Cahill, *Federal Fathers and Mothers;* Fear-Segal, *White Man's Club;* Anne Paulet, "'The Only Good Indian Is a Dead Indian': The

Use of United States Indian Policy as a Guide for the Conquest and Occupation of the Philippines, 1898–1905" (PhD dissertation, Rutgers University, 1995). On the rhetoric of "rescue" and women's involvement in reform see Peggy Pascoe, *Relations of Rescue: The Search for Female Moral Authority in the American West, 1874–1939* (New York: Oxford University Press, 1990).

20. Emma C. Lovewell to Mr. J. Whitwell, 9 April 1914, John Whitwell Folder 2, NPRC.

21. Adams, *Education for Extinction*, 82–84; Cahill, *Federal Fathers and Mothers*, chapter 3.

22. Carlisle Supervisor in Charge O. H. Lipps to Commissioner of Indian Affairs Cato Sells, 30 December 1914, Emma C. Lovewell Folder, NPRC.

23. Emma C. Lovewell to Commissioner of Indian Affairs Cato Sells, 10 December 1915, Emma C. Lovewell Folder, NPRC.

24. Emma C. Lovewell to E. B. Linnen, 5 September 1914, Emma C. Lovewell Folder, NPRC.

25. See Cahill, *Federal Fathers and Mothers*, chapter 3; Paulet, "'The Only Good Indian Is a Dead Indian,'" 336–338; Adams, "Fundamental Considerations," 2–3.

26. Frederick G. Behner, "Rags to Riches in the Ministry," Frederick G. Behner Biographical Information Folder, Bentley Historical Library, University of Michigan (BHL), 1–2.

27. Amparo Santamaria Lardizabal, "Pioneer American Teachers and Philippine Education" (PhD dissertation, Stanford University, 1956), 11–12; John Charles Muerman, "The Philippine School under the Americans" (PhD dissertation, George Washington University, 1922), 42, 144; Tarr, "The Education of Thomasites," 8–9, 195.

28. Frederick G. Behner, Diary Entries 25, 26, 28 September 1901, Diaries 1901–1902 Folder, BHL.

29. Frederick G. Behner, 5 October 1901, Diaries 1901–1902 Folder, BHL.

30. For illness, see Fredrick G. Behner, "Rags to Riches," 3–4; Behner, February to March, May, August, September 1902, Diaries 1901–1902 Folder, BHL. For village norms, see Behner 28 February 1902, Diaries 1901–1902 Folder, BHL. For environmental disturbances, see Behner, 3, 15 December 1901, 27 February, and 7–15 July 1902, Diaries 1901–1902 Folder, BHL.

31. Behner, 12 September 1902, Diaries 1901–1902 Folder, BHL.

32. Behner, 17, 31 October 1902, Diaries 1901–1902 Folder, BHL.

33. Behner, "Rags to Riches in the Ministry"; Diaries 1901–1902 Folder, BHL; Diaries 1903–1905 Folder, BHL.

34. Behner, 11 Tuesday 1902, Diaries 1901–1902 Folder, BHL.

35. Behner, 14 June 1904, Diaries 1903–1905 Folder, BHL.

36. Behner, 2 July 1904, Diaries 1903–1905 Folder, BHL.

37. Behner, 9 April 1905, Diaries 1903–1905 Folder, BHL.

38. Donna J. Amoroso, "Inheriting the 'Moro Problem': Muslim Authority and Colonial Rule in British Malaya and the Philippines," in Julian Go and Anne L. Foster,

eds., *The American Colonial State in the Philippines: Global Perspectives* (Durham, NC: Duke University Press, 2003), 118–147; Kenton J. Clymer, "Humanitarian Imperialism: David Prescott Barrows and the White Man's Burden in the Philippines," *Pacific Historical Review* 45, 4 (November 1976): 495–517; Julian Go, *American Empire and the Politics of Meaning: Elite Political Cultures in the Philippines and Puerto Rico during U.S. Colonialism* (Durham, NC: Duke University Press, 2008); Judith Raftery, "Textbook Wars: Governor-General James Francis Smith and the Protestant-Catholic Conflict in Public Education in the Philippines, 1904–1907," *History of Education Quarterly* 38, 2 (Summer 1998): 143–164.

39. Behner, 31 July 1902, Diaries 1901–1902 Folder, BHL.

40. Behner, 9 April 1905, Diaries 1903–1905 Folder, BHL.

41. Hoxie, *A Final Promise*, 53–54; Adams, "Fundamental Considerations," 2–4; For commentary on the usage of the term "Indian education," see K. Tsianina Lomawaima, "Estelle Reel, Superintendent of Indian Schools, 1898–1910," *Journal of American Indian Education* 35, 3 (1995): 5.

42. Cahill, *Federal Fathers and Mothers*, 30–32, 44–45. Cahill notes that the Indian Bureau was modeled upon the Freedmen's Bureau, also designed to fill needs presumed temporary.

43. Julian Go, "Introduction: Global Perspectives on the U.S. Colonial State in the Philippines," in Go and Foster, *The American Colonial State in the Philippines*, 8; Cahill, *Federal Fathers and Mothers*, 12.

44. Zimmerman, *Innocents Abroad*, 139: the largest number of US teachers in the Philippines reached 928 in 1902, with 4,000 having taught in the archipelago by 1941.

45. Eric Hobsbawm, *The Age of Empire: 1875–1914* (New York: Vintage Books, 1987); Go, "Introduction: Global Perspectives," 17–18. Anne L. Foster, *Projection and Power: The United States and Europe in Colonial Southeast Asia, 1919–1941* (Durham, NC: Duke University Press, 2010), 6–8, elaborates on a slightly later period referred to as "late high imperialism." Also see Michelle Morgan, "Americanizing the Teachers: Identity, Citizenship, and the Teaching Corps in Hawai'i, 1900–1941," *Western Historical Quarterly* 45 (Summer 2014), 147–167.

46. Walter Nugent, *Habits of Empire: A History of American Expansion* (New York: Knopf, 2008). Also see Niall Ferguson, *Colossus: The Price of America's Empire* (New York: Penguin Books, 2004); Foster and Go, eds., *The American Colonial State in the Philippines*; Hobsbawm, *The Age of Empire*; Go, "Introduction: Global Perspectives," 17–18; Go, *American Empire and the Politics of Meaning*; Matthew Frye Jacobson, *Barbarian Virtues: The United States Encounters Foreign Peoples at Home and Abroad, 1876–1917* (New York: Hill and Wang, 2000); Benjamin Justice, "Education at the End of a Gun: The Origins of American Imperial Education and the Case of the Philippines," in Noah W. Sobe, ed., *American Post-Conflict Educational Reform: From the Spanish-American War to Iraq* (New York: Palgrave Macmillan, 2009), 19–52; Ernest May, *Imperial Democracy: The Emergence of the United States as Great Power* (New York: Harper Torchbooks, 1973); Paul A. Kramer, "Power and Connection: Imperial Histories of the United States

in the World," *American Historical Review* (December 2011): 1348–1391; Charles S. Maier, *Among Empires: American Ascendancy and Its Predecessors* (Cambridge, MA: Harvard University Press, 2006); Alfred W. McCoy and Francisco A. Scarano, eds., *Colonial Crucible: Empire in the Making of the Modern American State* (Madison: University of Wisconsin Press, 2009); Alfred W. McCoy, Francisco A. Scarano, and Courtney Johnson, "On the Tropic of Cancer: Transitions and Transformations in the U.S. Imperial State," in McCoy and Scarano, eds., *Colonial Crucible*, 3–33.

47. William Appleman Williams, *The Tragedy of American Diplomacy* (New York: W. W. Norton, 1988); Frank Ninkovich, "The United States and Imperialism," in Robert D. Schulzinger, ed., *A Companion to American Foreign Relations* (Malden, MA: Blackwell Publishing, 2003), 80.

48. Justice, "Education at the End of a Gun"; Paulet, "To Change the World"; Paulet, "'The Only Good Indian Is a Dead Indian.'" Paulet credits Walter L. Williams as the first scholar to note parallels in policy. See Walter L. Williams, "United States Indian Policy and the Debate over Philippine Annexation: Implications for the Origins of American Imperialism," *Journal of American History* 66, 4 (March 1980): 810–831. Although not making specific comparisons between the Indian and Philippine Civil Service, Clymer's discussion of David Barrows—as a scholar, researcher, and friend of Native Americans, and how he utilized this knowledge in crafting Filipino education— is also relevant here. See Clymer, "Humanitarian Imperialism."

49. Go, "Introduction: Global Perspectives," 8; Julian Go, *Patterns of Empire: The British and American Empires, 1688 to the Present* (New York: Cambridge University Press, 2011); Go, *American Empire and the Politics of Meaning*. See Stoler's foundational study regarding the agency and influence of "colonized" peoples on power and empire, including the categories of "colonized" and "colonizer" as not fixed: Stoler, *Carnal Knowledge and Imperial Power*. Also see del Moral's study regarding empire building in Puerto Rico as one of negotiation, where imperial powers and Puerto Ricans crafted schooling: Solsiree del Moral, *Negotiating Empire: The Cultural Politics of Schools in Puerto Rico, 1898–1952* (Madison: University of Wisconsin Press, 2013). For a discussion on American and "Americanizing" teachers in Hawaii, see Morgan, "Americanizing the Teachers," 147–167.

50. Martin Carnoy, *Education as Cultural Imperialism* (New York: Longman, 1974): Carnoy argues that imperial powers consistently used schooling to dominate and reproduce politically and economically dependent colonized populations and in chapter 6 explores US internal colonialism. See also A. J. Angulo, *Empire and Education: A History of Greed and Goodwill from the War of 1898 to the War on Terror* (New York: Palgrave MacMillan, 2012); Michael B. Katz, *Class, Bureaucracy, and Schools: The Illusion of Educational Change in America* (New York: Praeger, 1971), xvi.

51. For more on "cultural imperialism" see Amy Kaplan, "Left Alone in America," in Amy Kaplan and Donald E. Pease, eds., *Cultures of United States Imperialism* (Durham, NC: Duke University Press, 1993), 3–21; Kristin L. Hoganson, *Fighting for American Manhood: How Gender Politics Provoked the Spanish-American and Philippine-American*

Wars (New Haven, CT: Yale University Press, 1998); Bederman, *Manliness and Civilization*.

52. Justice, "Education at the End of a Gun"; Paulet, "To Change the World"; Paulet, "'The Only Good Indian Is a Dead Indian.'" Justice and Paulet speak to empire in both American Indian and Filipino contexts. For more on empire and the American Indian experience see Cahill, *Federal Fathers and Mothers*; Carnoy, *Education as Cultural Imperialism*. For sources on empire and the Philippines see Angulo, *Empire and Education*; H. W. Brands, *Bound to Empire: The United States and the Philippines* (New York: Oxford University Press, 1992); Go, "Introduction: Global Perspectives"; Paul Kramer, *The Blood of Government: Race, Empire, the United States, and the Philippines* (Chapel Hill: University of North Carolina Press, 2006); May, *Social Engineering in the Philippines*; Stuart Creighton Miller, *"Benevolent Assimilation": The American Conquest of the Philippines, 1899–1903* (New Haven, CT: Yale University Press, 1982); William J. Pomeroy, *American Neocolonialism: Its Emergence in the Philippines and Asia* (New York: International Publishers, 1970); Peter Tarr, "The Education of Thomasites," particularly chapter 3, "'Democratic Education' in Comparative Colonial Context: Cuba, Puerto Rico, the Philippines," 98–234, and on Thomasites as "agents of empire," see 686. For examples of imperial education within other contexts, including how local actors shaped education and empire, see del Moral, *Negotiating Empire*; Stratton, *Education for Empire*.

53. For broader works that discuss empire, race, and gender beyond the Philippines but from a postcolonial perspective, see Frantz Fanon, *Black Skin, White Masks* (New York: Grove Press, 1967); Edward W. Said, *Orientalism* (New York: Pantheon Books, 1978); Stoler, *Carnal Knowledge and Imperial Power*.

54. Richard Hofstadter, *The Age of Reform: From Bryan to F.D.R.* (New York: Knopf, 1955); Anne Firor Scott, *Natural Allies: Women's Associations in American History* (Urbana: University of Illinois Press, 1991); Nell Irvin Painter, *Standing at Armageddon: The United States, 1877–1919* (New York: W. W. Norton, 1987); John Louis Recchiuti, *Civic Engagement: Social Science and Progressive-Era Reform in New York City* (Philadelphia: University of Pennsylvania Press, 2007); Daniel T. Rogers, "In Search of Progressivism," *Reviews in American History* 10, 4 (1982): 113–132; Lawrence A. Cremin, *The Transformation of the School: Progressivism in American Education, 1876–1957* (New York: Knopf, 1961).

55. Carl N. Degler, *In Search of Human Nature: The Decline and Revival of Darwinism in American Social Thought* (New York: Oxford University Press, 1991); Edward J. Larson, *Eugenics in the Deep South* (Baltimore: Johns Hopkins University Press, 1995); Angela Gonzales, Judy Kertész, and Gabrielle Tayac, "Eugenics as Indian Removal: Sociohistorical Processes and the De(con)struction of American Indians in the Southeast," *Public Historian* 29, 3 (Summer 2007): 53–67; Stephen Jay Gould, *The Mismeasure of Man* (New York: W. W. Norton, 1981); Pat Shipman, *The Evolution of Racism: Human Differences and the Use and Abuse of Science* (New York: Simon and Schuster, 1994); Ann Gibson Winfield, *Eugenics and Education in America: Institutionalised Rac-*

ism and the Implications of History, Ideology, and Memory (New York: Peter Lang, 2007); Daniel J. Kevles, *In the Name of Eugenics* (New York: Knopf, 1985); Steven Selden, "Inheriting Shame: The Story of Eugenics and Racism in America (New York: Teachers College Press, 1999). Also see Nell Irvin Painter, *The History of White People* (New York: W. W. Norton, 2010); Ibram Kendi, *Stamped from the Beginning: The Definitive History of Racist Ideas in America* (New York: Nation Books, 2016).

56. Michael B. Katz, *Reconstructing American Education* (Cambridge, MA: Harvard University Press, 1987); Cremin, *The Transformation of the School*; Lawrence A. Cremin, *American Education: The Metropolitan Experience, 1876–1980* (New York: Harper and Row, 1988); Carl Kaestle, *Pillars of the Republic: Common Schools and American Society, 1780–1860* (New York: Hill and Wang, 1983); Herbert M. Kliebard, *The Struggle for the American Curriculum, 1893–1958*, 2nd ed. (New York: Routledge, 1995); William J. Reese, *America's Public Schools: From the Common School to "No Child Left Behind"* (Baltimore: Johns Hopkins University Press, 2011); Joel Spring, *The American School: 1642–1985* (New York: Longman, 1986); David Tyack, *The One Best System: A History of American Urban Education* (Cambridge, MA: Harvard University Press, 1974); David Tyack and Elisabeth Hansot, *Managers of Virtue: Public School Leadership in America, 1820–1980* (New York: Basic Books, 1982); David Tyack and Elisabeth Hansot, *Learning Together: A History of Coeducation in American Schools* (New Haven, CT: Yale University Press, 1990).

57. Michael B. Katz, *Class, Bureaucracy, and Schools*, xvi–xvii; Kim Cary Warren, *The Quest for Citizenship: African American and Native American Education in Kansas, 1880–1935* (Chapel Hill: University of North Carolina Press, 2010); Paulet, "'The Only Good Indian Is a Dead Indian.'"

58. For more on US exceptionalism and empire see Anne L. Foster, *Projection and Power: The United States and Europe in Colonial Southeast Asia, 1919–1941* (Durham, NC: Duke University Press, 2010); Go "Introduction: Global Perspectives"; Go, *Patterns of Empire*; Kaplan, "Left Alone in America"; Justice, "Education at the End of a Gun"; Williams, *The Tragedy of American Diplomacy*; Akira Iriye, "Exceptionalism Revisited," *Reviews in American History* (June 1988): 291–297. Also see Daniel Rogers, "Exceptionalism," in Anthony Molho and Gordon S. Wood, eds., *Imagined Historians Interpret Their Past* (Princeton, NJ: Princeton University Press, 1998); Vicente L. Rafael, "The War of Translation: Colonial Education, American English, and Tagalog Slang in the Philippines," *Journal of Asian Studies* 74, 2 (May 2015): 283–302; Tarr, "The Education of Thomasites," 39–58.

59. Given the devastating rates of disease, decreasing access to land and resources, and warfare with white frontiersmen, the American Indian population declined precipitously over the course of the nineteenth century—almost to the point of extinction. See David J. Hacker and Michael R. Haines, "American Indian Mortality in the Late Nineteenth Century: The Impact of Federal Assimilation Policies on a Vulnerable Population," *Annales de Démographie Historique* 2 (2005); Russell Thornton, *American*

Indian Holocaust and Survival: A Population History since 1492 (Norman: University of Oklahoma Press, 1987).

60. Adams, *Education for Extinction*, x–xi.

61. Justice, "Education at the End of a Gun."

62. For further discussion on the significance of "benevolence" within imperial education "experiments" see Woolford, *This Benevolent Experiment*, 3.

63. Paulet, "'The Only Good Indian Is a Dead Indian,'" 196–204. More recently Paulet published on this same topic; see Paulet, "To Change the World." Paulet credits Walter L. Williams as the first scholar to connect American Indian and Filipino policy, but does not analyze education: Williams, "United States Indian Policy and the Debate over Philippine Annexation." Also see Jacobson, *Barbarian Virtues*, 6–8. Some scholars, including Paul Kramer, deride scholarship like Paulet's and Jacobson's for not framing the imperial experience accurately; see Kramer, *Blood of Government*, 27.

64. Adams, *Education for Extinction*, 6–11; Cahill, *Federal Fathers and Mothers*, 8, 68, 88, 209. As mentioned above, Kramer's *Blood of Government* criticizes Paulet's research for its narrow understanding of American empire, as one simply of "export" colonialism, 27. Although Paulet's assertions may be somewhat one-dimensional, her insights regarding the longer history of US empire as well as the continuities between American projects among American Indians and Filipinos are still useful. Also see Jacobson, *Barbarian Virtues*, 6–8.

65. Cahill, *Federal Fathers and Mothers*, 6. Cahill also notes how the Philippine Service, established in the early 1900s, was largely modeled on the Indian Service and that both incorporated a large teaching force; see 209; Stoler, *Carnal Knowledge and Imperial Power*. Moreover, in "Education at the End of a Gun," Benjamin Justice locates US schooling in the Philippines in a much longer history of American imperial education, including a fraught attempt to educate American Indians in seventeenth-century Massachusetts, thereby noting the connection between US internal colonialism and more formal imperial education projects. Still, similar to Cahill's treatment of the Indian Service, Justice does not explore teachers' personal experiences in the Philippines, leaving room for a more nuanced account of the meaning of empire building at an intimate level as well as an in-depth account of the multilayered challenges that teachers faced. Tarr, "'The Education of Thomasites," 148–152, notes connections between US imperial education aimed at Filipinos and Native Americans.

66. Margaret D. Jacobs, *White Mother to a Dark Race*.

67. Zimmerman, *Innocents Abroad*.

68. Also see Angulo, *Empire and Education*: Angulo provides a historical overview of American expansion over the course of the twentieth century, arguing that in the Philippines as elsewhere, humanitarian and commercial interests vied for control, with teachers forming the vanguard of the humanitarian forces. For a comparative framework between the United States and Canada, see Woolford, *This Benevolent Experiment*.

69. Zimmerman, *Innocents Abroad*, 18, similarly admits to his book's focus on teachers rather than the students.

70. Adams, *Education for Extinction*, ix.

71. Ibid., 1, 8, 48–57, 84, 337.

72. Fear-Segal, *White Man's Club*; Also see Jacqueline Fear-Segal and Susan D. Rose, eds., *Carlisle Indian Industrial School: Indigenous Histories, Memories, and Reclamations* (Lincoln, University of Nebraska Press, 2016).

73. Clifford E. Trafzer, Jean A. Keller, and Lorene Sisquoc, "Introduction: Origin and Development of the American Indian Boarding School System," in Clifford E. Trafzer, Jean A. Keller, and Lorene Sisquoc, eds., *Boarding School Blues: Revisiting American Indian Educational Experiences* (Lincoln: University of Nebraska Press, 2006).

74. For more on American Indian education see Cahill, *Federal Fathers and Mothers*; Brenda J. Child, *Boarding School Seasons: American Indian Families, 1900–1940* (Lincoln: University of Nebraska Press, 1998); Michael C. Coleman, *American Indian Children at School, 1850–1930* (Jackson: University Press of Mississippi, 1993); Jon Reyhner and Jeanne Eder, *A History of Indian Education* (Billings: Eastern Montana College, 1989); Fear-Segal, *White Man's Club*; Fear-Segal and Rose, *Carlisle Indian Industrial School*; Abigail Gundlack Graham, "The Power of Boarding Schools: A Historiographical Review," *American Educational History Journal* 38, 1/2 (2012): 467–481; Stephen W. Haycox, *Alaska: An American Colony* (Seattle: University of Washington Press, 2002); Jacobs, *White Mother to a Dark Race*; Paulet, "To Change the World"; Francis Paul Prucha, *American Indian Policy in Crisis: Christian Reformers and the Indian, 1865–1900* (Norman: University of Oklahoma Press, 1976); Trafzer et al., "Introduction: Origin and Development of the American Indian Boarding School System." Works on specific American Indian schools in this time period include Sonciray Bonnell, "Chemawa Indian Boarding School: The First One Hundred Years, 1880 to 1980" (PhD dissertation, Dartmouth College, 1997); Clyde Ellis, *To Change Them Forever: Indian Education at the Rainy Mountain Boarding School, 1893–1920* (Norman: University of Oklahoma Press, 1996); Sally Hyer, *One House, One Voice, One Heart: Native American Education at the Santa Fe Indian School, 1890–1990* (Santa Fe: Museum of New Mexico Press, 1990); Donal F. Lindsey, *Indians at Hampton Institute, 1877–1921* (Urbana: University of Illinois Press, 1995); K. Tsianina Lomawaima, *They Called It Prairie Light: The Story of the Chilocco Indian School* (Lincoln: University of Nebraska Press, 1994); Devon A. Mihesuah, *Cultivating the Rosebuds: The Education of Women at the Cherokee Female Seminary, 1851–1909* (Urbana: University of Illinois Press, 1993); Robert A. Trennert Jr., *The Phoenix Indian School: Forced Assimilation in Arizona, 1891–1935* (Norman: University of Oklahoma Press, 1988). Also see Bell, "Telling Stories out of School"; Matthew Bentley, "'Kill the Indian, Save the Man': Manhood at the Carlisle Indian Industrial School, 1879–1918" (PhD dissertation, University of East Anglia, 2012). Specific to Carlisle, these two notable doctoral dissertations highlight the varied ways that the school worked to establish new norms for Indian youth while recognizing student agency, though neither focuses on teachers. Bentley's "'Kill the Indian, Save the Man'" argues

that ideas regarding proper notions of masculinity changed over time and that initial efforts to promote "civilized" manliness were later supplanted by ideals that lauded physical strength and power, as shown through athletic prowess. Bell's "Telling Stories out of School" demonstrates how this first off-reservation institution functioned as a site of negotiation between the federal government and Indian children, drawing upon hundreds of student records and focusing on how the school's Native American students helped to define their own identities. Although these two scholarly works offer new insight into Carlisle as a place of contested and shifting meaning, neither explores the teachers' work to enact US policy in the classroom by assimilating youth into the dominant culture, nor do they illuminate the complexities of building an empire through the intimate and delicate negotiations more evident in a comparative project.

75. Justice, "Education at the End of a Gun"; Zimmerman, *Innocents Abroad*; Angulo, *Empire and Education*.

76. Focusing more on military interventions, and referencing education, see Stanley Karnow, *In Our Image: America's Empire in the Philippines* (New York: Random House, 1989), 196–209; Stanley Karnow, "The Philippines," *Dissent* 56 1 (Winter 2009): 39; Kramer, *Blood of Government*, 148–150; Miller, *Benevolent Assimilation*, 263. John Morgan Gates, *Schoolbooks and Krags: The United States Army in the Philippines, 1898–1902* (Westport, CT: Greenwood Press, 1973). On deepening class and other divisions see Go, *Patterns of Empire*, 70–71; Amoroso, "Inheriting the 'Moro Problem.'" For further information on US intervention in Filipino education see Encarnacion Alzona, *A History of Education in the Philippines* (Manila: University of the Philippines Press, 1932); Clymer, "Humanitarian Imperialism"; Kenton J. Clymer, *Protestant Missionaries in the Philippines, 1898–1916: An Inquiry into the American Colonial Mentality* (Urbana: University of Illinois Press, 1986); Jane A. Margold, "Egalitarian Ideals and Exclusionary Practices: U.S. Pedagogy in the Colonial Philippines," *Journal of Historical Sociology* 8, 4 (December 1995): 375–394; Geronima T. Pecson and Maria Racelis, eds., *Tales of the American Teachers in the Philippines* (Manila: Carmelo and Bauermann, 1959); René Romero, "The Flowering of Philippine Education under the American Regime (1898–1923)," *American Historical Collection* 4, 2 (April 1976); Tarr, "The Education of Thomasites." For further discussion of the impact of war on the Philippines experiment, see Chapters 1 and 4.

77. May, *Social Engineering in the Philippines*.

78. Glenn Anthony May, "The Business of Education in the Colonial Philippines, 1909–30," in McCoy and Scarano, *Colonial Crucible*, 152: here May focuses on efforts to institute industrial education in the Philippines around the turn of the century without consistent leadership, infrastructure, or planning to make it successful. Instituted in part due to beliefs at the turn of the twentieth century that "industrial education was valuable in the instruction of 'backward races,'" May notes that Filipino students produced many artisanal wares, but that ultimately there was little to no market or demand for these goods. Thus, notions of creating an industrial system whereby the production and selling of goods would lead to economic independence, one of the pur-

ported goals of American intervention in the islands, proved flawed. Also see Lardiza-bal, "Pioneer American Teachers and Philippine Education"; John Charles Muerman, "The Philippine School under the Americans" (PhD dissertation, George Washington University, 1922): Muerman provides a romanticized insider's look into teachers' experiences, as he taught in the islands alongside other Thomasites beginning in 1901. Similarly Lardizabal assumes the success and benevolence of US teachers' work and their mission in the Philippines, and she created and conducted an extensive survey of teachers' memories of their experiences—some of which have proved useful for this study—but in her analysis, Lardizabal focuses almost solely on teachers' positive recollections, leaving little room for a balanced account of US schooling in the Philippines. Tarr, "The Education of Thomasites," 196–198, also comments on flaws within Lardizabal's study. Also see Paulet, "To Change the World"; Williams, "United States Indian Policy and the Debate over Philippine Annexation." For further information on Philippine education see Kramer, *Blood of Government*.

79. Kramer, *Blood of Government*, 27.

80. Paul A. Kramer, "Race, Empire, and Transnational History," in McCoy and Scarano, *Colonial Crucible*, 200 [199–209]; also see Kramer, *The Blood of Government*; Vicente L. Rafael, *White Love and Other Events in Filipino History* (Durham, NC: Duke University Press, 2000).

81. McCoy and Scarano, *Colonial Crucible*; Kramer, "Race, Empire, and Transnational History," 200.

82. Kramer, "Race, Empire, and Transnational History."

83. Fear-Segal, *White Man's Club*, 121–123. Also see Philip J. Deloria, *Playing Indian* (New Haven, CT: Yale University Press, 1998). Beyond the confines of education and race, Deloria discusses several moments in American history where whites selectively claimed and repurposed certain traits of "Indianness"—what they viewed as the "good" of Indian culture while simultaneously distancing themselves from what they viewed as "bad" or "backward" Indian—as a means of creating a uniquely American identity, in this way showing how this making of race and identity occurred throughout US history and for varying purposes.

84. Cahill, *Federal Fathers and Mothers*, 3–7; Stoler, *Carnal Knowledge and Imperial Power*; Linda Gordon, *Pitied but Not Entitled: Single Mothers and the History of Welfare, 1890–1935* (Cambridge, MA: Harvard University Press, 1994); Theda Skocpol, *Protecting Soldiers and Mothers: The Political Origins of Social Policy in the United States* (Cambridge, MA: Harvard University Press, 1992). Also see Jacobs's analysis regarding how white women were central to Indian reform, *White Mother to a Dark Race*.

85. Zimmerman, *Innocents Abroad*, 94–96, 104. For further comparative discussion of "settler colonialism" see Woolford, *This Benevolent Experiment*.

86. Rafael, *White Love and Other Events in Filipino History*, especially chapter 2.

87. Hoganson, *Fighting for American Manhood*.

1. Ralph Wendell Taylor to Mother, 21 June 1901, Box 1, Taylor Family Correspondence June to December 1901 Folder, Taylor Family Papers, Bentley Historical Library, University of Michigan (BHL).

2. Ibid.

3. *The Log of the "Thomas," July 23–August 21, 1901*, ed. Ronald P. Gleason, 67–68, http://openlibrary.org. Peter Tarr, "The Education of the Thomasites: American School Teachers in Philippine Colonial Society, 1901–1913" (PhD dissertation, Cornell University, 2006), 9, 195: Tarr cites the number of teachers aboard the USS *Thomas* at 523, according to the records of the first general superintendent of education in the Philippines, Fred W. Atkinson. Other scholars identify different numbers of teachers who were aboard the USS *Thomas* in July to August 1901. Amparo Santamaria Lardizabal, "Pioneer American Teachers and Philippine Education" (PhD dissertation, Stanford University, 1956), 21, cites 509 teachers; Jonathan Zimmerman, *Innocents Abroad: American Teachers in the American Century* (Cambridge, MA: Harvard University Press, 2006), 1, cites 526 teachers.

4. Cathleen D. Cahill, *Federal Fathers and Mothers: A Social History of the United States Indian Service, 1869–1933* (Chapel Hill: University of North Carolina Press, 2011), 88; Anne Paulet, "To Change the World": The Use of American Indian Education in the Philippines," *History of Education Quarterly* 47, 2 (May 2007); Anne Paulet, "'The Only Good Indian Is a Dead Indian': The Use of United States Indian Policy as a Guide for the Conquest and Occupation of the Philippines, 1898–1905" (PhD dissertation, Rutgers University, 1995); Walter L. Williams, "United States Indian Policy and the Debate over Philippine Annexation: Implications for the Origins of American Imperialism," *Journal of American History* 66, 4 (March 1980): 810–831.

5. Elaine Goodale Eastman, *Pratt: The Red Man's Moses* (Norman: University of Oklahoma Press, 1935), 102.

6. Ibid., 106.

7. David Wallace Adams, *Education for Extinction: American Indians and the Boarding School Experience, 1875–1928* (Lawrence: University of Kansas, 1995), 11–12; Cahill, *Federal Fathers and Mothers*, 25–26, 54–55, 209; Paulet, "'The Only Good Indian Is a Dead Indian,'" 232. Also see Julian Go, "Introduction: Global Perspectives on the U.S. Colonial State in the Philippines," in Julian Go and Anne L. Foster, *The American Colonial State in the Philippines*, (Durham, NC: Duke University Press, 2003).

8. Frederick E. Hoxie, *A Final Promise: The Campaign to Assimilate the Indians, 1880–1920* (Lincoln: University of Nebraska Press, 1984), 53–54. Also see Adams, *Education for Extinction*, 18–27; David Wallace Adams, "Fundamental Considerations: The Deep Meaning of Native American Schooling, 1880–1900," *Harvard Educational Review* 58, 1 (February 1988): 2–3; Cahill, *Federal Fathers and Mothers*, 2; Michael C. Coleman, *American Indian Children at School, 1850–1930* (Jackson: University Press of Mississippi, 1993), 41; Francis Paul Prucha, *American Indian Policy in Crisis: Christian Reformers and the Indian, 1865–1900* (Norman: University of Oklahoma Press, 1976). For

nineteenth-century indigenous-white encounters, see Francis Paul Prucha, *The Great Father: The United States Government and the American Indians* (Lincoln: University of Nebraska Press, 1984); Robert M. Utley, *The Indian Frontier of the American West, 1846–1890* (Albuquerque: University of New Mexico Press, 1984); Robert F. Berhhofer Jr., *The White Man's Indian: Images of the American Indian from Columbus to the Present* (New York: Knopf, 1978); Brian W. Dippie, *The Vanishing American: White Attitudes and U.S. Indian Policy* (Middletown, CT: Wesleyan University Press, 1982).

9. Adams, *Education for Extinction*, 38. For a different framework regarding reformers' efforts to "save" or "civilize" the Indian, see Adams, "Fundamental Considerations," 1–3.

10. Ibid., 36–43. For more on education at Fort Marion see Diane Glancy, *Fort Marion Prisoners and the Trauma of Native Education* (Lincoln: University of Nebraska Press, 2014).

11. Adams, *Education for Extinction*, 44–48. Also see Cahill, *Federal Fathers and Mothers*, 11, 22, 32; Paulet, "'The Only Good Indian Is a Dead Indian,'" 12, 338.

12. Richard Henry Pratt, *Battlefield and Classroom: Four Decades with the American Indian, 1867–1904*, Robert M. Utley, ed. (1964; repr., Norman: University of Oklahoma Press, 2003), 195–197.

13. Over his twenty years as superintendent of Carlisle, Pratt would repeat this journey west countless times.

14. Pratt, *Battlefield and Classroom*, 213.

15. Adams, *Education for Extinction*, 47–48. Also see Cahill, *Federal Fathers and Mothers*, 11, 22, 32; Paulet, "'The Only Good Indian Is a Dead Indian,'" 11–12.

16. Richard Henry Pratt to Laura Pratt, 21 August 1879, Box 18, Folder 613, Richard Henry Pratt Papers, Beinecke Rare Book and Manuscript Library (BRBML), Yale University. On Sherman and "total war," see Paulet, "'The Only Good Indian Is a Dead Indian,'" 157.

17. Richard Henry Pratt to Laura Pratt, 22 August 1879, Box 18, Folder 613, BRBML.

18. R. H. Pratt, "Report of School at Carlisle," *59th Annual Report of the Commissioner of Indian Affairs to the Secretary of the Interior, 1890* (Washington, DC: Government Printing Office, 1890), 309, University of Wisconsin Digital Collections, http://digital.library.wisc.edu/1711.dl/History. For more on the Bureau of Indian Affairs moving from the Department of War into the Department of the Interior, see Paulet, "'The Only Good Indian Is a Dead Indian,'" 133, 137–138.

19. Adams, *Education for Extinction*, 53.

20. David J. Hacker and Michael R. Haines, "American Indian Mortality in the Late Nineteenth Century: The Impact of Federal Assimilation Policies on a Vulnerable Population," *Annales de Démographie Historique* 2 (2005), 19; Adams, "Fundamental Considerations," 2–3; Russell Thornton, *American Indian Holocaust and Survival: A Population History since 1492* (Norman: University of Oklahoma Press, 1987); Daniel Richter, *Facing East from Indian Country: A Native History of Early America* (Cambridge, MA: Harvard University Press, 2001), 7. For a discussion of population and cultural

decimation as genocide see Andrew Woolford, *This Benevolent Experiment: Indigenous Boarding Schools, Genocide, and Redress in Canada and the United States* (Lincoln: University of Nebraska Press, 2015), 21–45.

21. Adams, *Education for Extinction*, 7; Cahill, *Federal Fathers and Mothers*, 9–10, 18; Paulet, "'The Only Good Indian Is a Dead Indian,'" 143–146; Theda Perdue, "Cherokee Women and the Trail of Tears," *Journal of Women's History* 1, 1 (1989): 14–30; Rose Stremlau, "Rape Narratives on the Northern Paiute Frontier: Sarah Winnemucca, Sexual Sovereignty, and Economic Autonomy, 1844–1891," in Dee Garceau-Hagen, ed., *Portraits of Women in the American West* (New York: Routledge, 2005), 37–62.

22. Hacker and Haines, "American Indian Mortality in the Late Nineteenth Century," 17. See also Stremlau's account of Northern Paiute Sarah Winnemucca's survival and campaign against sexual violence and rape on the Western frontier. For more on the largest mass hanging in American history, which was perpetrated against the Dakota, see Paulet, "The Only Good Indian Is a Dead Indian," 144–146; and John Biewen, "Little War on the Prairie," *This American Life*, November 23, 2012, https:// www.thisamericanlife.org/479/little-war-on-the-prairie.

23. Hacker and Haines, 33: 62 percent higher mortality rate for American Indians compared to whites.

24. Devon A. Mihesuah, "'Too Dark to Be Angels': The Class System among the Cherokees at the Female Seminary," *American Indian Culture and Research Journal* 15, 1 (1991): 29–52; Stremlau, "Rape Narratives on the Northern Paiute Frontier"; Zitkala-Sa, "Impressions of an Indian Childhood," *Atlantic Monthly* 85, 507 (January 1900): 37–47; Zitkala-Sa, "School Days of an Indian Girl," *Atlantic Monthly* 85, 508 (February 1900): 185–194; Zitkala-Sa, "An Indian Teacher among Indians," *Atlantic Monthly* 85, 509 (March 1900): 381–387.

25. Adams, *Education for Extinction*, 7.

26. Ibid., 5–9.

27. Paulet, "To Change the World," 174–175; Paulet, "'The Only Good Indian Is a Dead Indian'"; Williams, "United States Indian Policy and the Debate over Philippine Annexation."

28. Julian Go, "Imperial Power and Its Limits: America's Colonial Empire in the Early Twentieth Century," in Craig Calhoun, Frederick Cooper, and Kevin W. Moore, eds., *Lessons of Empire: Imperial Histories and American Power* (New York: Social Science Research Council, 2006), 202–203.

29. Paulet, "'The Only Good Indian Is a Dead Indian,'" ii, 6–8.

30. As quoted in Benjamin Justice, "Education at the End of a Gun : The Origins of American Imperial Education and the Case of the Philippines," in Noah W. Sobe, ed., *American Post-Conflict Educational Reform: From the Spanish-American War to Iraq* (New York: Palgrave Macmillan, 2009), 35. Also see Tarr, "The Education of the Thomasites," 59–74.

31. For more on American imperial "exceptionalism" in the Philippines see Go, "Introduction: Global Perspectives," 1, 12 13, 15; Go, "Imperial Power and Its Limits, 206;

Paul Kramer, *The Blood of Government: Race, Empire, the United States, and the Philippines* (Chapel Hill: University of North Carolina Press, 2006, 23–29; Thomas McCormick, "From Old Empire to New: The Changing Dynamics and Tactics of American Empire," in Alfred W. McCoy and Francisco A. Scarano, eds., *Colonial Crucible: Empire in the Making of the Modern American State* (Madison: University of Wisconsin Press, 2009), 63; Tarr, "The Education of the Thomasites," 39–58. Of course, anti-imperialist momentum grew as well. On anti-imperialist movement, see Matthew Frye Jacobson, *Barbarian Virtues: The United States Encounters Foreign Peoples at Home and Abroad, 1876–1917* (New York: Hill and Wang, 2000), 227–234; Stanley Karnow, *In Our Image: America's Empire in the Philippines* (New York: Random House, 1989), 109–110, 136, 164–165; Stuart Creighton Miller, *"Benevolent Assimilation": The American Conquest of the Philippines, 1899–1903* (New Haven, CT: Yale University Press, 1982), 13–30; McCormick, "From Old Empire to New," 70–72; Jim Zwick, "The Anti-Imperialist Movement, 1898–1921," in Virginia M. Bouvier, ed., *Whose America? The War of 1898 and the Battles to Define the Nation* (Westport, CT: Praeger, 2001).

32. "Finding Aid for Dean C. Worcester Papers, 1887–1925," Dean C. Worcester Papers, BHL, accessed June 30, 2013, http://quod.lib.umich.edu; Marjorie Barritt, "American-Philippine Relations: A Guide to the Resources in the Michigan Historical Collections," BHL, accessed June 28, 2013, http://bentley.umich.edu/research/guides /philippines/philint.php; Daniel Roderick Williams, *The Odyssey of the Philippine Commission* (Chicago: A. C. McClurg, 1913); Glenn Anthony May, *Social Engineering in the Philippines*, xxii, xxvi, 3, 8–23, 41–56; Justice, "Education at the End of Gun"; Paul A. Kramer, "Race, Empire, and Transnational History," in Alfred W. McCoy and Francisco A. Scarano, eds., *Colonial Crucible: Empire in the Making of the Modern American State* (Madison: University of Wisconsin Press, 2009), 204; John Charles Muerman, "The Philippine School under the Americans" (PhD dissertation, George Washington University, 1922), 22, 26–28; Tarr, "The Education of the Thomasites," especially 59–97 and 200.

33. Lardizabal, "Pioneer American Teachers and Philippine Education," 8–16; Paulet, "'The Only Good Indian Is a Dead Indian,'" 288, 292–293, 323; Tarr, "The Education of the Thomasites," 59–97.

34. Justice, "Education at the End of a Gun"; Glenn Anthony May, *Social Engineering in the Philippines*, xxvi. May discusses US involvement in building infrastructure, including installing sanitation services. Muerman, "The Philippine School under the Americans," 25: Muerman wrote of US soldiers' involvement in teaching Filipinos English, arguing that they "made no attempt to organize a system of public instruction" but were ordered to teach "conversational English" in existing Filipino schools. For more on soldiers' involvement in education see John Morgan Gates, *Schoolbooks and Krags: The United States Army in the Philippines, 1898–1902* (Westport, CT: Greenwood Press, 1973); Tarr, "The Education of the Thomasites," 153–155, 195. For more on the Philippine-American War see H. W. Brands, *Bound to Empire: The United States and the Philippines* (New York: Oxford University Press, 1992), 49–59; Karnow, *In Our Image*,

139–195; Kramer, *The Blood of Government*, 82–140; Miller, *"Benevolent Assimilation"*; Paulet, "'The Only Good Indian Is a Dead Indian,'" 269–281. Paul Kramer, "Decoloniz-ing the History of the Philippine-American War," in Leon Wolff, *Little Brown Brother: How the United States Purchased and Pacified the Philippine Islands at the Century's Turn* (New York: History Book Club, 1961), ix–xvii, cites the earliest critiques of the US role, ambition, and cruelty in the Philippine-American War. See also Peter W. Stanley, *A Nation in the Making: The Philippines and the United States, 1899–1921* (Cambridge, MA: Harvard University Press, 1974); Richard E. Welch, "American Atrocities in the Philip-pines: The Indictment and the Response," *Pacific Historical Review* 43 (1974): 233–255; Wolff, *Little Brown Brother*.

35. Karnow, *In Our Image*, 194: the Philippine-American war "ended officially on July 4, 1902." However, Karnow writes, "The American conquest of the Philippines was not to be completed for another decade," as violent unrest continued on Samar, Luzon, and Mindanao, prompting American military response, including a 1913 battle against the Moros on Mindanao.

36. Muerman, "The Philippine School under the Americans," 35; Lardizabal, "Pio-neer American Teachers and Philippine Education," 11–12, 298–300; Tarr, "The Educa-tion of the Thomasites," 196–200, 656–690.

37. For example, several teachers in this study were appointed by their respective universities, including Ralph Taylor from the University of Michigan and Clara Don-aldson of Cornell; see Taylor to Mother, 21 June 1901; Clara R. Donaldson to Chief of Bureau of Insular Affairs, Washington, DC, 18 September 1920, Clara R. Donaldson File, Record Group 350, Box 365, Entry 21, National Archives at College Park, Maryland (NAMD). As valedictorian of his graduating class, it is likely that Frederick Behner was nominated by administrators at North Central College in Naperville, Illinois. Also see Tarr, "The Education of the Thomasites," 17–19, 196–198, and 656–690.

38. For more on how humanitarian and commercial interests vied for power as the US empire expanded to include the Philippines, see A. J. Angulo, *Empire and Educa-tion: A History of Greed and Goodwill from the War of 1898 to the War on Terror* (New York: Palgrave MacMillan, 2012). Also see Tarr, "The Education of the Thomasites," 690.

39. On the anti-imperialist movement see Jacobson, *Barbarian Virtues*, 227–234; Karnow, *In Our Image*, 109–110, 136, 164–165; Miller, *"Benevolent Assimilation,"* 13–30; McCormick, "From Old Empire to New," 70–72; Zwick, "The Anti-Imperialist Move-ment, 1898–1921."

40. *Log of the "Thomas,"* 55.

41. Muerman, "The Philippine School under the Americans," 42.

42. Lardizabal, "Pioneer American Teachers and Philippine Education," 17–22; Zimmerman, *Innocents Abroad*, 124–125, demonstrates how Thomasites' credentials did not always indicate "success" in the classroom.

43. Muerman, "The Philippine School under the Americans," 144.

44. Lardizabal, "Pioneer American Teachers and Philippine Education," 29: inter-estingly, John Muerman did not initiate his application but was instead nominated by

former students (who had become army lieutenants) bent on securing their former teacher a job offer.

45. Muerman, "The Philippine School under the Americans," 117–118.

46. Lardizabal, "Pioneer American Teachers and Philippine Education," 314–15, 316. On November 15, 1955, Lardizabal sent out a cover letter and survey in hopes of finding out more about the Thomasites' experiences. Considering that Lardizabal completed the dissertation five months later, in April 1956, and that she describes herself as "racing against time," her collection and analysis of the fifty responders was hurried. For other accounts of Thomasites see Karnow, *In Our Image*, 200–205; Jane A. Margold, "Egalitarian Ideals and Exclusionary Practices: U.S. Pedagogy in the Colonial Philippines," *Journal of Historical Sociology* 8, 4 (December 1995): 375–394; Muerman, "The Philippine School under the Americans"; Tarr, "The Education of the Thomasites," 196–199, 690; Zimmerman, *Innocents Abroad*, 1–3, 23, 123–125, 155–156.

47. Lardizabal, "Pioneer American Teachers and Philippine Education," 31–32.

48. Ibid., 7, 5: among the obstacles detailed, Lardizabal lists "floods, typhoons, poor roads, and lack of transportation facilities . . . cholera and smallpox epidemics" that Thomasites faced as well their work that went well beyond the classroom, where they essentially served as "health officers, guidance counselors, justices of the peace, and jacks-of-all-trades."

49. Questionnaire: Walter W. Marquardt, Box 7, Biographical Folder, BHL. See Appendix 2 for complete list of Thomasites studied here.

50. Mary Helen Fee, *A Woman's Impressions of the Philippines* (Chicago: A. C. McClurg, 1910), 12.

51. Miller, *Benevolent Assimilation*, 134. Significantly, other Thomasites examined here used the term "little brown brother" in their personal writing, demonstrating its relative commonality: Blaine Free Moore to Pa and Ma, 2 April 1902, Blaine Free Moore Papers, Box 1, Correspondence January to June 1902 Folder, Library of Congress (LOC), Washington, DC; Blaine Free Moore to Brother, 11 May 1903, Box 1, Correspondence January to June 1903 Folder, LOC; Blaine Free Moore to Pa and Ma, 8 July 1903, Box 1, Correspondence July to December 1903, LOC; Harrie Cole to Mother, 22 April 1904, Harry Newton Cole Papers, 1904 Folder, BHL. Also see Wolff, *Little Brown Brother*.

52. John C. Early, "Reminiscences of John C. Early," John C. Early Papers, John Early Reminiscences Folder, BHL. Also see Tarr, "The Education of the Thomasites," chapter 7, "John Early and Roy Barton: The True Believer and the Skeptic."

53. George Ezra Carrothers, interview, July 27, 1965, transcript, 1, George E. Carrothers Papers, BHL; Carrothers, "A Sojourn in the Philippines," 3, Biographical Reminiscences 1952–1955 and 1964 Folder, BHL. For more on Carrothers, see Tarr, "The Education of the Thomasites," chapter 8, "Conclusion: A Certain Blindness."

54. Taylor to Mother, 21 June 1901; Harrie Cole to Mother, 20 October 1901, October to November 1901 Folder, BHL. For more on Carrothers, see Tarr, "The Education of the Thomasites," chapter 8, and chapter 5, "Leyte: Harrie Cole's Philippine Nightmare."

55. H. A. Bordner, "Transportation Request," Lingayen, 20 January 1914, NARA II—Harvey A Bordner and Wife Maude M. Bordner Folder, RG 350, Entry 21, Box 71; John C. Early and wife, "NOTE: For P.I. Report for the Month of June, 1932, from the Dir. of Civil Service, Manila," NARA II, RG 350, Entry 21; Harrie Cole to Mother, 20 October 1901; Mary Cole to Folks at Home, 10 April 1902, April to May 1902 Folder, BHL; Marquardt, Diary entries 18 March, 1904, 1 April 1904, Diary 1 September 1903 to 21 March 1905, Box 6, Diaries and Notes 1900–1935 Folder, BHL; Marquardt, Diary entry 10 August 1904, Box 7, untitled bound book.

56. Blaine Free Moore, Notes about numbers of letters per year, Box 1, Diary 1/4 Folder, LOC. For more on Blaine Moore see Tarr, "The Education of the Thomasites," chapter 8.

57. "Two contributions" and "A Sense of Humor," Clips about Evans Family Folder, Evans Family Papers 1904–1974, BHL; "John H. Evans Dies Today at Home of Son: Was Formerly Governor of Mountain Provinces in Philippines," Report/Letter 1909 Folder, BHL.

58. Untitled Newspaper Clipping, 2 September 1965, Frank W. Cheney Papers, BHL; James T. Golden, "Colorful, Versatile 'Unk' Cheney,'" Frank W. Cheney Papers, BHL.

59. Regarding archival history, men's personal papers seem to have been preserved more formally and are more accessible to scholars and the general public. For more on male Thomasites as supervisors see Tarr, "The Education of the Thomasites," 193–194.

60. "The Bureau of Education: A Statement of Organization and Aims Published for General Information," *Philippine Teacher* 1, 1 (December 15, 1904), Library Materials Vol. 674, Record Group 350, Philippines Miscellaneous, NAMD.

61. For example, see Jurgen Herbst, *Women Pioneers of Public Education: How Culture Came to the Wild West* (New York: Palgrave MacMillan, 2008); Margaret D. Jacobs, *White Mother to a Dark Race: Settler Colonialism, Maternalism, and the Removal of Indigenous Children in the American West and Australia, 1880–1940* (Lincoln: University of Nebraska Press, 2009); Peggy Pascoe, *Relations of Rescue: The Search for Female Moral Authority in the American West, 1874–1939* (New York: Oxford University Press, 1990).

62. Muerman, "The Philippine School under the Americans," 54.

63. Yet, the historical record too often masks such independence. Most of the female Thomasites' records were buried in their respective husbands' personal papers or personnel files, including Alice Hollister Marquardt, Mary Cole, Maude Ethel Martin Bordner, and Willa Rhodes Early. Also see Sarah Steinbrock-Pratt, "'We Were All Robinson Crusoes': American Women Teachers in the Philippines," *Women's Studies* 41 (June 2012): 379–392.

64. Genevieve Bell, "Telling Stories out of School: Remembering the Carlisle Indian Industrial School, 1879–1918" (PhD dissertation, Stanford University, 1998), 158.

65. In the mid-nineteenth century, female teachers, on average, earned wages that were 40 to 60 percent of what males earned. Reformers argued that female teachers were needed not only to save money but also because women would help to ease the

transition from home to school for children. Presumed to be nurturing by nature, female teachers would be more motherly and help young children adjust to their new school environment. Some people objected to having female teachers and argued that women would not be able to teach the higher subjects or control a classroom of older, rowdier students. To quell such concerns, male overseers were installed to help discipline students and meet the academic needs of more advanced students. These male overseers, or principals, became more common as the number of female teachers rose. Except for dame schools or private lessons, in 1800 most teachers were male. By 1900 most teachers were women—about 70 percent of instructors below the college level were women nationwide. In general, female teachers' careers were brief. Young women often began teaching in their late teenage years and would stop in their early twenties upon marriage, usually only teaching for a total of two to three years. See B. A. Hinsdale, *Horace Mann and the Common School Revival in the United States* (New York: Charles Scribner's Sons, 1900); Carl Kaestle, *Pillars of the Republic: Common Schools and American Society, 1780–1860* (New York: Hill and Wang, 1983); Joel Spring, *The American School: 1642–1985* (New York: Longman, 1986); David Tyack, *The One Best System: A History of American Urban Education* (Cambridge, MA: Harvard University Press, 1974).

66. Pratt, *Battlefield and Classroom*, 231.

67. Sarah Mather to Richard Henry Pratt, n.d., Richard Henry Pratt Papers, Box 6, Letters from SA Mather to Pratt, Undated Folder 195, BRBML.

68. Pratt, *Battlefield and* Classroom, 231.

69. J. W. Gibbs to Miss Perritt, October 15 (likely 1879), Richard Henry Pratt Papers, Box 13, Folder 455, BRBML: Gibbs asked to begin her work at Carlisle in January 1880 to give her time to rest after having cared for her children, who had recently been ill.

70. Pratt, *Battlefield and Classroom*, 121: Pratt references Mrs. Cooper Gibbs and Mrs. King Gibbs, "widows of two brothers in the Confederate service during the Civil War" who supported his endeavors in St. Augustine. Likely one of these "Gibbs" was the same who joined Carlisle. Another early Carlisle hire was Miss Perritt (also originally from New England), who had worked with Pratt in St. Augustine.

71. This was particularly important since Pratt often left the school grounds for weeks on end as he recruited students to fill the classrooms, thus leaving the teachers on their own to run the school.

72. Mark S. Granovetter, "The Strength of Weak Ties," *American Journal of Sociology* 78, 6 (May 1973): 1374, 1377; Paul McLean, "Using Network Analysis in Comparative-Historical Research," *Trajectories: Newsletter of the ASA Comparative and Historical Sociology Section* 22, 1 (Fall 2010): 10–14.

73. Marianne Burgess to Richard Henry Pratt, 21 October 1879, Richard Henry Pratt Papers, Box 2, Folder 42, BRBML.

74. Ibid. Burgess was also eager to leave the "sickly climate," which contributed to her bout with malaria over the previous year.

75. For a critique of Marianne Burgess, see Fear-Segal, *White Man's Club*, 206–230.

76. "In the Spotlight," *FW Programmer* 82, 2 (December/March 1982), 2, Carlisle

Barracks, PA, PI-2-8-10 Folder, Cumberland County Historical Society, Carlisle, Pennsylvania (CCHS).

77. Pratt, *Battlefield and Classroom*, 232. Burgess taught among the Pawnee where her father served as the Indian agent. It is unknown how Ely came to work among the Pawnee. Both women were originally from Pennsylvania. See Marianna Burgess, "Service Record Card," and Anne S. Ely, "Service Record Card," Service Record Cards Folder, NPRC.

78. Pratt, *Battlefield and Classroom*, 232; Anne S. Ely "Service Record Card," Service Record Cards Folder, National Personnel Records Center (NPRC), Saint Louis, MO.

79. Burgess to Richard Henry Pratt, 21 October 1879, Richard Henry Pratt Papers, Box 2, Folder 42, BRBML.

80. Jacobs, *White Mother to a Dark Race*.

81. Pratt, *Battlefield and Classroom*, 236.

82. Ibid.

83. Ibid.

84. *Carlisle Arrow* 11, 1 (September 4, 1914), CCHS.

85. Emma A. Cutter to R. L. Brunhouse, 17 April 1933, Box 13, Folder 450, BRBML.

86. Ibid.; Pratt, *Battlefield and Classroom*, 231.

87. Bell, "Telling Stories out of School," 65, 158. According to scholar Genevieve Bell, all twelve teachers in 1885 were single white women between the ages of twenty-two and fifty-five. By 1904 there were twenty-one teachers—all white—seventeen of whom were female, with only one having taught at the school since its opening and three others with the school since the 1890s. However, Bell writes elsewhere in her dissertation, "Pratt had a staff of thirty teachers in 1882; this number increased to forty by 1885 and sixty by 1893—the number remained constant until the end of his tenure." Primary sources suggest that Bell's lower numbers (twelve teachers in 1885) count academic teachers while the higher numbers (thirty teachers in 1882) count both academic and industrial teachers; see "Daily Morning Reports," 1 July 1887 to 1 July 1891, Record Group 75, Entry 1331, National Archives, Washington, DC (NADC).

88. *58th Annual Report of the Commissioner of Indian Affairs 1889* (Washington, DC: Government Printing Office, 1889), 4–5, University of Wisconsin Digital Collections, http://digital.library.wisc.edu/1711.dl/History.

89. Ibid., 6.

90. Several of Carlisle's early employees were Quakers, including Marianne Burgess and Anne Ely, as was Pratt's assistant superintendent, Alfred J. Standing. See Pratt, *Battlefield and Classroom*, 230, 236; Marianna Burgess to Richard Henry Pratt, 4 August 1917, Richard Henry Pratt Papers, Box 2, Folder 42, BRBML; Good Bear to Anne Ely, 4 April 1894, Richard Henry Pratt Papers, Box 13, Folder 456, BRBML. Others professed and exhibited their Christian devotion, as discussed further in Chapter 2.

91. Cahill, *Federal Fathers and Mothers*, 109–111. Cahill discusses civil service employee exemptions from the exam in 1895, which suggests that the exam had, by that time, been made mandatory.

92. Richard Henry Pratt to Knute Nelson, 19 April 1897, Richard Henry Pratt Papers, Box 10, Folder 343, BRBML.

93. Ibid.

94. R. H. Pratt, "Report of School at Carlisle, PA," 28 September 1898, *19th Annual Report of the Commissioner of Indian Affairs*, in *Annual Reports of the Department of the Interior for the Fiscal Year Ended June 30, 1898: Indian Affairs*, 55th Congress, 3rd Session, House of Representatives, Document No. 5 (Washington, DC: Government Printing Office, 1899), 390, The Internet Archive, http://www.archive.org.

95. "Report of the Commissioner of Indian Affairs," in *Annual Reports of the Department of the Interior for the Fiscal Year Ended June 30, 1901: Indian Affairs Part I, Report of the Commissioner and Appendixes* (Washington, DC: Government Printing Office, 1902), 31, University of Wisconsin Digital Collections, http://digital.library.wisc.edu/1711.dl/History.

96. Adams, *Education for Extinction*, 323, 388.

97. Ibid. See note 54 for details on public schools.

98. Cahill, *Federal Fathers and Mothers*, 89.

99. Employment Card, Jessie W. Cook, Jessie W. Cook Folder, NPRC.

100. Emma C. Lovewell to Commissioner of Indian Affairs Francis Leupp, 28 February 1908, Emma C. Lovewell Folder, NPRC.

101. Gwen Williams, "Request for Transfer," 21 May 1913, Gwen Williams Folder, NPRC.

102. Margaret M. Sweeney to US Senator Boies Penrose, 13 January 1913, Margaret M. Sweeney Folder, NPRC; Sweeney to Superintendent of Mount Pleasant Indian School R. A. Cochran, 10 June 1909, Margaret M. Sweeney Folder, NPRC; Emma K. Hetrick to Commissioner of Indian Affairs, 20 September 1909, Emma Hetrick Folder, NPRC; Superintendent of Tomah Indian School L. M. Compton to R. H. Pratt, 18 April 1909, Emma Hetrick Folder, NPRC; US Representative Simeon D. Fess to Commissioner of Indian Affairs, 11 May 1914, Clara Donaldson Folder, NPRC; May D. McKitrick to Assistant to the Commissioner of Indian Affairs E. B. Merritt, 15 May 1914, and 5 July 1914, Clara Donaldson Folder, NPRC.

103. Commissioner of Indian Affairs to Reverend F. S. Spalding, 7 September 1909, Jessie Cook Folder, NPRC. Jessie's husband was an Episcopal minister who worked among the Shoshone Indians.

104. "Teaching Music Can Fill Your Life: At the Indian School the Pupils Wanted to Sing with Their Mouths Closed," untitled newspaper clipping, n.d., Mrs. Edward Whistler Folder, Waidner-Spahr Library, Dickinson College, Carlisle, Pennsylvania (WDC).

105. Muerman, "The Philippine School under the Americans," 144; Lardizabal, "Pioneer American Teachers and Philippine Education," 17.

106. Personal Record of Nellie R. Denny, 1 May 1914, and "Efficiency Report of Nellie R. Denny," 1 November 1916, Record Group 75, Entry 1344A, Records Relating to Carlisle School–Personnel, Nellie Robertson Denny Folder, NADC; Wallace Denny Personal Information Card, Record Group 75, Entry 1344A, Records Relating to Car-

lisle School–Personnel, Wallace Denny Folder, NADC. Wallace Denny, Nellie's husband and an Oneida Indian from Wisconsin, was also a Carlisle graduate (1906) and later served as an assistant disciplinarian at the school.

107. "Efficiency Report of Nellie R. Denny," 1 November 1916.

108. Wallace Denny, "Personal Information Card," Wallace Denny Folder, Entry 1344A, Record Group 75, NADC; Elizabeth Bender, "Service Record Card" and "Report of Edgar A. Allen, Special Indian Agent: General Inspection of Blackfeet, Agency, Montana," 23 February 1910, Elizabeth Bender Folder, NPRC. Dietz, DeCora, Wheelock, and Nellie and Wallace Denny are discussed in Bell, "Telling Stories out of School," 83, 90, 108–110, 158. For more on Angel DeCora's teaching career at Carlisle, see Suzanne Alene Shope, "American Indian Artist Angel DeCora: Aesthetics, Power, and Transcultural Pedagogy in the Progressive Era" (EdD dissertation, University of Montana, 2009)," 117–118, 130–131, 247. And, for other Native American perspectives on Carlisle, see Jacqueline Fear-Segal and Susan D. Rose, eds., *Carlisle Indian Industrial School: Indigenous Histories, Memories, and Reclamations* (Lincoln: University of Nebraska Press, 2016).

109. Ellen Carol Dubois and Lynn Dumenil, *Through Women's Eyes: An American History, Volume One*, 3rd ed. (Boston: Bedford St. Martin's), 421; Adams, *Education for Extinction*, 311–313; Kevin Claesgens, "Zitkala-Sa (Gertrude Simmons Bonnin) Biography" (State College: Pennsylvania Center for the Book, Penn State University, 2005), http://pabook.libraries.psu.edu/palitmap/bios/Zitkala_Sa.html.

110. Zitkala-Sa, "Impressions of an Indian Childhood," "School Days of an Indian Girl," and "An Indian Teacher among Indians."

111. Zitkala Sa, "An Indian Teacher among Indians," 383.

112. Ibid., 385.

113. Ibid., 385–386.

114. Adams, *Education for Extinction*, 313, 308–313.

115. Dubois and Dumenil, *Through Women's Eyes*, 421; Adams, *Education for Extinction*, 311–313; Claesgens, "Zitkala-Sa (Gertrude Simmons Bonnin) Biography."

116. United States Congressional Inquiry, "*Carlisle Indian School*, Charges by R. H. Pratt, Brigadier General, United States Army," Report on the Carlisle Indian School, by Inspector E. B. Linnen, 24 February 1914, 1373–1374. In fact, Pratt remained committed to the school well after his forced departure. He visited the school over the years, and in 1914 he submitted a report to Linnen that testified against then superintendent Moses Friedman, and also revealed his continued commitment to Indian education, in particular at Carlisle.

117. Zitkala-Sa's move to the Pennsylvania Indian boarding school was significant in that it helped to inspire feelings of ambivalence about having rejected much of her Sioux heritage, and ultimately led her to campaign against Carlisle and white efforts to assimilate Indians.

118. *Indian Helper* 4, 43 (June 14, 1889), 3 CCHS.

119. Commissioner of Indian Affairs Cato Sells to Clara R. Donaldson, 26 August 1914, Clara Donaldson Folder, NPRC.

120. Mrs. Edward L. Whistler (Verna Dunagan), interview, 29–30, WDC.

121. Norman W. Cameron, Diaries 1–5, Special Collections Library, University of Michigan (SCLM); Norman Cameron (grandson), "The U.S. Military Occupation of Bohol: 1900–1902," George Percival Scriven: An American in Bohol, The Philippines, 1899–1901, An On-line Archival Collection, Special Collections Library, Duke University, May 1997, http://library.duke.edu/rubenstein/scriptorium/scriven/bohol-history .html.

122. Mary Cole to Folks at Home, 16 March 1902, January to March 1902 Folder, Harry Newton Cole Papers, BHL; Mary Cole to Brother Leon and Mother, n.d. (likely November or December 1901), Undated Folder, Harry Newton Cole Papers, BHL. Also see Tarr, "The Education of Thomasites," chapter 5.

123. Blaine Free Moore Papers, LOC; Jules Theophile Frelin, Diaries, University Archives, University of Minnesota, (UAUM); Herman Hespelt Papers, Special Collections Library, Binghamton University (SCLB); H. O. Whiting Letters in James Hardy Papers, Indiana State Library, Indianapolis (ISL).

124. Cameron, Diary 1, SCLM.

125. H. O. Whiting to Dear Ones in America, 24 October 1906, James Hardy Papers, ISL.

126. Harrie Cole to Mother, 20 July 1901, Harry Newton Cole Papers, July 1901 Folder, BHL.

127. Blaine Free Moore to Pa and Ma, 15 July 1901, Box 1, Correspondence 1901 Folder, LOC.

128. Cameron, Diary 1, SCLM.

129. Ibid.

130. Harrie Cole to Mother, 20 and 29 July 1901, July 1901 Folder, BHL.

131. Herman Hespelt to Parents and Willie, 2 May 1911, SCLB.

132. Ibid. Hespelt also met "two newly married couples also going to the Philippines," although about a decade after the first Thomasites ventured overseas; Harrie Cole to Mother, 20 July 1901; Harrie Cole to Mother, 29 July 1901, BHL.

133. Mary Cole to Folks at Home, 24 July 1901, July 1901 Folder, Harry Newton Cole Papers, BHL.

134. Harrie Cole to Mother, 29 July 1901, BHL.

135. Mary Cole to Folks at Home, 24 July 1901, BHL. Although years later teachers did not travel in as large of groups, they, too, wrote of games like deck sports, which involved obstacle courses and pillow fights. For example, see H. O. Whiting to Dear Ones in America, 24 October 1906, ISL. Also see Tarr, "The Education of Thomasites," chapter 5.

136. Blaine Free Moore, 27 and 29 July 1901, Box 1, Diary 1/4 Folder, LOC.

137. Blaine Free Moore, 22 July 1901, Box 1, Diary 1/4 Folder, LOC; H. O. Whiting to Ones in America, 24 October 1906, ISL; Mary to Dear Folks at home, 24 July 1901, BHL.

138. Cameron, 21 August 1901, Diary 1, SCLM. Considering the accuracy in which the first of the two songs is remembered by Cameron, when compared to the version

recorded elsewhere, it is reasonable to assume that he participated in the singing and was one of the "'boys'" (or, at least, heard them often enough to remember the lyrics verbatim). Zimmerman, *Innocents Abroad*, 2. Although relationships were formed on the journey, rumors of such relationships also abounded, including a newspaper headline that suggested that thirty couples had met on the *Thomas* and wed in Hawaii on their way to the Philippines, though this proved to be false. For a discussion on minstrel songs, see Rhae Lynn Barnes, "Darkology: The Hidden History of Amateur Blackface Minstrelsy and the Making of Modern America" (PhD dissertation, Harvard University, 2016).

139. *Log of the "Thomas,"* 49; Cameron, 21 August 1901, Diary 1, SCLM. Also see the discussion of song and racial epithets in Kramer, *Blood of Government*, 114–115.

140. Cameron, 21 August 1901, Diary 1, SCLM.

141. *Log of the "Thomas,"* 25.

142. Jules Theophile Frelin, 14 August 1901, Diary 1899, University of Minnesota Archives, Minneapolis (UMA).

143. *Log of the "Thomas,"* 25.

144. After the Philippines, Mary Helen Fee volunteered for the Red Cross in France, where she also worked as a writer, before returning to the United States and teaching in the Indian Service. See Katherine Steinbock-Pratt, "'A Great Army of Instruction': American Teachers and the Negotiation of Empire in the Philippines" (PhD dissertation, University of Texas at Austin, 2013), 284–285.

145. Taylor to Mother, 1 January 1908, Taylor Family Correspondence 1908 Folder, BHL: "Their house party included the Armes of Cavite, the Cushmands of Zambales, an unmarried woman who had taught in the same Indian school with them, and half a dozen bachelors of the province."

146. Blaine Free Moore, 14 August 1901, Box 1, Diary 1/4, LOC.

147. Williams, "United States Indian Policy and the Debate over Philippine Annexation: Implications for the Origins of American Imperialism"; Paulet, "To Change the World"; and Paulet, "'The Only Good Indian Is a Dead Indian'"; see US policy among American Indians as a precedent for interventions in the Philippines. Here, teachers see the projects as somewhat comparable, at least regarding their work as teachers in both locations. This sense of comparability is also true for the crossover teachers studied here.

148. Clara R. Donaldson to Chief of Bureau of Insular Affairs, 18 September 1920, Record Group 350, Entry 21, Box 365, Clara R. Donaldson Folder, NAMD.

149. McKitrick, 15 May 1914, Clara Donaldson Folder, NPRC; *Carlisle Arrow* 11, 2 (September 11, 1914), CCHS.

150. Muerman, "The Philippine School under the Americans," 54.

151. McKitrick, 15 May 1914, Clara Donaldson Folder, NPRC.

152. Commissioner of Indian Affairs Cato Sells to U.S. Representative Frank B. Willis, 27 July 1914, Clara Donaldson Folder, NPRC.

153. At their time of hire, Anne Ely was forty-six years old: *FW Programmer* 82, 2 (December/March 1982): 2, Carlisle Barracks, PA, PI-2-8-10 Folder, CCHS; Sarah Mathers

was sixty-three years old: Pratt, *Battlefield and Classroom,* 220; Marianna Burgess was in her twenties but had years of experience teaching among the Pawnee: Burgess to Richard Henry Pratt, 21 October 1879, BRBML.

154. US Representative Frank B. Willis to Commissioner of Indian Affairs Cato Sells, 24 July 1914, Clara Donaldson Folder, NPRC; May D. McKitrick to Commissioner Sells, 17 July 1914, Clara Donaldson Folder, NPRC.

155. Principal Teacher John D. DeHuff to Supervisor O. H. Lipps Carlisle Indian School, 21 August 1914, Clara Donaldson Folder, NPRC; US Representative Simeon D. Fess, 11 May 1914, Clara Donaldson Folder, NPRC.

156. Commissioner of Indian Affairs Cato Sells to US Representative Frank B. Willis, 18 August 1914, Clara Donaldson Folder, NPRC; Clara R. Donaldson to Commissioner Sells, 22 August 1914, telegram, Clara Donaldson Folder, NPRC: She was first offered a position at the Pipestone Indian School in Minnesota, which she accepted; see Commissioner Sells to Clara R. Donaldson, 26 August 1914, telegram, Clara Donaldson Folder, NPRC.

157. John D. DeHuff to Supervisor Lipps, 21 August, 1914, NPRC.

158. John DeHuff to Commissioner of Indian Affairs Cato Sells, 20 January 1913, John DeHuff Folder, NPRC; Supervisor in the Philippines William R. Rosenhaus to Commissioner Sells, 19 January 1914, John DeHuff Folder, NPRC.

159. Edwin A. Schell to Commissioner of Indian Affairs Cato Sells, 5 February 1914, John DeHuff Folder, NPRC.

160. John DeHuff to Commissioner of Indian Affairs Cato Sells, 20 January 1913, NPRC.

161. John DeHuff to Commissioner Indian Affairs Cato Sells, 23 April 1914, John DeHuff Folder, NPRC.

162. Supervisor of Carlisle O. H. Lipps to Commissioner of Indian Affairs Cato Sells, 31 July 1914, John DeHuff Folder, NPRC.

163. Record of J. D. DeHuff, 5 June 1918, John DeHuff Folder, NPRC; John DeHuff to Commissioner of Indian Affairs Cato Sells, 24 July 1916, John DeHuff Folder, NPRC; Superintendent of Santa Fe Indian School C. E. Faris to Commissioner of Indian Affairs, 6 December 1934, Elizabeth DeHuff Folder, NPRC.

164. Record of Fernando G. Tranbarger, 11 May 1911, Fernando G. Tranbarger Folder 2, NPRC.

165. Fernando G. Tranbarger to Commissioner of Indian Affairs, 30 September 1911, Fernando G. Tranbarger Folder 2, NPRC.

166. Commissioner of Indian Affairs Cato Sells to Moses Friedman, 18 May 1914, Moses Friedman Folder, NPRC; Inspector E. B. Linnen, Western Union Telegram in code, 9 February 1914, Translation Telegram from Inspector Linnen. 11 February 1914, Moses Friedman Folder, NPRC.

167. Recommendation Letter for Moses Friedman, Superintendent C. W. Goodman (US Indian School, Phoenix, Arizona) to Whom It May Concern, 6 April 1903, Moses Friedman Folder, NPRC.

168. Principal J. Frank Daniel (Secondary School Cebu, Philippine Islands) to General Superintendent of Education Manila, 23 September 1904, Moses Friedman Folder, NPRC.

169. Division Superintendent Samuel McClintock to Moses Friedman, 13 February 1906, Moses Friedman Folder, NPRC.

170. Moses Friedman to Commissioner of Indian Affairs, 23 June 1906, Moses Friedman Folder, NPRC.

171. Commissioner of Indian Affairs F. E. Leupp to Secretary of the Interior, 7 March 1908, Moses Friedman Folder, NPRC.

172. *Carlisle Arrow* 7, 1 (September 9, 1910): 4, CCHS: "Announcement has been received of the marriage, on August 3, of Miss Katharine C. Bingley to Mr. Fernando G. Tranbarger, the wedding taking place at Greensboro, North Carolina. Both Mr. and Mrs. Tranbarger were teachers here last year, and we extend them our heartiest congratulations and best wishes."

173. Commissioner Jose Gil to Secretary of the President (Manila), 21 June 1906, Record Group 350, Entry 21, Box 215, Moses Friedman Folder, NAMD: Moses Friedman served as a teacher from January 13, 1904, to June 9, 1906; Record of Fernando G. Tranbarger, Fernando G. Tranbarger Folder, NPRC: Tranbarger taught in the Philippine Service from June 12, 1906, to November 17, 1909.

174. Fernando G. Tranbarger to Commissioner of Indian Affairs, 30 August 1911, Fernando G. Tranbarger Folder 2, NPRC; Fernando G. Tranbarger to Superintendent Moses Friedman, 30 September 1911, Fernando G. Tranbarger Folder 2, NPRC; Fernando G. Tranbarger to Commissioner of Indian Affairs, 24 October 1911, Fernando G. Tranbarger Folder 2, NPRC.

CHAPTER 2. LIFE AT CARLISLE, 1879–1918

1. "Report of the Commissioner of Indian Affairs," 1901, 31–32.

2. Philip J. Deloria, *Playing Indian* (New Haven, CT: Yale University Press, 1998): Deloria explores the historical significance of particular moments when white Americans have donned disguises, performing or "playing Indian," as a means of both rejecting the "other" and claiming a unique identity. Following Deloria's example, I use the term "being Indian" to illustrate how Carlisle teachers sought to erase students' Indian identities. The term acknowledges the fluidity of students' identities (what it meant to "be Indian") as well as how white reformers' beliefs and tactics changed over time.

3. Clifford E. Trafzer, "Introduction: Origin and Development of the American Indian Boarding School System," in Clifford E. Trafzer, Jean A. Keller, and Lorene Sisquoc, eds., *Boarding School Blues: Revisiting American Indian Educational Experiences* (Lincoln: University of Nebraska Press, 2006), 15; Jacqueline Fear-Segal, *White Man's Club: Schools, Race, and the Struggle of Indian Acculturation* (Lincoln: University of Nebraska, 2007), 122, 160–161.

4. American Indian peoples, including the children at boarding schools like Carlisle, have created their own identities as well as varied meanings of "Indian" or "being

Indian," demonstrating their agency. As my study focuses on teachers' agency, I defer to the following scholars to better understand "Indian" agency from an indigenous perspective. See David Wallace Adams, *Education for Extinction: American Indians and the Boarding School Experience, 1875–1928* (Lawrence: University of Kansas, 1995); David Wallace Adams, "Beyond Bleakness: The Brighter Side of Indian Boarding Schools, 1870–1940," in Trafzer et al., *Boarding School Blues*; Genevieve Bell, "Telling Stories out of School: Remembering the Carlisle Indian Industrial School, 1879–1918" (PhD dissertation, Stanford University, 1998); Cathleen D. Cahill, *Federal Fathers and Mothers: A Social History of the United States Indian Service, 1869–1933* (Chapel Hill: University of North Carolina Press, 2011); Michael C. Coleman, *American Indian Children at School, 1850–1930* (Jackson: University Press of Mississippi, 1993); Fear-Segal, *White Man's Club*; Trafzer, "Introduction: Origin and Development of the American Indian Boarding School System"; Jacqueline Fear-Segal and Susan D. Rose, eds., *Carlisle Indian Industrial School: Indigenous Histories, Memories, and Reclamations* (Lincoln: University of Nebraska Press, 2016).

5. Bell, "Telling Stories out of School," 158.

6. Ibid., 65: the school's first newspaper, *Eadle Keatah Toh* (later known by its English translation, "Morning Star") was distributed within a few months of Carlisle's opening. By 1893 there were two publications: The *Red Man*, a monthly with a circulation of 2,000 to 3,000; and a weekly, the *Indian Helper*, with a circulation of 9,000. See Jon Reyhner and Jeanne Eder, *A History of Indian Education* (Billings: Eastern Montana College, 1989), 141; "Carlisle Indian Industrial School: Periodicals and Newspapers," CCHS website, accessed September 25, 2015, http://www.historicalsociety.com/CIIS_Newspapers.html. Other publications also circulated within and beyond Carlisle over the years, including the *Craftsmen*, the *Arrow*, and the *Carlisle Arrow*; Fear-Segal, *White Man's Club*, 206: "These periodicals were the public voice of Carlisle, which sought to inform whites about the goals, activities and achievements of the school"; for further critique of the school's newspapers, see chapter 8, "Man-on-the-Bandstand: Surveillance, Concealment, and Resistance," in Fear-Segal, *White Man's Club*, 206–230.

7. Coleman, *American Indian Children at School*, 38–40; Fear-Segal, *White Man's Club*, 1; Francis Paul Prucha, *American Indian Policy in Crisis: Christian Reformers and the Indian, 1865–1900* (Norman: University of Oklahoma Press, 1976). For autobiographic accounts of indigenous peoples regarding missionaries, see Francis La Flesche, *The Middle Five: Indian Schoolboys of the Omaha Tribe* (1900; repr., Lincoln: University of Nebraska Press, 1963); Zitkala-Sa, "Impressions of an Indian Childhood," *Atlantic Monthly* 85, 507 (January 1900): 37–47; Zitkala-Sa, "School Days of an Indian Girl," *Atlantic Monthly* 85, 508 (February 1900): 185–194.

8. Coleman, *American Indian Children at School*, 41. Also see Adams, *Education for Extinction*, 18–27; Adams, "Fundamental Considerations," 2–3; Frederick E. Hoxie, *A Final Promise: The Campaign to Assimilate the Indians, 1880–1920* (Lincoln: University of Nebraska Press, 1984), 53–54.

9. Cahill, *Federal Fathers and Mothers*, 3–6; Coleman, *American Indian Children at School*, 38–40.

10. Cahill, *Federal Fathers and Mothers*, 55–56.

11. Coleman, *American Indian Children at School*, 40. See chapter 1 for discussion of real threats that faced American Indians in the nineteenth century.

12. Richard Henry Pratt, *Battlefield and Classroom: Four Decades with the American Indian, 1867–1904*, Robert M. Utley, ed. (1964; repr., Norman: University of Oklahoma Press, 2003).

13. Sarah A. Mather to Richard Henry Pratt, Letter, 21 August 1879, Richard Henry Pratt Papers, Box 6, Folder 195, BRBML.

14. Pratt, *Battlefield and Classroom*, 121, 220.

15. Ibid., 220, 222–228. Of course, this is Pratt's account. Native American accounts of the same experience likely do not highlight the adventure and triumph but instead might point to threats or lies perpetrated by these white outsiders.

16. Luther Standing Bear, *My People the Sioux*, edited by E. A. Brininstool (1928; repr., Lincoln: University of Nebraska Press, 1975), 133, 127.

17. Zitkala-Sa, "Impressions of an Indian Childhood," 46–47; Zitkala-Sa, "School Days of an Indian Girl," 185.

18. Standing Bear, *My People the Sioux*, 130–131.

19. Ibid., 129–130. For Standing Bear's account of the longer journey from his home to Carlisle, see 125–132.

20. Pratt, *Battlefield and Classroom*, 228–229; Fear-Segal, *White Man's Club*, 181.

21. Pratt, *Battlefield and Classroom*, 258–260: Richard Henry Pratt to US Representative Thaddeaus C. Pound, reprinted letter, 13 January 1881.

22. "Letter from Theo Schwan, Capt. 11th Infantry, Acting US Indian Agent dated 20 August 1879," *Eadle Keatah Toh* 1, 3 (May 1880): 1–2, CCHS.

23. Richard Henry Pratt, interview by Mr. Spears (N.Y. Sun), October 7, 1896, Transcript, 6, Richard Henry Pratt Papers, Box 19, Folder 679, BRBML.

24. Fear-Segal, *White Man's Club*; Margaret L. Archuleta, Brenda Child, and K. Tsianina Lomawaima, eds., *Away from Home: American Indian Boarding School Experiences, 1879–2000* (Phoenix: Heard Museum, 2000). For a more complex understanding of Carlisle's history and memory see Jacqueline Fear-Segal and Susan D. Rose, *Carlisle Indian Industrial School: Indigenous Histories, Memories, and Reclamations* (Lincoln: University of Nebraska Press, 2016).

25. Adams, *Education for Extinction*, 8–24.

26. *Indian Helper* 15, 18 (March 2, 1900), CCHS.

27. Ibid.

28. Emma A. Cutter to R. L. Brunhouse, 29 March 1933, Richard Henry Pratt Papers, Box 13, Folder 450, BRBML.

29. Pratt, *Battlefield and Classroom*, 229–236, 274–475.

30. David B. Tyack and Elisabeth Hansot, *Learning Together: A History of Coeducation*

in American Schools (New Haven, CT: Yale University Press, 1990). David B. Tyack and Larry Cuban, *Tinkering toward Utopia: A Century of Public School Reform* (Cambridge, MA: Harvard University Press, 1995).

31. Standing Bear, *My People the Sioux*, 127–129, recalled boys and girls sleeping on opposite sides of a room aboard a steamboat and occupying separate train cars according to sex. Although Standing Bear's sister ultimately refused to board the steamboat and continue the journey east, choosing instead to remain with her parents who had accompanied them thus far, other sisters and brothers were divided by sex, which would have added to the children's profound anxiety as they headed toward Carlisle. Standing Bear writes that some of the Sioux "big boys" explained that the train would fall off the edge of the Earth and sang "brave songs" as they anticipated their deaths, hurtling toward the end of the Earth, 131. For more on the impact of family separation at boarding schools for indigenous peoples in the United States and Australia, see Margaret D. Jacobs, *White Mother to a Dark Race: Settler Colonialism, Maternalism, and the Removal of Indigenous Children in the American West and Australia, 1880–1910* (Lincoln: University of Nebraska Press, 2009).

32. Standing Bear, *My People the Sioux*, 229–236, 274–475, 232. Mrs. Platt, a former missionary teacher, volunteered her services and was hired to work the kitchen and dining room during the school's first five years; Emma A. Cutter to R. L. Brunhouse, 29 March 1933, BRBML.

33. Standing Bear, *My People the Sioux*, 137–138.

34. Ibid. While Luther Standing Bear's memoir offers insights into his experiences at Carlisle, it also reflects the romanticization of memory that often occurs decades after an event.

35. Jason Betzinez (with Wilber Sturtevant Nye), *I Fought with Geronimo* (1959; repr., Lincoln: University of Nebraska Press, 1987), 154.

36. Asa Daklugie memoir in Eve Ball (with Nora Henn and Lynda A. Sánchez), *Indeh: An Apache Odyssey* (Norman: University of Oklahoma Press, 1988), 150, 144.

37. Bell, "Telling Stories out of School," 5.

38. Matthew Bentley, "'Kill the Indian, Save the Man': Manhood at the Carlisle Indian Industrial School, 1879–1918" (PhD dissertation, University of East Anglia, 2012).

39. "The Indian Training School," *Eadle Keatah Toh* 1, 1 (January 1880): 1, CCHS.

40. Standing Bear, *My People the Sioux*, 141–142; Asa Daklugie memoir in Ball, *Indeh: An Apache Odyssey*, 144.

41. Asa Daklugie memoir in Ball, *Indeh: An Apache Odyssey*, 149, 151. Ball's interview with Asa Daklugie includes his use of the term "White Eyes," a derogatory term that describes white people who took lands away from his people, including white authorities at Carlisle, and suggests the constant sense of white surveillance of Indian children at the school.

42. Emma A. Cutter to R. L. Brunhouse, 29 March 29 1933, BRBML.

43. Standing Bear, *My People the Sioux*, 133, 146.

44. Richard Henry Pratt, interview, 13, BRBML.

45. "Is It Right," *Indian Helper* 3, 4 (September 2, 1887): 2, CCHS.

46. *58th Annual Report of the Commissioner of Indian Affairs 1889* (Washington, DC: Government Printing Office, 1889), 6.

47. "Is It Right," *Indian Helper*, 2.

48. Ibid., 1.

49. Dennison Wheelock to Richard Henry Pratt, 11 August 1922, Richard Henry Pratt Papers, Box 9, Folder 323, BRBML; Cahill, *Federal Fathers and Mothers*, 229; Clarke Garrett, *In Pursuit of Pleasure: Leisure in Nineteenth-Century Cumberland County* (Carlisle, PA: Cumberland County Historical Society, 1997), 97–98.

50. Mrs. Edward L. Whistler (Verna Dunagan), interview, 4, 34.

51. Emma A. Cutter to Nana Pratt, 15 February 1937, Richard Henry Pratt Papers, Box 15, Folder 505, BRBML.

52. Betzinez, *I Fought with Geronimo*, 154.

53. *Indian Helper* 4, 21 (January 11, 1889); *Indian Helper* 4, 29 (March 8, 1889); *Indian Helper* 15, 18 (March 2, 1900); *Indian Helper* 15, 23 (April 6, 1900); *Indian Helper* 15, 24 (April 13, 1900).

54. Asa Daklugie memoir in Ball, *Indeh: An Apache Odyssey*, 144.

55. Standing Bear, *My People the Sioux*, 138.

56. William J. Reese, *America's Public Schools: From the Common School to "No Child Left Behind"* (Baltimore: Johns Hopkins University Press, 2011), 85–89, on Johann Pestalozzi education reformer and "objective methods."

57. Emma A. Cutter to R. L. Brunhouse, 29 March 1933, BRBML.

58. "First Annual Report," 5 October 1880, *Eadle Keatah Toh* 1, 7 (November 1880), CCHS; Levi Seeley, *Grube's Method of Teaching Arithmetic* (New York: E. L. Kellogg, 1891), 11–16, https://archive.org/details/grubesmethodofteooseelrich; Elaine Goodale Eastman, *Pratt: The Red Man's Moses* (Norman: University of Oklahoma Press, 1935), 85. Emma A. Cutter to Nana, 15 February 1937, BRBML. Miss Semple and Sarah Mather are both credited with introducing such methods to Carlisle.

59. Standing Bear, *My People the Sioux*, 155.

60. Asa Daklugie memoir in Ball, *Indeh: An Apache Odyssey*, 144–145.

61. "First Annual Report," 5 October 1880, *Eadle Keatah Toh*: teachers used maps, oral lessons, and drawing to teach geography.

62. Fear-Segal, *White Man's Club*, 49–50.

63. See Table 2.1 for more on Carlisle student attendance.

64. Although this book focuses on the teachers of academic subjects, industrial training held a particular significance in the nineteenth-century imagination. Following the Civil War, industrial training like that developed at Carlisle was heralded by champions of the "new education" who believed that public schools should teach students skills that would help them in the so-called real world. Northern reformers targeted immigrant communities while southern educators focused on African Americans, both believing that these groups were particularly suited for industrial training. Of course, racial biases regarding immigrants' and African Americans' ca-

pabilities largely influenced such beliefs, as they did for Indians at Carlisle. Just as missionaries had instituted both academic and manual training with their Indian students utilizing a "half-and-half" day model years before Carlisle opened, the industrial training program at Carlisle reflected larger educational trends that developed over the course of the nineteenth century. See Reese, *America's Public Schools*, 99–107.

65. Hattie M. McDowell to Commissioner of Indian Affairs Cato Sells, 20 July 1918, Hattie McDowell Folder, NPRC: Carlisle eliminated the lower grades in 1915; Carlisle Supervisor O. H. Lipps to Commissioner of Indian Affairs, 13 April 1915, Lucy Case Folder, NPRC; Reese, *America's Public Schools*, 181–183.

66. Adapted from Bell, "Telling Stories out of School": 45, 77, 333, 400, 402, 158: According to Bell, the Bureau of Indian Affairs defunded teachers' summer leave in 1911. See also *Indian Helper* 14, 39 (July 21, 1899): 2; "Personals about Educational Leave," *Carlisle Arrow* 10, 1 (September 5, 1913), John Whitwell Folder 2, NPRC.

67. See Table 2.1.

68. Emma Lovewell to E. B. Linnen, 5 September 1914, Emma C. Lovewell Folder, NPRC.

69. Mattie Lane to Commissioner of Indian Affairs, 1 July 1912, Mattie Lane Folder, NPRC.

70. In fact, low graduation rates at the school suggest that most students did not demonstrate mastery in key areas at Carlisle. See Appendix 3.

71. Cahill, *Federal Fathers and Mothers*, 220: in 1912, the Efficiency Report forms were revised.

72. Efficiency Report: Emma C. Lovewell, 15 January 1912, Emma C. Lovewell Folder, NPRC; Efficiency Report: Emma C. Lovewell, 19 December 1914, Emma C. Lovewell Folder, NPRC.

73. Efficiency Report: 20 February 1911, Emma C. Lovewell Folder, NPRC.

74. Acting Commissioner of Indian Affairs F. H. Abbot to US Senator Carroll S. Page, 6 March 1912, Emma C. Lovewell Folder, NPRC. Abbot repeated the exact phrasing as listed on the Efficiency Report of February 20, 1911: "work lacks the life and spirit necessary for complete success."

75. Efficiency Report: 19 December 1914, Emma C. Lovewell Folder, NPRC.

76. See Table 2.2 on Efficiency Reports.

77. R. H. Pratt, "Report of School at Carlisle, PA," 25 August 1894, *Annual Report of the Commissioner of Indian Affairs 1894* (Washington, DC: Government Printing Office, 1895), 48, University of Wisconsin Digital Collections, http://digital.library.wisc.edu/1711.dl/History.

78. Bell, "Telling Stories out of School," 158.

79. Cahill, *Federal Fathers and Mothers*, 84–98.

80. Commissioner Chas. H. Burke to Superintendent Port Apache Agency Charles L. Davis, 29 September 1925, Lydia A. Dittes Folder, NPRC.

81. Cahill, *Federal Fathers and Mothers*, 84–85.

82. Carlisle Co-workers to Richard Henry Pratt, 20 June 1904, Richard Henry Pratt Papers, Box 9, Folder 332, BRBML.

83. "Notes from Room No. 8," *Carlisle Arrow* 11, 30 (April 2, 1915), CCHS.

84. Good Bear to Ann Ely, 4 April 1894, Richard Henry Pratt Papers, Box 13, Folder 456, BRBML.

85. Standing Bear, *My People the Sioux*, 161.

86. Louis J. Paul to Mrs. Laura Pratt, 30 May 1924, in *Indian Trails*, Richard Henry Pratt Papers, Box 21, Folder 699, BRBML.

87. Pratt, *Battlefield and Classroom*, 233; *Morning Star* 4, 2 (September 1883), CCHS; Richard Henry Pratt to Chief S. Bear Rosebud, 15 December 1880, Richard Henry Pratt Papers, Box 10-4, Bound Letters (24 December 1879 to 28 June 1881): 203; *Indian Helper* 3, 22 (January 13, 1888), CCHS.

88. Fear-Segal, *White Man's Club*, 258–263. The school separated "Jack" (Mather) from his biological sister when they arrived at the school; "Daily Morning Reports July 1, 1887 to July 1, 1891," 5 February 1888: 16–17, Record Group 75, Entry 1331: "Jack Mather died 5 pm," NADC.

89. Emma Lovewell to E. B. Linnen, 5 September 1914, NPRC; Pratt, *Battlefield and Classroom*, 233. Pratt described a former mission teacher employed at Carlisle "in charge of the dining room and kitchen" for the school's first five years as "motherly to the individual students" and emphasized other teachers' love for their students.

90. In *White Man's Club*, Fear-Segal analyzes the role that school newspapers played in surveying students, particularly through that of Burgess's "Man-on-the-Bandstand" persona, which served a particularly invasive and eerie role for fifteen years. Fear-Segal writes on page 207, "This anonymous, invisible, white male persona brazenly located himself on the school bandstand [located in the center of the school grounds], claiming it as both home and editorial site. From here he watched the children and commented on their activities."

91. Marianna Burgess, *Stiya, a Carlisle Indian Girl at Home; Founded on the Author's Actual Observations* (1891; repr., Memphis: General Books, 2010), 30.

92. *Indian Helper* 4, 34 (May 1, 1891), CCHS.

93. Pratt, *Battlefield and Classroom*, 229; Standing Bear, *My People the Sioux*, 127.

94. These skills often did not apply to students' lives after Carlisle, particularly if students returned to reservations. Standing Bear, *My People the Sioux*, 147: Luther Standing Bear explained that he was trained to be a tinsmith while a student at Carlisle but that afterward "this trade did not benefit me any."

95. Fear-Segal, *White Man's Club*, 207; Bell, "Telling Stories out of School," 65–66, 115; Adams, "Beyond Blackness," 51.

96. Asa Daklugie memoir in Ball, *Indeh: An Apache Odyssey*, 147.

97. Moses Friedman to Matron Gaither, 22 November 1912, Moses Friedman Folder, NPRC.

98. Moses Friedman to Major James McLaughlin, Indian Inspector, Department of the Interior, 5 December 1912, Moses Friedman Folder, NPRC.

99. Moses Friedman to John Whitwell, 9 September 1913, John Whitwell Folder 1, NPRC.

100. Supervisor John B. Brown to Commissioner of Indian Affairs, 23 January 1914, Moses Friedman Folder, NPRC.

101. United States Congressional Inquiry, *Carlisle Indian School*, Testimony of Miss Emma C. Lovewell, 1183–1184.

102. Bell calculated the average age of Carlisle students from 1879 to 1918. The average age range was from 11 to 18 years old. For more, see Table 2.1: Student Attendance at Carlisle, compiled from Bell's calculations, 45, 77, 333, 400, 402.

103. United States Congressional Inquiry, *Carlisle Indian School*, 949–1390; Teachers' Testimony, Emma C. Lovewell, 1182–1185; "Report on the Carlisle Indian School, by Inspector E. B. Linnen, Feb. 24, 1914," 1359.

104. Teachers oversaw many clubs and extracurricular activities outside of their classroom duties. For examples, see *Carlisle Arrow* 10, 1 (September 5, 1913), CCHS: Young Women's Christian Association; *Indian Helper* 4, 11 (October 26, 1888), CCHS: Missionary Society, "to help the Indian children of Alaska who have not yet as many advantages as we have in Education's Road."

105. Richard Henry Pratt, interview, 9, BRBML.

106. *Indian Helper* 13, 51 (October 7, 1898): 4, CCHS.

107. Teachers also served as "official visitors" and advisors of debate clubs and reportedly "gave helpful remarks," some of which could be quite critical of students' "lack of conformity to parliamentary usage" at meetings. See *Indian Helper*, 14, 11 (January 6, 1899); *Indian Helper* 15, 18 (March 2, 1900); *Carlisle Arrow* 11, 6 (October 9, 1914); *Carlisle Arrow* 11, no. 30 (April 2, 1915), CCHS.

108. *Indian Helper* 5, 21 (January 24, 1890), CCHS.

109. *Carlisle Arrow* 11, 17 (January 1, 1915), CCHS.

110. R. H. Pratt, "Report of School at Carlisle, PA," 25 August 1894, *Annual Report of the Commissioner of Indian Affairs 1894*, 408; Adams, "Beyond Bleakness," 51: "Other than in the classroom, and perhaps the dining room, the sexes were generally kept apart, except in carefully monitored moments, such as on Saturday evenings when smaller children tossed bean bags and played other innocent games and older ones came together for waltzes, square dances, and Virginia reels." For one example of student enjoyment see Betzinez, *I Fought with Geronimo*, 155.

111. *Indian Helper* 13, 50 (September 30, 1898), CCHS.

112. As cited in Bell, "Telling Stories out of School," 84; United States Congressional Inquiry, *Carlisle Indian School, Hearings Before the Joint Commission of the Congress of the United States to Investigate Indian Affairs, Feb. 6–8 and March 25, 1914.* 63rd Congress, 2nd Session. Part II (Washington, DC: Government Printing Office, 1914), 1047–1048. Genevieve Bell found that such rules regarding respectability were not enforced equally under all of the school's administrations. She argued, "Seemingly at odds with this adherence to military discipline, Mercer relaxed many of the social restrictions that had been common practice . . . permitting male and female pupils 'to

dance as many as two to three times a week and just have a general good time' (US Congress 1914: 1047–48)"; Moses Friedman to John Whitwell, 29 September 1913, John Whitwell Folder, NPRC.

113. *Eadle Keatah Toh* 1, 1 (January 1880): 1, CCHS.

114. Estelle Reel (Superintendent of Indian Schools), 10 August 1901, in *Course of Study for Indian Schools of the United States; Industrial and Literary* (Washington, DC: Government Printing Office, 1901): 5–6, CCHS. For a discussion of Reel (including her background and racist perspective) see K. Tsianina Lomawaima, "Estelle Reel, Superintendent of Indian Schools, 1898–1910," *Journal of American Indian Education* 35, 3 (1995): 5–31.

115. *Carlisle Arrow* 11, 2 (September 11, 1914), CCHS; Betzinez, *I Fought with Geronimo*, 156, suggests that church attendance was mandatory.

116. *Indian Helper* 15, 18 (March 2, 1900), CCHS; "General School News," *Carlisle Arrow* 11, 11 (November 13, 1914): "Miss Snoddy, Mrs. Ewing, and Miss Roberts have been chosen to act as an advisory committee for the Y.W.C.A.," CCHS; *Carlisle Arrow* 11, 14 (December 4, 1914), CCHS; R. H. Pratt, "Report of School at Carlisle, PA," 25 August 1894, *Annual Report of the Commissioner of Indian Affairs 1894*, 406; Eastman, *Pratt: The Red Man's Moses*, 85.

117. Institute for Government Research with Technical Director Lewis Meriam, *The Problem of Indian Administration: Report of a Survey made at the request of Honorable Hubert Work, Secretary of the Interior, and submitted to him, February 21, 1928* (Baltimore: Johns Hopkins University Press, 1928), 16.

118. Margaret Connell Szasz, *Education and the American Indian: The Road to Self-Determination since 1928* (Santa Fe: University of New Mexico Press), 67.

119. Eastman, *Pratt: The Red Man's Moses*, 85.

120. Theodore D. Sargent, *The Life of Elaine Goodale Eastman* (Lincoln: University of Nebraska Press, 2005).

121. Katherine S. Bowersox to Richard Henry Pratt, 20 August 1902, Richard Henry Pratt Papers, Box 1, Folder 36, BRBML.

122. Ibid.

123. Carlisle Co-workers to Richard Henry Pratt, 20 June 1904, BRBML.

124. Standing Bear, *My People the Sioux*, 146–147.

125. *Indian Helper* 3, 19 (December 23, 1887): 2, CCHS; *Indian Helper* 3, 21 (January 6, 1888): 3, CCHS; *Indian Helper* 4, 20 (January 4, 1889): 1, 4, CCHS.

126. *Indian Helper* 3, 19 (December 23, 1887): 2, CCHS; *Indian Helper* 3, 21 (January 6, 1888): 3, CCHS; *Indian Helper* 4, 20 (January 4, 1889): 1, 4, CCHS; "Chips from Christmas '99," *Indian Helper* 15, 10 (January 5, 1900), CCHS.

127. *Indian Helper* 4, 20 (January 4, 1889), CCHS; *Indian Helper* 15, 10 (January 5, 1900), CCHS; *Carlisle Arrow* 11, 17 (January 1, 1915), CCHS; John Whitwell to Moses Friedman, 29 December 1910, John Whitwell Folder 1, NPRC.

128. Good Bear to Ely, 4 April 1894, BRBML.

129. Betzinez, *I Fought with Geronimo*, 156.

130. Ibid., 150.

131. Although Superintendent Moses Friedman's own personal religion is not directly revealed in the historical record, the anti-Semitism that he suffered at the hands of students (and likely staff members) complicate the school's reliance upon Christianity as a means of disciplining students, at least during his tenure. See Alice Beck Kehoe, *A Passion for the True and Just: Felix and Lucy Kramer Cohen and the Indian New Deal* (Phoenix: University of Arizona Press, 2014), 127.

132. Peter Nabokov, ed., *Native American Testimony: A Chronicle of Indian-White Relations from Prophesy to the Present, 1492–2000* (New York: Penguin Books, 1999), 49–53.

133. For more on the trauma and resilience of indigenous communities impacted by Carlisle, see Fear-Segal, *Carlisle Indian Industrial School.*

CHAPTER 3. DISCIPLINE AT CARLISLE, 1879–1918

1. *Eadle Keatah Toh* 1, 2. (April 1880), CCHS.

2. Jacqueline Fear-Segal, *White Man's Club: Schools, Race, and the Struggle of Indian Acculturation* (Lincoln: University of Nebraska, 2007), 65–66, for an analysis on the "Man-on-the-Bandstand" persona that served to enforce student compliance, and which first appeared in the school newspaper the *Indian Helper*, in 1885.

3. Richard Henry Pratt, interview by Mr. Spears (N.Y. Sun), October 7, 1896, Transcript, 6, Richard Henry Pratt Papers, Box 19, Folder 679, BRBML.

4. Ibid.

5. For more on punishment at Indian schools, see Trafzer, et al., "Introduction: Origin and Development of the American Indian Boarding School System," 21.

6. Clifford E. Trafzer, "Introduction: Origin and Development of the American Indian Boarding School System," in Clifford E. Trafzer, Jean A. Keller, and Lorene Sisquoc, eds., *Boarding School Blues: Revisiting American Indian Educational Experiences* (Lincoln: University of Nebraska Press, 2006), 21.

7. Michael C. Coleman, *American Indian Children at School, 1850–1930* (Jackson: University Press of Mississippi, 1993), 86–88; Mrs. Edward L. Whistler (Verna Dunagan), interview, 3–4, WDC; Jason Betzinez (with Wilber Sturtevant Nye), *I Fought with Geronimo* (1959; repr., Lincoln: University of Nebraska Press, 1987), 150.

8. Richard Henry Pratt, interview, 1, BRBML.

9. "Rules for Indian Schools," *59th Annual Report of the Commissioner of Indian Affairs to the Secretary of the Interior, 1890* (Washington, DC: Government Printing Office, 1890), CLII, University of Wisconsin Digital Collections, http://digital.library.wisc.edu/1711.dl/History.

10. Betzinez, *I Fought with Geronimo*, 50.

11. Trafzer, "Introduction: Origin and Development of the American Indian Boarding School System," 21.

12. *59th Annual Report of the Commissioner of Indian Affairs to the Secretary of the Interior 1890*, CLII, University of Wisconsin Digital Collections, http://digital.library.wisc.edu/1711.dl/History; Sonciray Bonnell, "Chemawa Indian Boarding School: The

First One Hundred Years, 1880 to 1980" (PhD dissertation, Dartmouth College, 1997); David Wallace Adams, "The Federal Indian Boarding School: A Study of Environment and Response, 1879–1918" (EdD dissertation, Indiana University, 1975), 124. In *Boarding House Blues*, Trafzer notes that "company officers and others also confined children to stockades, jails, or guardhouses—often hidden from plain view of curious visitors to the schools," 21.

13. Asa Daklugie memoir in Eve Ball (with Nora Henn and Lynda A. Sánchez), *Indeh: An Apache Odyssey* (University of Oklahoma Press, 1988), 150–151.

14. Richard Henry Pratt, interview, 1, BRBML.

15. Elaine Goodale Eastman, *Pratt: The Red Man's Moses* (Norman: University of Oklahoma Press, 1935), 209.

16. Ibid.

17. Asa Daklugie memoir in Ball, *Indeh: An Apache Odyssey*, 151.

18. United States Congressional Inquiry, *Carlisle Indian School*, Testimony of Miss Emma C. Lovewell, 1183–1184.

19. John Whitwell to Moses Friedman, 31 July 1913, John Whitwell Folder 1, NPRC. Testimony and reports on undernourishment can be found in the United States Congressional Inquiry, *Carlisle Indian School*, Testimony of Alvis Martin, Student, 993–996, and Report on the Carlisle Indian School, by Inspector E. B. Linnen, 24 February 1914, "The Dining Room—Lack of Sufficient Food for the Students," 1352–1355.

20. John Whitwell to Commissioner of Indian Affairs, 14 April 1914, John Whitwell Folder 2, NPRC.

21. Ibid.

22. Bonnell, "Chemawa Indian Boarding School," 23.

23. John Whitwell to Commissioner of Indian Affairs, 14 April 1914, NPRC.

24. Emma C. Lovewell to John Whitwell, 9 April 1914, John Whitwell Folder 2, NPRC.

25. Mattie Lane to Commissioner of Indian Affairs, 1 July 1912, NPRC.

26. Ibid.

27. Bell, "Telling Stories out of School," 246; Trafzer, "Introduction: Origin and Development of the American Indian Boarding School System," 21.

28. William J. Reese, *America's Public Schools: From the Common School to "No Child Left Behind"* (Baltimore: Johns Hopkins University Press, 2011); John L. Rury, *Education and Social Change: Contours in the History of American Schooling*, 5th ed. (New York: Routledge, 2016); David Tyack, *The One Best System: A History of American Urban Education* (Cambridge, MA: Harvard University Press, 1974); Quincy Adams Kuehner, "The Evolution of the Modern Concept of School Discipline" (PhD dissertation, University of Pennsylvania, 1913).

29. Bell, "Telling Stories out of School," 212: "On average, ninety students per year deserted during Friedman's tenure, compared to Pratt's average of twenty students per year (1879–1904). . . . William Mercer averaged eighty-seven students per year

(1904–1908); Oscar Lipps, sixty-four (1914–1916); and John Francis had 115 students deserted during his sixteen months in charge of Carlisle (1917–1918)."

30. Ibid., chapter 6, 209–248, specifically 209, 211, 214.

31. *Indian Helper* 15, 13 (January 26, 1900), CCHS.

32. Center for Disease Control, "Achievements in Public Health, 1900–1999: Impact of Vaccines Universally Recommended for Children—United States, 1990–1998," *Morbidity and Mortality Weekly Report* 48, 12 (April 2, 1999): 243–248, https://www.cdc.gov/mmwr/preview/mmwrhtml/00056803.htm.

33. Bell, "Telling Stories out of School," 387–388.

34. Robert A. Trennert Jr., *The Phoenix Indian School: Forced Assimilation in Arizona, 1891–1935* (Norman: University of Oklahoma Press, 1988), 77, 102; Trafzer, "Introduction: Origin and Development of the American Indian Boarding School System," 20.

35. Cathleen D. Cahill, *Federal Fathers and Mothers: A Social History of the United States Indian Service, 1869–1933* (Chapel Hill: University of North Carolina Press, 2011), 222.

36. Bell, "Telling Stories out of School," 64.

37. For a personalized account of death and disease at a missionary school see Francis La Flesche, *The Middle Five: Indian Schoolboys of the Omaha Tribe* (1900; repr., Lincoln: University of Nebraska Press, 1963), 152. Also see Jacqueline Fear-Segal and Susan D. Rose, eds., *Carlisle Indian Industrial School: Indigenous Histories, Memories, and Reclamations* (Lincoln: University of Nebraska Press, 2016), particularly the chapters by Barbara Landis, "Death at Carlisle: Naming the Unknowns in the Cemetery," and Warren Petoskey, "Response to Visiting Carlisle: Experiencing Intergenerational Trauma."

38. *Eadle Keatah Toh* 1, 1 (January 1880), CCHS; *Eadle Keatah Toh* 1, 2 (April 1880), CCHS.

39. *Eadle Keatah Toh* 1, 7 (November 1880), CCHS; "First Annual Report," 5 October 1880, *Eadle Keatah Toh*, CCHS.

40. Richard Henry Pratt to Chief S. Bear Rosebud, 13 December 1880, Richard Henry Pratt Papers, Box 10-4, Bound Letters (24 December 1879 to 28 June 1881), 190; Richard Henry Pratt to Chief S. Bear Rosebud, 15 December 1880, 203–205, BRBML.

41. Richard Henry Pratt to Chief White Thunder, 14 December 1880, Richard Henry Pratt Papers, Box 10-4, Bound Letters (24 December 1879 to 28 June 1881): 195–197; Richard Henry Pratt to Chief White Thunder, 15 December 1880, 199–200, BRBML.

42. Richard Henry Pratt to Chief Swift Bear, 14 December 1880, Richard Henry Pratt Papers, Box 10-4, Bound Letters (24 December 1879 to 28 June 1881), 193–194, BRBML.

43. R. H. Pratt, "Report of School at Carlisle, PA," 1 September 1889, *58th Annual Report of the Commissioner of Indian Affairs 1889* (Washington, DC: Government Printing Office, 1889), 367, University of Wisconsin Digital Collections, http://digital.library.wisc.edu/1711.dl/History.

44. Richard Henry Pratt to Nana Hawkins, 12 April 12 1891, Richard Henry Pratt Papers, Box 17, Folder 584, BRBML.

45. *Indian Helper* 6, 33 (April 24, 1891), CCHS.

46. Ibid.

47. *Indian Helper* 3, 39 (May 11, 1888): 3, CCHS.

48. Richard Henry Pratt, interview, 9, BRBML. Although "scrofula" does not always indicate a tuberculosis infection, here Pratt likely used "scrofula" in reference to tuberculosis.

49. R. H. Pratt, "Report of School at Carlisle, PA," 28 September 1898, *19th Annual Report of the Commissioner of Indian Affairs*, 392.

50. *Indian Helper* 15, 13 (January 26, 1900): 3, CCHS.

51. J. E. Henderson (Disciplinarian) to John Whitwell, 19 December 1910, John Whitwell Folder 1, NPRC.

52. David Wallace Adams, "Beyond Bleakness: The Brighter Side of Indian Boarding Schools, 1870–1940," in Trafzer et al., *Boarding School Blues*, 53–57.

53. *Indian Helper* 3, 23 (January 20, 1888): 3, CCHS.

54. Richard Henry Pratt, interview, 5, BRBML.

55. Bell, "Telling Stories out of School," 138, 140, 143–144, 197. It is also important to consider the number of students who sent their own children to Carlisle, suggesting perhaps that, at least in their experience, the school's benefits outweighed its risks.

56. *Indian Helper* 3, 39 (May 11, 1888): 3; *Indian Helper* 3, 23 (January 20, 1888): 3; *Indian Helper* 3, 37 (April 27, 1888): 3.

57. *Indian Helper* 4, 15 (November 23, 1888): 3; *Indian Helper* 3, 39 (May 11, 1888), CCHS.

58. *Indian Helper* 3, 41 (May 25, 1888): 2, CCHS.

59. *Indian Helper* 4, 21 (January 11, 1889): 3, CCHS.

60. For examples see *Indian Helper* 3, 37 (April 27, 1888): 3; *Indian Helper* 6, 33 (April 24, 1891): 3; *Indian Helper* 15, 14 (February 2, 1900): 3.

61. Katherine S. Bowersox to Richard Henry Pratt, 22 August 1902, Richard Henry Pratt Papers, Box 1, Folder 36, BRBML; Also see Emma Lovewell to E. B. Linnen, 5 September 1914, NPRC.

62. For example, see Emma Lovewell to E. B. Linnen, 5 September 1914, NPRC.

63. Moses Friedman to Marianna Moore, 26 May 1913, John Whitwell Folder 2, NPRC; Record of Marianne Craig Moore, 3 June 1913, Marianna C Moore Folder, NPRC; "Biographical Note," Archives and Special Collections Dickinson College Carlisle, PA, Marianne Craig Moore Collection, WDC.

64. Bell, "Telling Stories out of School," 107–108; prior to Carlisle, Sarah Mather and her friend, Miss Perritt, moved to St. Augustine, Florida, and opened a boarding school for young ladies before teaching Pratt's Indian prisoners (see Fear-Segal, *White Man's Club*, 262). Like Burgess and Ely, Mather and Perritt also had a close relationship. Such female relationships were not unusual in the nineteenth century and were referred to as "Boston marriages." Women lived together, vacationed together, and had deep friendships, although it is not known whether they had intimate sexual relationships. See Carroll Smith-Rosenberg, "The Female World of Love and Ritual: Relations between Women in Nineteenth-Century America," *Signs* 1, 1 (Autumn 1975): 1–29. Smith-Rosen-

berg draws from "the correspondence and diaries of (middle class) women and men in thirty-five families between the 1760s and the 1880s" and analyzes same-sex friendships "within a cultural and social setting rather than from an exclusively individual psychosexual perspective"; also see Helen Lefkowitz Horowitz, *The Power and Passion of M. Carey Thomas* (Urbana: University of Illinois Press, 1999); Helen Lefkowitz Horowitz, *Rereading Sex: Battles over Sexual Knowledge and Suppression in Nineteenth-Century America* (New York: Vintage Books, 2002).

65. Emma Cutter to Nana Pratt Hawkins, 11 December 1934, Richard Henry Pratt Papers, Box 15, Folder 505, BRBML.

66. Katherine S. Bowersox to Richard Henry Pratt, 22 August 1902, Richard Henry Pratt Papers, Box 1, Folder 36, BRBML.

67. Royal L. Mann, "Request for Transfer," 4 March 1914, Royal L. Mann Folder, NPRC.

68. Ibid.

69. Personal Record of Royal LeBau Mann, Royal L. Mann Folder, NPRC.

70. Mattie Lane to Commissioner of Indian Affairs, 1 July 1912, NPRC.

71. David Wallace Adams, *Education for Extinction: American Indians and the Boarding School Experience, 1875–1928* (Lawrence: University of Kansas, 1995), 323.

72. "Special Orders, No. 137," War Department, 11 June 1904, Records Relating to Carlisle School—Personnel, Record Group 75, Entry 1344A, William A. Mercer File, NADC.

73. Bell, "Telling Stories out of School," 78–86.

74. Anna Hoffman, "Notarized Statement," 14 December 1907, Associated Executive Committee of Friends on Indian Affairs Papers, Box 5, Folder 3 (Letters 1909 January to March), Haverford College (QSCH).

75. Marie MacCloud, "Notarized Letter," 16 December 1907, Box 5, Folder 3 (Letters 1909 January to March), QSCH.

76. William A. Mercer to Lucretia Ross, 31 December 1907, Box 5, Folder 3 (Letters 1909 January to March), QSCH.

77. Ibid.

78. Commissioner F. E. Leupp to William A. Mercer, 24 December 1907, Box 5, Folder 3 (Letters 1909 January to March), QSCH.

79. Anne S. Ely to Lucretia Ross, 2 February 1909, Box 5, Folder 3 (Letters 1909 January to March), QSCH.

80. Lucretia Ross to Mr. Herbert Welsh (Haskell Institute, Kansas), 11 March 1909, Box 5, Folder 3 (Letters 1909 January to March), QSCH.

81. S. M. Brosino (Agent Indian Rights Association) to Honorable Secretary of the Interior, 27 March 1909, Box 5, Folder 3 (Letters 1909 January to March), QSCH.

82. Medical Service, Bureau Indian Affairs, *Serial Two: Hearings Before the Joint Commission of Congress of the United States, Sixty-Third Congress, Second Session to Investigate Indian Affairs,* July 15, 1914, Part 16-A (Washington, DC: Government Printing Office, 1914): 2219–2236.

83. MacCloud, 16 December 1907, Box 5, Folder 3 (Letters 1909 January to March), QSCH.

84. Emma Hetrick to Commissioner of Indian Affairs, 5 February 1912, Emma Hetrick Folder, NPRC.

85. Alice Beck Kehoe, *A Passion for the True and Just: Felix and Lucy Kramer Cohen and the Indian New Deal* (Phoenix: University of Arizona Press, 2014), 127; *Carlisle Indian School: Hearings*, 985, 1000, 1066, 1158, 1189, 1245, 1335, 1360, 1388; Bell, "Telling Stories out of School," 94–95.

86. Jose Gil, 21 June 1939, NAMD.

87. Memorandum: Mariette Wood, 17 June 1909, Mariette Wood Folder, NPRC.

88. Ibid.

89. Hetrick to Commissioner, 5 February 1912, NPRC.

90. Fernando G. Tranbarger to Commissioner of Indian Affairs, 14 December 1911, Fernando G. Tranbarger Folder 2, NPRC.

91. Mattie Lane to Commissioner of Indian Affairs Cato Sells, 22 July 1912, Mattie Lane Folder, NPRC; Fernando G. Tranbarger to Superintendent Moses Friedman, 30 September 1911, Fernando G. Tranbarger Folder 2, NPRC; Frances Scales to Commissioner of Indian Affairs, 17 December 1910, Frances Scales Folder, NPRC.

92. John Whitwell to Moses Friedman, 29 December 1910, John Whitwell Folder 1, NPRC.

93. John Whitwell to Commissioner of Indian Affairs Cato Sells, 15 October 1913, John Whitwell Folder 2, NPRC.

94. Moses Friedman to Commissioner of Indian Affairs Cato Sells, 17 October 1913, John Whitwell Folder 2, NPRC.

95. Commissioner of Indian Affairs Cato Sells to John Whitwell, 25 November 1913, John Whitwell Folder 2, NPRC; Sells to John Whitwell, 20 March 1914, John Whitwell Folder 2, NPRC.

96. *Carlisle Indian School: Hearings Before the Joint Commission of Congress of the United States, Sixty-Third Congress, Second Session to Investigate Indian Affairs*, February 6, 7, 8, and March 25, 1914, Part 11 (Washington, DC: Government Printing Office, 1914): 949–1390, http://books.google.com. Teachers' testimonies against Friedman include Bertha D. Canfield, 1058–1062; John Whitwell, 1063–1100; Angel Dietz, 1106–1111; Lydia E. Kaup, 1112–1114; Emma C. Lovewell, 1182–1185; Hattie M. McDowell, 1185–1186; and Margaret M. Sweeney, 1193–1195. Testimonies defending Friedman include Emma H. Foster, 1219–1222; Lelah Burns, 1280–1285; and Adelaide B. Reichel, 1285–1292.

97. *Carlisle Indian School: Hearings*, Testimonies of Bertha D. Canfield, 1058–1062; John Whitwell, 1063–1100; Angel Dietz, 1106–1111; Lydia E. Kaup, 1112–1114; Emma C. Lovewell, 1182–1185; Hattie M. McDowell, 1185–1186; Miss Margaret M. Sweeney, 1193–1195.

98. *Carlisle Indian School: Hearings*, Emma H. Foster, 1219–1222; other testimony defending Friedman: Lelah Burns, 1280–1285; Adelaide B. Reichel, 1285–1292.

99. Commissioner of Indian Affairs Cato Sells to Moses Friedman, 18 May 1914, Moses Friedman Folder, NPRC; Sergeant A. A. Jones (First Assistant Secretary) to Samuel J. Graham (Assistant Attorney General), 23 March 1914, Moses Friedman Folder, NPRC.

100. Kehoe, *A Passion for the True and Just*, 127; *Carlisle Indian School: Hearings*, 985, 1000, 1066, 1158, 1189, 1245, 1335, 1360, 1388.

101. Bell, "Telling Stories out of School," 94–95.

102. Ibid.

103. Ibid., 99–100.

104. Memorandum Concerning Oscar A. Lipps, 11 May 1915, Record Group 75, Entry 1344A, Oscar Lipps Folder, NADC.

105. Dennison Wheelock to Commissioner of Indian Affairs, 17 March 1917, Record Group 75, Entry 1344A, John Francis, Jr. Folder, NADC.

106. Dennison Wheelock to Commissioner of Indian Affairs, 17 March 1917, Record Group 75, Entry 1344A, John Francis, Jr. Folder, NADC.

107. Record of John Francis Jr., 1 July 1911, Record Group 75, Entry 1344A, John Francis Jr. Folder; Record of Oscar H. Lipps, Record Group 75, Entry 1344A, Oscar Lipps Folder, NADC.

108. John Francis Jr. to Commissioner Cato Sells, 28 January 1918, Record Group 75, Entry 1344A, John Francis Jr. Folder, NADC.

109. Employment Record, 11 February 1917, Record Group 75, Entry 1344A, John Francis Jr. Folder, NADC.

110. E. B. Merritt (Assistant Commissioner) to Secretary of the Treasury, 17 July 1918, John Francis Jr. Folder, NADC.

111. Bell, "Telling Stories out of School," 45, 65, 77, 333, 400, 402.

CHAPTER 4. LIFE AND DEATH ON THE ISLANDS, 1901–1918

1. Mary Helen Fee, *A Woman's Impressions of the Philippines* (Chicago: A. C. McClurg, 1910), 12, 42.

2. Jane A. Margold, "Egalitarian Ideals and Exclusionary Practices: U.S. Pedagogy in the Colonial Philippines," *Journal of Historical Sociology* 8, 4 (December 1995): 381–382; Glenn Anthony May, *Social Engineering in the Philippines: The Aims, Execution, and Impact of American Colonial Policy, 1900–1913* (Westport, CT: Greenwood Press, 1980, 78; Judith Raftery, "Textbook Wars: Governor-General James Francis Smith and the Protestant-Catholic Conflict in Public Education in the Philippines, 1904–1907," *History of Education Quarterly* 38, 2 (Summer 1998): 143–164. For more on US educational and diplomatic intervention in the Philippines, see Peter Tarr, "The Education of the Thomasites: American School Teachers in Philippine Colonial Society, 1901–1913" (PhD dissertation, Cornell University, 2006), 59–97.

3. A. J. Angulo, *Empire and Education: A History of Greed and Goodwill from the War of 1898 to the War on Terror* (New York: Palgrave MacMillan, 2012); Benjamin Justice, "Education at the End of a Gun: The Origins of American Imperial Education and

the Case of the Philippines," in Noah W. Sobe, ed., *American Post-Conflict Educational Reform: From the Spanish-American War to Iraq* (New York: Palgrave Macmillan, 2009); May, *Social Engineering in the Philippines*; Jonathan Zimmerman, *Innocents Abroad: American Teachers in the American Century* (Cambridge, MA: Harvard University Press, 2006); Tarr, "The Education of the Thomasites": Tarr's dissertation is an exception as it provides a broad overview on US policy and military interventions and explores several Thomasites' experiences. He discusses Harrie and Mary Cole, John Early, and Ralph Taylor at length, plus Frederick Behner, George Carrothers, and Blaine Moore among others.

4. Norman Cameron, 21 August 1901, Diary 1, Special Collections Library, University of Michigan (SCLM).

5. Ralph Wendell Taylor to Mother, 21 August 21 1901, BHL. For more on Ralph Taylor see Tarr, "The Education of the Thomasites," 415–521. For more on the spectacle of the Thomasites' arrival see Stanley Karnow, *In Our Image: America's Empire in the Philippines* (New York: Random House, 1989), 196; Zimmerman, *Innocents Abroad*, 1–3. For more on teachers' work and settling in to their new environment see Margold, "Egalitarian Ideals and Exclusionary Practices."

6. Elizabeth Winifred Mitchell (Campbell) to Twentieth Century Club, n.d., 1901 File, Wisconsin Historical Society (WHS).

7. For more on the making of race in the Philippines see Paul Kramer, *The Blood of Government: Race, Empire, the United States, and the Philippines* (Chapel Hill: University of North Carolina Press, 2006), 14, 15, 27; Paul A. Kramer, "Race, Empire, and Transnational History," in Alfred W. McCoy and Francisco A. Scarano, eds., *Colonial Crucible: Empire in the Making of the Modern American State* (Madison: University of Wisconsin Press, 2009), 204.

8. Tarr, "The Education of the Thomasites," 679: regarding the Thomasites in particular, Tarr disagrees with Paul Kramer's analysis of race in the Philippines and argues, "Philippine experience was more likely than not to reinforce or even accentuate preexisting racial prejudices. In fact, it is probably that some of the Americanizing zeal routinely attributed to the Thomasites is an oblique reflection of a rather pervasive racism and intolerance." Also see Carl N. Degler, *In Search of Human Nature: The Decline and Revival of Darwinism in American Social Thought* (New York: Oxford University Press, 1991); Edward J. Larson, *Eugenics in the Deep South* (Baltimore: Johns Hopkins University Press, 1995; Angela Gonzales, Judy Kertész, and Gabrielle Tayac, "Eugenics as Indian Removal: Sociohistorical Processes and the De(con)struction of American Indians in the Southeast," *Public Historian* 29, 3 (Summer 2007); Stephen Jay Gould, *The Mismeasure of Man* (New York: W. W. Norton, 1981); Pat Shipman, *The Evolution of Racism: Human Differences and the Use and Abuse of Science* (New York: Simon and Schuster, 1994); Ann Gibson Winfield, *Eugenics and Education in America: Institutionalised Racism and the Implications of History, Ideology, and Memory* (New York: Peter Lang, 2007); Daniel J. Kevles, *In the Name of Eugenics* (New York: Knopf, 1985); Steven Selden, *Inheriting Shame: The Story of Eugenics and Racism in America* (New York:

Teachers College Press, 1999; Nell Irvin Painter, *The History of White People* (New York: W. W. Norton, 2010); Ibram Kendi, *Stamped from the Beginning: The Definitive History of Racist Ideas in America* (New York: Nation Books, 2016); Walter David Greason, *Suburban Erasure: How the Suburbs Ended the Civil Rights Movement in New Jersey* (Madison, NJ: Farleigh Dickinson University Press, 2013).

9. David P. Barrows, "Instructions for Volunteer Field Workers," Bureau of Non-Christian Tribes of the Philippine Islands (Manila, 1901), 3, 9–14.

10. David P. Barrows, *A History of the Philippines* (New York: American Book Co., 1905), 25–41. For a discussion on Barrows's work, including a citation regarding his doctoral work on the Cahuilla Indians, see Kenton J. Clymer, "Humanitarian Imperialism: David Prescott Barrows and the White Man's Burden in the Philippines," *Pacific Historical Review* 45, 4 (November 1976): 499.

11. Also see Tarr, "The Education of the Thomasites," 216–234.

12. Mary Cole to Folks at Home, 28 August 1901, Harry Newton Cole Papers, August to September 1901 Folder, BHL. Also see Tarr, "The Education of the Thomasites," chapter 5, "Leyte: Harrie Cole's Philippine Nightmare."

13. Cameron, 27 August 1901, Diary 1, SCLM.

14. Cameron, 23 August 1901, Diary 1, SCLM; Ralph W. Taylor to Mother, 6 September 1901, Taylor Family Papers, Box 1, Correspondence June to Dec. 1901 Folder, BHL; Mary Cole to Folks at Home, 28 August 1901; Harrie Cole to Mother, 12 September 1901, Harrie Newton Cole Papers, August to September 1901 Folder, BHL.

15. Mitchell to Twentieth Century Club, WHS.

16. "Guide to Twentieth Century Club Records, 1920–1982," La Crosse Public Library Archives, La Crosse, Wisconsin, accessed September 25, 2015, http://archives.lacrosselibrary.org/collections/sports-and-recreation/mss-142/.

17. Annie Firor Scott, *Natural Allies: Women's Associations in American History* (Urbana: University of Illinois Press, 1991); Nancy Hewitt and Suzanne Lebsock, eds., *Visible Women: New Essays on American Activism* (Urbana: University of Illinois Press, 1993). For a discussion of African American clubwomen see Deborah Gray White, *Too Heavy a Load: Black Women in Defense of Themselves, 1894–1994* (New York: W. W. Norton, 1999).

18. Mary Cole to Folks at Home, 28 August 1901, Harry Newton Cole Papers, August to September 1901 Folder, BHL.

19. Zimmerman, *Innocents Abroad*, 191–192, uses Harrie Cole's racially charged language. For information on US soldiers' racial prejudices see Stuart Creighton Miller, *"Benevolent Assimilation": The American Conquest of the Philippines, 1899–1903* (New Haven, CT: Yale University Press, 1982), 58–59, 176–177; Karnow, *In Our Image*, 142, 174; Kramer, *The Blood of Government*, 34–35, 124–130; Kramer, "Race, Empire, and Transnational History," 204.

20. Harrie Cole to Mother, 12 September 12 1901; Mary Cole to Folks at Home, 17 September 1901, Harry Newton Cole Papers, August to September 1901 Folder, BHL.

21. Cameron, September 1, Diary 1, SCLM.

22. Ibid.; 31 August and 6 September 1901.

23. David Silbey, *A War of Frontier and Empire: the Philippine-American War, 1899–1902* (New York: Hill and Wang, 2007), xvii; Karnow, *In Our Image*, 48–195; Kramer, *Blood of Government*, 34–35, 125–135; May, *Social Engineering in the Philippines*, xxv–xxvi; Miller, *"Benevolent Assimilation,"* in entirety, especially chapter 9. The same racism that shaped teachers' sense of benevolent purpose similarly influenced soldiers' beliefs regarding the justifiability of violence; H. W. Brands, *Bound to Empire: The United States and the Philippines* (New York: Oxford University Press, 1992), 53–58. On US military interventions in Philippines overlapping with early Thomasites, see Tarr, "The Education of the Thomasites," 4–8.

24. Miller, *"Benevolent Assimilation,"* chapters 2 and 9, particularly 14–17 and 174–176. Also see Karnow, *In Our Image*; Kramer, *Blood of Government*, 105–115.

25. Harrie to Leon Cole (brother), 21 October 1901, Harry Newton Cole Papers, October to November 1901 Folder, BHL.

26. John C. Early, "Reminiscences of John C. Early," 6, John C. Early Papers, John Early Reminiscences Folder, BHL.

27. George E. Carrothers, "A Sojourn in the Philippines," 4, George Ezra Carrothers Papers, Biographical Reminiscences 1952–1955 and 1964 Folder, BHL.

28. Ibid., 4–5.

29. "The Bureau of Education: A Statement of Organization and Aims Published for General Information," *Philippine Teacher* 1, 1 (December 15, 1904), Library Materials Vol. 674, Record Group 350, Philippines Miscellaneous, National Archives at College Park, Maryland (NAMD).

30. Ibid.

31. For a more in-depth analysis on US women teachers in the Philippines see Sarah Steinbrock-Pratt, "'We Were All Robinson Crusoes': American Women Teachers in the Philippines," *Women's Studies* 41 (June 2012): 379–392.

32. Fee, *A Woman's Impressions*, 12, 61, 93–94, 107–108, 239.

33. Walter W. Marquardt to Unknown, 19 August 1901 (edited transcription), Walter W. Marquardt Papers, Box 7, Bound Papers: 19–20, BHL.

34. May D. McKitrick to Mr. E. B. Merritt, 15 May 1914, Clara Donaldson Folder, NPRC.

35. Mitchell to Twentieth Century Club, WHS: in a handwritten note at the bottom of the letter, it is noted that Mitchell married fellow Thomasite Louis J. Campbell during her time teaching in Manila. She died in 1923 and is buried in Washington, DC.

36. Early, "Reminiscences of John C. Early," 7–8, BHL.

37. Ibid., 10–11; "carabao" refers to water buffalo that live in the Philippines. For more on John Early see Tarr, "The Education of the Thomasites," chapter 7, "John Early and Roy Barton: The True Believer and the Skeptic."

38. Fee, *A Woman's Impressions*, 73.

39. Behner, 21–22 September 1901, Diaries 1901–1902 Folder, BHL.

40. Behner, 26 September 1901, Diaries 1901–1902 Folder, BHL.

41. Behner, 30 September 1901, Diaries 1901–1902 Folder, BHL.

42. Harvey Bordner to Brother, 6 May 1902, Harvey A. Bordner Papers, Box 1, Personal Correspondence 1902, Indiana University Archives, Bloomington (IUA).

43. Bordner to Brother, 2 December 1902, IUA.

44. H. O. Whiting to Home Folks, 4 August 1907, H. O. Whiting Letters in James Hardy Papers, Indiana State Library, Indianapolis (ISL).

45. Fee, *A Woman's Impressions*, 75.

46. Laura Gibson Smith, "Point of View," Box 2, Writings Notes on Philippines Folder, Iowa Women's Archives, University of Iowa Libraries, Iowa City (IWA).

47. Carrothers, interview, 6, BHL.

48. Mary and Harry Cole to Dear Folks at Home, 4 August 1901, August to September 1901 Folder, BHL.

49. H. O. Whiting to Mother, 25 December 25 1906, ISA. Although Whiting provides his address on this and other letters in the same time period as "Larena, Oriental Negros, P.I.," Larena is on the island of Siquifor.

50. Mary Cole to Folks at Home, 17 February 1902, January to March 1902 Folder, BHL.

51. Whiting to Mother, November 1907, ISL.

52. Ibid.

53. Blaine Free Moore to Pa and Ma, 15 August 1903, Box 1, Correspondence July to December 1903 Folder, Library of Congress (LOC).

54. Bordner, "Discipline," July 1916, Box 1; Bordner, "Teacher Qualifications Sought by Superintendents," 30 September 1918, Box 1, IUA.

55. Bordner to Mr. Tilon D. Bordner, 17 April 1903, IUA.

56. Mary Cole to Brother and Sister, 15 October 15 1901, Harry Newton Cole Papers, October to November 1901 Folder, BHL.

57. G. W. Evans, Diary 22 July 1914, Evans Family Papers, BHL.

58. Behner, 4 February 1902, Diaries 1901–1902 Folder, BHL; Mary Cole to Brother and Sister, 15 October 1901, Harry Newton Cole Papers, October to November 1901 Folder, BHL; Fee, *A Woman's Impressions*; Behner, 4 February 1902, Diaries 1901–1902 Folder, BHL.

59. Harrie Cole to Mother, 18 November 1901, October to November 1901 Folder, BHL.

60. Glen Evans, 3 August 1904, Diary of G. W. Evans, 1904–1905 Folder, Evans Family Papers, BHL; Mary Cole to Brother and Sister, 15 October 1901, Harry Newton Cole Papers, October to November 1901 Folder, BHL; Mary Cole to Dear Folks at Home, 17 October 1901, Harry Newton Cole Papers, October to November 1901 Folder, BHL.

61. Fee, *A Woman's Impressions*, 81.

62. Tarr, "The Education of the Thomasites," 204–207: Tarr describes overcrowded classrooms and other complaints in the Thomasites' early years.

63. Harrie and Mary Cole; Glen Evans; Fee, *A Woman's Impressions*; Blaine Free Moore.

64. Fee, *A Woman's Impressions*, 85. Tarr, "The Education of the Thomasites," 204–

207, describes both overcrowding in some schools and lack of local interest and under-enrollment in other Philippine communities.

65. Mary Cole to Folks at Home, 9 February 1902, Harry Newton Cole Papers, BHL.

66. Blaine Free Moore to Pa and Ma, 23 August 1903, Box 1, Correspondence July to December 1903 Folder, LOC. Also see Margold, "Egalitarian Ideas and Exclusionary Practices," 382; John Charles Muerman, "The Philippine School under the Americans" (PhD dissertation, George Washington University, 1922), 101; May, *Social Engineering*, 78.

67. Marquardt, 12 September 1901, Box 7, Untitled bound book of transcribed letters and personal documents, 25, BHL. Also see May, *Social Engineering*, 93.

68. Marquardt, 18 July and 3 August 1901, Box 7, Untitled bound book of transcribed letters and personal documents, 14, 17; Behner, January to April 1902, Diaries 1901 to 1902 Folder, BHL; Harrie Cole to Mother, 20 October 1901, October to November 1901 Folder, BHL. Also see Tarr, "The Education of the Thomasites," 194–195 and 203–205, where he describes Thomasites' initial work in the field as well as multiple challenges.

69. Harrie Cole to Folks at Home, 5 November 1901, October to November 1901 Folder, BHL.

70. Behner, 24 January 1902, Diaries 1901 to 1902 Folder, BHL.

71. Blaine Free Moore to brother, 17 January 1903, Box 1, January to June 1903 Folder, LOC. In the context of this letter, it sounds as if Moore was referring to intellectual decline when he commented on the risk of going "backward." He may have also been referring to moral decline, as much of his other correspondence condemns behaviors he sees as deleterious, and perhaps this was a way for him to admit his own moral missteps to his brother.

72. Whiting to "Loved Ones," 12 August 1907, ISL.

73. Bordner to Sister and Brother, 15 October 1905, IUA.

74. Behner, 13 October 1902, Diaries 1901 to 1902 Folder, BHL.

75. Blaine Free Moore to Pa and Ma, 2 April 1902, Correspondence January to June 1902 Folder, LOC.

76. For more on American influences on Manila, and sentiments regarding the city's embodiment of "civilization" see Kenneth Kasperski, "Chapter 3: Pearl of the Orient," in "Noble Colonials: Americans and Filipinos, 1901–1940" (PhD dissertation, University of Florida, 2012), 40–70.

77. George E. Carrothers, "A Sojourn in the Philippines," 23, Biographical Reminiscences 1952–1955 and 1964 Folder, BHL. Also see Miller, *"Benevolent Assimilation,"* 58–59, 187–188, 191–192.

78. On Victorian notions of women's moral virtue see Peggy Pascoe, *Relations of Rescue: The Search for Female Moral Authority in the American West, 1874–1939* (New York: Oxford University Press, 1990), xv–xviii; Nancy Cott, *The Bonds of Womanhood: "Woman's Sphere" in New England, 1780–1835* (New Haven, CT: Yale University Press, 1987); Nancy Hewitt, *Women's Activism and Social Change: Rochester, New York, 1822–1872* (Ithaca, NY: Cornell University Press); Lori D. Ginzberg, *Women and the Work of*

Benevolence: Morality, Politics, and Class in the Nineteenth-Century United States (New Haven, CT: Yale University Press, 1990); Barbara Leslie Epstein, *The Politics of Domesticity: Women, Evangelism, and Temperance in Nineteenth-Century America* (Middletown, CT: Wesleyan University Press, 1981).

79. George E. Carrothers, Record of some events in the life of George E. Carrothers prepared at the suggestion of family members, March 1964, BHL.

80. Isaac Adams (Office of the Attorney-General) to Mr. John Cheesborough, 1 April 1908, John Cheesborough Papers, 1886–1914 Folder, David M. Rubenstein Rare Book and Manuscript Library, Duke University (RDU).

81. Carrothers, "A Sojourn in the Philippines," 23.

82. Early, "Reminiscences of John C. Early," 14–15, BHL.

83. Behner, 13 December 1902, Diaries 1901 to 1902 Folder, BHL.

84. Zimmerman, *Innocents Abroad*, 190–191.

85. Jules Theophile Frelin, 8 December 1901, Diary 1899, University of Minnesota Archives, Minneapolis (UMA).

86. Frelin, 22 December 1901, Diary 1899, UMA: Frelin wrote of an American who was "lost" with a woman as a euphemism to his sexual encounter. Also see Miller, *"Benevolent Assimilation,"* 191–192; Zimmerman, *Innocents Abroad*, 190–191.

87. Behner, 14 June 1904, Diaries 1903 to 1905 Folder, BHL.

88. Bordner to Brother, 6 May 1902, IUA.

89. Brands, *Bound to Empire*, 72; Kenton J. Clymer, *Protestant Missionaries in the Philippines, 1898–1916: An Inquiry into the American Colonial Mentality* (Urbana: University of Illinois Press, 1986), 162–164; Karnow, *In Our Image*, 199.

90. Blaine Free Moore to Ma and Pa, 6 November 1901, Box 1, Correspondence 1901, LOC.

91. Mary Cole to Mother, May 1904, Harry Newton Cole Papers, 1904 Folder, BHL.

92. Cameron, Diary 1, SCLM.

93. Describing soldiers: Cameron, 15 October 1901 and 16 January 1902, Diary 2. Describing civilians: Cameron, 2 February 1902, Diary 2; Cameron, 19 January 1903 and 16 February 1903, Diary 4, SCLM.

94. Cameron, 25 and 28 January 1902, Diary 2, SCLM.

95. Marquardt, 30 September 1902, Box 6, Diaries and Notes 1900 to 1935, BHL; Marquardt, Diaries and Notes, 1900–1935, Source Material, Travel, Food, Superstitions, W. W. Marquardt; Marquardt, Diary August 9, 1902–September 13, 1903; Marquardt, Extracts from Diary; Harrie Cole to Mother and Leon, 30 June 1902, June 1902 Folder, BHL; Mary Cole to Folks at Home, 24 August 1902, July to August 1902 Folder, BHL. Zimmerman, *Innocents Abroad*, 191–192, cites Harrie Cole's racially charged language. For information on US soldiers' racial prejudices, see Brands, *Bound to Empire*, 61–62; Miller, *"Benevolent Assimilation,"* 58–59, 176–177; Karnow, *In Our Image*, 142, 174; Kramer, *The Blood of Government*, 34–35, 124–130; Kramer, "Race, Empire, and Transnational History," 204.

96. Blaine Free Moore to Pa and Ma, 1 March 1903, Correspondence January to June 1903 Folder, LOC.

97. Blaine Free Moore to Pa and Ma, 25 July 1903, Correspondence July to December 1903 Folder, LOC.

98. Harrie Cole to Mother, 17 November 1902, September to December 1902 Folder, BHL.

99. Harrie Cole to Mother, 8 April 1904, 1904 Folder, BHL. For more on Anglo-Saxon identity, see Kramer, "Race, Empire, and Transnational History," 204; May, *Social Engineering in the Philippines*, 11.

100. Harrie Cole to Mother, 17 October 1903, 1903 Folder, BHL.

101. Harrie Cole to Mother, 8 April 1904, 1904 Folder, BHL. Also see Kramer, *Blood of Government*, 20, 33, 109–110; Kramer, "Race, Empire, and Transnational History," 204; May, *Social Engineering*, 11; Miller, "*Benevolent Assimilation*," 6, 18–19.

102. Today, the "water cure" is known as "water boarding" and is classified as a method of torture; Paul Kramer, "The Water Cure," *Social Science Diliman* 13, 2 (July–December 2017): Kramer recounts how Americans in the mainland who were shocked by reporting and soldier's accounts of US torture perpetrated against Filipinos, including the water cure. Just as quickly as such alarm was raised in 1900, Kramer argues, Americans' concerns over the nation's mistreatment of Filipinos largely faded away by 1902 and 1903, as such atrocities seemed distant and congressional investigations were called off. Also see Brands, *Bound to Empire*, 55–58; Karnow, *In Our Image*, 154–155, 179–180; Kramer, *Blood of Government*, 125–135.

103. Miller, "*Benevolent Assimilation*," 210–230. Also see Tarr, "The Education of the Thomasites," 201–202.

104. Mary Cole, 11 November 1901, Diary 1901–1902, Harry Newton Cole Papers, BHL.

105. Mary Cole, 24 and 28 October, 12 November 1901 and 2 January 1902, Diary 1901–1902, Harry Newton Cole Papers, BHL.

106. Harrie Cole to Mother and Leon, 30 June 1902, BHL

107. Cameron, 15 October 1901, Diary 1, SCLM.

108. Ibid., 13 November 1901.

109. Ibid., 23 December 1901.

110. Ibid., 27 January 1902.

111. Glen Evans, 1, 22–25 and 30 August 1904, Diary 1904 to 1905 Folder, BHL.

112. Ibid., 22 September 1904.

113. Ibid., 22 September, 1 October, 4 November 1904, 22 January and 24 February 1905.

114. Blaine Free Moore to Pa and Ma, 28 January 1902, Correspondence January to June 1902 Folder, LOC.

115. Blaine Free Moore to Brother, 20 August 1902, Correspondence July to December 1902 Folder, LOC.

116. Blaine Free Moore to Brother, 17 January 1903, Correspondence January to June 1903 Folder, LOC.

117. Blaine Free Moore to Ma and Pa, 15 February 1903, Correspondence January to June 1903 Folder, LOC.

118. Ibid.

119. Fee, *A Woman's Impressions*, 213: Mary Fee's memoir reveals that during a trip to explore an abandoned mine, she was given a gun to "to see that the excavating department kept busy." To counter the notion that women of the time period were not accustomed to guns, Mary further wrote: "I had n't [*sic*] felt so close to childhood for many a long year." She then fired the pistol "to hurry up" the laborers who then "seemed to think a bond of friendship had been established between us." She allegedly fired again for good measure, again causing a reaction among the men. Also see Tarr, "The Education of the Thomasites," chapter 4, "Philanda Rand among the Hacenderos of Negros: Imperial Role-Reversal." Although Philanda Rand was a Thomasite who is not featured in this book, she bucked several gender norms, including gun toting.

120. Marquardt, 20 July 1901, Box 7, Untitled Bound Documents, 15, BHL.

121. Ibid.; Marquardt, 17 February 1903, Box 6, Bound Diaries and Notes 1900–1935, 24, BHL.

122. Marquardt, "Dangers," Box 7, Biographical, Questionnaire Folder, BHL.

123. Carrothers, interview, BHL.

124. Brands, *Bound to Empire*, 55–58; Karnow, 179–180; Kramer, *Blood of Government*, 125–135; Miller, *"Benevolent Assimilation,"* 227–238.

125. Harrie Cole to Mother and Leon, 16 February 1902, January to March 1902 Folder, BHL.

126. Mary Cole, 20 January 1902, Diary 1901–1902, Harry Newton Cole Papers, BHL.

127. Cameron, 20 October 1902, Diary 2, SCLM.

128. Daniel Roderick Williams, *The Odyssey of the Philippine Commission* (Chicago: A. C. McClurg, 1913), 71–72.

129. Bordner, January 1914, News Clipping about Indiana University Alumni, Box 3, IUA.

130. For more on disease and empire see Ann Laura Stoler, *Carnal Knowledge and Imperial Power: Race and the Intimate in Colonial Rule* (Berkeley: University of California Press, 2002); Kramer, 35, 38, 92; Stanley Karnow, "The Philippines," *Dissent* 56, 1 (Winter 2009): 38; Kristin L. Hoganson, *Fighting for American Manhood: How Gender Politics Provoked the Spanish-American and Philippine-American Wars* (New Haven, CT: Yale University Press, 1998), 7; Zimmerman, *Innocents Abroad*, 67–68.

131. Tarr, "The Education of the Thomasites," 202: Tarr details that one of the difficulties retaining US teachers in the Philippines was disease. According to Tarr's research, from 1901 to 1905, forty-two Thomasites (2 percent) died, mostly from disease. In 1902 there were sixteen deaths, and in 1903, fourteen teachers died from smallpox,

cholera, dysentery, or typhoid while six others were killed, four drowned, and two committed suicide.

132. Mary Cole to Folks at Home, 17 October 1901, October to November 1901 Folder, BHL.

133. Mary Cole to Mother and Leon, 27 January 1902, January to March Folder 1902, BHL.

134. Mary Cole, 15 February 1902, Diary 1901–1902, Harry Newton Cole Papers, BHL.

135. Harrie Cole to Mother and Leon, 16 February 1902, January to March Folder 1902, BHL; Mary Cole, 11 February 1902, Diary 1901–1902, Harry Newton Cole Papers, BHL.

136. Mary Cole, 13 February 1902, Diary 1901–1902, Harry Newton Cole Papers, BHL; Mary Cole to Mother, 10 March 1902, January to March Folder 1902, Harry Newton Cole Papers, BHL.

137. Harrie Cole to Mother and Leon, 16 February 1902, January to March Folder 1902, Harry Newton Cole Papers, BHL.

138. Mary Cole to Folks at Home, 24 March 1902, January to March Folder 1902, BHL.

139. Mary Cole to Folks at Home, 11 May 1902, April to May 1902 Folder, BHL.

140. Harrie Cole to Mother and Leon, 11 June 1902, June 1902 Folder, BHL.

141. Ibid., 15 June 1902.

142. Blaine Free Moore to Pa and Ma, 15 May 1902, Correspondence January to June 1902 Folder, LOC. Also see Zimmerman, *Innocents Abroad*, 67–68.

143. Taylor to Mother, 7 August 1902, Correspondence 1902 Folder, BHL.

144. Taylor to Mother, 17 October 1903, Correspondence 1903 Folder, BHL.

145. Ibid.; Taylor to Mother, 1 April 1903, Correspondence 1903 Folder, BHL.

146. Tarr, "The Education of the Thomasites," 414–521: for more on Ralph Taylor, see Tarr's chapter 6, "Emerson Christie and Ralph Taylor: Ironies of Intervention."

147. Behner, Diaries 1901 to 1902 Folder, BHL.

148. Ibid., 12 September 1902.

149. Ibid., 17 December 1902.

150. Bordner to Brother, 20 February 1903, IUA.

151. Bordner to Mr. Tilon D. Bordner, 17 April 1903, IUA.

152. Harrie Cole to Mother and Leon, 26 May 1902, April to May 1902 Folder; Marquardt to Unknown (transcription), 12 June 1902, 52, untitled Book, Box 7, Walter W. Marquardt, BHL.

153. Harrie Cole to Mother and Leon, 21 July 1902, July to August 1902 Folder, BHL.

154. Marquardt, January 1903, Box 6, Bound Diaries and Notes 1900 to 1935, 21, BHL.

155. Carrothers, "Incidents in the Life of a Hoosier Schoolmaster," 1963, 3–4, BHL.

156. Carrothers, interview, 7, BHL.

157. Behner, 30 January 1902, Diaries 1901 to 1902 Folder, BHL.

158. Ibid., 22 February, 1902.

159. Bordner to Sister and Brother, 15 October 1905, IUA; Muerman, "The Philippine School under the Americans," 71: "A destructive typhoon in 1905 damaged and destroyed many school houses but it taught the American engineers valuable lessons in school house construction."

160. Marquardt, "Questionnaire Re: 'Thomasites,'" Box 7, Biographical Folder, BHL.

161. Fee, *A Woman's Impressions*, 42.

162. Ibid., 187.

163. Behner, 14 and 18 March 1902, Diaries 1901 to 1902 Folder, BHL.

CHAPTER 5. AFTER THE(IR) SERVICE: REFLECTIONS
ON IMPERIAL EDUCATION

1. John DeHuff to Commissioner of Indian Affairs Charles J. Rhoads, 21 July 1930, John DeHuff Folder, NPRC.

2. Ibid.; C. E. Faris (Superintendent Santa Fe Indian School) to Commissioner of Indian Affairs, 6 December 1934, Elizabeth DeHuff Folder, NPRC.

3. "Overview: Guide to the Elizabeth Willis DeHuff Collection of American Indian Art," BRBML, http://hdl.handle.net/10079/fa/beinecke.dehuff.

4. John DeHuff to Commissioner of Indian Affairs Charles J. Rhoads, 21 July 1930; General Superintendent H. B. Peairs to Commissioner of Indian Affairs, 24 July 1926, John DeHuff Folder, NPRC.

5. John DeHuff to Commissioner of Indian Affairs Charles J. Rhoads, 21 July 1930; Faris to Commissioner of Indian Affairs, 6 December 1934; *Indian Detours* Pamphlet, n.d., University of Arizona Library, accessed September 25, 2015, http://www.library .arizona.edu/exhibits/pams/pdfs/detsanfe.pdf.

6. Faris to Commissioner of Indian Affairs, 6 December 1934.

7. Elizabeth W. DeHuff to C. E. Faris (Superintendent of Northern Pueblos Indian Agency), 28 November 1934, Elizabeth DeHuff Folder, NPRC.

8. Meriam Lewis, *The Problem of Indian Administration* (Baltimore: Johns Hopkins University Press, 1928).

9. Faris to Commissioner of Indian Affairs, 6 December 1934; *Indian Detours* Pamphlet.

10. Chas C. Walcutt (Assistant to Chief of Bureau) to Moses Friedman, 31 January 1914, Record Group 350, Entry 21, Box 215, Moses Friedman Folder, NAMD; Friedman to Major Shelton, n.d., Record Group 350, Entry 21, Box 215, Moses Friedman Folder, NAMD.

11. Alice Beck Kehoe, *A Passion for the True and Just: Felix and Lucy Kramer Cohen and the Indian New Deal* (Phoenix: University of Arizona Press, 2014), 127–129.

12. Mrs. Edward L. Whistler (Verna Dunagan), interview, 41, WDC. Perhaps such a rumor was also influenced by anti-Semitic associations regarding wealth.

13. Kehoe, *A Passion for the True and Just*, 129.

14. Lewis, *The Problem of Indian Administration*, 11. Also see also David Wallace

Adams, *Education for Extinction: American Indians and the Boarding School Experience, 1875–1928* (Lawrence: University Press of Kansas, 1995), 331; Cathleen D. Cahill, *Federal Fathers and Mothers: A Social History of the United States Indian Service, 1869–1933* (Chapel Hill: University of North Carolina Press, 2011), 248–249.

15. Katherine Bingley Tranbarger to Commissioner of Indian Affairs Cato Sells, 10 January 1914: while several letters from the Tranbargers to the commissioner of Indian affairs reveal their strained relationship with Carlisle's superintendent, Katharine claimed in a letter a few years later that she had resigned from Carlisle due to her health. It is likely that she resigned, in part, due to pregnancy, as she would later write of her "little daughter."

16. Katherine Bingley Tranbarger, "Request for Reinstatement," 11 August 1913; Telegraph, 4 September 1913; K. B. Tranbarger to Commissioner of Indian Affairs, 28 September 1913; K. B. Tranbarger to Commissioner of Indian Affairs, 9 January 1914, Katherine Bingley Tranbarger Folder, NPRC.

17. K. B. Tranbarger, "Request for Reinstatement," 11 August 1913, NPRC.

18. K. B. Tranbarger to Commissioner of Indian Affairs, 28 September 1913. NPRC.

19. K. B. Tranbarger to Commissioner of Indian Affairs, 9 January 1914, NPRC.

20. "Indian Schools Support, 1918," Letter from the Secretary of the Interior Transmitting Report for the Fiscal Year Ended June 30, 1918, Relating to the Appropriation "Indian Schools, Support, 1918," 2 December 1918, 4.

21. Fernando G. Tranbarger, "Qualification Record," Fernando G. Tranbarger Folder 1, NPRC.

22. Clara Donaldson to Commissioner of Indian Affairs Cato Sells, 25 July 1918, containing "Indian Commissioner Plans Details of Transfer," *Carlisle Evening Herald* (July 22, 1918), Clara Donaldson Folder, NPRC; "Changes in Employees at U.S. Indian School Carlisle, PA, September 1918," in Monthly Time Book 1918, Record Group 75, Entry 1344, NADC; Commissioner Cato Sells to Clara A. Snoddy, 9 August 1918, Clara A. Snoddy Folder, NPRC. After Carlisle's closing, the majority of teachers either went west, like Donaldson, to work in various Indian schools; or to Washington, DC, to work for the Office of Indian Affairs or other government agencies. Alongside Donaldson, Principal Teacher Clyde M. Blaire was transferred to Chilocco while other teachers were sent to positions similar to those they held at Carlisle, including Sadie Robertson, transferred to the Phoenix Indian School; Hattie McDowell to Chemawa; Rey Heagy to Mt. Pleasant; and Clara Snoddy to the Haskell Institute. Teachers sent to Washington, DC, included Verna Dunagan, Gwen Williams, and Emma Foster.

23. Donaldson to Sells, 25 July 1918, NPRC.

24. Commissioner Sells to Donaldson, 15 August 1918, Clara Donaldson Folder, NPRC.

25. Commissioner Sells to US Representative Frank B. Willis, 27 July 1918, Clara Donaldson Folder, NPRC.

26. C. M. Blair (Chilocco Assistant Superintendent in Charge) to Commissioner of Indian Affairs, 28 August 1920, Clara Donaldson Folder, NPRC; Elizabeth Jones

to Commissioner of Indian Affairs, September 1925, Elizabeth Jones Folder, NPRC. Other teachers, like Donaldson and Jones, sought verification from the Office of Indian Affairs regarding their work in the Indian Service for the purpose of receiving teacher retirement benefits. Jones, who taught at Carlisle 1913–1914, sought such verification in order to receive retirement benefits (which she would receive from the state of North Dakota after proving her twenty-five years of teaching service).

27. C. M. Blair (Chilocco Assistant Superintendent in Charge) to Commissioner of Indian Affairs, 28 August 1920, Clara Donaldson Folder, NPRC.

28. Donaldson to Commissioner of Indian Affairs, 23 August 1921, Clara Donaldson Folder, NPRC.

29. Donaldson to Commissioner of Indian Affairs, 14 September 1921, Clara Donaldson Folder, NPRC. Donaldson's letter suggests that she received a late appointment elsewhere in the Indian Service but as she had already begun teaching high school Latin and Spanish (presumably in Ohio public schools) that she could "not professionally resign until the close of the school year in May." The historical record suggests that Donaldson never returned to the Indian Service.

30. H. B. Peairs (Superintendent at the Haskell Institute) to Commissioner of Indian Affairs, 6 September 1921, Clara Donaldson Folder, NPRC.

31. E. B. Merritt (Assistant to Commissioner of Indian Affairs) to Clara Donaldson, 19 September 1921, Clara Donaldson Folder, NPRC.

32. For eleven of the remaining Carlisle teachers the next part of their career is unknown, while four others went into miscellaneous work, two retired, and one died.

33. And, of the remaining fourteen teachers who worked in the Philippines, seven pursued fields outside of education, six are unknown, and one is considered "other."

34. "Mrs. Foster Ends 38 Years of Duty," *Washington Post* (July 31, 1929), in Emma H. Foster Folder, NPRC: Foster spent sixteen years at Carlisle, until its closing in 1918, before going to Washington, DC, to work for the Indian Office and later the War Department; Jessie Cooke to Commissioner of Indian Affairs Burke, 7 June 1924, Jessie Cook Folder, NPRC.

35. Other Thomasites who married while in the islands, including John Evans, left due to illness. In fact, although high marriage rates were not found at Carlisle, Cathleen Cahill argues that in addition to the Indian Service, "Significantly, the only other federal agency that was similar in terms of the marital status and racial make-up of its workforce was the Philippine Civil Service Commission, founded in 1900. The personnel of this agency—whose goals were similarly colonial—mirrored that of the Indian Service." See Cahill, *Federal Fathers and Mothers*, 88.

36. Harrie Cole to Mother, 22 December 1902, September to December 1902 Folder, BHL.

37. Mary to Mother, n.d., 1904 Folder, BHL; Marquardt, March 18 and 1 April, 1904, Box 6, Bound Book Diaries and Notes 1900 to 1935, 87, BHL.

38. Marquardt, 15 March and 1 April 1904, Box 6, Bound Book Diaries and Notes

1900 to 1935, 87, BHL; Marquardt, "Questionnaire Re: 'Thomasites,'" Box 7, Biographical Folder, BHL.

39. Marquardt, "Places of Service," Box 7, Biographical Folder, 2, BHL.

40. Perhaps Alice did not write to loved ones back home. More likely, such letters are held privately and not archived like her husband's, or were not preserved by relatives and friends.

41. Bordner, January 1914, News clipping about Indiana University Alumni, Box 3, IUA. Maude was in the class of 1899 and Harvey in the class of 1896 at Indiana University.

42. Harvey Bordner to Sister and Brother, 15 October 1905, IUA.

43. H. Bordner to Brother and Sister, 16 August 1907, IUA.

44. H. Bordner to Brother, 11 September 1918, IUA.

45. "P. I. Official Gazette," 25 December 1918, Record Group 350, Entry 21, Box 71, Harvey A. Bordner and Wife Maude M. Bordner Folder; "Biographical Note," Harvey A. Bordner Papers Finding Aid, IUA.

46. Bordner, "Biographical Note," IUA.

47. Willa Rhode Early, "For P.I report for the month of June, 1932," Record Group 350, Entry 21, Box 173, John C. Early and wife Folder, NAMD.

48. Peter Tarr, "The Education of the Thomasites: American School Teachers in Philippine Colonial Society, 1901–1913" (PhD dissertation, Cornell University, 2006), 202.

49. Early, "For P. I. report."

50. Miscellanea of Willa R. Early Folder, John C. Early Papers, BHL: in John Early's personal papers held at the University of Michigan's Bentley Library, Willa has a thin folder dedicated to her alone, and at the National Archives in College Park, Maryland, she is referred to on the label of her husband's file titled "John C Early and wife." Both of these sources, however, simply list dates of employment and salaries and are void of anything more personal about Willa.

51. "Address of the Honorable Joseph Ralston Hayden, Vice-Governor of the Philippine Islands, upon the dedication of a memorial window in the Cathedral of St. Mary and St. John, Manila," 1 September 1935, Miscellanea Folder, John C. Early Papers, BHL.

52. Early, "Reminiscences of John C. Early," BHL; "Summary: Early, John C., For Vice Governor of the Philippine Islands," Record Group 350, Entry 21, Box 173, John C. Early and Wife Folder, NAMD.

53. J. C. Early to Dr. J. Paul Goode (Department of Geography, University of Chicago), 3 January 1931, BHL.

54. "Address of the Honorable Joseph Ralston Hayden," John C. Early Papers, BHL.

55. Walter Robb, "A Brief Tribute to John C. Early," Record Group 350, Entry 21, Box 173, John C. Early and Wife Folder, NAMD.

56. Ibid.; Certificate of Death: John C. Early, 2 January 1932, Record Group 350, Entry 21, Box 173, John C. Early and Wife Folder, NAMD.

57. "Address of the Honorable Joseph Ralston Hayden," BHL.

58. Willa Rhode Early, "For P.I report for the month of June, 1932," NAMD; for more on John Early see Peter Tarr, "The Education of the Thomasites: American School Teachers in Philippine Colonial Society, 1901–1913" (PhD dissertation, Cornell University, 2006), chapter 7, "John Early and Roy Barton: The True Believer and the Skeptic."

59. Harrie Cole to Mother, 14 May 1903, 1903 Folder, BHL.

60. Mary Cole to Mother, 23 September 1903, 1903 Folder, BHL. Like the Marquardts, Bordners, and Earlys, Mary Cole's personal writing is archived within her husband's papers. However, her writing—diaries and letters—is much more extensive than that of the other wives.

61. Mary Cole to Mother, May 1904, 1904 Folder, BHL; Harrie Cole to Leon, 25 June 1904, 1904 Folder, BHL.

62. Margaret Jolly Cole, 20 August 1980, Harry Newton Cole Papers, BHL.

63. Ibid. Margaret Cole claims to have preserved the entire historical record of her parents' writings from the Philippines and wrote, "The temptation to edit was almost overpowering. It was with a great deal of self-control that I am able to give them to you intact. Warts and all."

64. "4,000 Know Him as a Thorough Teacher," *Michigan Alumnus* 38, 34 (July 9, 1932): 671; Wilfred B. Shaw, ed., *The University of Michigan Encyclopedic Survey: Volume II* (Ann Arbor: University of Michigan Press, 1951): 524.

65. For more on Harrie and Mary Cole see Tarr, "The Education of the Thomasites," chapter 5, "Leyte: Harrie Cole's Philippine Nightmare."

66. John Charles Muerman, "The Philippine School under the Americans" (PhD dissertation, George Washington University, 1922).

67. Contrasting this with Carlisle teachers, few of whom pursued higher education after their years in the Indian Service, suggests the unique qualifications of the Thomasites—even their elite status within the field of education—and sometimes beyond.

68. Carrothers, interview, 27 July 1965, Biographical reminiscences, 1952–55 and 1964 Folder, 1–2, BHL.

69. Carrothers, "Incidents in the Life of a Hoosier Schoolmaster," Biographical reminiscences, 1952–55 and 1964 Folder, 12, BHL.

70. Carrothers, "Record of some events in the life of George E. Carrothers," March 1964, BHL.

71. For more on George Carrothers see Tarr, "The Education of the Thomasites," 656–732.

72. Cameron, 4 August and 20 May 1903, Diary 3; Diary 5, SCLM.

73. Norman Cameron, "The U.S. Military Occupation of Bohol: 1900–1902," Special Collections Library, Duke University, May 1997, http://library.duke.edu/rubenstein/scriptorium/scriven/bohol-history.html; "School Superintendent Appointed," *Midland Journal*, 62, 31 (February 14, 1936); *Indiana Evening Gazette*, November 21, 1935.

74. "Biographical Sketch of Jules Theophile Frelin," in Finding Aid: Jules Theophile

Frelin Diaries, 1899, 1918, University of Minnesota Archives, http://special.lib.umn.edu/findaid/xml/uarc00724.xml.

75. Ernest H. Hespelt to the War Department, Washington DC (Telegram), 31 July 1919, Record Group 350, Entry 21, Box 281, Ernest H. Hespelt Folder, NAMD; Ernest H. Hespelt to Governor-General, Manila P.I., 2 May 1919, Record Group 350, Entry 21, Box 281, Ernest H. Hespelt Folder, NAMD.

76. James O. Swain, "E. Herman Hespelt (1886–1961)," *Hispania* 45, 1 (March 1962): 19–21: Hespelt married another Spanish-language academic, Miriam Hespelt.

77. Blaine Free Moore, "The Supreme Court and Unconstitutional Legislation" (PhD dissertation, Columbia University, 1913); Law Book Exchange, "The Supreme Court and Unconstitutional Legislation, Blaine Free Moore," accessed September 27, 2015, http://www.lawbookexchange.com/pages/books/27935/blaine-free-moore/the-supreme-court-and-unconstitutional-legislation.

78. Frederick G. Behner, "Rags to Riches in the Ministry," 4–6, BHL.

79. James T. Golden, "Colorful, Versatile 'Unk' Cheney," newspaper clipping (September 2, 1956), Frank W. Cheney Papers, Frank Cheney Folder, BHL.

80. Frank W. Cheney to Director Bureau of Insular Affairs, 18 April 1927, RG 350, Entry 21, Box 113, Frank W. Cheney Folder, NAMD.

81. James T. Golden, "Colorful, Versatile 'Unk' Cheney," Frank Cheney Folder, BHL.

82. Ibid.

83. Mary Helen Fee, *The Locusts Years* (Chicago: A. C. McClurg, 1912); Fee, *A Woman's Impressions*.

84. Sarah Katherine Steinbock-Pratt, "'A Great Army of Instruction': American Teachers and the Negotiation of Empire in the Philippines" (PhD dissertation, University of Texas at Austin, 2013), 284–285.

85. Mary Helen Fee, "Night Raids from the Air," *The Forum* (1918), in Francis J. Reynolds and Allen L. Churchill, eds., *World's War Events, Volume III Recorded by Statesmen, Commanders, Historians and by Men Who Fought or Saw the Great Campaigns*, Gutenberg Ebook, August 12, 2005, 229, http://www.gutenberg.org/files/16513/16513-h/16513-h.htm#Page_229.

86. Steinbock-Pratt, "'A Great Army of Instruction,'" 285.

87. "Finding Aid: Reece A. Oliver," Oliver Family Letters, Indiana State Library.

88. Donaldson to Commissioner Sells, 25 July 1918, containing "Indian Commissioner Plans Details of Transfer," *Carlisle Evening Herald* (July 22, 1918).

89. Adams, *Education for Extinction*, 328–333; Kim Cary Warren, *The Quest for Citizenship: African American and Native American Education in Kansas, 1880–1935* (Chapel Hill: University of North Carolina Press, 2010), 146–147. Of course, segregated education was still very much supported and practiced more broadly until the 1954 *Brown v. Board of Education* US Supreme Court decision, after which significant and violent efforts resisted school integration.

90. John Whitwell to Commissioner of Indian Affairs Cato Sells, 20 April 1917, John Whitwell Folder 2, NPRC.

91. Employment Record: John Whitwell, John Whitwell Folder, NPRC.

92. Marianne Burgess to R. H. Pratt, 14 March 1918, Box 2, Folder 42, Richard Henry Pratt Papers, BRBML.

93. Ibid.

94. Burgess (unsigned) to Lucretia S. Franklin (Chairman of the Committee for Philanthropic Labor, Illinois Yearly Meeting of Friends), 9 August 1917, Box 2, Folder 42, Richard Henry Pratt Papers, BRBML.

95. Burgess to Mason Pratt, 25 November 1919, Box 17, Folder 570, Richard Henry Pratt Papers, BRBML.

96. Cahill, *Federal Fathers and Mothers*, 229.

97. Burgess to Richard Henry Pratt, 27 January 1920, Box 2, Folder 42, Richard Henry Pratt Papers, BRBML; Burgess to Richard and Laura Pratt, 30 August 1921, Box 2, Folder 42, Richard Henry Pratt Papers, BRBML.

98. Cahill, *Federal Fathers and Mothers*, 223.

99. Ibid., 224.

100. Adams, *Education for Extinction*, 145–146.

101. Ibid., 87–93; Cahill, *Federal Fathers and Mothers*, 89.

102. Adams, *Education for Extinction*, 87.

103. Also see record of Mabel E. Curtis. Curtis sought to transfer elsewhere in the Indian Service but was likely not missed by school authorities or may even have been pushed out. Prior to her time at Carlisle, she transferred three times within six years at her "own request." But, her supervisors at Carlisle gave her mediocre, even damaging teacher evaluations. One described Curtis as "a fairly good teacher, but she is lacking in life and energy in the school room. She is pleasant, kind and patient with pupils, but is inclined to do too much of the reciting herself. She is not of a happy, contented disposition and is inclined to see the dark or unfavorable side of others." Curtis soon after transferred again to another Indian school. See "Request for Transfer: Mabel E. Curtis," 14 June 1910, Efficiency Report: Mabel Curtis, 20 February 1911, and Commissioner of Indian Affairs R. G. Valentine to Mabel Curtis, 2 August 1911, Mabel E. Curtis Folder, NPRC.

104. John DeHuff, Principal, Academic Department, "Efficiency Report, Case," 19 December 1914; O. H. Lipps to Commissioner of Indian Affairs, 13 April 1915, Lucy A. Case Folder, NPRC.

105. Efficiency Report: Lucy Case, 1 November 1915, Lucy A. Case Folder, NPRC.

106. Superintendent Charles W. Buchanan (Tulalip Indian Agency, Washington) to Commissioner of Indian Affairs Cato Sells, 16 September 1918, Lucy A. Case Folder, NPRC.

107. Efficiency Report: Lucy Case, 1 May 1918, Lucy A. Case Folder, NPRC.

108. Lucy Case to Sirs of the United States Indian Service, 25 July 1921, Lucy A. Case Folder, NPRC.

109. R. A. Cochran, Superintendent (Mt. Pleasant Indian School), to Commissioner

of Indian Affairs, 28 October 1909; F. H. Abbott (Action Commissioner) to Miss Margaret M. Sweeney, 15 November 1909, Margaret M. Sweeney Folder, NPRC.

110. Chas. F. Peirce, Efficiency Report, Margaret M. Sweeney, 15 January 1912, Margaret M. Sweeney Folder, NPRC.

111. James Sweeney to Hon. Boies Penrose, 13 January 1913, Margaret Sweeney Folder, NPRC.

112. Moses Friedman, Efficiency Report, Margaret M. Sweeney, 1 October 1913, Margaret M. Sweeney Folder, NPRC.

113. United States Congressional Inquiry, *Carlisle Indian School*, 1193.

114. John DeHuff, Efficiency Report, Margaret Sweeney, 19 December 1914, Margaret Sweeney Folder, NPRC.

115. Assistant Commissioner E. B. Merritt to Civil Service Commission, 27 September 1920, Margaret M. Sweeney Folder, NPRC.

116. Ibid.

117. Commissioner Chas. H. Burke to Margaret Sweeney, 23 May 1923, and Sweeney to Commissioner Burke, 28 May 1923, Margaret M. Sweeney Folder, NPRC.

118. Margaret M. Sweeney to Commissioner Charles H. Burke, 13 June 1923, Margaret M. Sweeney Folder, NPRC.

119. United States congressional inquiry, *Carlisle Indian School*, 1193–1194.

120. Efficiency Report: Margaret Sweeney, 1 May 1926, Margaret M. Sweeney Folder, NPRC.

121. Ibid.; Efficiency Report: Margaret Sweeney, 1 November 1926, Margaret M. Sweeney Folder, NPRC.

122. Superintendent (Carson School) to Commissioner of Indian Affairs Collier, 29 March 1935, Margaret M. Sweeney Folder, NPRC.

123. Employment Record Notecard: Gwen Williams, n.d., Gwen Williams Folder, NPRC.

124. Chas. F. Peirce, Efficiency Report for Indian Office status file, Gwen Williams, 22, July 1914, NPRC.

125. Letter, Principal, Academic Department, John DeHuff to Mr. Lipps, 30 December 1914, Gwen Williams Folder, NPRC.

126. Efficiency Report, 1 November 1917, Gwen Williams Folder, NPRC.

127. B. Garber (Chief Education Division) to C. F. Hauke, 3 January 1920, Gwen Williams Folder, NPRC.

128. Gwen Williams to My Superior Officers, 8 April 1922, Gwen Williams Folder, NPRC.

129. B. Garber (Chief Education Division) to C. F. Hauke, 3 January 1920, Gwen Williams Folder, NPRC.

130. Gwen Williams to My Superior Officers, 8 April 1922, Gwen Williams Folder, NPRC.

131. Adams, *Education for Extinction*, 91–93.

132. "Brief of charges filed by Major G. L. Scott, U.S. Indian Agent, Lake Leech Agency, Minnesota, against Charles L. Davis, Superintendent of the Red Lake School and his answer to the same," November 1903, Charles L. Davis Folder 1, NPRC.

133. Memorandum: Retirement of Miss Gwen Williams (Office of Indian Affairs), 27 February 1939, Gwen Williams Folder, NPRC. Adelaide Reichel refused a similar transfer from Carlisle to DC in 1918, believing that the increase in salary "would be insufficient to enable her to live in Washington under present conditions." See Chief Clerk to Secretary of the Interior, 12 April 1918, Adelaide Reichel Folder, NPRC; "Changes in Employees at U.S. Indian School Carlisle, PA, September 1918," in Monthly Time Book 1918, Record Group 75, Entry 1344, NADC.

134. For a concise account of US imperial education efforts, see Michelle Morgan, "Americanizing the Teachers: Identity, Citizenship, and the Teaching Corps in Hawai'i, 1900–1941," *Western Historical Quarterly* 45 (Summer 2014): 148–149.

135. Dora LeCrone to Commissioner of Indian Affairs R. G. Valentine, 20 July 1912, Dora S. LeCrone Folder, NPRC.

136. H. E. Wadsworth (Superintendent Salem Indian Training School) to Commissioner of Indian Affairs, 4 January 1913, Dora S. LeCrone Folder, NPRC.

137. Wadsworth to Commissioner of Indian Affairs, 4 August 1913, Dora S. LeCrone Folder, NPRC.

138. Abigal Gundlack Graham, "The Power of Boarding Schools: A Historiographical Review," *American Educational History Journal* 38, 1/2 (2012): 467–481; Stephen W. Haycox, *Alaska: An American Colony* (Seattle: University of Washington Press, 2002).

139. In 1909 Amelia McMichael transferred from Carlisle to teach in the Alaskan Educational Service, and like LeCrone, she received a raise in salary (from $660 to $900). See F. H. Abbott (Acting Commissioner of Indian Affairs) to Amelia McMichael, 31 August 1909, and McMichael to Commissioner of Indian Affairs, 8 August 1912, Amelia McMichael Folder, NPRC.

140. "A Christmas Letter from Miss Ericson in Porto Rico," *Indian Helper* 15, 10 (January 5, 1900): 4, CCHS.

141. Ibid.

142. For information regarding Carlisle's involvement with Puerto Rico, see Pablo Navarro-Rivera, "The Imperial Enterprise and Educational Policies in Colonial Puerto Rico," in Alfred W. McCoy and Francisco A. Scarano, eds., *Colonial Crucible: Empire in the Making of the Modern American State* (Madison: University of Wisconsin Press, 2009), 163–174.

143. Emma Hetrick to Commissioner of Indian Affairs, 17 October 1910 and 21 November 1910, Emma Hetrick Folder, NPRC.

144. Emma Hetrick to Commissioner of Indian Affairs, 17 July 1911, 5 February 1912, and 12 July 1912, Emma Hetrick Folder, NPRC.

145. Felix Periva (Acting Principal of Schools, Porto Rico) to Office of Indian Affairs, 31 January 1911, Emma Hetrick Folder, NPRC.

146. Hetrick to Commissioner of Indian Affairs, 27 November 1911, Emma Hetrick

Folder, NPRC; in the colonial and early federalist era, Anglo settlers identified the "Five Civilized Tribes" as the Cherokee, Chicksaw, Choctaw, Creek, and Seminole, as these indigenous peoples were assessed as having, at least in part, assimilated to European norms (including religion, family structure, etc.). Of course, this did not protect these indigenous peoples from removal from their lands, breaking of treaties, or other inequitable and devastating treatment. Genevieve Bell, "Telling Stories out of School: Remembering the Carlisle Indian Industrial School, 1879–1918" (PhD dissertation, Stanford University, 1998), 27, 32, 128; Tarr, "The Education of the Thomasites," 122; Grant Foreman, *The Five Civilized Tribes* (Norman: University of Oklahoma Press, 1934).

147. Carey Hickle (Secretary, Porto Rico Commissioner of Education) to Whom It May Concern, 1 February 1912, Emma Hetrick Folder, NPRC.

148. Hetrick to Commissioner of Indian Affairs, 12 July 1912, Emma Hetrick Folder, NPRC; C. F. Hauke (Acting Commissioner of Indian Affairs) to Mr. J. F. House (Superintendent Rapid City School, South Dakota), 29 August 1912, Emma Hetrick Folder, NPRC.

149. "John H. Evans Dies Today at Home of Son: Was Formerly Governor of Mountain Provinces in Philippines," and "A Sense of Humor," n.d., newspaper clipping, Clips about Evans Family Folder, Evans Family Papers, BHL.

150. "Edward Sharp," n.d., Edward Sharp Papers (General) 1901–1904 Folder, Edward Sharp Papers, RDU.

151. "Application for Retirement from the Civil Service on Account of Total Disability: John Whitwell," 19 June 1929, John Whitwell Folder 2, NPRC.

152. Similarly, John DeHuff, one of the crossover teachers, had left Carlisle due to tuberculosis in 1916: John DeHuff to Commissioner of Indian Affairs, 24 July 1916, John DeHuff Folder, NPRC.

153. Idilla Wilson to Commissioner of Indian Affairs Cato Sells, 3 August 1918, Idilla Wilson Folder, NPRC.

154. John Francis Jr. to Commissioner of Indian Affairs, 18 June 1918, Idilla Wilson Folder, NPRC.

155. Idilla Wilson to Commissioner of Indian Affairs Cato Sells, 3 August 1918, NPRC.

156. US Civil Service Commission (Department of Interior), "Abstract of Official Record of Employee: Idilla Wilson," 29 December 1922, Idilla Wilson Folder, NPRC.

157. See Chapter 1 regarding teachers Margaret Sweeney, Emma Hetrick, and Clara Donaldson, who assisted elderly parents or other dependent family members.

158. Employee Card: Frances Scales; Scales to Mr. Goodman, 24 July 1909; F. H. Abbott (Acting Commissioner to Frances), 1 September 1909; Scales to Commissioner of Indian Affairs, 17 December 1910, all in Frances Scales Folder, NPRC.

159. Efficiency Report: Clara A. Snoddy, 1 May 1921; Snoddy to Superintendent of the Phoenix Indian School, 29 September 1941; Paul L. Fickinger (Associate Director of Education, Office of Indian Affairs) to Snoddy, 20 October 1941, all in Clara A. Snoddy Folder, NPRC.

160. Hattie McDowell to Mrs. Harper, 6 February 1924, and Employee Card: Hattie McDowell, Hattie McDowell Folder, NPRC; Emma Cutter to Nana Pratt, 15 February 1937 (round robin letter, original date 30 January 1935), Box 13, Folder 450, Richard Henry Pratt Papers, BRBML: "While Sister Charlotte was living, we had several Carlisle parties, but later, owing to Sister Ruth's condition, I was not able to entertain much."

161. C. F. Hauke (Assistant Commissioner of Indian Affairs) to Mr. Peyton Carter (Superintendent Wahpeton), 6 June 1918, Margaret Roberts Folder, NPRC.

162. Superintendent Harvey K. Meyer (Leech Lake Agency, Minnesota) to Commissioner of Indian Affairs, 14 May 1918, Margaret Roberts Folder, NPRC.

163. Margaret Roberts to Mr. Peyton Carter (Superintendent Wahpeton), 11 August 1918, Margaret Roberts Folder, NPRC.

164. Bell, "Telling Stories out of School," 158; Cahill, *Federal Fathers and Mothers*, 91.

165. Superintendent Crandall (Santa Fe) to Commissioner of Indian Affairs, 14 October 1909, Mariette Wood Folder, NPRC.

166. Efficiency Report: Mariette Wood, 1 November 1909, Mariette Wood Folder, NPRC. Gendered assumptions similarly guided hiring practices in the Philippines, as discussed in chapter 3.

167. Efficiency Report: Royal Man, 1 December 1915, Royal L. Mann Folder, NPRC.

168. Efficiency Report: Royal Mann, 19 December 1916, and E. B. Merritt (Assistant to Commissioner of Indian Affairs) to Royal Mann, 28 July 1920, Royal Mann Folder, NPRC.

169. Fannie Peter to Richard Henry Pratt, 2 October 1904, Box 7, Folder 248, Richard Henry Pratt Papers, BRBML.

170. Ibid.

171. Emma Cutter to Nana Pratt, 10 June 1934, 15 February 1937, Box 15, Folder, 505, Richard Henry Pratt Papers, BRBML. In addition to maintaining ties with fellow teachers, some Carlisle teachers kept in touch with former students. Emma Cutter "enjoyed many letters from returned students" while still at Carlisle. She explained, "During my fifteen years in Washington, I saw many Carlisle students who came to do business for their tribe, at the Indian Bureau." (See Cutter to Nana Pratt, 15 February 1937.) Similarly, Fannie Peter wrote of being in touch with former students when working in Washington, DC. See Peter to Richard Henry Pratt, 27 December 1916, Box 7, Folder 248, Richard Henry Pratt Papers, BRBML.

172. *Carlisle Arrow* 11, 1 (September 4, 1914), CCHS.

173. Ibid.

174. Marianne Burgess to Richard Henry Pratt and Laura Pratt, 24 July 1914, Box 2, Folder 42, Richard Henry Pratt Papers, BRBML.

175. Burgess to R. H. Pratt, 14 March 1918, Box 2, Folder 42, Richard Henry Pratt Papers, BRBML.

176. *FWProgrammer* 82, no. 2 (December/March 1982), PI 2-8-10, Miscellaneous FWProgrammer Folder, CCHS.

177. Walter William Marquardt Plaque at dedication (photograph), 4 April 1987, Box 7, Biographical Folder, Walter W. Marquardt Papers, BHL.

CONCLUSION: LEGACIES OF IMPERIAL EDUCATION

1. Jessie Cook to Commissioner of Indian Affairs Burke, 7 June 1924, Jessie Cook Folder, NPRC.

2. Indian Citizenship Act of 1924, Pub. L. No. 68-175, 43 Stat. 253 (1924).

3. For more on controversy over amendment, see Vine Deloria Jr. and Clifford M. Lytle, *American Indians, American Justice* (Austin: University of Texas Press, 1983), 221.

4. Jessie Cook to Moses Friedman, 12 December 1912, Jessie Cook Folder, NPRC.

5. Walter Marquardt, "Advice to New Teachers" and "Mental Degeneracy," Scrap Book, Talks and Papers, by W. W. Marquardt, 1896–1916," 156, 160, Box 5, Walter W. Marquardt Papers, BHL.

6. Paulo Freire, *Pedagogy of the Oppressed* (1971; repr., New York: Continuum Press, 2001).

7. Oath: Clara Donaldson, Form 1-280, 8 September 1914, Clara Donaldson Folder, NPRC.

8. Benedict Anderson, *Imagined Communities: Reflections on the Origin and Spread of Nationalism* (1983; repr., London: Verso, 2006).

9. Mary Helen Fee, *A Woman's Impressions of the Philippines* (Chicago: A. C. McClurg, 1910), 12.

10. Ibid.

11. Bureau of Indian Education, Riverside Indian School Application for Admission 2019–2020 School Year, "Social Summary," 14, https://ris.bie.edu/Student_Applica tion_2019_20.pdf; Bureau of Indian Education, Riverside Indian School Application for Admission 2018–2019 "Riverside Indian School: Parent-Student-School Compact," https://ris.bie.edu/Student_Application_2018_19.pdf.

12. Jon Reyhner and Jeanne Eder, *American Indian Education: A History* (Norman: University of Oklahoma Press, 2004), 143.

13. Rosalinda L. Oroso, "The Thomasites Remembered," *Philippine Star*, September 16, 2001, http://www.philstar.com/starweek-magazine/133925/thomasites-remem bered.

14. Fee, *A Woman's Impressions*, 101.

15. Julian Go, *Patterns of Empire: The British and American Empires, 1688 to the Present* (New York: Cambridge University Press, 2011), x.

BIBLIOGRAPHY

PRIMARY SOURCES

Archives

Associated Executive Committee of Friends on Indian Affairs Collection. Quaker and Special Collections, Haverford College, Haverford, Pennsylvania (QSCH).

Bentley Historical Library, University of Michigan. University of Michigan. Ann Arbor, Michigan (BHL).

   Behner, Frederick G., Papers.

   Carrothers, George E., Papers.

   Cheney, Frank W., Papers.

   Cole, Harry (Harrie) Newton, Papers.

   Early, John C., Papers.

   Evans, Glen, Evans Family Papers.

   Marquardt, Walter W., Papers.

   Taylor, Ralph Wendell, Taylor Family Papers.

   Worcester, Dean C., Papers,

Bordner, Harvey A., Papers. Office of University Archives and Records Management, Indiana University, Bloomington, Indiana (IUA).

Cameron, Norman W., Diaries. Special Collections Library, University of Michigan, Ann Arbor, Michigan (SCLM).

Campbell, Elizabeth Winifred (Mitchell), File. Wisconsin Historical Society, Madison, Wisconsin (WHS).

Carlisle Indian Industrial School Collection. Cumberland County Historical Society, Carlisle, Pennsylvania (CCHS).

   Carlisle School Newspapers:

   Carlisle Arrow (1910, 1913–1915)

   Eadle Keatah Toh (1880)

   Indian Helper (1887–1891; 1900)

   Morning Star (1883)

Carlisle Indian School Papers. Archives and Special Collections, Waidner-Spahr Library, Dickinson College, Carlisle, Pennsylvania (WDC).

Cheesborough, John, Papers. Rubenstein Library, Duke University, Durham, North Carolina (RDU).

Frelin, Jules Theophile, Diaries. University Archives, University of Minnesota, Twin Cities, Minnesota (UAUM).

Hespelt, Herman, Papers. Special Collections Library, Binghamton University, Binghamton, New York (SCLB).

Moore, Blaine Free, Papers. Library of Congress Manuscript Division, Washington, DC (LOC).

Moore, Marianne Craig, Collection. Archives and Special Collections, Dickinson College, Carlisle, Pennsylvania (WDC).

National Archives, Washington, DC (NADC).

> Preliminary Inventory of the Records of the Bureau of Indian Affairs, Carlisle Indian Industrial School, Record Group 75, Entry 1331.

> Records Relating to Carlisle School Personnel, Records of the Bureau of Indian Affairs, Record Group 75, Entries 1344 and 1344A.

> > Denny, Nellie Robertson, Folder.

> > Denny, Wallace, Folder.

> > Francis Jr., John, Folder.

> > Lipps, Oscar A., Folder.

> > Mercer, William A., Folder.

National Archives at College Park, Maryland (NAMD).

> Philippine Civil Service, Records of the Bureau of Insular Affairs, Record Group 350.

> > Bordner, Harvey A., and Wife (Maude M. Bordner), File.

> > Cheney, Frank W., File.

> > Donaldson, Clara R., File.

> > Early, John C., and Wife (Willa Rhodes Early), File.

> > Friedman, Moses, File.

> > Hespelt, Ernest Herman, File.

National Personnel Records Center, Indian School Service, Carlisle Indian Industrial School Collection, St. Louis, Missouri (NPRC).

> Bender, Elizabeth, File.

> Case, Lucy A., File.

> Cook, Jessie W., File.

> Curtis, Mabel E., File.

> Davis, Charles L., File.

> DeHuff, Elizabeth, File.

> DeHuff, John, File.

> Dittes, Lydia E., File.

> Donaldson, Clara, File.

> Ely, Ann S., Record card.

> Emery, Hazel, File.

> Foster, Emma H., File.

> Friedman, Moses, File.

> Hetrick, Emma K., File.

> Jones, Elizabeth, File.

> Lane, Mattie, File.

> LeCrone, Dora S., File.

Lovewell, Emma C., File.

Mann, Royal LeBau, File.

McDowell, Hattie, File.

McMichael, Amelia, File.

Reichel, Adelaide B., File.

Roberts, Margaret, File.

Scales, Frances, File.

Snoddy, Clara A., File.

Sweeney, Margaret M., File.

Tranbarger, Fernando G., File.

Tranbarger, Katherine Bingley, File.

Whitwell, John, File.

Williams, Gwen, File.

Wilson, Idilla, File.

Wood, Mariette, File.

Oliver, Reese (Reece) A., Oliver Family Papers. Indiana State Library, Indianapolis, Indiana (ISL).

Pratt, Richard Henry, Papers. Beinecke Rare Book and Manuscript Library, Yale University. New Haven, Connecticut (BRBML).

Sharp, Edward, Papers. Rubenstein Library, Duke University, Durham, North Carolina (RDU).

Smith, Laura Gibson, Papers. Iowa Women's Archives, University of Iowa Libraries, Iowa City, Iowa (IWA).

Whistler, Mrs. Edward L., Folder. Carlisle Indian School Papers, Archives and Special Collections, Dickinson College, Carlisle, Pennsylvania (WDC).

Whiting, H. O., Letters. James Hardy Papers, Indiana State Library, Indianapolis, Indiana (ISL).

Memoirs

Betzinez, Jason, with Wilbur Sturtevant Nye. *I Fought with Geronimo*. 1959; repr., Lincoln: University of Nebraska Press, 1959.

Daklugie, Asa, in Eve Ball with Nora Henn and Lynda A. Sánchez. *Indeh: An Apache Odyssey*. Norman: University of Oklahoma Press, 1988.

Fee, Mary Helen. *The Locusts' Years*. Chicago: A. C. McClurg, 1912.

———. *A Woman's Impressions of the Philippines*. Chicago: A. C. McClurg, 1910.

La Flesche, Francis. *The Middle Five: Indian Schoolboys of the Omaha Tribe*. 1900; repr., Lincoln: University of Nebraska Press, 1963.

Pratt, Richard Henry. *Battlefield and Classroom: Four Decades with the American Indian, 1867–1904*, ed. Robert M. Utley. 1964; repr., Norman: University of Oklahoma Press, 2003.

Standing Bear, Luther. *My People the Sioux*, ed. E. A. Brininstool. 1928; repr., Lincoln: University of Nebraska Press, 1975.

Williams, Daniel Roderick. *The Odyssey of the Philippine Commission.* Chicago: A. C. McClurg, 1913.

Zitkala-Sa. "Impressions of an Indian Childhood," *Atlantic Monthly* 85, 507, January 1900, 37–47.

———. "An Indian Teacher among Indians," *Atlantic Monthly* 85, 509, March 1900, 381–387.

———. "School Days of an Indian Girl," *Atlantic Monthly* 85, 508, February 1900, 185–194.

Government Documents

Annual Report of the Commissioner of Indian Affairs. Office of Indian Affairs, Washington, DC, 1889, 1890, 1894, 1898, 1901. University of Wisconsin Digital Collections, http://digital.library.wisc.edu/1711.dl/History and the Internet Archive, http://www.archive.org.

Course of Study for Indian Schools of the United States: Industrial and Literary. Washington, DC: Government Printing Office, 1901.

Hearings Before the Joint Commission of the Congress of the United States, 63rd Cong. Second Session to Investigate Indian Affairs, February 6, 7, 8, and March 25, 1914, Part 11. Washington, DC: Government Printing Office, 1914.

Hearings Before the Joint Commission of Congress of the United States, 63rd Cong. Second Session to Investigate Indian Affairs, July 15, 1914, Part 16-A. Washington, DC: Government Printing Office, 1914.

House of Representatives Report No. 1502, Indian Schools Support 1918, 65th Congress. Third Session, December 3, 1918. Washington, DC: Government Printing Office, 1918.

Indian Citizenship Act of 1924, Pub. L. No. 68-175, 43 Stat. 253 (1924).

Meriam, Lewis (Institute for Government Research with Technical Director). *The Problem of Indian Administration: Report of a Survey Made at the Request of Honorable Hubert Work, Secretary of the Interior, and Submitted to Him, February 21, 1928.* Baltimore: Johns Hopkins University Press, 1928.

Other Primary Sources

Barrows, David P. *A History of the Philippines.* New York: American Book Co., 1905.

———. "Instructions for Volunteer Field Workers." Bureau of Non-Christian Tribes of the Philippine Islands, Manila, 1901, 3, 9–14.

"The Bureau of Education: A Statement of Organization and Aims Published for General Information." *Philippine Teacher* 1, 1, December 15, 1904. Library Materials Vol. 674, Record Group 350, Philippines Miscellaneous, NAMD.

[Burgess, Marianna]. *Stiya, A Carlisle Indian Girl at Home; Founded on the Author's Actual Observations.* 1891; repr. Memphis: General Books, 2010.

Cameron, Norman. "The U.S. Military Occupation of Bohol: 1900–1902," George Percival Scriven: An American in Bohol, the Philippines, 1899–1901. An On-line

Archival Collection, Special Collections Library, Duke University. May 1997. http://
library.duke.edu/rubenstein/scriptorium/scriven/bohol-history.html.

Fee, Mary Helen. "Night Raids from the Air." *The Forum* (1918). In *World's War Events,
Volume III, Recorded by Statesmen, Commanders, Historians and by Men Who Fought
or Saw the Great Campaigns*, ed. Francis J. Reynolds and Allen L. Churchill. Ebook, August 12, 2005, http://www.gutenberg.org/files/16513/16513-h/16513-h.htm
#Page_229.

Indian Detours Roundabout Old Santa Fe New Mexico. Chicago: Rand McNally; repr.
1940. Southwestern Wonderland University of Arizona Library Special Collections
Pamphlet, http://www.library.arizona.edu/exhibits/pams/pdfs/detsanfe.pdf.

"In the Spotlight." *FWProgrammer* 82, 2, December/March 1982. PI-2-8-10 Folder,
CCHS.

"Just Because She Made Dem Goo-Goo Eyes." Charles Templeton Sheet Music Collection, Mississippi State University Libraries (1900), http://cdm16631.contentdm
.oclc.org/cdm/ref/collection/SheetMusic/id/26074.

The Log of the "Thomas," July 23–August 21, 1901, ed. Ronald P. Gleason, accessed June
15, 2019, http://openlibrary.org/books/OL25302238M/The_log_of_the_Thomas_July
_23_to_August_21_1901.

Seeley, Levi. *Grube's Method of Teaching Arithmetic*. New York: E. L. Kellogg, 1891, 11–16,
https://archive.org/details/grubesmethodofteooseelrich.

SECONDARY SOURCES

Books and Book Chapters

Adams, David Wallace. "Beyond Bleakness: The Brighter Side of Indian Boarding
Schools, 1870–1940." In Clifford. E. Trafzer, Jean A. Keller, and Lorene Sisquoc,
eds., *Boarding School Blues: Revisiting American Indian Educational Experiences*. Lincoln: University of Nebraska Press, 2006.

———. *Education for Extinction: American Indians and the Boarding School Experience,
1875–1928*. Lawrence: University Press of Kansas, 1995.

Alzona, Encarnacion. *A History of Education in the Philippines*. Manila: University of the
Philippines Press, 1932.

Amoroso, Donna J. "Inheriting the 'Moro Problem': Muslim Authority and Colonial
Rule in British Malaya and the Philippines." In Julian Go and Anne L. Foster, eds.,
The American Colonial State in the Philippines: Global Perspectives. Durham, NC:
Duke University Press, 2003, 118–147.

Anderson, Benedict. *Imagined Communities: Reflections on the Origin and Spread of Nationalism*. 1983; repr., London: Verso, 2006.

Angulo, A. J. *Empire and Education: A History of Greed and Goodwill from the War of 1898
to the War on Terror*. New York: Palgrave Macmillan, 2012.

Archuleta, Margaret L., Brenda Child, and K. Tsianina Lomawaima, eds. *Away from
Home: American Indian Boarding School Experiences, 1879–2000*. Phoenix: Heard
Museum, 2000.

Bederman, Gail. *Manliness and Civilization: A Cultural History of Gender and Race in the United States, 1880–1917.* Chicago: University of Chicago Press, 1995.

Berghofer Robert F., Jr. *The White Man's Indian: Images of the American Indian from Columbus to the Present.* New York: Knopf, 1978.

Brands, H. W. *Bound to Empire: The United States and the Philippines.* New York: Oxford University Press, 1992.

Cahill, Cathleen D. *Federal Fathers and Mothers: A Social History of the United States Indian Service, 1869–1933.* Chapel Hill: University of North Carolina Press, 2011.

Carnoy, Martin. *Education as Cultural Imperialism.* New York: Longman, 1974.

Child, Brenda J. *Boarding School Seasons: American Indian Families, 1900–1940.* Lincoln: University of Nebraska Press, 1998.

Clymer, Kenton J. *Protestant Missionaries in the Philippines, 1898–1916: An Inquiry into the American Colonial Mentality.* Urbana: University of Illinois Press, 1986.

Coleman, Michael C. *American Indian Children at School, 1850–1930.* Jackson: University Press of Mississippi, 1993.

Cott, Nancy. *The Bonds of Womanhood: "Woman's Sphere" in New England, 1780–1835.* New Haven, CT: Yale University Press, 1987.

Cremin, Lawrence A. *American Education: The Metropolitan Experience 1876–1980.* New York: Harper and Row, 1988.

———. *The Transformation of the School: Progressivism in American Education, 1876–1957.* New York: Knopf, 1961.

Degler, Carl N. *In Search of Human Nature: The Decline and Revival of Darwinism in American Social Thought.* New York: Oxford University Press, 1991.

Delmendu, Sharon. *The Star-Entangled Banner: One Hundred Years of America in the Philippines.* New Brunswick: Rutgers University Press, 2004.

del Moral, Solsiree. *Negotiating Empire: The Cultural Politics of Schools in Puerto Rico, 1898–1952.* Madison: University of Wisconsin Press, 2013.

Deloria, Philip J. *Playing Indian.* New Haven, CT: Yale University Press, 1998.

Deloria, Vine, and Clifford M. Lytle. *American Indians, American Justice.* Austin: University of Texas Press, 1983.

Dippie, Brian W. *The Vanishing American: White Attitudes and U.S. Indian Policy.* Middletown, CT: Wesleyan University Press, 1982.

Dubois, Ellen Carol, and Lynn Dumenil. *Through Women's Eyes: An American History, Volume I,* 3rd ed. Boston: Bedford St. Martin, 2012.

Eastman, Elaine Goodale. *Pratt: The Red Man's Moses.* Norman: University of Oklahoma Press, 1935.

Ellis, Clyde. *To Change Them Forever: Indian Education at the Rainy Mountain Boarding School, 1893–1920.* Norman: University of Oklahoma Press, 1996.

Epstein, Barbara Leslie. *The Politics of Domesticity: Women, Evangelism, and Temperance in Nineteenth-Century America.* Middletown, CT: Wesleyan University Press, 1981.

Fanon, Frantz. *Black Skin, White Masks.* New York: Grove Press, 1967.

Fear-Segal, Jacqueline. *White Man's Club: Schools, Race, and the Struggle of Indian Acculturation.* Lincoln: University of Nebraska Press, 2007.

Fear-Segal, Jacqueline, and Susan D. Rose. *Carlisle Indian Industrial School: Indigenous Histories, Memories, and Reclamations.* Lincoln: University of Nebraska Press, 2016.

Ferguson, Niall. *Colossus: The Price of America's Empire.* New York: Penguin Books, 2004.

Foreman, Grant. *The Five Civilized Tribes.* Norman: University of Oklahoma Press, 1934.

Foster, Anne L. *Projection and Power: The United States and Europe in Colonial Southeast Asia, 1919–1941.* Durham, NC: Duke University Press, 2010.

Foster, Anne L., and Julian Go, eds. *The American Colonial State in the Philippines,* Durham, NC: Duke University Press, 2003.

Freire, Paulo. *Pedagogy of the Oppressed.* 1971; repr., New York: Continuum Press, 2001.

Garrett, Clarke. *In Pursuit of Pleasure: Leisure in Nineteenth-Century Cumberland County.* Carlisle, PA: Cumberland County Historical Society, 1997.

Gates, John Morgan. *Schoolbooks and Krags: The United States Army in the Philippines, 1898–1902.* Westport, CT: Greenwood Press, 1973.

Ginzberg, Lori D. *Women and the Work of Benevolence: Morality, Politics, and Class in the Nineteenth-Century United States.* New Haven, CT: Yale University Press, 1990.

Glancy, Diane. *Fort Marion Prisoners and the Trauma of Native Education.* Lincoln: University of Nebraska Press, 2014.

Go, Julian. *American Empire and the Politics of Meaning: Elite Political Cultures in the Philippines and Puerto Rico during U.S. Colonialism.* Durham, NC: Duke University Press, 2008.

———. "Imperial Power and Its Limits: America's Colonial Empire in the Early Twentieth Century." In Craig Calhoun, Frederick Cooper, and Kevin W. Moore, eds., *Lessons of Empire: Imperial Histories and American Power.* New York: Social Science Research Council, 2006.

———. "Introduction: Global Perspectives on the U.S. State in the Philippines." In Julian Go and Anne L. Foster, eds., *The American Colonial State in the Philippines,* 1–42. Durham, NC: Duke University Press, 2003.

———. *Patterns of Empire: The British and American Empires, 1688 to the Present.* New York: Cambridge University Press, 2011.

Gordon, Linda. *Pitied but Not Entitled: Single Mothers and the History of Welfare, 1890–1935.* Cambridge, MA: Harvard University Press, 1994.

Gould, Stephen Jay. *The Mismeasure of Man.* New York: Norton, 1981.

Greason, Walter David. *Suburban Erasure: How the Suburbs Ended the Civil Rights Movement in New Jersey.* Madison, NJ: Farleigh Dickinson University Press, 2013.

Haycox, Stephen W. *Alaska: An American Colony.* Seattle: University of Washington Press, 2002.

Herbst, Jurgen. *Women Pioneers of Public Education: How Culture Came to the Wild West.* New York: Palgrave Macmillan, 2008.

Hewitt, Nancy A. *Women's Activism and Social Change: Rochester, New York, 1822–1872.* Ithaca, NY: Cornell University Press, 1984.

Hewitt, Nancy A., and Suzanne Lebsock, eds. *Visible Women: New Essays on American Activism.* Urbana: University of Illinois Press, 1993.

Hinsdale, B. A. *Horace Mann and the Common School Revival in the United States.* New York: Charles Scribner's Sons, 1900.

Hobsbawm, Eric. *The Age of Empire: 1875–1914.* New York: Vintage Books, 1987.

Hofstadter, Richard. *The Age of Reform.* New York: Knopf, 1955.

Hoganson, Kristin L. *Fighting for American Manhood: How Gender Politics Provoked the Spanish-American and Philippine-American Wars.* New Haven, CT: Yale University Press, 1998.

Horowitz, Helen Lefkowitz. *The Power and Passion of M. Carey Thomas.* Urbana: University of Illinois Press, 1999.

———. *Rereading Sex: Battles over Sexual Knowledge and Suppression in Nineteenth-Century America.* New York: Vintage Books, 2002.

Hoxie, Frederick E. *A Final Promise: The Campaign to Assimilate the Indians, 1880–1920.* Lincoln: University of Nebraska Press, 1984.

Hyer, Sally. *One House, One Voice, One Heart: Native American Education at the Santa Fe Indian School, 1890–1990.* Santa Fe: Museum of New Mexico Press, 1990.

Jacobs, Margaret D. *White Mother to a Dark Race: Settler Colonialism, Maternalism, and the Removal of Indigenous Children in the American West and Australia, 1880–1910.* Lincoln: University of Nebraska Press, 2009.

Jacobson, Matthew Frye. *Barbarian Virtues: The United States Encounters Foreign Peoples at Home and Abroad, 1876–1917.* New York: Hill and Wang, 2000.

Justice, Benjamin. "Education at the End of a Gun: The Origins of American Imperial Education and the Case of the Philippines." In Noah W. Sobe, ed., *American Post-Conflict Educational Reform: From the Spanish-American War to Iraq,* 19–52. New York: Palgrave Macmillan, 2009.

Kaestle, Carl. *Pillars of the Republic: Common Schools and American Society, 1780–1860.* New York: Hill and Wang, 1983.

Kaplan, Amy. "Left Alone in America." In Amy Kaplan and Donald E. Pease, eds., *Cultures of United States Imperialism,* 3–21. Durham, NC: Duke University Press, 1993.

Karnow, Stanley. *In Our Image: America's Empire in the Philippines.* New York: Random House, 1989.

Katz, Michael B. *Class, Bureaucracy, and Schools: The Illusion of Educational Change in America.* New York: Praeger, 1971.

———. *Reconstructing American Education.* Cambridge, MA: Harvard University Press, 1987.

Kehoe, Alice Beck. *A Passion for the True and Just: Felix and Lucy Kramer Cohen and the Indian New Deal.* Phoenix: University of Arizona Press, 2014.

Kendi, Ibram. *Stamped from the Beginning: The Definitive History of Racist Ideas in America.* New York: Nation Books, 2016.

Kevles, Daniel J. *In the Name of Eugenics*. New York: Knopf, 1985.

Kliebard, Herbert M. *The Struggle for the American Curriculum, 1893–1958,* 2nd ed. New York: Routledge, 1995.

Kramer, Paul. *The Blood of Government: Race, Empire, the United States, and the Philippines*. Chapel Hill: University of North Carolina Press, 2006.

———. "Decolonizing the History of the Philippine-American War." In Leon Wolff, *Little Brown Brother: How the United States Purchased and Pacified the Philippine Islands at the Century's Turn*. New York: History Book Club, 1961, ix–xvii.

———. "Race, Empire, and Transnational History." In Alfred W. McCoy and Francisco A. Scarano, eds., *Colonial Crucible: Empire in the Making of the Modern American State*. Madison: University of Wisconsin Press, 2009.

Larson, Edward J. *Eugenics in the Deep South*. Baltimore: Johns Hopkins University Press, 1995.

Maier, Charles S. *Among Empires: American Ascendancy and Its Predecessors*. Cambridge, MA: Harvard University Press, 2006.

May, Ernest. *Imperial Democracy: The Emergence of the United States as Great Power*. New York: Harper Torchbooks, 1973.

May, Glenn Anthony. "The Business of Education in the Colonial Philippines, 1909–30." In Alfred W. McCoy and Francisco A. Scarano, eds., *Colonial Crucible: Empire in the Making of the Modern American State*. Madison: University of Wisconsin Press, 2009.

———. *Social Engineering in the Philippines: The Aims, Execution, and Impact of American Colonial Policy, 1900–1913*. Westport, CT: Greenwood Press, 1980.

McCormick, Thomas. "From Old Empire to New: The Changing Dynamics and Tactics of American Empire." In Alfred W. McCoy and Francisco A. Scarano, eds., *Colonial Crucible: Empire in the Making of the Modern American State*. Madison: University of Wisconsin Press, 2009.

McCoy, Alfred W., and Francisco A. Scarano, eds. *Colonial Crucible: Empire in the Making of the Modern American State*. Madison: University of Wisconsin Press, 2009.

McCoy, Alfred W., Francisco A. Scarano, and Courtney Johnson. "On the Tropic of Cancer: Transitions and Transformations in the U.S. Imperial State." In Alfred W. McCoy and Francisco A. Scarano, eds., *Colonial Crucible: Empire in the Making of the Modern American State*. Madison: University of Wisconsin Press, 2009, 3–33.

Mihesuah, Devon A. *Cultivating the Rosebuds: The Education of Women at the Cherokee Female Seminary, 1851–1909*. Chicago: University of Illinois Press, 1993.

Miller, Stuart Creighton. *Benevolent Assimilation: The American Conquest of the Philippines, 1899–1903*. New Haven, CT: Yale University Press, 1982.

Nabokov, Peter, ed. *Native American Testimony: A Chronicle of Indian-White Relations from Prophesy to the Present, 1492–2000*. New York: Penguin Books, 1999.

Navarro-Rivera, Pablo. "The Imperial Enterprise and Educational Policies in Colonial Puerto Rico." In Alfred W. McCoy and Francisco A. Scarano, eds., *Colonial Crucible:*

Empire in the Making of the Modern American State. Madison: University of Wisconsin Press, 2009, 163–174.

Ninkovich, Frank. "The United States and Imperialism." In Robert D. Schulzinger, ed., *A Companion to American Foreign Relations*. Malden, MA: Blackwell, 2003.

Nugent, Walter. *Habits of Empire: A History of American Expansion*. New York: Knopf, 2008.

Painter, Nell Irvin. *The History of White People*. New York: W. W. Norton, 2010.

———. *Standing at Armageddon: The United States, 1877–1919*. New York: W. W. Norton, 1987.

Pascoe, Peggy. *Relations of Rescue: The Search for Female Moral Authority in the American West, 1874–1939*. New York: Oxford University Press, 1990.

Pecson, Geronima T., and Maria Racelis, eds. *Tales of the American Teachers in the Philippines*. Manila: Carmelo and Bauermann, 1959.

Pomeroy, William J. *American Neo-colonialism: Its Emergence in the Philippines and Asia*. New York: International Publishers, 1970.

Prucha, Francis Paul. *American Indian Policy in Crisis: Christian Reformers and the Indian, 1865–1900*. Norman: University of Oklahoma Press, 1976.

———. *The Great Father: The United States Government and the American Indians, Vol. 2*. Lincoln: University of Nebraska Press, 1983.

Rafael, Vicente L. *White Love and Other Events in Filipino History*. Durham, NC: Duke University Press, 2000.

Recchiuti, John Louis. *Civic Engagement: Social Science and Progressive-Era Reform in New York City*. Philadelphia: University of Pennsylvania Press, 2007.

Reese, William J. *America's Public Schools: From the Common School to "No Child Left Behind,"* 2nd ed. Baltimore: Johns Hopkins University Press, 2011.

Reyhner, Jon, and Jeanne Eder. *American Indian Education: A History*. Norman: University of Oklahoma Press, 2004.

Richter, Daniel. *Facing East from Indian Country: A Native History of Early America*. Cambridge, MA: Harvard University Press, 2001.

Rogers, Daniel. "Exceptionalism." In Anthony Molho and Gordon S. Wood, eds., *Imagined Historians Interpret Their Past*. Princeton, NJ: Princeton University Press, 1998.

Rury, John L. *Education and Social Change: Contours in the History of American Schooling*, 5th ed. New York: Routledge, 2016.

Said, Edward W. *Orientalism*. New York: Pantheon Books, 1978.

Sargent, Theodore D. *The Life of Elaine Goodale Eastman*. Lincoln: University of Nebraska Press, 2005.

Scott, Anne Firor. *Natural Allies: Women's Associations in American History*. Urbana: University of Illinois Press, 1991.

Selden, Steven. Inheriting Shame: The Story of Eugenics and Racism in America. New York: Teachers College Press, 1999.

Shaw, Wilfred B., ed. *The University of Michigan Encyclopedic Survey: Volume II*. Ann Arbor: University of Michigan Press, 1951.

Shipman, Pat. *The Evolution of Racism: Human Differences and the Use and Abuse of Science*. New York: Simon and Schuster, 1994.

Silbey, David. *A War of Frontier and Empire: The Philippine-American War, 1899–1902*. New York: Hill and Wang, 2007.

Skocpol, Theda. *Protecting Soldiers and Mothers: The Political Origins of Social Policy in the United States*. Cambridge, MA: Harvard University Press, 1992.

Spring, Joel. *The American School: 1642–1985*. New York: Longman, 1986.

Stanley, Peter W. *A Nation in the Making: The Philippines and the United States, 1899–1921*. Cambridge, MA: Harvard University Press, 1974.

Stoler, Ann Laura. *Carnal Knowledge and Imperial Power: Race and the Intimate in Colonial Rule*. Berkeley: University of California Press, 2002.

Stratton, Clif. *Education for Empire: American Schools, Race, and the Paths of Good Citizenship*. Oakland: University of California Press, 2016.

Stremlau, Rose. "Rape Narratives on the Northern Paiute Frontier: Sarah Winnemucca, Sexual Sovereignty, and Economic Autonomy, 1844–1891." In Dee Garceau-Hagen, ed., *Portraits of Women in the American West*. New York: Routledge, 2005, 37–62.

Szasz, Margaret Connell. *Education and the American Indian: The Road to Self-Determination since 1928*. Santa Fe: University of New Mexico Press, 1999.

———. *Indian Education in the American Colonies, 1607–1783*. Lincoln: University of Nebraska Press, 2007.

Thornton, Russell. *American Indian Holocaust and Survival: A Population History since 1492*. Norman: University of Oklahoma Press, 1987.

Trafzer, Clifford E., Jean A. Keller, and Lorene Sisquoc. *Boarding School Blues: Revisiting American Indian Educational Experiences*. Lincoln: University of Nebraska Press, 2006.

Trennert, Robert A., Jr. *The Phoenix Indian School: Forced Assimilation in Arizona, 1891–1935*. Norman: University of Oklahoma Press, 1988.

Tyack, David. *The One Best System: A History of American Urban Education*. Cambridge, MA: Harvard University Press, 1974.

Tyack, David B., and Larry Cuban. *Tinkering Toward Utopia: A Century of Public School Reform*. Cambridge, MA: Harvard University Press, 1995.

Tyack, David, and Elisabeth Hansot. *Learning Together: A History of Coeducation in American Schools*. New Haven, CT: Yale University Press, 1990.

———. *Managers of Virtue: Public School Leadership in America, 1820–1980*. New York: Basic Books, 1982.

Warren, Kim Cary. *The Quest for Citizenship: African American and Native American Education in Kansas, 1880–1935*. Chapel Hill: University of North Carolina Press, 2010.

White, Deborah Gray. *Too Heavy a Load: Black Women in Defense of Themselves, 1894–1994*. New York: W. W. Norton, 1999.

Williams, William Appleman. *The Tragedy of American Diplomacy*. 1959; repr., New York: W. W. Norton, 1988.

Winfield, Ann Gibson. *Eugenics and Education in America: Institutionalized Racism and the Implications of History, Ideology, and Memory.* New York: Peter Lang, 2007.

Wolff, Leon. *Little Brown Brother: How the United States Purchased and Pacified the Philippine Islands at the Century's Turn.* New York: Doubleday, 1961.

Woolford, Andrew. *This Benevolent Experiment: Indigenous Boarding Schools, Genocide, and Redress in Canada and the United States.* Lincoln: University of Nebraska Press, 2015.

Zimmerman, Jonathan. *Innocents Abroad: American Teachers in the American Century.* Cambridge, MA: Harvard University Press, 2006.

Zwick, Jim. "The Anti-Imperialist Movement, 1898–1921." In Virginia M. Bouvier, ed., *Whose America? The War of 1898 and the Battles to Define the Nation.* Westport, CT: Praeger, 2001.

Dissertations and Theses

Adams, David Wallace. "The Federal Indian Boarding School: A Study of Environment and Response, 1879–1918." EdD dissertation, Indiana University, 1975.

Barnes, Rhae Lynn. "Darkology: The Hidden History of Amateur Blackface Minstrelsy and the Making of Modern America, 1860–1970." PhD dissertation, Harvard University, 2016.

Bell, Genevieve. "Telling Stories out of School: Remembering the Carlisle Indian Industrial School, 1879–1918." PhD dissertation, Stanford University, 1998.

Bentley, Matthew. "'Kill the Indian, Save the Man': Manhood at the Carlisle Indian Industrial School, 1879–1918." PhD dissertation, University of East Anglia, 2012.

Bonnell, Sonciray. "Chemawa Indian Boarding School: The First One Hundred Years, 1880 to 1980." PhD dissertation, Dartmouth College, 1997.

Kasperski, Kenneth. "Noble Colonials: Americans and Filipinos, 1901–1940." PhD dissertation, University of Florida, 2012.

Kuehner, Quincy Adams. "The Evolution of the Modern Concept of School Discipline." PhD dissertation, University of Pennsylvania, 1913.

Lardizabal, Amparo Santamaria. "Pioneer American Teachers and Philippine Education." PhD dissertation, Stanford University, 1956.

Moore, Blaine Free. "The Supreme Court and Unconstitutional Legislation." PhD dissertation, Columbia University, 1913.

Muerman, John Charles. "The Philippine School under the Americans." PhD dissertation, George Washington University, 1922.

Paulet, Anne. "'The Only Good Indian Is a Dead Indian': The Use of United States Indian Policy as a Guide for the Conquest and Occupation of the Philippines, 1898–1905." PhD dissertation, Rutgers University, 1995.

Shope, Suzanne Alene. "American Indian Artist Angel DeCora: Aesthetics, Power, and Transcultural Pedagogy in the Progressive Era." EdD dissertation, University of Montana, 2009.

Steinbock-Pratt, Sarah Katherine. "'A Great Army of Instruction': American Teachers and the Negotiation of Empire in the Philippines." PhD dissertation, University of Texas at Austin, 2013.

Tarr, Peter. "The Education of the Thomasites: American School Teachers in Philippine Colonial Society, 1901–1913." PhD dissertation, Cornell University, 2006.

Journal and Magazine Articles

Adams, David Wallace. "Fundamental Considerations: The Deep Meaning of Native American Schooling, 1880–1900." *Harvard Educational Review* 58, 1 (February 1988).

Clymer, Kenton. "Humanitarian Imperialism: David Prescott Barrows and the White Man's Burden in the Philippines." *Pacific Historical Review* 45, 4 (November 1976), 495–517.

"4,000 Know Him as a Thorough Teacher." *Michigan Alumnus* 38, 34 (July 9, 1932).

Gonzales, Angela, Judy Kertész, and Gabrielle Tayac. "Eugenics as Indian Removal: Sociohistorical Processes and the De(con)struction of American Indians in the Southeast." *Public Historian* 29, 3 (Summer 2007), 53–67.

Graham, Abigail Gundlack. "The Power of Boarding Schools: A Historiographical Review." *American Educational History Journal* 38, 1/2 (2012), 467–481.

Granovetter, Mark S. "The Strength of Weak Ties," *American Journal of Sociology* 78, 6 (May 1973), 1360–1380.

Hacker, David J., and Michael R. Haines. "American Indian Mortality in the Late Nineteenth Century: The Impact of Federal Assimilation Policies on a Vulnerable Population." *Annales de Démographie Historique* 2 (2005), 17–45.

Iriye, Akira. "Exceptionalism Revisited." *Reviews in American History* 93, 3 (June 1988), 291–297.

Karnow, Stanley. "The Philippines." *Dissent* 56, 1 (Winter 2009).

Kramer, Paul A. "Power and Connection: Imperial Histories of the United States in the World." *American Historical Review* (December 2011), 1348–1391.

———. "The Water Cure." *Social Science Diliman* 13, 2 (July–December 2017).

Lomawaima, K. Tsianina. "Estelle Reel, Superintendent of Indian Schools, 1898–1910." *Journal of American Indian Education* 35, 3 (1995).

Margold, Jane A. "Egalitarian Ideals and Exclusionary Practices: U.S. Pedagogy in the Colonial Philippines." *Journal of Historical Sociology* 8, 4 (December 1995), 375–394.

McLean, Paul. "Using Network Analysis in Comparative Historical Research." *Trajectories: Newsletter of the ASA Comparative and Historical Sociology Section* 22, 1 (Fall 2010), 10–14.

Mihesuah, Devon A. "'Too Dark to Be Angels': The Class System among the Cherokees at the Female Seminary." *American Indian Culture and Research Journal* 15, 1 (1991), 29–52.

Morgan, Michelle. "Americanizing the Teachers: Identity, Citizenship, and the Teaching Corps in Hawai'i, 1900–1941." *Western Historical Quarterly* 45 (Summer 2014), 147–167.

Paulet, Anne. "To Change the World: The Use of American Indian Education in the Philippines." *History of Education Quarterly* 47, 2 (May 2007), 173-202.

Perdue, Theda. "Cherokee Women and the Trail of Tears." *Journal of Women's History* 1, 1 (1989), 14–30.

Rafael, Vicente L. "The War of Translation: Colonial Education, American English, and Tagalog Slang in the Philippines." *Journal of Asian Studies* 74, 2 (May 2015), 283–302.

Raftery, Judith. "Textbook Wars: Governor-General James Francis Smith and the Protestant-Catholic Conflict in Public Education in the Philippines, 1904–1907." *History of Education Quarterly* 38, 2 (Summer 1998), 143–164.

Rogers, Daniel T. "In Search of Progressivism," *Reviews in American History* 10, 4 (December 1982), 113–132.

Romero, René. "The Flowering of Philippine Education under the American Regime (1898–1923)." *American Historical Collection* 4, 2 (April 1976).

"School Superintendent Appointed," *Midland Journal* 62, 31 (February 14, 1936).

Smith-Rosenberg, Carroll. "The Female World of Love and Ritual: Relations between Women in Nineteenth-Century America." *Signs* 1, 1 (Autumn 1975), 1–29.

Steinbrock-Pratt, Sarah. "'We Were All Robinson Crusoes': American Women Teachers in the Philippines." *Women's Studies*, 41 (June 2012), 379–392.

Swain, James O. "E. Herman Hespelt (1886–1961)." *Hispania* 45, 1 (March 1962), 19–21.

Welch, Richard E. "American Atrocities in the Philippines: The Indictment and the Response." *Pacific Historical Review*, 43 (1974), 233–255.

Williams, Walter L. "United States Indian Policy and the Debate over Philippine Annexation: Implications for the Origins of American Imperialism." *Journal of American History* 66, 4 (March 1980), 810–831.

Other Secondary Sources

Barritt, Marjorie. "American-Philippine Relations: A Guide to the Resources in the Michigan Historical Collections." Bentley Historical Library, University of Michigan.

Biewen, John. "Little War on the Prairie." *This American Life*, November 23, 2012, https://www.thisamericanlife.org/479/little-war-on-the-prairie.

Bureau of Indian Education. Riverside Indian School Application for Admission 2018–2019 School Year, "Riverside Indian School: Parent-Student-School Compact," 22, https://ris.bie.edu/Student_Application_2018_19.pdf.

Bureau of Indian Education. Riverside Indian School Application for Admission 2019–2020 School Year, "Social Summary," 14, https://ris.bie.edu/Student_Application_2018_19.pdf.

Claesgens, Kevin. "Zitkala-Sa (Gertrude Simmons Bonnin) Biography." Pennsylvania Center for the Book, Penn State University, Fall 2005, http://pabook.libraries.psu.edu/palitmap/bios/Zitkala_Sa.html.

La Crosse Public Library Archives. "Guide to the Twentieth Century Club Records, 1920–1982," La Cross, Wisconsin, http://archives.lacrosselibrary.org/collections /sports-and-recreation/mss-142/.

Law Book Exchange. "The Supreme Court and Unconstitutional Legislation, Blaine Free Moore," accessed September 27, 2015, http://www.lawbookexchange.com /pages/books/27935/blaine-free-moore/the-supreme-court-and-unconstitutional -legislation.

Oroso, Rosalinda L. "The Thomasites Remembered." *Philippine Star*, September 16, 2001, http://www.philstar.com/starweek-magazine/133925/thomasites-remembered.

"Overview: Guide to the Elizabeth Willis DeHuff Collection of American Indian Art." Elizabeth Willis DeHuff Collection, Beinecke Rare Book and Manuscript Library, Yale University. New Haven, CT (BRBML), http://hdl.handle.net/10079/fa/bei necke.dehuff.

INDEX